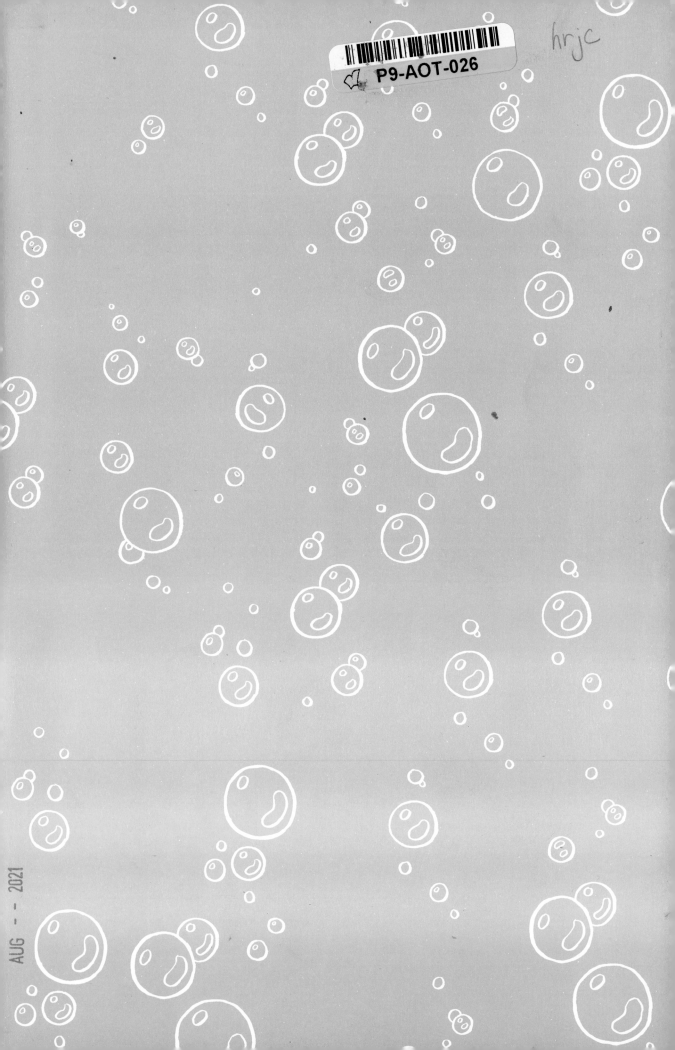

hrjc

Cataloging-in-Publication Data has been applied for and may be
obtained from the Library of Congress.

ISBN 978-1-4197-2561-6

ACKNOWLEDGMENTS: Thank you to Karen and Clay for their tenacity, sense of humor, and love
in sharing me with SpongeBob and his world in Bikini Bottom for so many years; to Chris Duffy
for his deft care and editing of the comics; to all the creative contributors to the comics; and to
Charlie Kochman, Orlando Dos Reis, Pamela Notarantonio, Amy Vreeland, and Alison Gervais
at Abrams for shepherding the comics stories into these amazing books.

Content Editor: Chris Duffy
Cover Artist: Jacob Chabot

Editor: Orlando Dos Reis
Project Manager: Charles Kochman
Book Design: Pamela Notarantonio
Managing Editor: Amy Vreeland
Production Manager: Alison Gervais

Photograph of Stephen Hillenburg on page 5 by Craig Matthew/Nickelodeon
Illustrations on title page and page 208 by Jacob Chabot

Featuring stories and art by: Graham Annable, Stephen Bissette, James Campbell,
Jacob Chabot, Comicraft, Vanessa Davis, Vince Deporter, Stephen DeStefano, Mike DeVito, Derek
Drymon, Bob Flynn, Ramona Fradon, Cat Garza, Gary Gianni, Sam Henderson, Hi-Fi, Stephen
Hillenburg, Shane Houghton, Al Jaffee, Paul Karasik, Kaz, James Kochalka, Monica Kubina, Jacob
Lambert, Rob Leigh, Robert Leighton, Mark Martin, Tony Millionaire, Raul the Third, Brian Murnane,
Jerry Ordway, Andy Rementer, Scott Roberts, Gregg Schigiel, R. Sikoryak,
Brian Smith, Tim Truman, Joey Weiser, and Maris Wicks.

The stories included in this collection were originally published in SpongeBob Comics no. 2 (April
2011), 11 (August 2012), 12 (September 2012), 13 (October 2012), 14 (November 2012),
15 (December 2012), 17 (February 2013), 18 (March 2013), 22 (July 2013),
26 (November 2013), 27 (December 2013), 29 (February 2014), 32 (May 2014),
33 (June 2014), 34 (July 2014), 35 (August 2014), 36 (September 2014), 42 March 2015); Annual
Super-Giant Spectacular 2 (June 2014) and 3 (June 2015); and Freestyle Funnies
(Free Comic Book Day, May 2013). Comics production by Paul Tutrone.

Bonus pinups created specially for this edition by: Sergio Aragonés, Hilary Barta,
Dave Cooper, Stephen DeStefano, Renée French, Nathan Hale, Kaz, James Kochalka,
Ross MacDonald, Jason Millet, Rick Nielsen, Gregg Schigiel, and Skottie Young.

Printed and bound in China
1 2 3 4 5 6 7 8 9 10

Abrams ComicArts books are available at special discounts when purchased in
quantity for premiums and promotions as well as fundraising or educational use.
Special editions can also be created to specification. For details,
contact specialsales@abramsbooks.com or the address below.

ABRAMS The Art of Books
115 West 18th Street, New York, NY 10011
abramsbooks.com

Contents

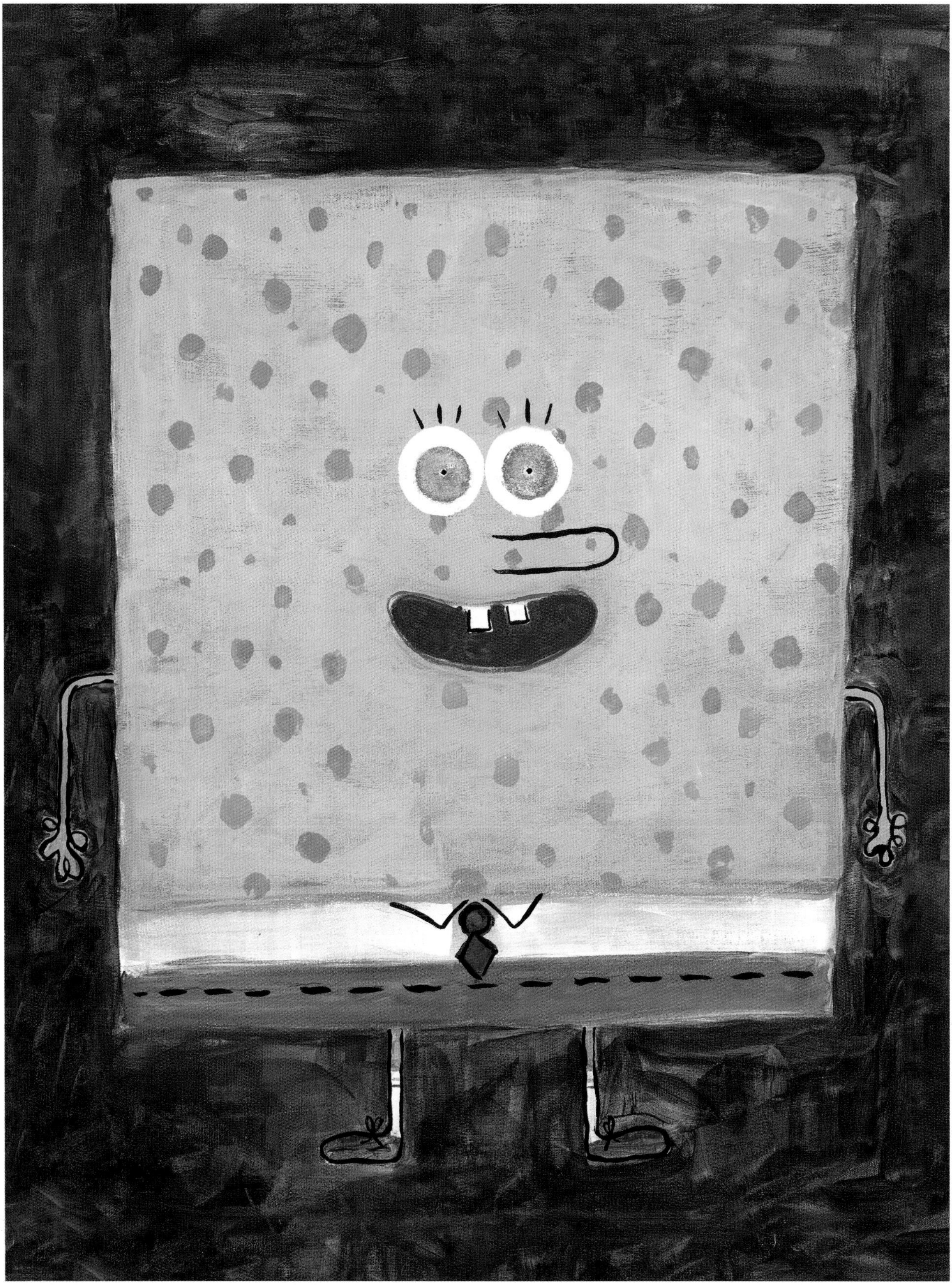

Painting of SpongeBob SquarePants by Stephen Hillenburg, 2011

Introduction

Ahoy there! My name is Stephen Hillenburg, and I created SpongeBob SquarePants. I was always interested in the ocean and in art. I love surfing and diving. But I never figured all these things would come together. When I went to Humboldt State University in California, my teachers would say, "What are you doing? You should be an artist!" Well, I ended up working at the Orange County Marine Institute (now called the Ocean Institute) in Dana Point and really enjoyed it. My last year there, I made a comic to teach about tide pools. It was called "The Intertidal Zone," and in it there was a character called Bob the Sponge.

Then I went to CalArts and studied experimental animation with the program's founder, Jules Engel. After I graduated, I got a job on the animated series *Rocko's Modern Life*, created by Joe Murray. It was a great experience for me; I definitely learned a lot about running a show. I had the "Intertidal" comic hanging in my office, and one day the famous TV producer Martin Olson saw it and said, "This is your show!" It wasn't my show, but I started to think that if I was going to make a show, it would be under the sea . . . and SpongeBob was born. And when we started SpongeBob Comics, I was really excited—I think it gives a chance for more people to see the characters. I love the different styles used in the SpongeBob Comics and the hilarious stories. I invite you to enjoy the adventures of SpongeBob and friends!

Stephen Hillenburg

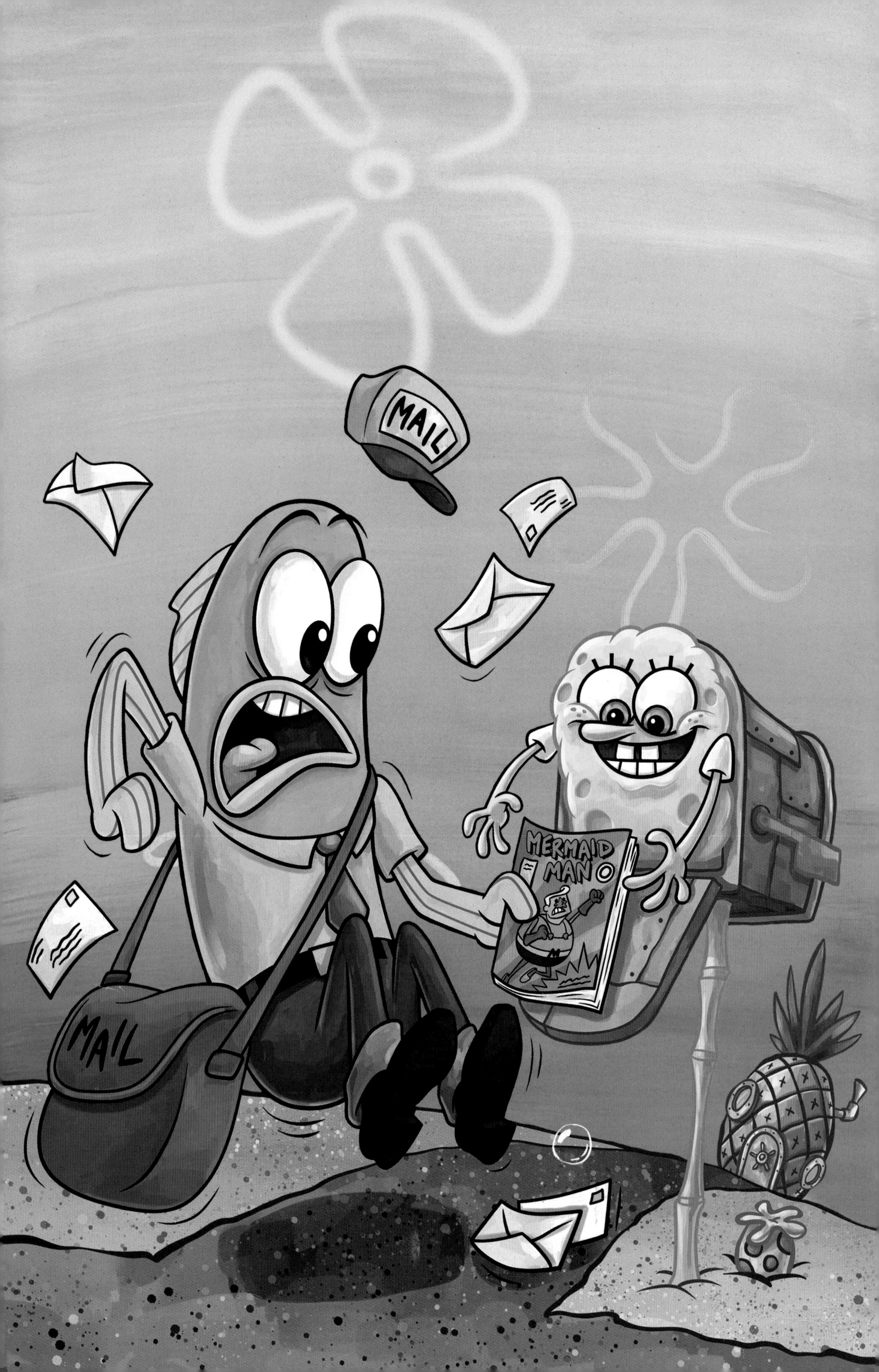
MAIL
MERMAID MAN
MAIL

UNDERSEA ADVENTURES

Featuring
the comic exploits of SpongeBob
SquarePants and his aquatic friends!

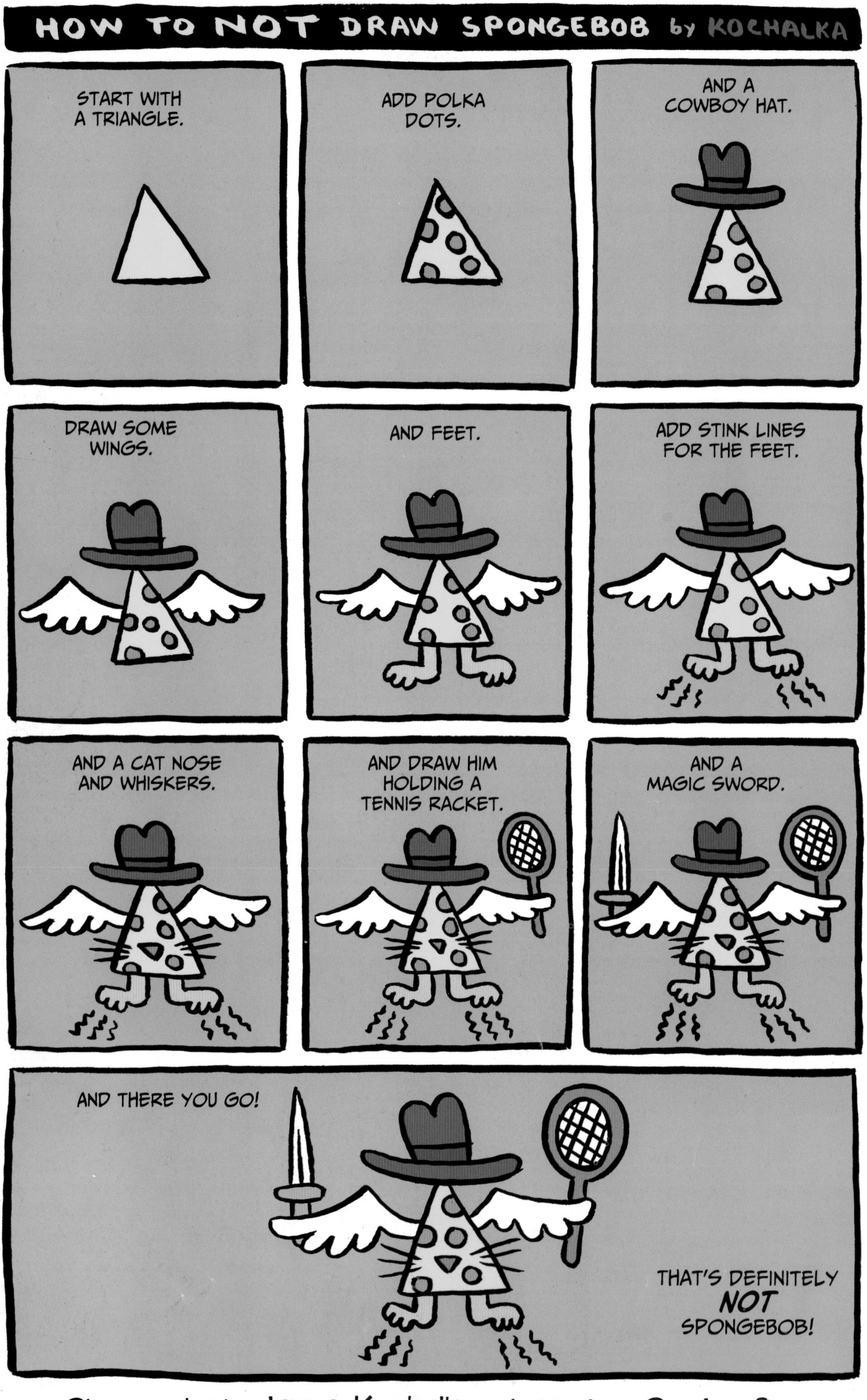
HOW TO NOT DRAW SPONGEBOB by KOCHALKA
START WITH A TRIANGLE.
ADD POLKA DOTS.
AND A COWBOY HAT.
DRAW SOME WINGS.
AND FEET.
ADD STINK LINES FOR THE FEET.
AND A CAT NOSE AND WHISKERS.
AND DRAW HIM HOLDING A TENNIS RACKET.
AND A MAGIC SWORD.
AND THERE YOU GO!
THAT'S DEFINITELY NOT SPONGEBOB!

Story and art: James Kochalka Lettering: Comicraft

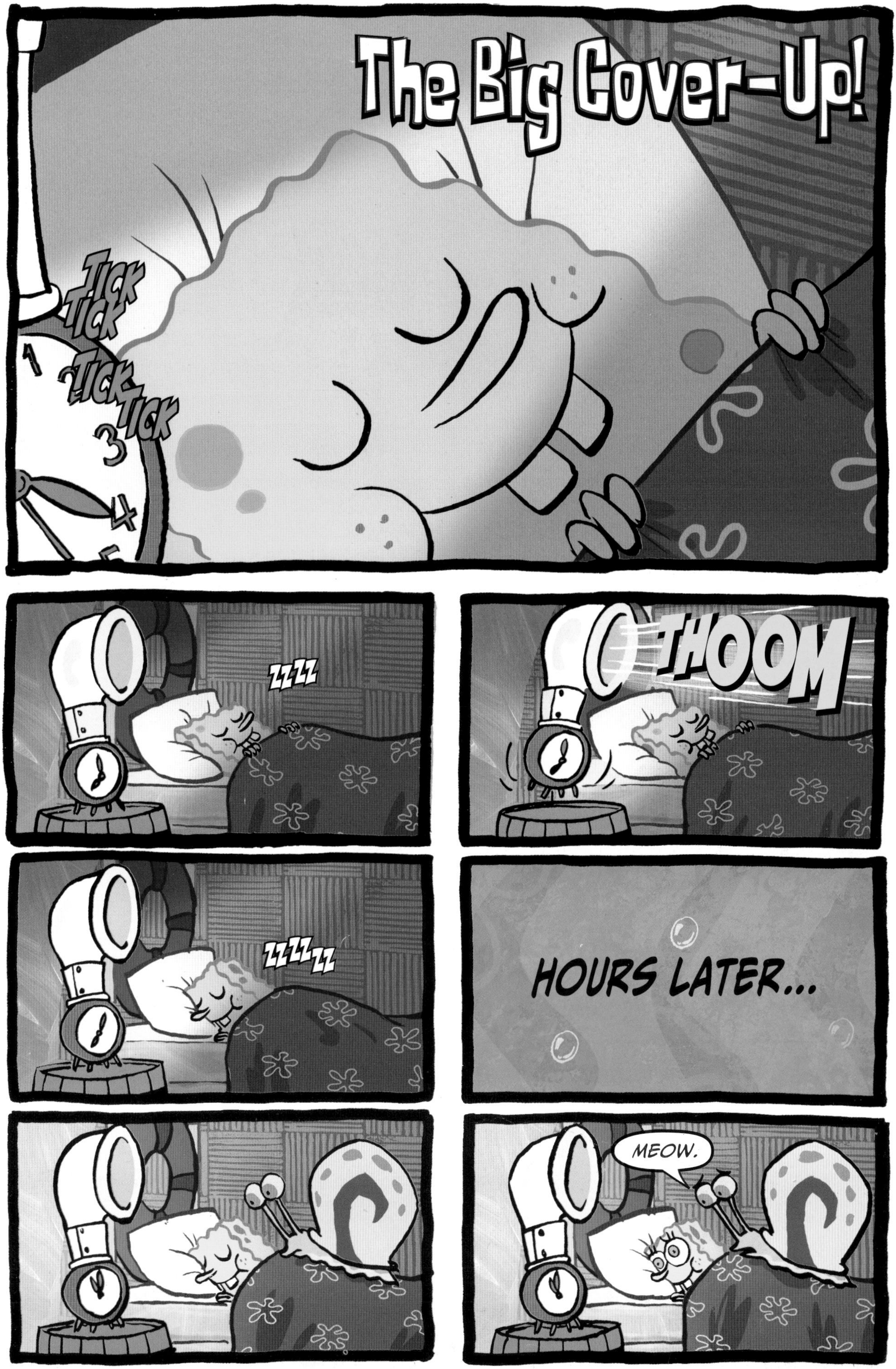
The Big Cover-Up!
TICK TICK TICK TICK
ZZZZ
THOOM
ZZZZZZ
HOURS LATER...
MEOW.

STORY, PENCILS, INKS: GRAHAM ANNABLE COLOR: MARK MARTIN LETTERING: COMICRAFT

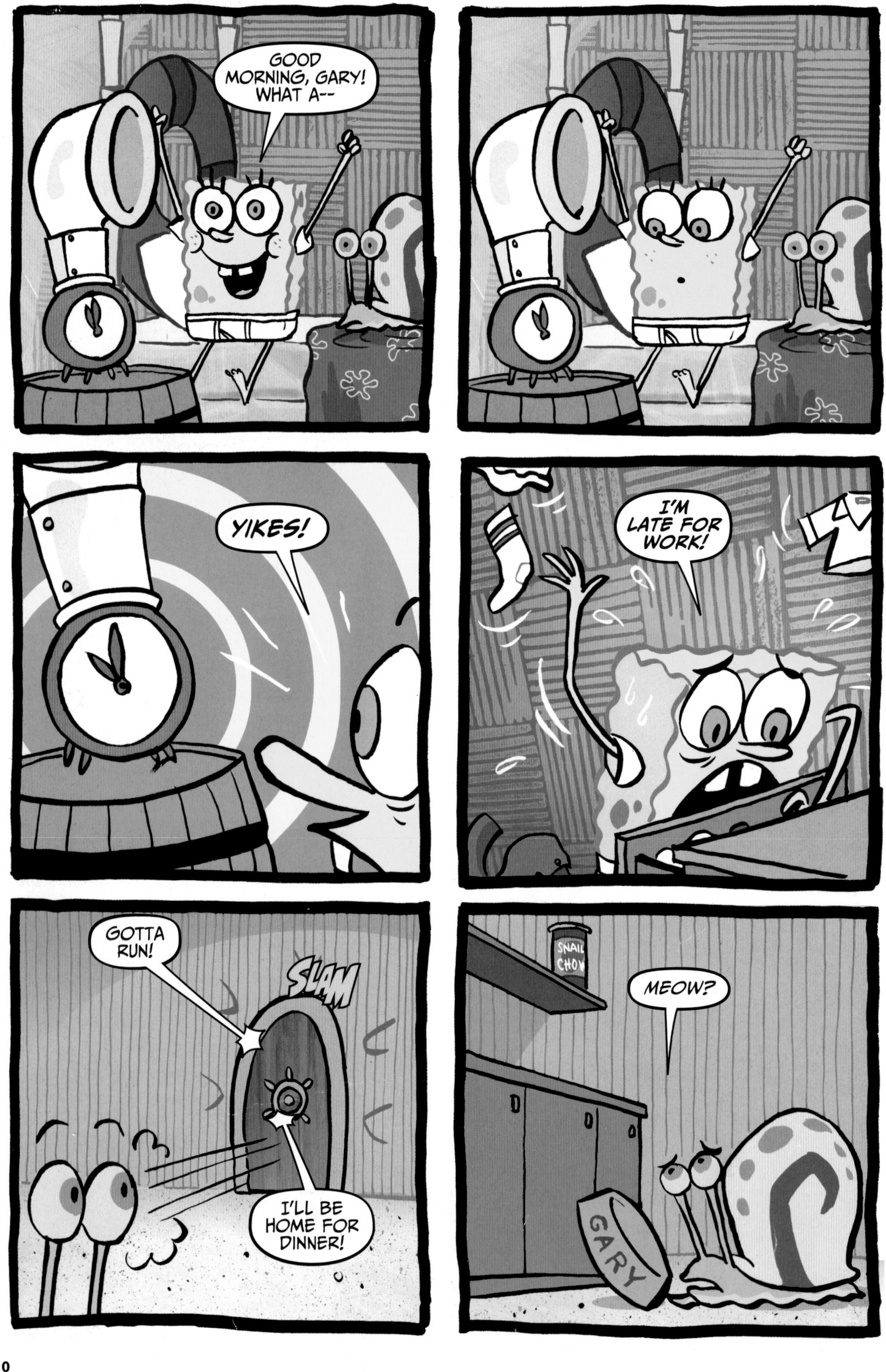
GOOD MORNING, GARY! WHAT A--
YIKES!
I'M LATE FOR WORK!
GOTTA RUN!
SLAM
I'LL BE HOME FOR DINNER!
SNAIL CHOW
MEOW?
GARY

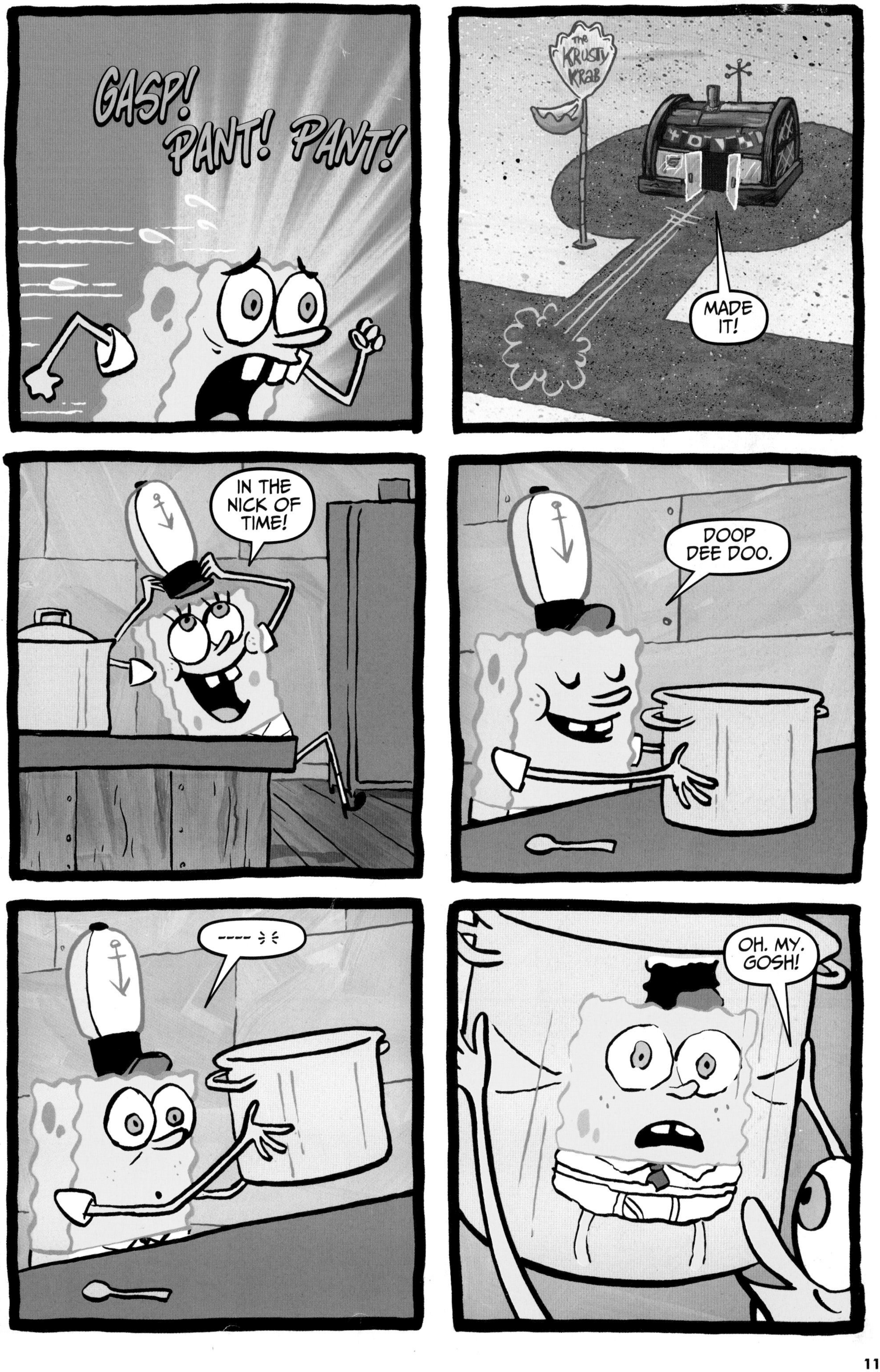
GASP! PANT! PANT!
The Krusty Krab
MADE IT!
IN THE NICK OF TIME!
DOOP DEE DOO.
OH. MY. GOSH!

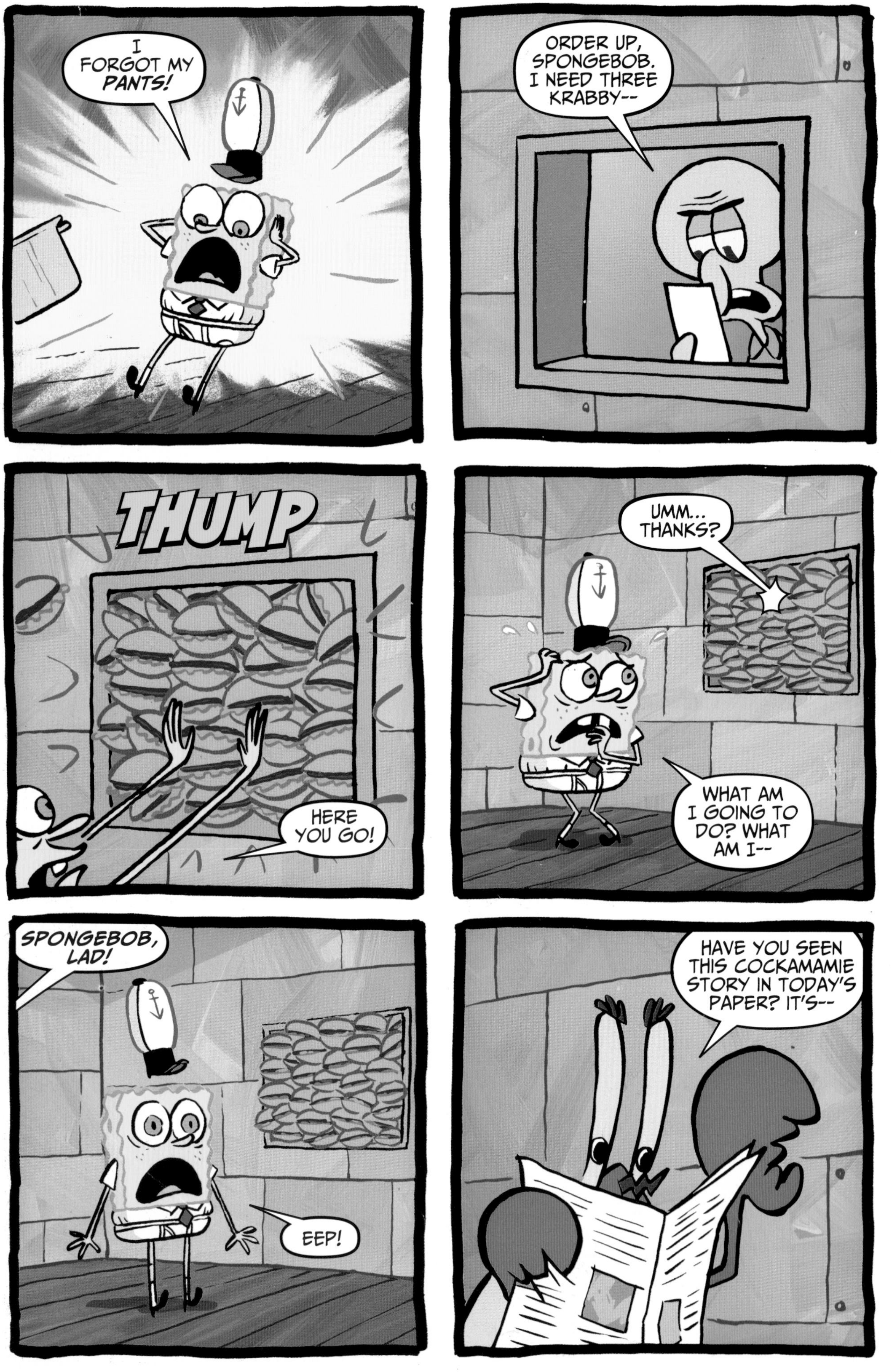
I FORGOT MY PANTS!
ORDER UP, SPONGEBOB. I NEED THREE KRABBY--
THUMP
HERE YOU GO!
UMM... THANKS?
WHAT AM I GOING TO DO? WHAT AM I--
SPONGEBOB, LAD!
EEP!
HAVE YOU SEEN THIS COCKAMAMIE STORY IN TODAY'S PAPER? IT'S--

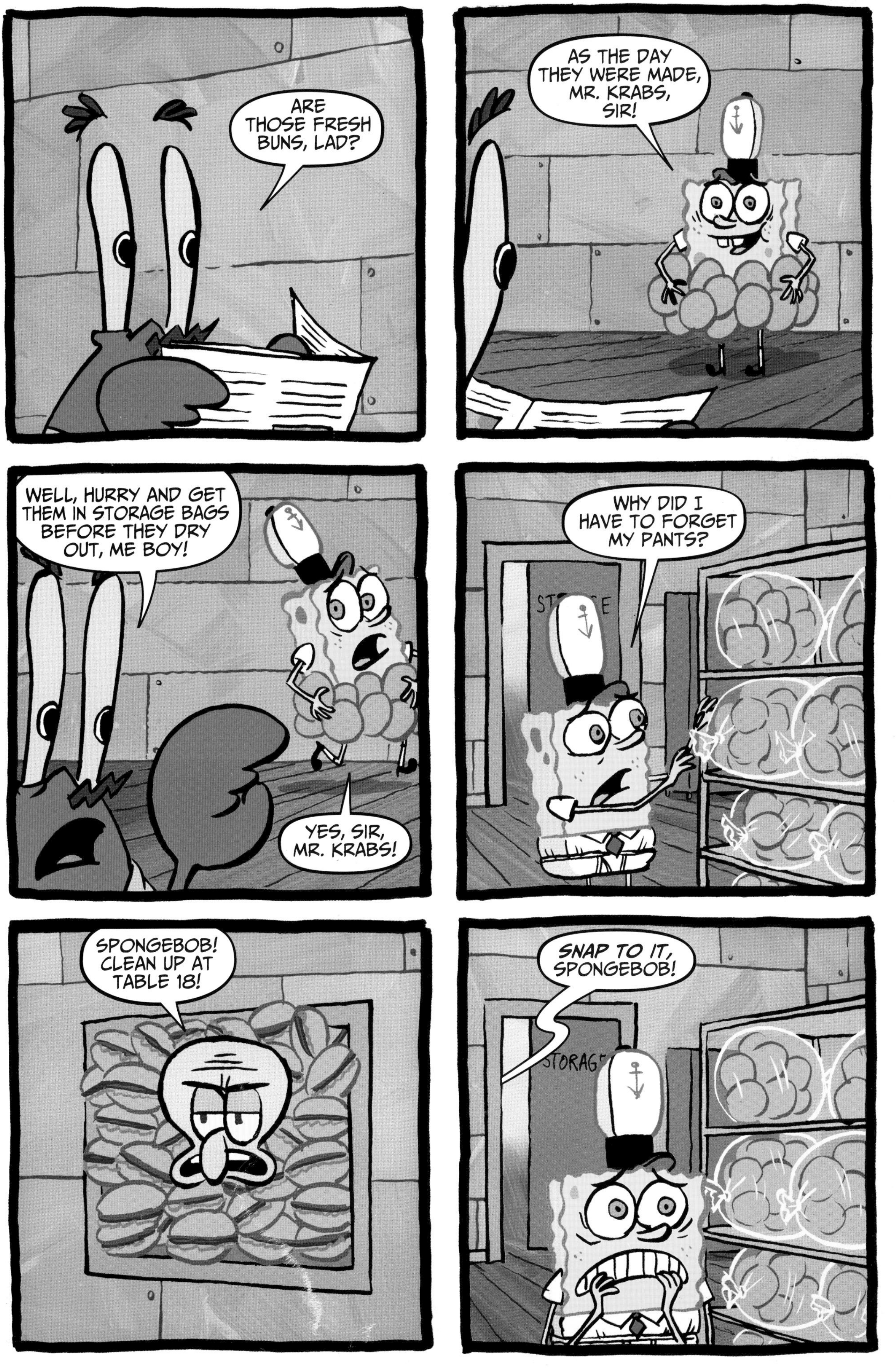
ARE THOSE FRESH BUNS, LAD?
AS THE DAY THEY WERE MADE, MR. KRABS, SIR!
WELL, HURRY AND GET THEM IN STORAGE BAGS BEFORE THEY DRY OUT, ME BOY!
YES, SIR, MR. KRABS!
WHY DID I HAVE TO FORGET MY PANTS?
SPONGEBOB! CLEAN UP AT TABLE 18!
SNAP TO IT, SPONGEBOB!

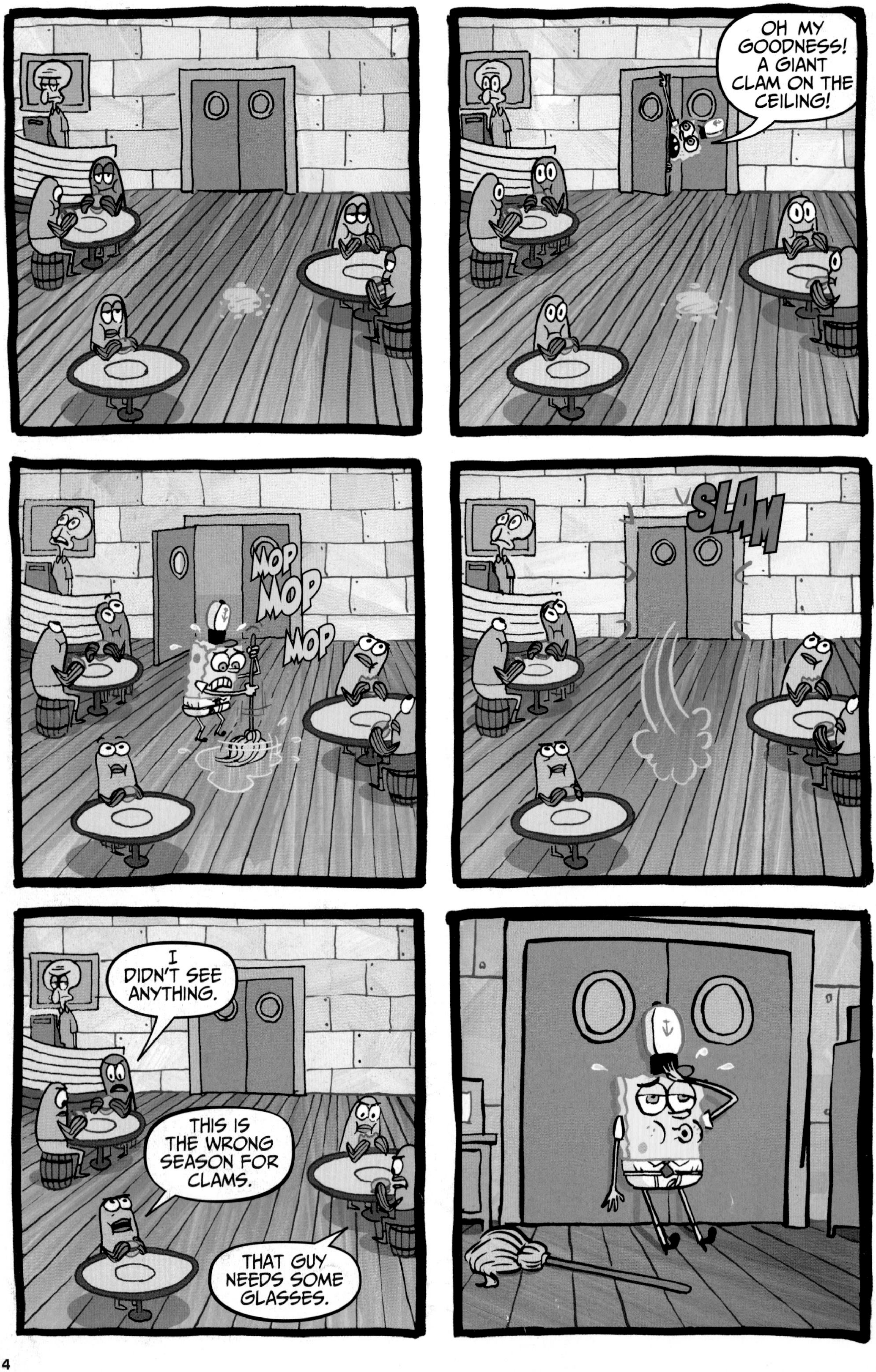
OH MY GOODNESS! A GIANT CLAM ON THE CEILING!
MOP MOP MOP
SLAM
I DIDN'T SEE ANYTHING.
THIS IS THE WRONG SEASON FOR CLAMS.
THAT GUY NEEDS SOME GLASSES.

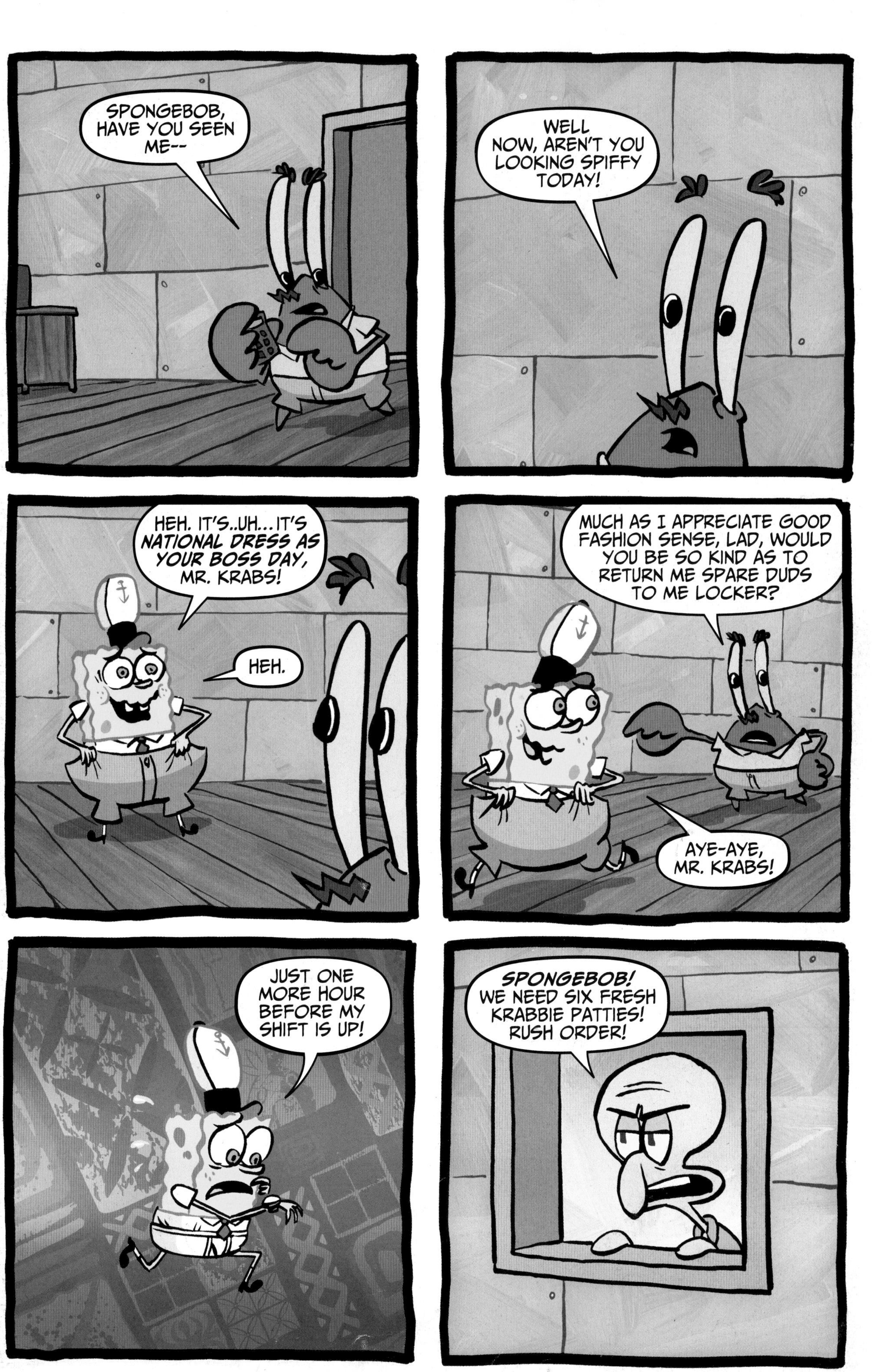
SPONGEBOB, HAVE YOU SEEN ME--
WELL NOW, AREN'T YOU LOOKING SPIFFY TODAY!
HEH. IT'S..UH...IT'S NATIONAL DRESS AS YOUR BOSS DAY, MR. KRABS!
HEH.
MUCH AS I APPRECIATE GOOD FASHION SENSE, LAD, WOULD YOU BE SO KIND AS TO RETURN ME SPARE DUDS TO ME LOCKER?
AYE-AYE, MR. KRABS!
JUST ONE MORE HOUR BEFORE MY SHIFT IS UP!
SPONGEBOB! WE NEED SIX FRESH KRABBIE PATTIES! RUSH ORDER!

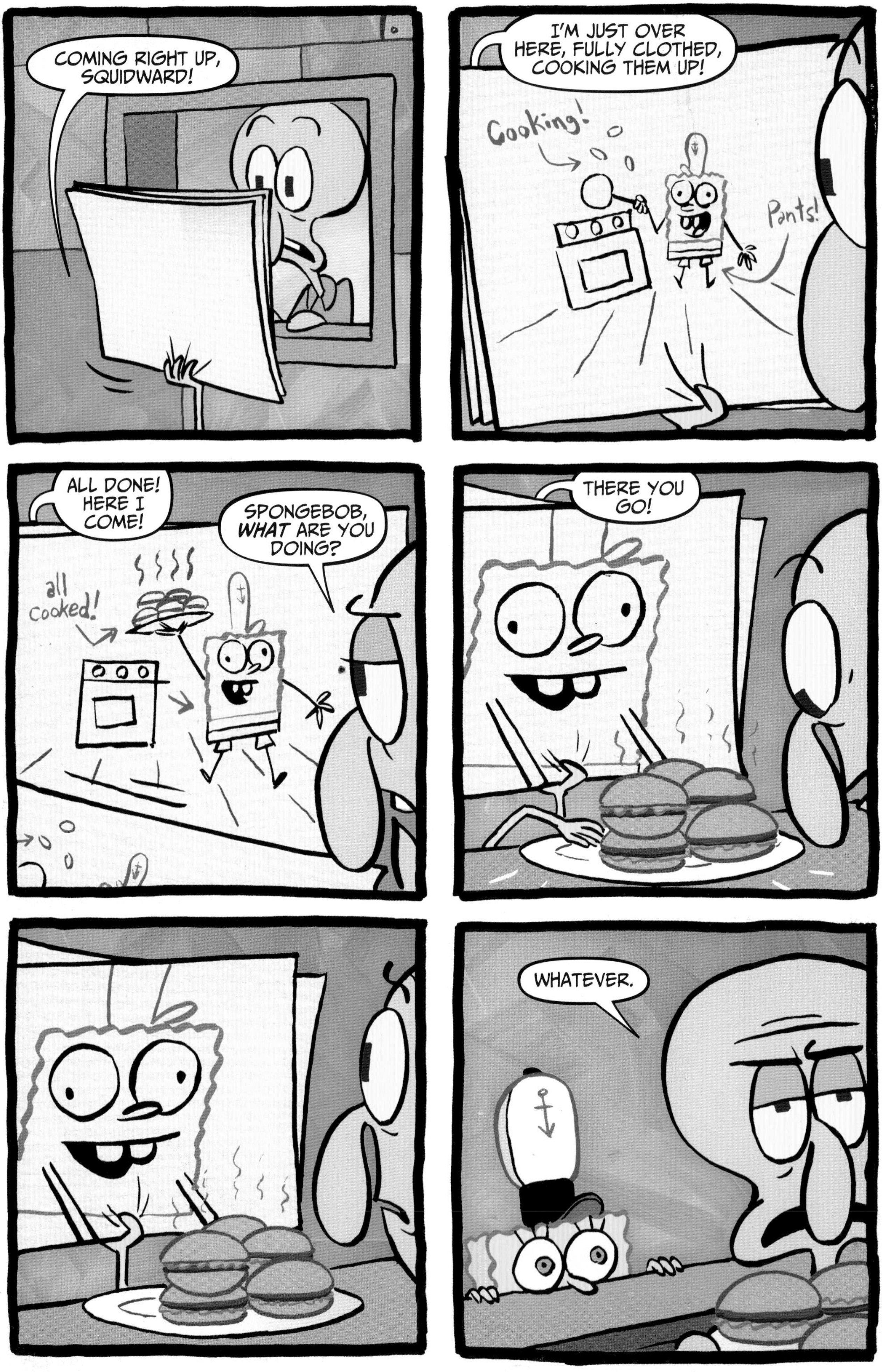
COMING RIGHT UP, SQUIDWARD!
I'M JUST OVER HERE, FULLY CLOTHED, COOKING THEM UP!
Cooking!
Pants!
ALL DONE! HERE I COME!
all cooked!
SPONGEBOB, *WHAT* ARE YOU DOING?
THERE YOU GO!
WHATEVER.

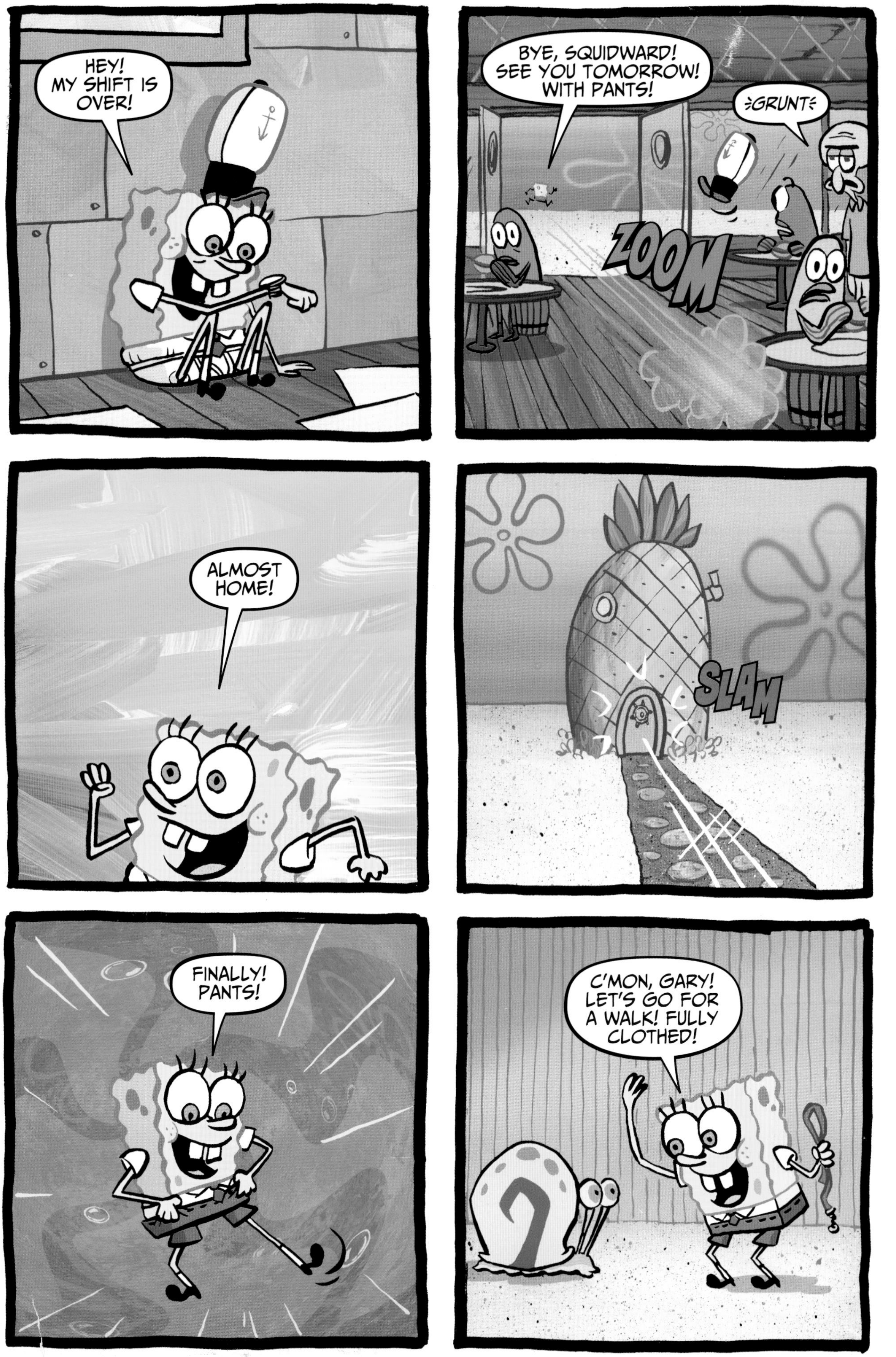
HEY! MY SHIFT IS OVER!
BYE, SQUIDWARD! SEE YOU TOMORROW! WITH PANTS!
GRUNT
ZOOM
ALMOST HOME!
SLAM
FINALLY! PANTS!
C'MON, GARY! LET'S GO FOR A WALK! FULLY CLOTHED!

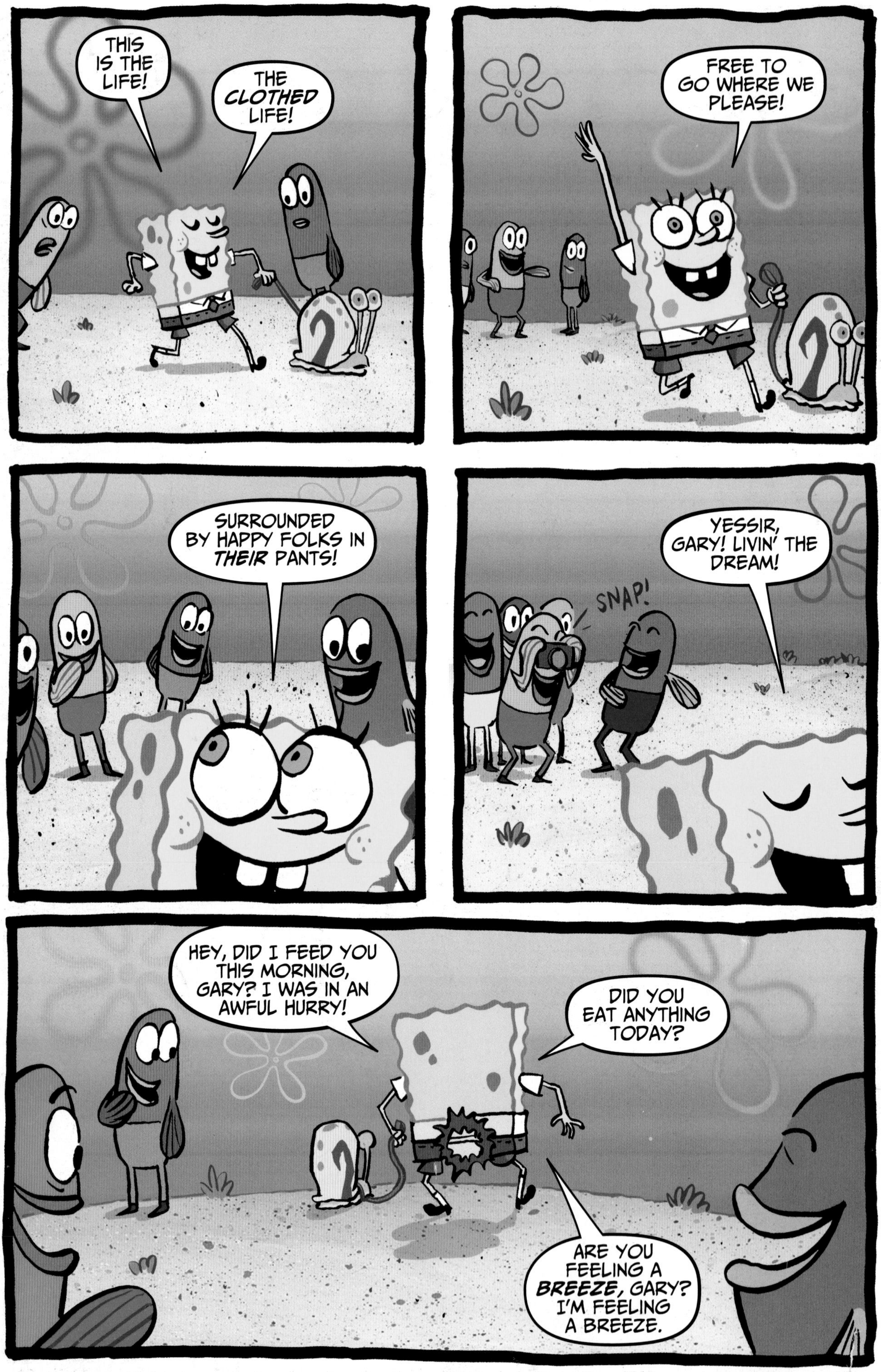
THIS IS THE LIFE!
THE *CLOTHED* LIFE!
FREE TO GO WHERE WE PLEASE!
SURROUNDED BY HAPPY FOLKS IN *THEIR* PANTS!
YESSIR, GARY! LIVIN' THE DREAM!
SNAP!
HEY, DID I FEED YOU THIS MORNING, GARY? I WAS IN AN AWFUL HURRY!
DID YOU EAT ANYTHING TODAY?
ARE YOU FEELING A *BREEZE*, GARY? I'M FEELING A BREEZE.

END

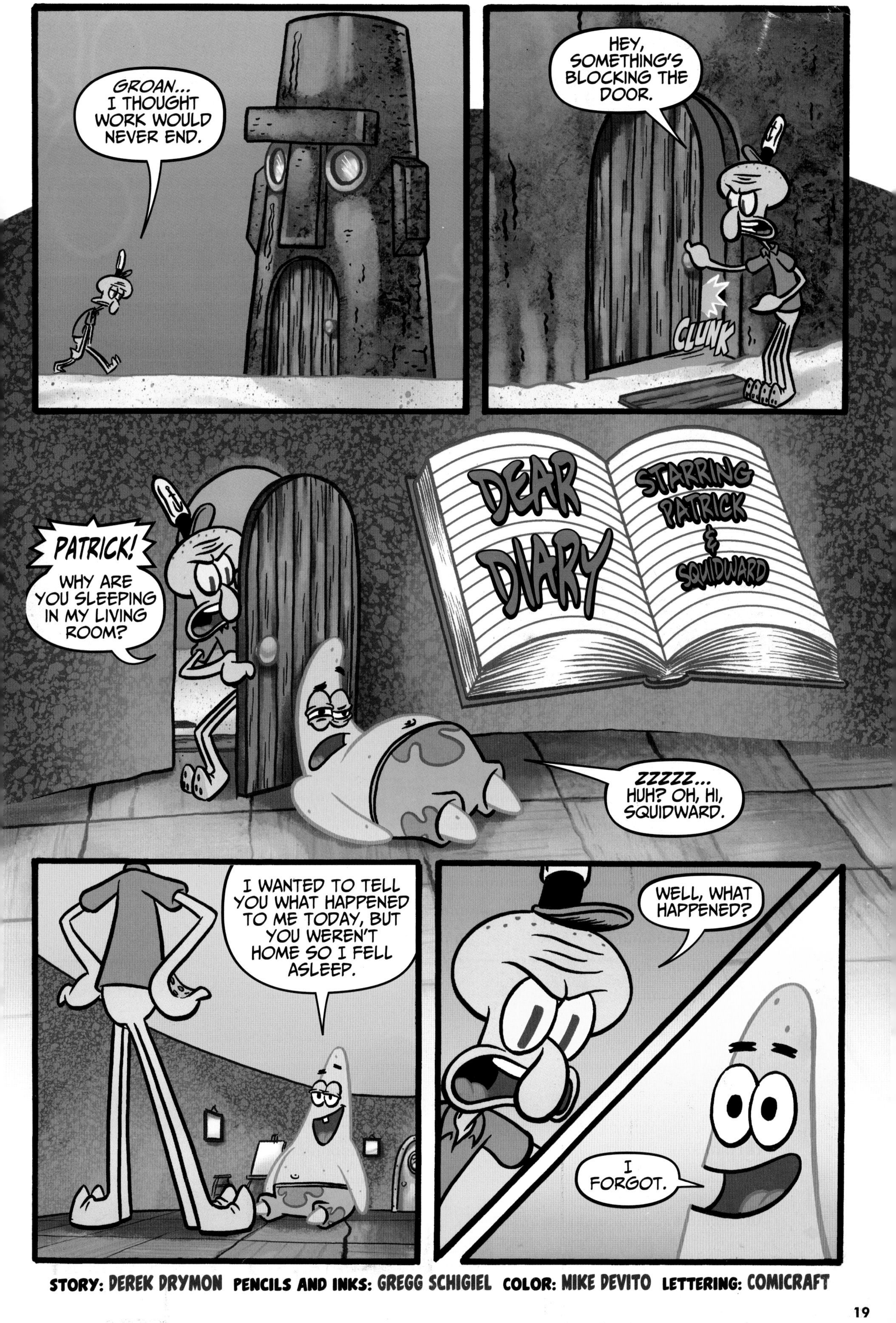
GROAN... I THOUGHT WORK WOULD NEVER END.
HEY, SOMETHING'S BLOCKING THE DOOR.
CLUNK
DEAR DIARY
STARRING PATRICK & SQUIDWARD
PATRICK! WHY ARE YOU SLEEPING IN MY LIVING ROOM?
ZZZZZ... HUH? OH, HI, SQUIDWARD.
I WANTED TO TELL YOU WHAT HAPPENED TO ME TODAY, BUT YOU WEREN'T HOME SO I FELL ASLEEP.
WELL, WHAT HAPPENED?
I FORGOT.

STORY: DEREK DRYMON **PENCILS AND INKS:** GREGG SCHIGIEL **COLOR:** MIKE DEVITO **LETTERING:** COMICRAFT

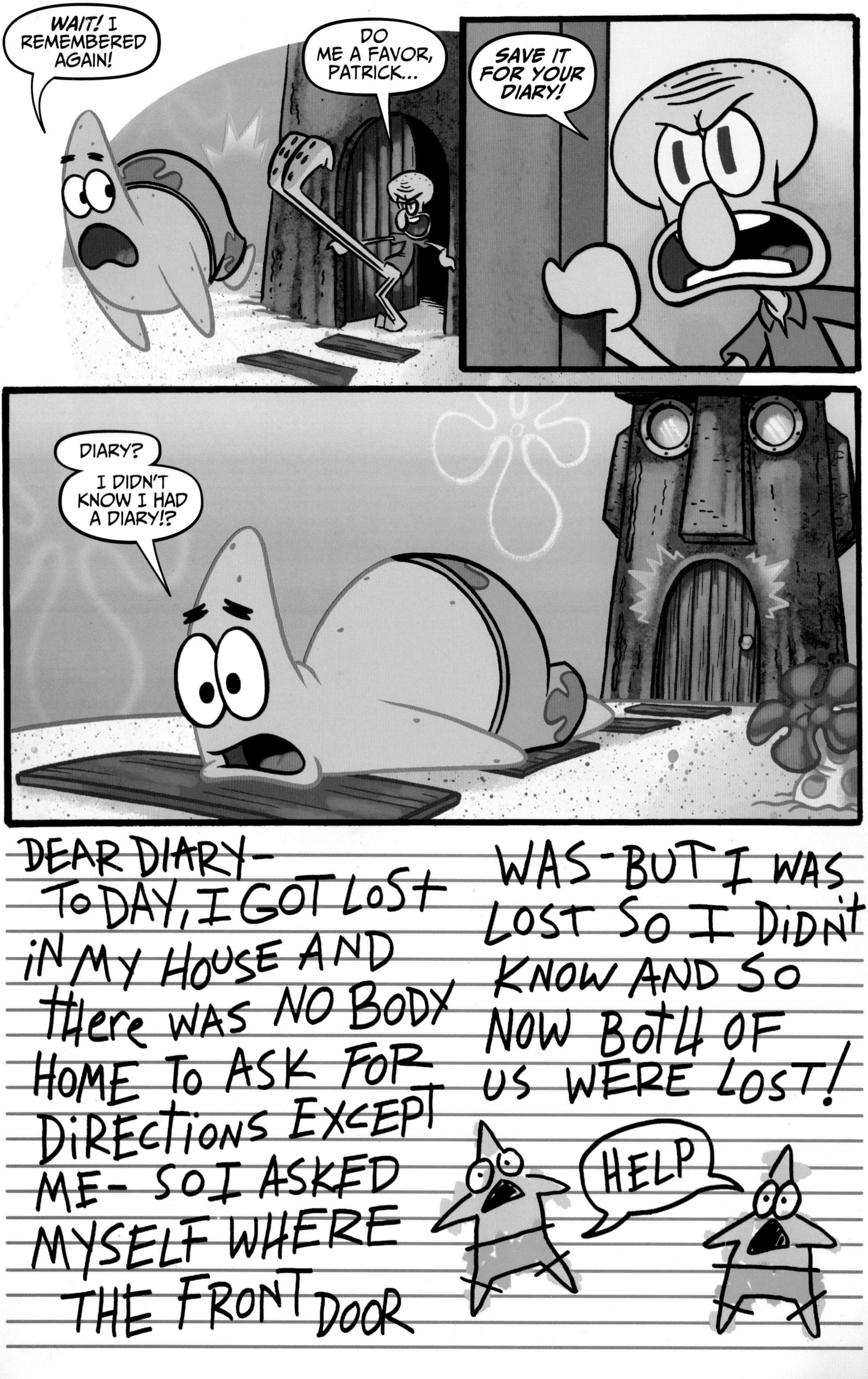
WAIT! I REMEMBERED AGAIN!
DO ME A FAVOR, PATRICK...
SAVE IT FOR YOUR DIARY!
DIARY?
I DIDN'T KNOW I HAD A DIARY!?
DEAR DIARY-
TODAY, I GOT LOST IN MY HOUSE AND there WAS NO BODY HOME TO ASK FOR DIRECTIONS EXCEPT ME- SO I ASKED MYSELF WHERE THE FRONT DOOR WAS- BUT I WAS LOST SO I DIDN't KNOW AND SO NOW BOTH OF US WERE LOST!
HELP

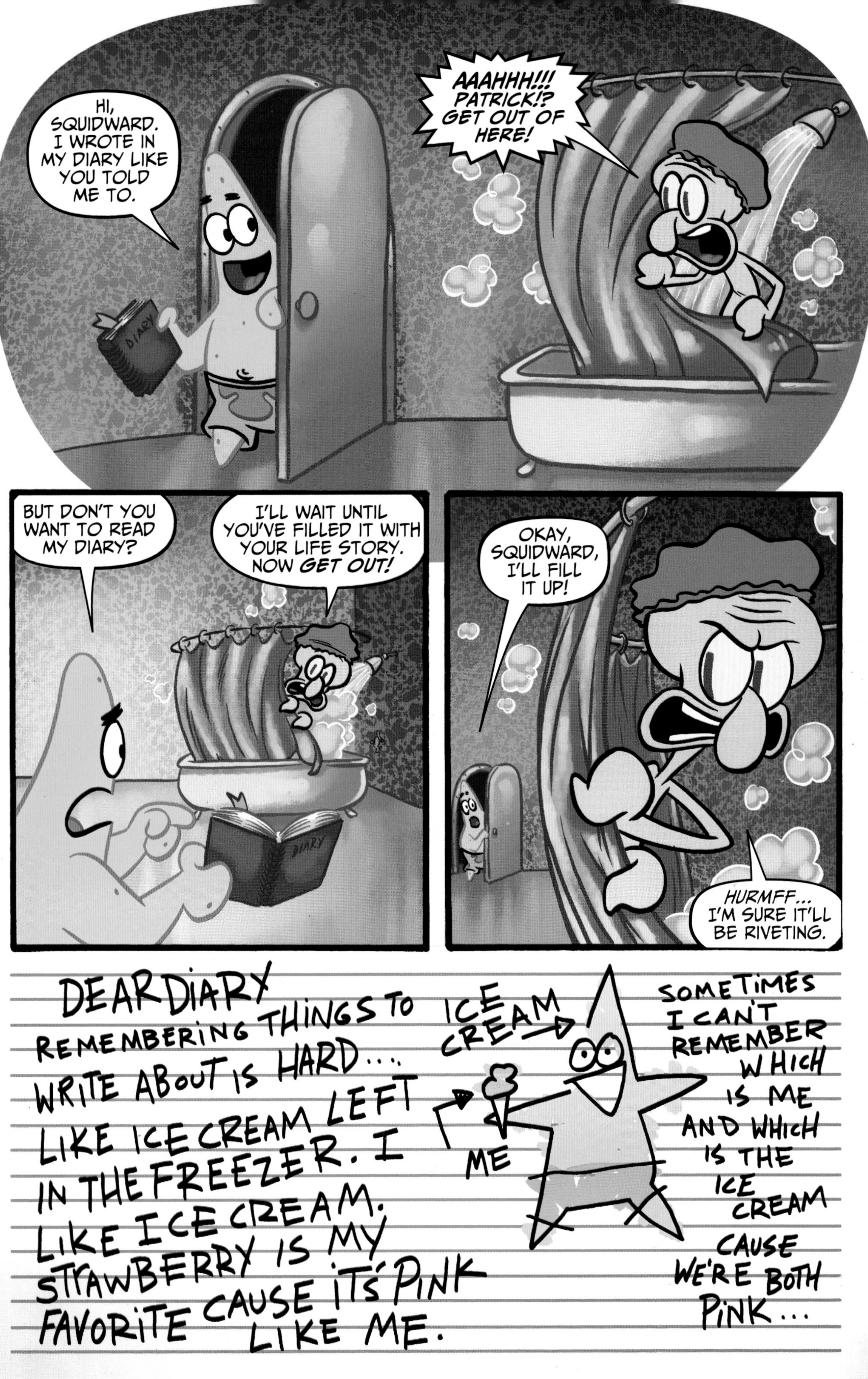
HI, SQUIDWARD. I WROTE IN MY DIARY LIKE YOU TOLD ME TO.
AAAHHH!!! PATRICK!? GET OUT OF HERE!
DIARY
BUT DON'T YOU WANT TO READ MY DIARY?
I'LL WAIT UNTIL YOU'VE FILLED IT WITH YOUR LIFE STORY. NOW GET OUT!
DIARY
OKAY, SQUIDWARD, I'LL FILL IT UP!
HURMFF... I'M SURE IT'LL BE RIVETING.
DEAR DIARY
REMEMBERING THINGS TO WRITE ABOUT IS HARD.... LIKE ICE CREAM LEFT IN THE FREEZER. I LIKE ICE CREAM. STRAWBERRY IS MY FAVORITE CAUSE IT'S PINK LIKE ME.
ICE CREAM
ME
SOMETIMES I CAN'T REMEMBER WHICH IS ME AND WHICH IS THE ICE CREAM CAUSE WE'RE BOTH PINK...

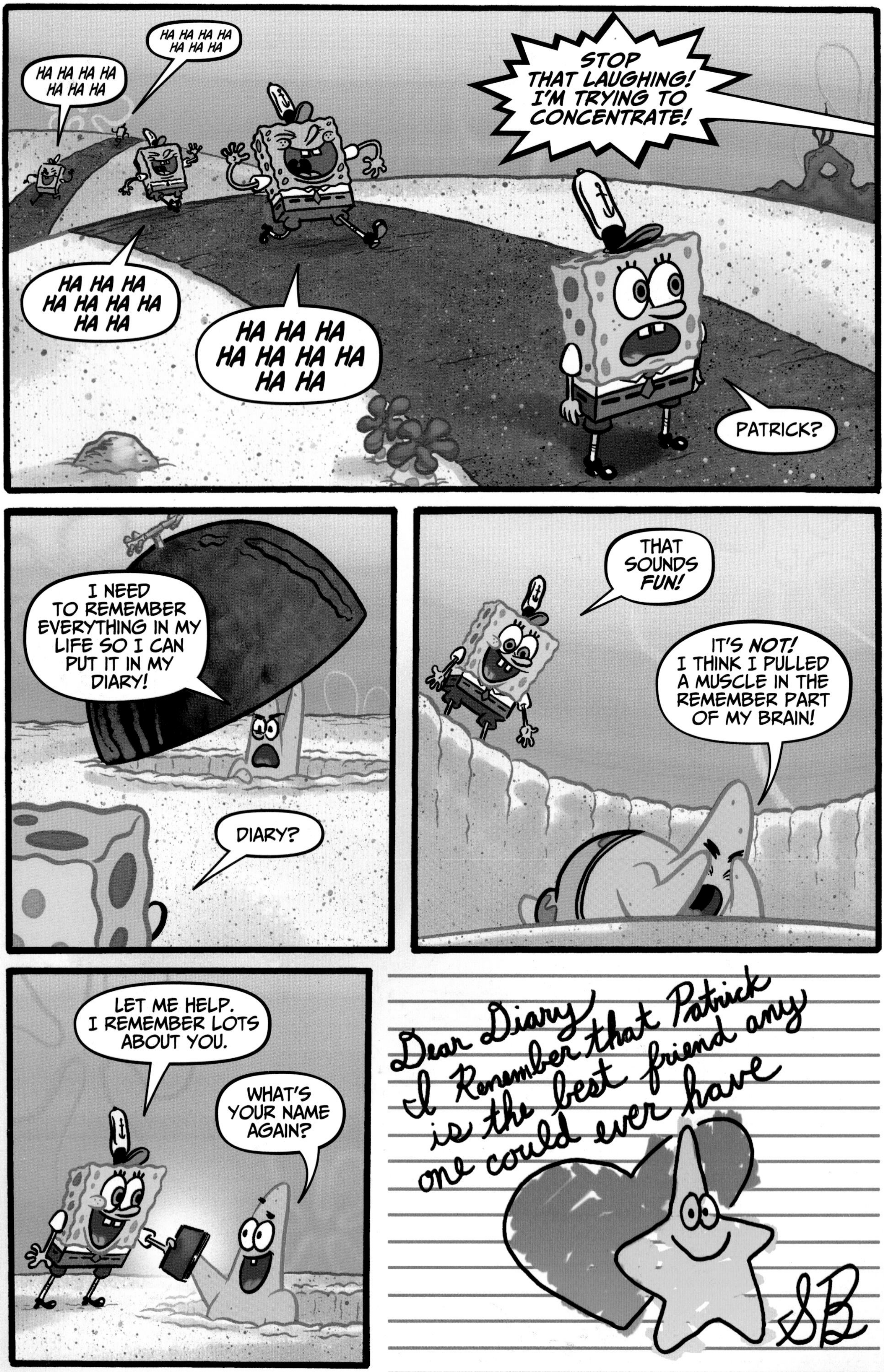
HA HA HA HA
HA HA HA
HA HA HA HA
HA HA HA
STOP THAT LAUGHING! I'M TRYING TO CONCENTRATE!
HA HA HA
HA HA HA HA
HA HA
HA HA HA
HA HA HA HA
HA HA
PATRICK?
I NEED TO REMEMBER EVERYTHING IN MY LIFE SO I CAN PUT IT IN MY DIARY!
DIARY?
THAT SOUNDS FUN!
IT'S NOT! I THINK I PULLED A MUSCLE IN THE REMEMBER PART OF MY BRAIN!
LET ME HELP. I REMEMBER LOTS ABOUT YOU.
WHAT'S YOUR NAME AGAIN?
Dear Diary
I Remember that Patrick
is the best friend any
one could ever have
SB

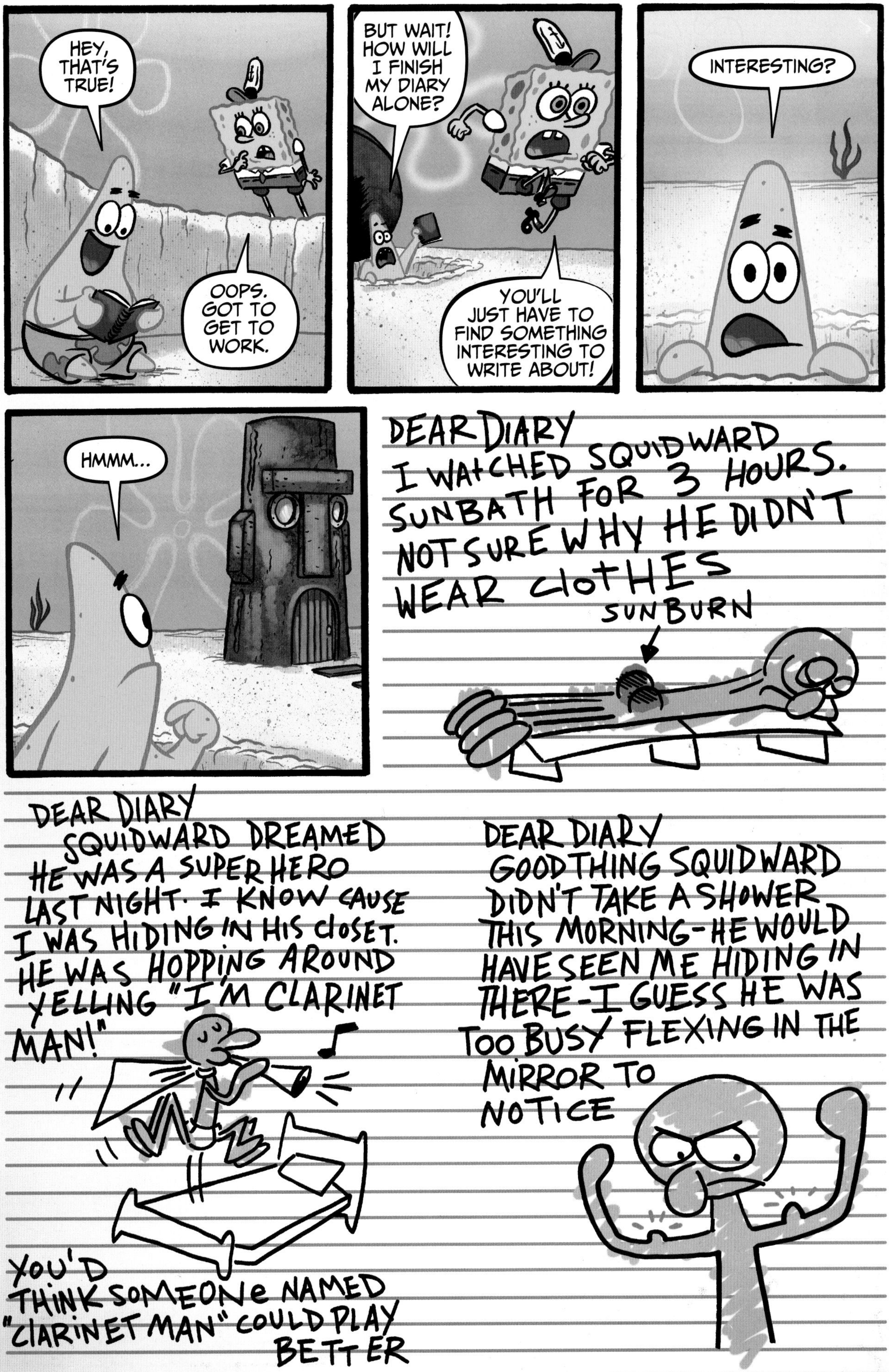
HEY, THAT'S TRUE!
OOPS. GOT TO GET TO WORK.
BUT WAIT! HOW WILL I FINISH MY DIARY ALONE?
YOU'LL JUST HAVE TO FIND SOMETHING INTERESTING TO WRITE ABOUT!
INTERESTING?
HMMM...
DEAR DIARY
I WATCHED SQUIDWARD SUNBATH FOR 3 HOURS. NOT SURE WHY HE DIDN'T WEAR CLOTHES
SUNBURN
DEAR DIARY
SQUIDWARD DREAMED HE WAS A SUPER HERO LAST NIGHT. I KNOW CAUSE I WAS HIDING IN HIS CLOSET. HE WAS HOPPING AROUND YELLING "I'M CLARINET MAN!"
YOU'D THINK SOMEONE NAMED "CLARINET MAN" COULD PLAY BETTER
DEAR DIARY
GOOD THING SQUIDWARD DIDN'T TAKE A SHOWER THIS MORNING-HE WOULD HAVE SEEN ME HIDING IN THERE-I GUESS HE WAS TOO BUSY FLEXING IN THE MIRROR TO NOTICE

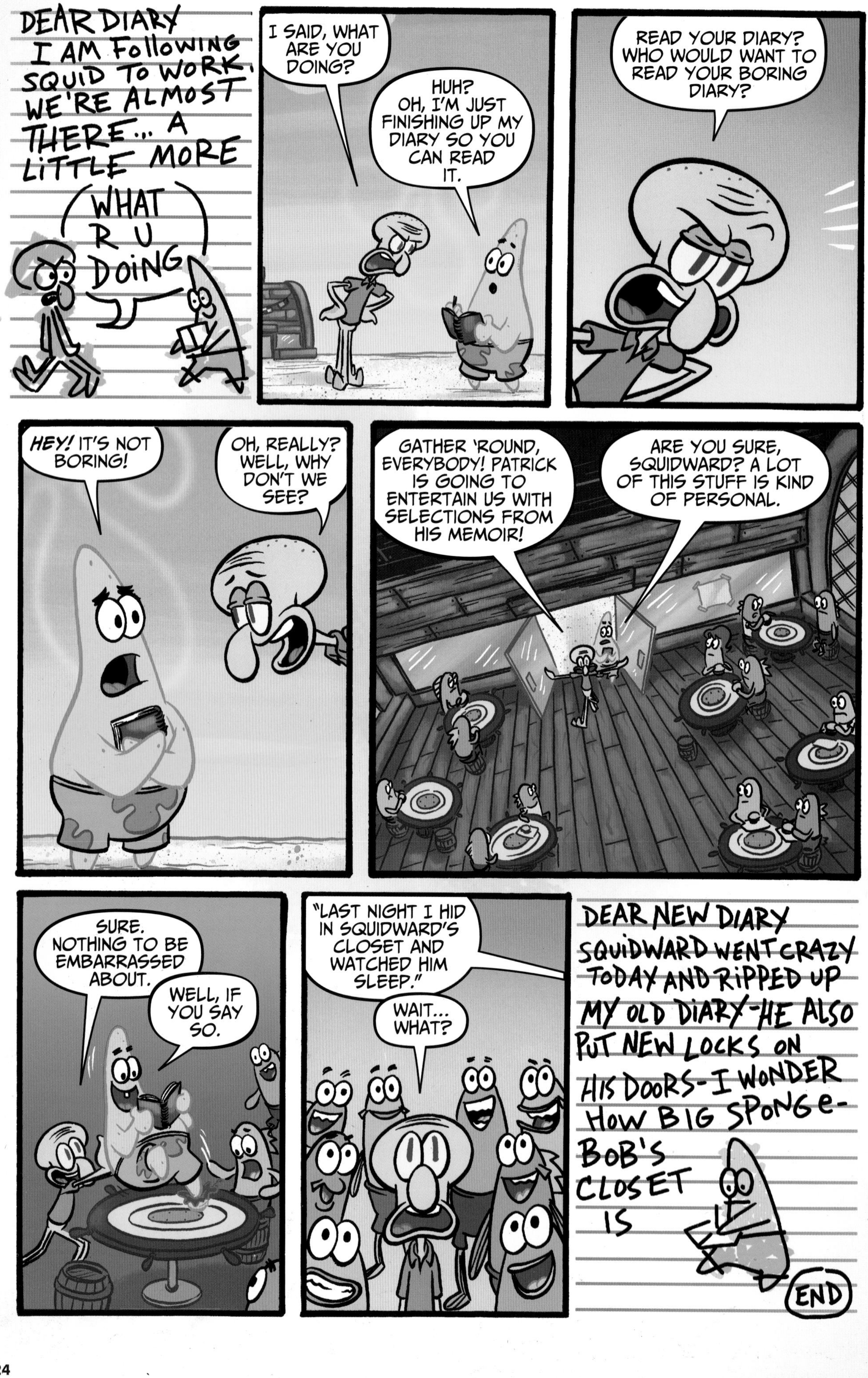
DEAR DIARY I AM Following SQUID TO WORK. WE'RE ALMOST THERE... A LITTLE MORE
(WHAT R U DOING)
I SAID, WHAT ARE YOU DOING?
HUH? OH, I'M JUST FINISHING UP MY DIARY SO YOU CAN READ IT.
READ YOUR DIARY? WHO WOULD WANT TO READ YOUR BORING DIARY?
HEY! IT'S NOT BORING!
OH, REALLY? WELL, WHY DON'T WE SEE?
GATHER 'ROUND, EVERYBODY! PATRICK IS GOING TO ENTERTAIN US WITH SELECTIONS FROM HIS MEMOIR!
ARE YOU SURE, SQUIDWARD? A LOT OF THIS STUFF IS KIND OF PERSONAL.
SURE. NOTHING TO BE EMBARRASSED ABOUT.
WELL, IF YOU SAY SO.
"LAST NIGHT I HID IN SQUIDWARD'S CLOSET AND WATCHED HIM SLEEP."
WAIT... WHAT?
DEAR NEW DIARY SQUIDWARD WENT CRAZY TODAY AND RIPPED UP MY OLD DIARY-HE ALSO PUT NEW LOCKS ON HIS DOORS-I WONDER HOW BIG SPONGE-BOB'S CLOSET IS
END

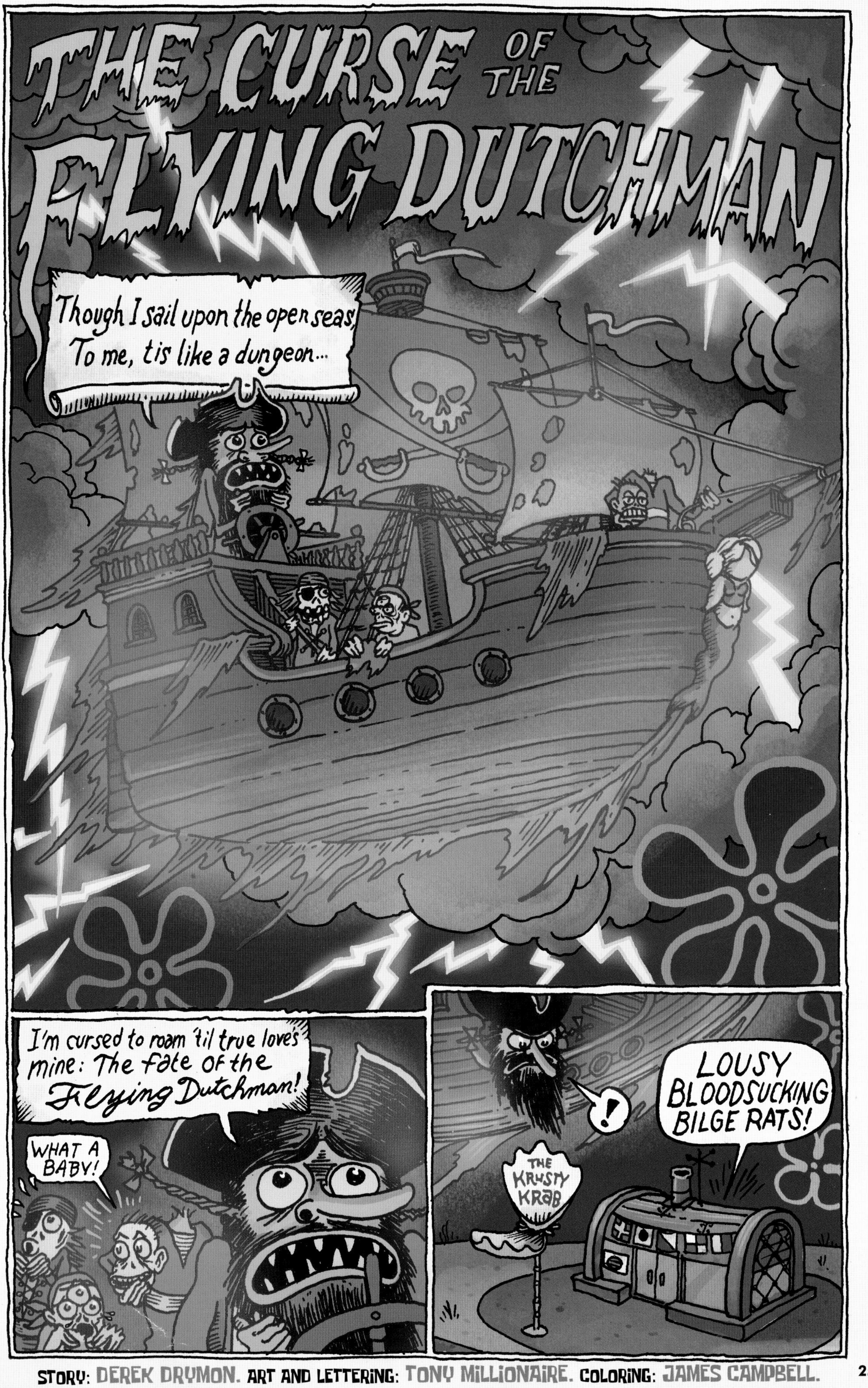
THE CURSE OF THE FLYING DUTCHMAN
Though I sail upon the open seas, To me, tis like a dungeon...
I'm cursed to roam 'til true love's mine: The fate of the Flying Dutchman!
WHAT A BABY!
!
LOUSY BLOODSUCKING BILGE RATS!
THE KRUSTY KRAB

STORY: DEREK DRYMON. ART AND LETTERING: TONY MILLIONAIRE. COLORING: JAMES CAMPBELL.

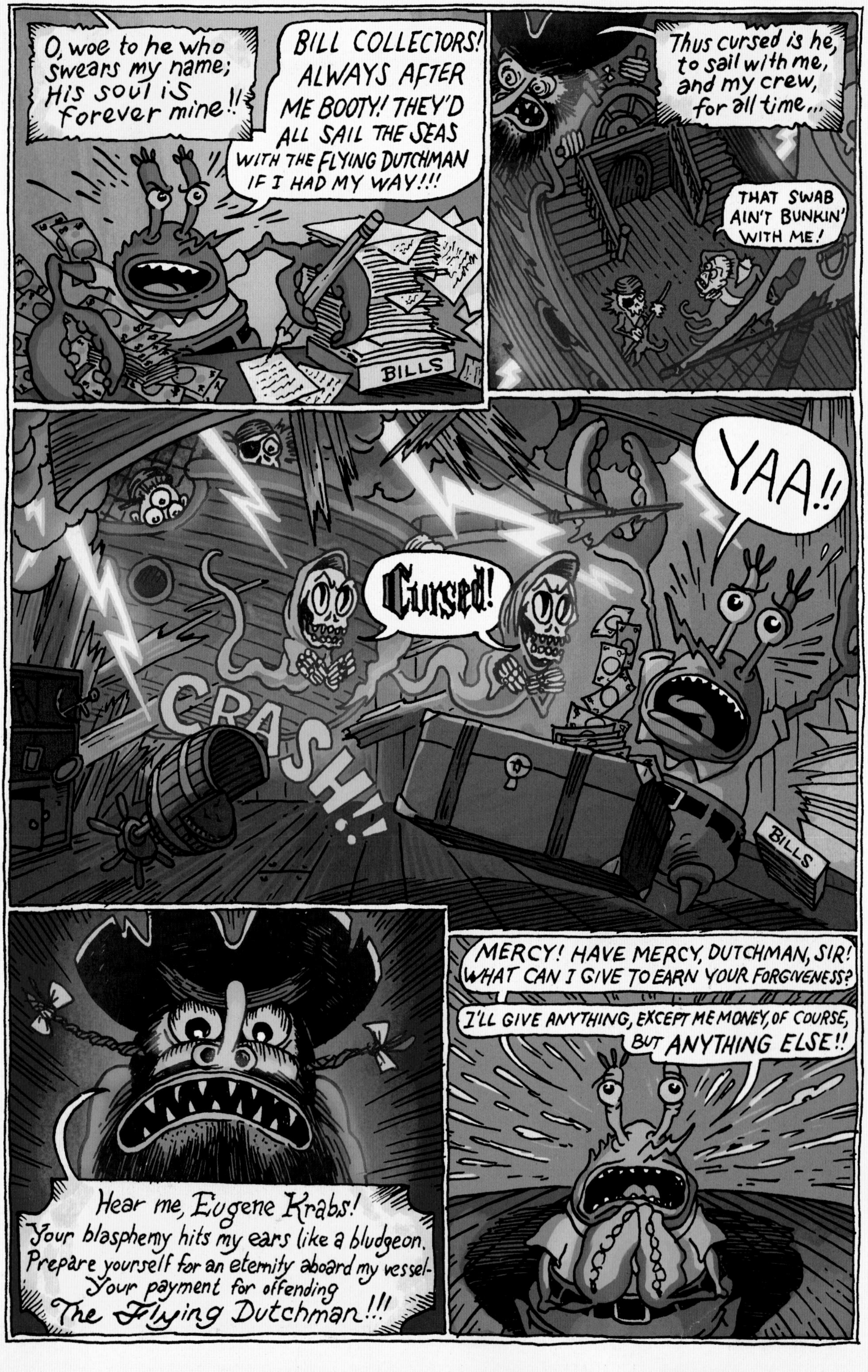

O, woe to he who swears my name; His soul is forever mine!!
BILL COLLECTORS! ALWAYS AFTER ME BOOTY! THEY'D ALL SAIL THE SEAS WITH THE FLYING DUTCHMAN IF I HAD MY WAY!!!
BILLS
Thus cursed is he, to sail with me, and my crew, for all time...
THAT SWAB AIN'T BUNKIN' WITH ME!
YAA!!
Cursed!
CRASH!!
BILLS
Hear me, Eugene Krabs! Your blasphemy hits my ears like a bludgeon. Prepare yourself for an eternity aboard my vessel- Your payment for offending The Flying Dutchman!!!
MERCY! HAVE MERCY, DUTCHMAN, SIR! WHAT CAN I GIVE TO EARN YOUR FORGIVENESS?
I'LL GIVE ANYTHING, EXCEPT ME MONEY, OF COURSE, BUT ANYTHING ELSE!!

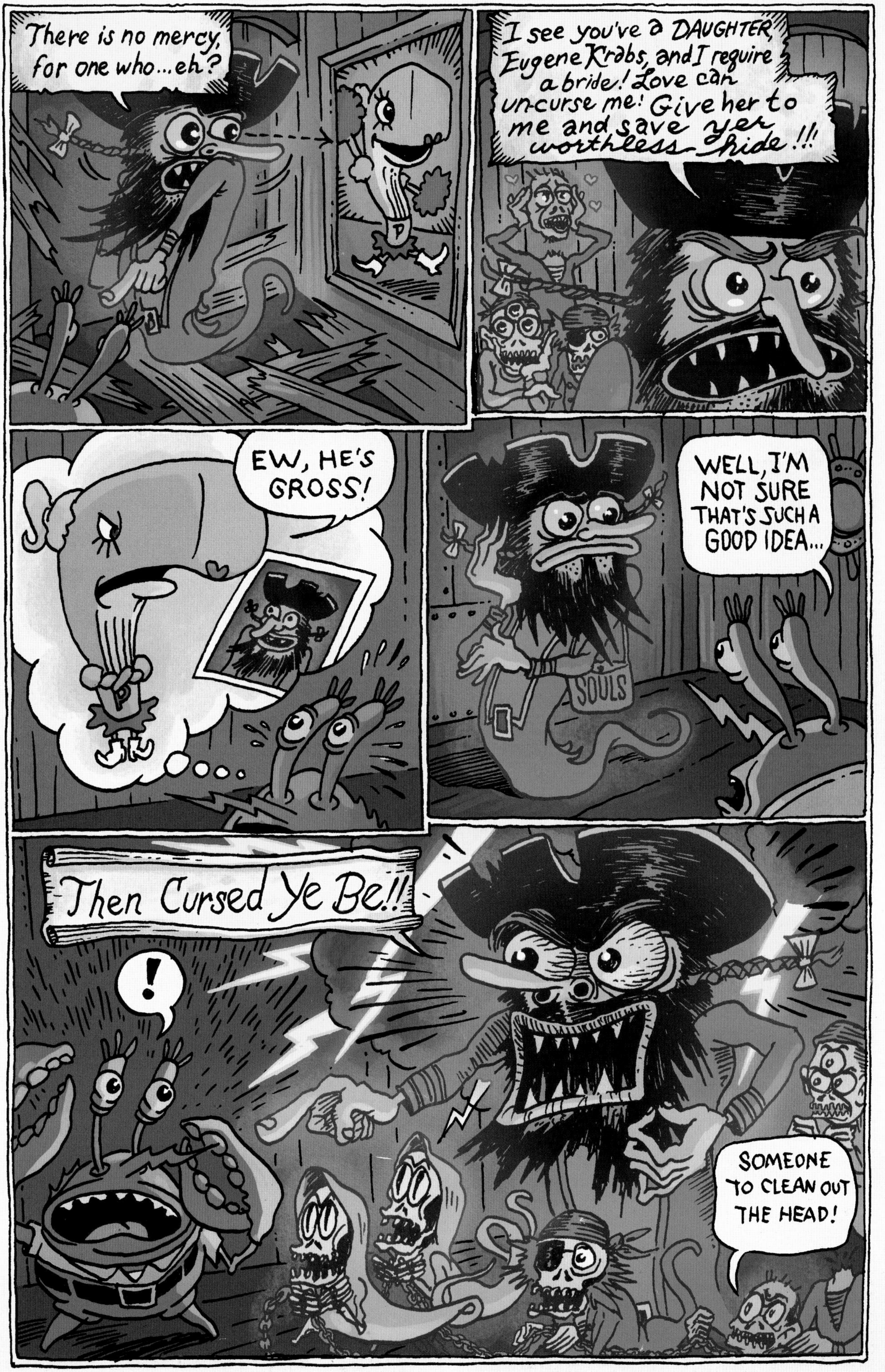

There is no mercy, for one who...eh?
I see you've a DAUGHTER, Eugene Krabs, and I require a bride! Love can un-curse me! Give her to me and save yer worthless hide!!!
EW, HE'S GROSS!
WELL, I'M NOT SURE THAT'S SUCH A GOOD IDEA...
SOULS
Then Cursed Ye Be!!
!
SOMEONE TO CLEAN OUT THE HEAD!

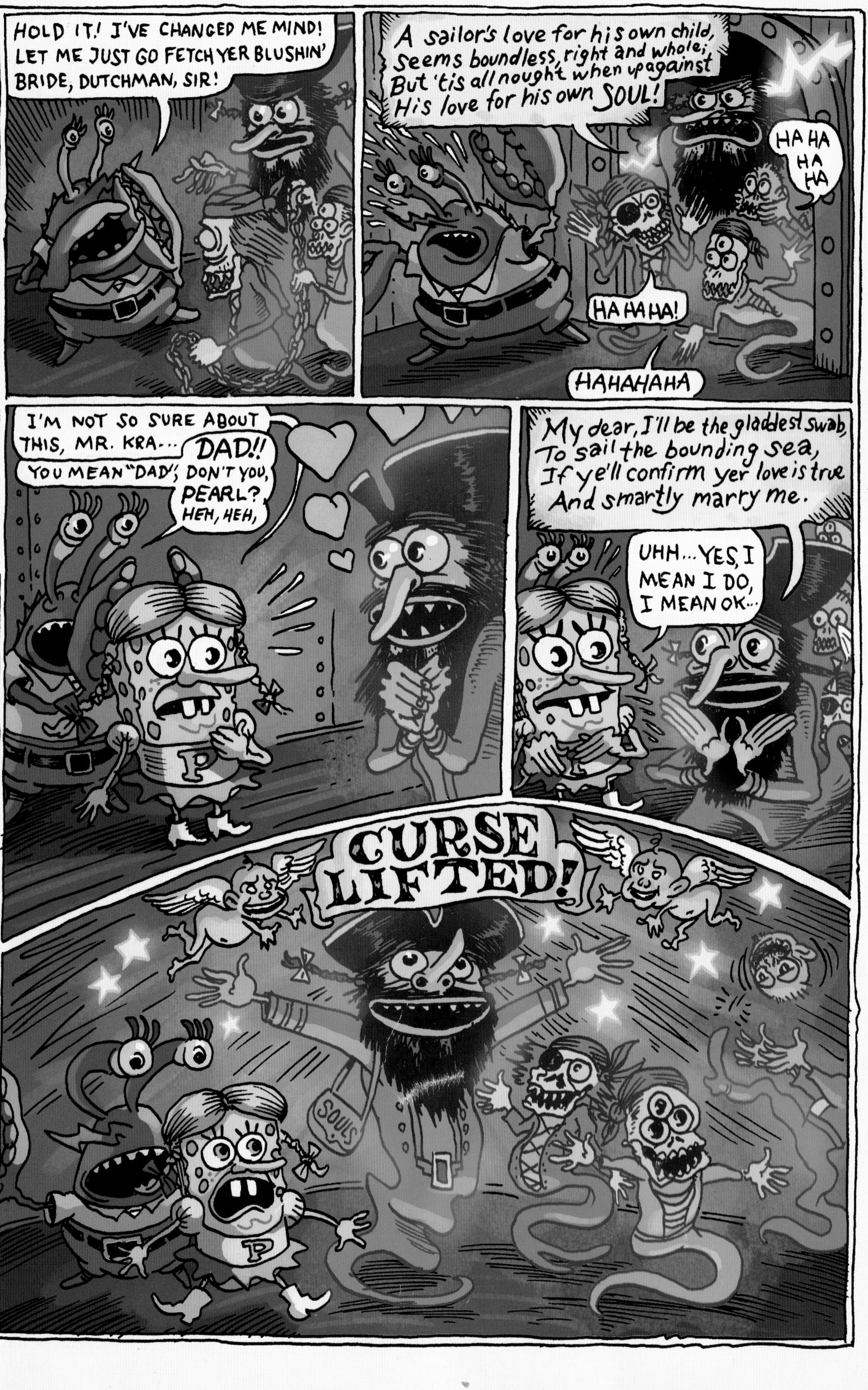
HOLD IT! I'VE CHANGED ME MIND! LET ME JUST GO FETCH YER BLUSHIN' BRIDE, DUTCHMAN, SIR!
A sailor's love for his own child, Seems boundless, right and whole; But 'tis all nought when up against His love for his own SOUL!
HA HA HA HA
HAHAHA!
HAHAHAHA
I'M NOT SO SURE ABOUT THIS, MR. KRA...
DAD!! YOU MEAN "DAD", DON'T YOU, PEARL? HEH, HEH,
My dear, I'll be the gladdest swab, To sail the bounding sea, If ye'll confirm yer love is true And smartly marry me.
UHH... YES, I MEAN I DO, I MEAN OK...
CURSE LIFTED!
SOULS

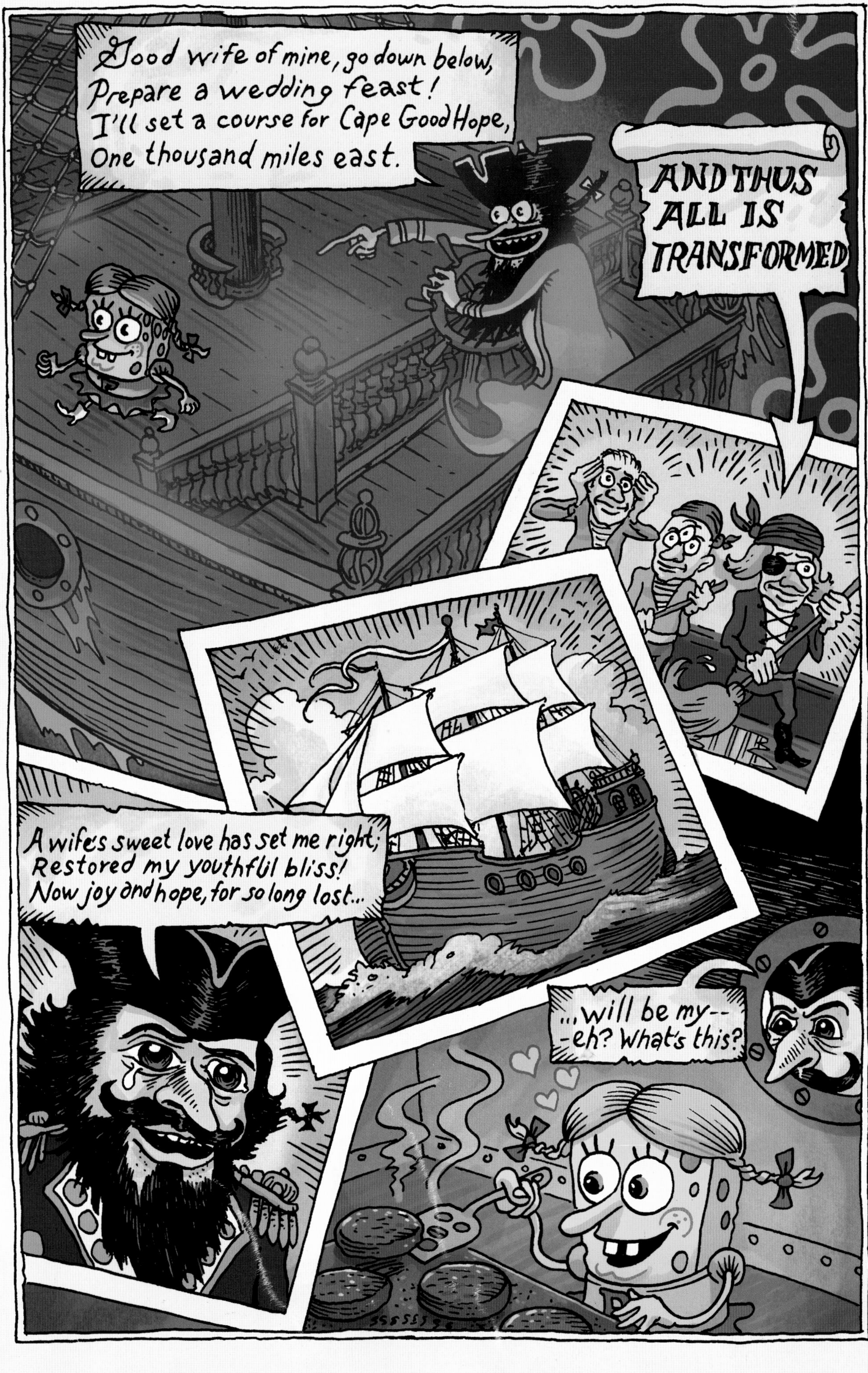
Good wife of mine, go down below, Prepare a wedding feast! I'll set a course for Cape Good Hope, One thousand miles east.
AND THUS ALL IS TRANSFORMED
A wife's sweet love has set me right; Restored my youthful bliss! Now joy and hope, for so long lost...
...will be my-- -eh? What's this?

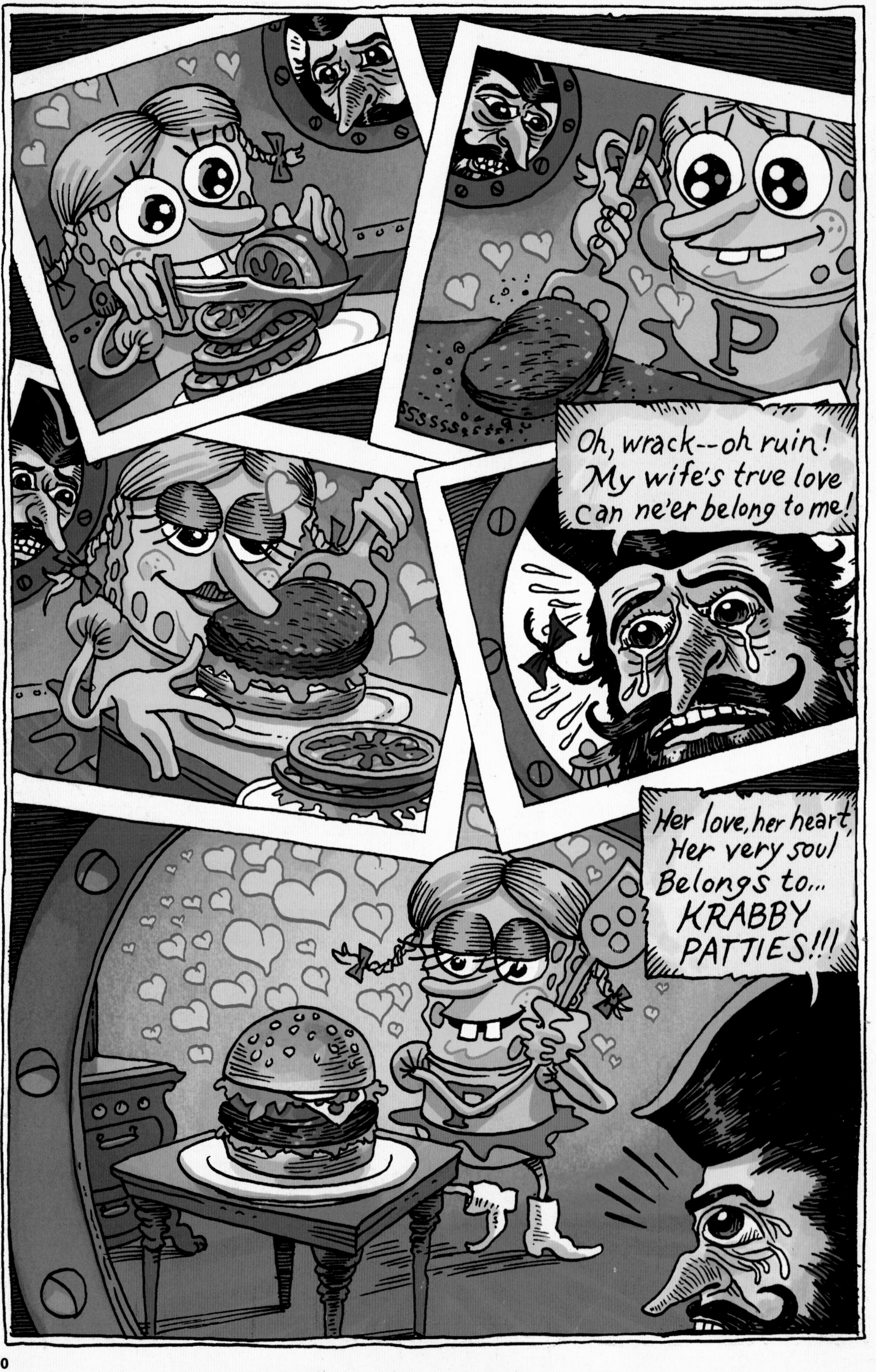
SSSSSSSSSSS
Oh, wrack--oh ruin! My wife's true love can ne'er belong to me!
Her love, her heart, Her very soul Belongs to... KRABBY PATTIES!!!

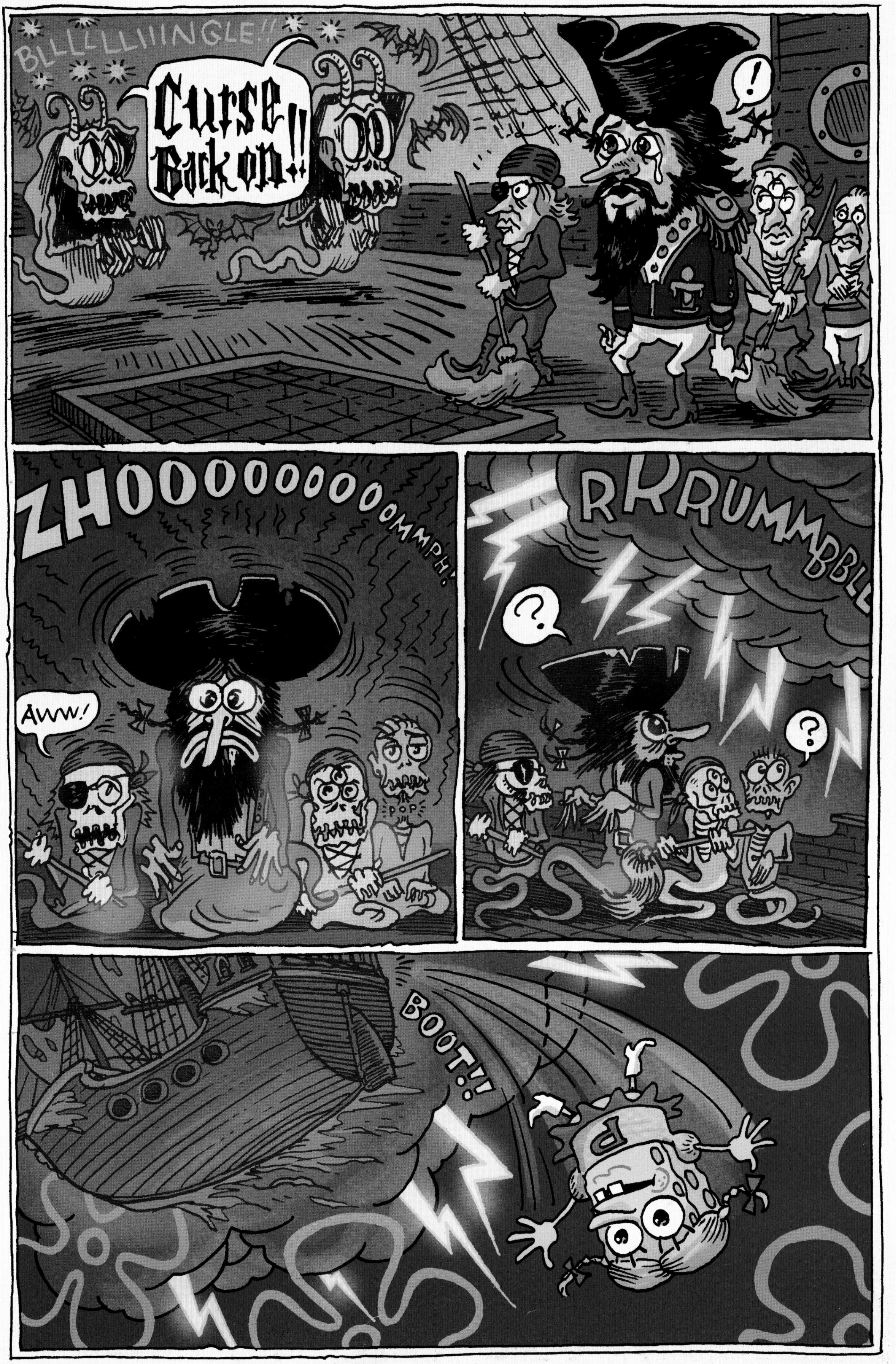
BLLLLLLIIINGLE!!
Curse Back on!!
!
ZHOOOOOOOOOOOMMPH!
AWW!
POP
RRRUMMBBLE
?
?
BOOT!!

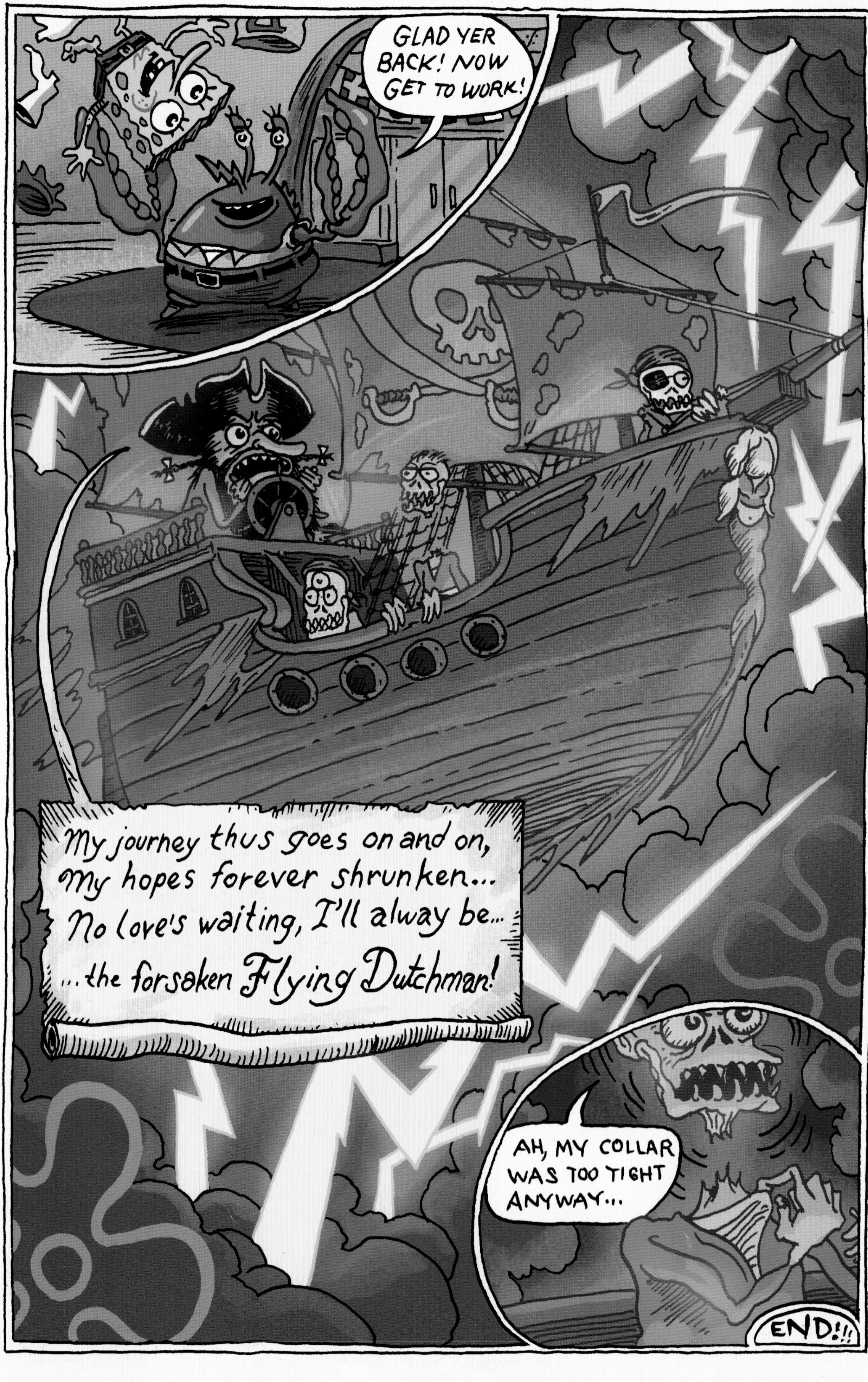
GLAD YER BACK! NOW GET TO WORK!
My journey thus goes on and on, my hopes forever shrunken... No love's waiting, I'll alway be... ...the forsaken Flying Dutchman!
AH, MY COLLAR WAS TOO TIGHT ANYWAY...
END!!!

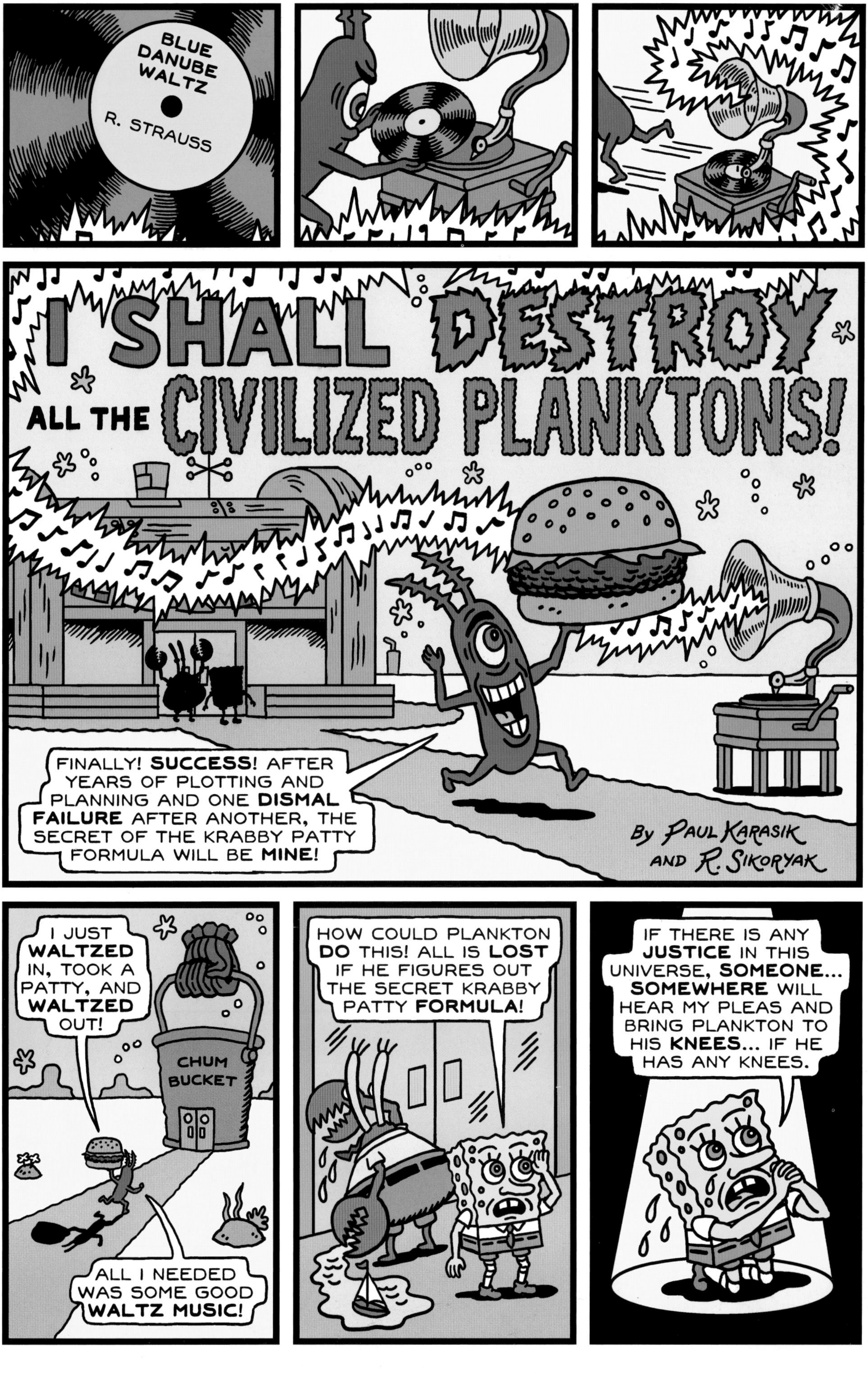
BLUE DANUBE WALTZ
R. STRAUSS
I SHALL DESTROY ALL THE CIVILIZED PLANKTONS!
FINALLY! SUCCESS! AFTER YEARS OF PLOTTING AND PLANNING AND ONE DISMAL FAILURE AFTER ANOTHER, THE SECRET OF THE KRABBY PATTY FORMULA WILL BE MINE!
By PAUL KARASIK AND R. SIKORYAK
I JUST WALTZED IN, TOOK A PATTY, AND WALTZED OUT!
CHUM BUCKET
ALL I NEEDED WAS SOME GOOD WALTZ MUSIC!
HOW COULD PLANKTON DO THIS! ALL IS LOST IF HE FIGURES OUT THE SECRET KRABBY PATTY FORMULA!
IF THERE IS ANY JUSTICE IN THIS UNIVERSE, SOMEONE... SOMEWHERE WILL HEAR MY PLEAS AND BRING PLANKTON TO HIS KNEES... IF HE HAS ANY KNEES.

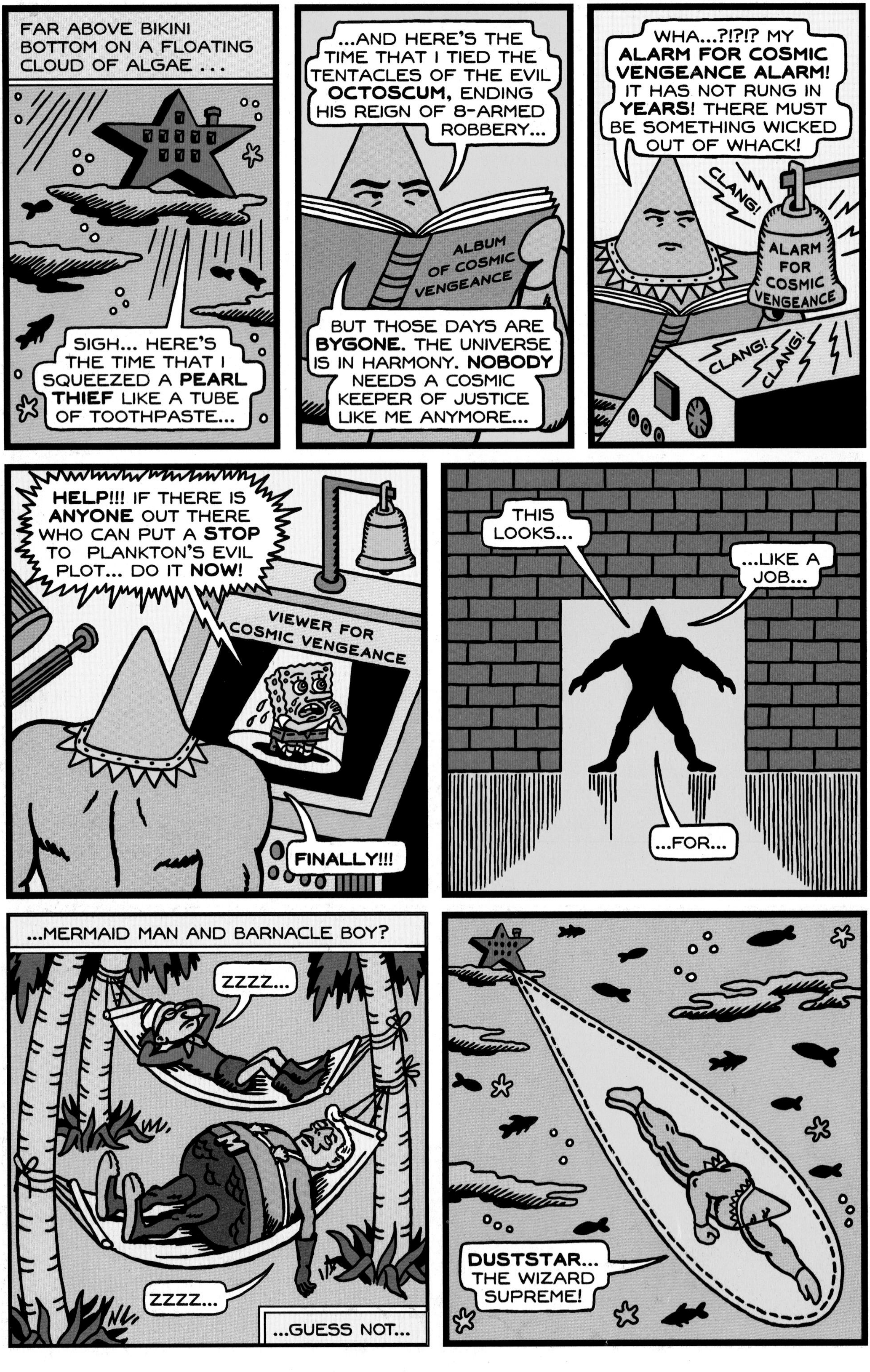
FAR ABOVE BIKINI BOTTOM ON A FLOATING CLOUD OF ALGAE . . .
SIGH... HERE'S THE TIME THAT I SQUEEZED A **PEARL THIEF** LIKE A TUBE OF TOOTHPASTE...
...AND HERE'S THE TIME THAT I TIED THE TENTACLES OF THE EVIL **OCTOSCUM**, ENDING HIS REIGN OF 8-ARMED ROBBERY...
ALBUM OF COSMIC VENGEANCE
BUT THOSE DAYS ARE **BYGONE**. THE UNIVERSE IS IN HARMONY. **NOBODY** NEEDS A COSMIC KEEPER OF JUSTICE LIKE ME ANYMORE...
WHA...?!?!? MY **ALARM FOR COSMIC VENGEANCE ALARM**! IT HAS NOT RUNG IN **YEARS**! THERE MUST BE SOMETHING WICKED OUT OF WHACK!
CLANG!
ALARM FOR COSMIC VENGEANCE
CLANG!
CLANG!
HELP!!! IF THERE IS **ANYONE** OUT THERE WHO CAN PUT A **STOP** TO PLANKTON'S EVIL PLOT... DO IT **NOW**!
VIEWER FOR COSMIC VENGEANCE
FINALLY!!!
THIS LOOKS...
...LIKE A JOB...
...FOR...
...MERMAID MAN AND BARNACLE BOY?
ZZZZ...
ZZZZ...
...GUESS NOT...
DUSTSTAR... THE WIZARD SUPREME!

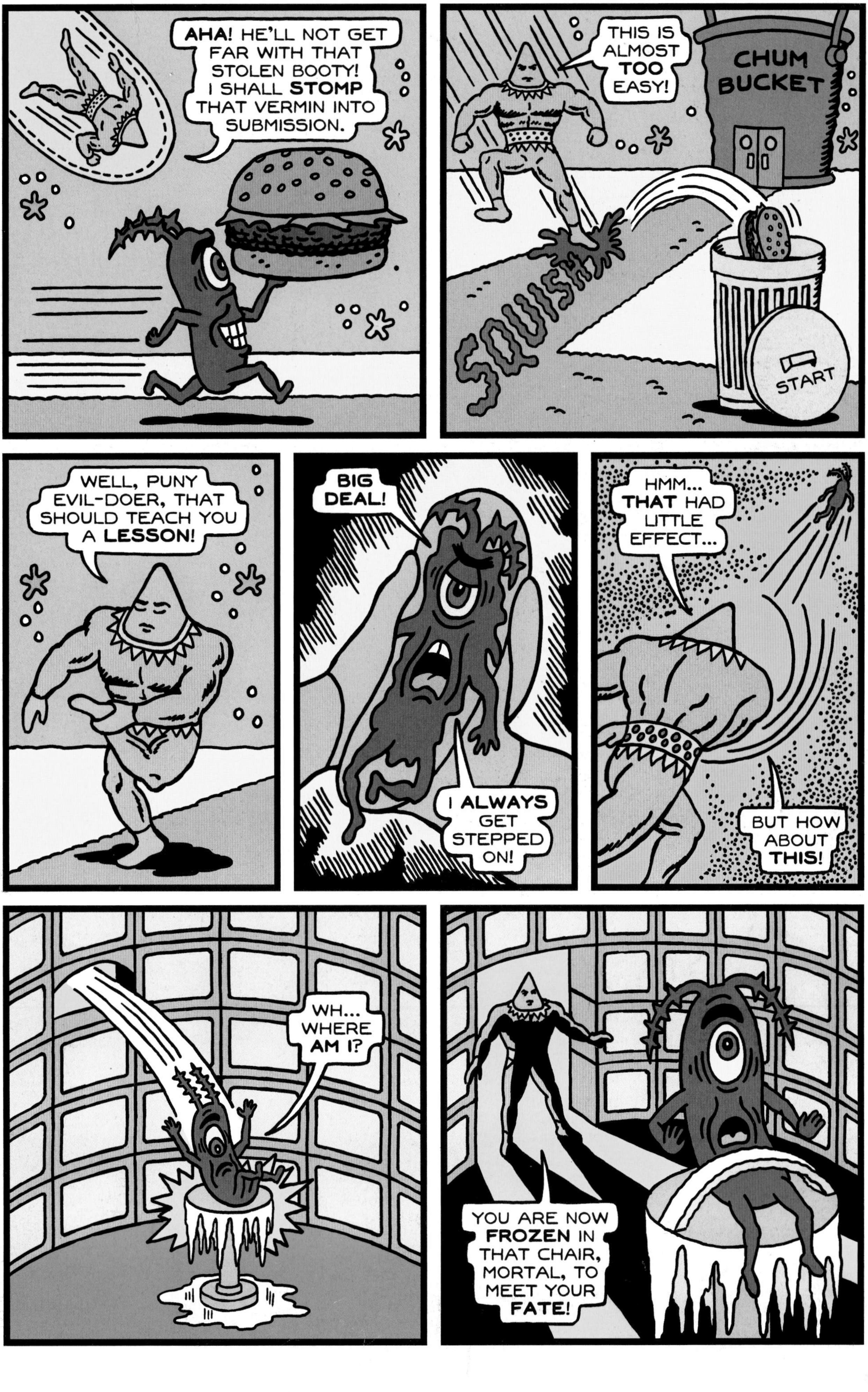
AHA! HE'LL NOT GET FAR WITH THAT STOLEN BOOTY! I SHALL STOMP THAT VERMIN INTO SUBMISSION.
THIS IS ALMOST TOO EASY!
CHUM BUCKET
SQUISH
START
WELL, PUNY EVIL-DOER, THAT SHOULD TEACH YOU A LESSON!
BIG DEAL!
I ALWAYS GET STEPPED ON!
HMM... THAT HAD LITTLE EFFECT...
BUT HOW ABOUT THIS!
WH... WHERE AM I?
YOU ARE NOW FROZEN IN THAT CHAIR, MORTAL, TO MEET YOUR FATE!

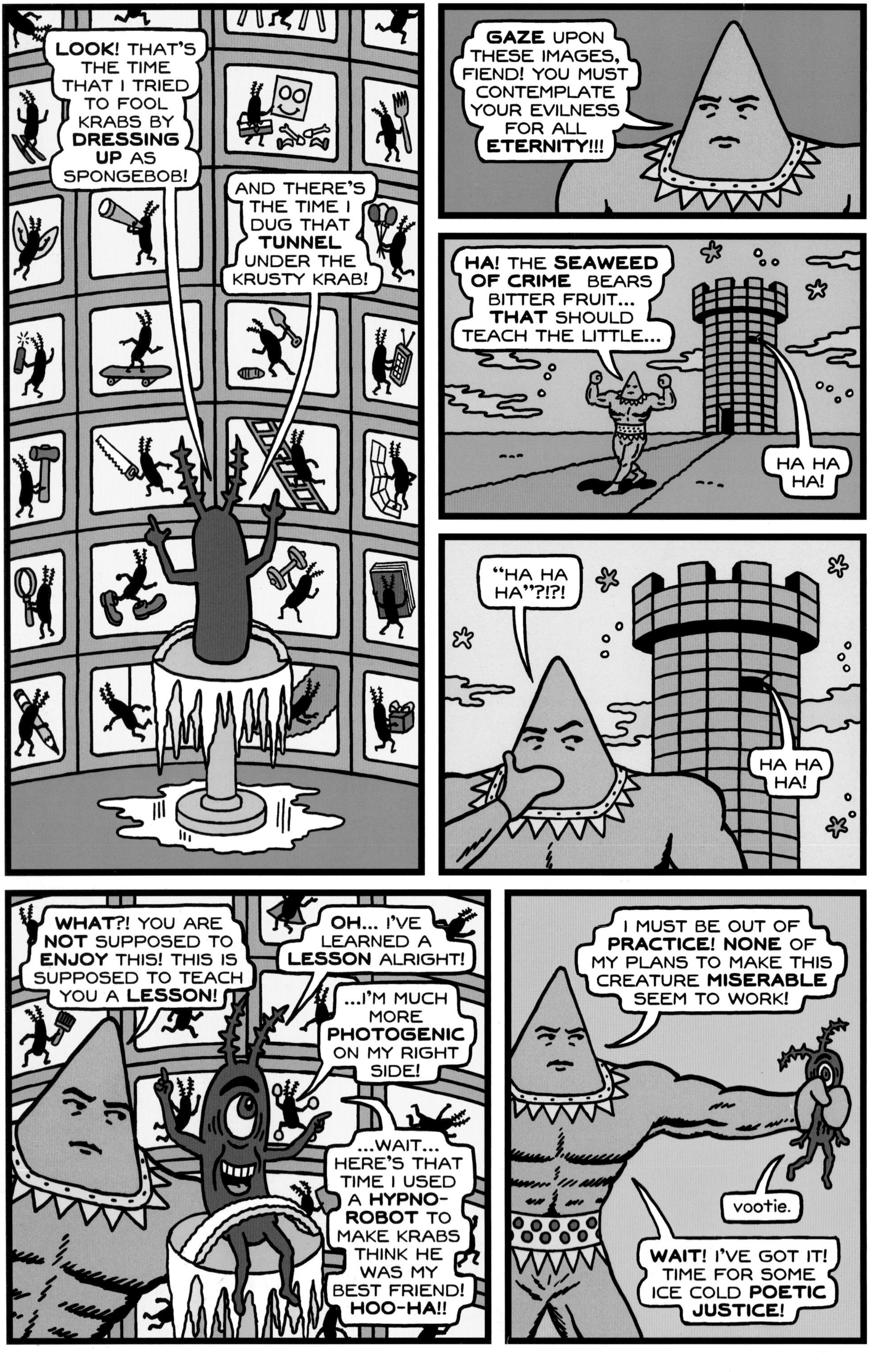
LOOK! THAT'S THE TIME THAT I TRIED TO FOOL KRABS BY DRESSING UP AS SPONGEBOB!
AND THERE'S THE TIME I DUG THAT TUNNEL UNDER THE KRUSTY KRAB!
GAZE UPON THESE IMAGES, FIEND! YOU MUST CONTEMPLATE YOUR EVILNESS FOR ALL ETERNITY!!!
HA! THE SEAWEED OF CRIME BEARS BITTER FRUIT... THAT SHOULD TEACH THE LITTLE...
HA HA HA!
"HA HA HA"?!?!
HA HA HA!
WHAT?! YOU ARE NOT SUPPOSED TO ENJOY THIS! THIS IS SUPPOSED TO TEACH YOU A LESSON!
OH... I'VE LEARNED A LESSON ALRIGHT!
...I'M MUCH MORE PHOTOGENIC ON MY RIGHT SIDE!
...WAIT... HERE'S THAT TIME I USED A HYPNO-ROBOT TO MAKE KRABS THINK HE WAS MY BEST FRIEND! HOO-HA!!
I MUST BE OUT OF PRACTICE! NONE OF MY PLANS TO MAKE THIS CREATURE MISERABLE SEEM TO WORK!
vootie.
WAIT! I'VE GOT IT! TIME FOR SOME ICE COLD POETIC JUSTICE!

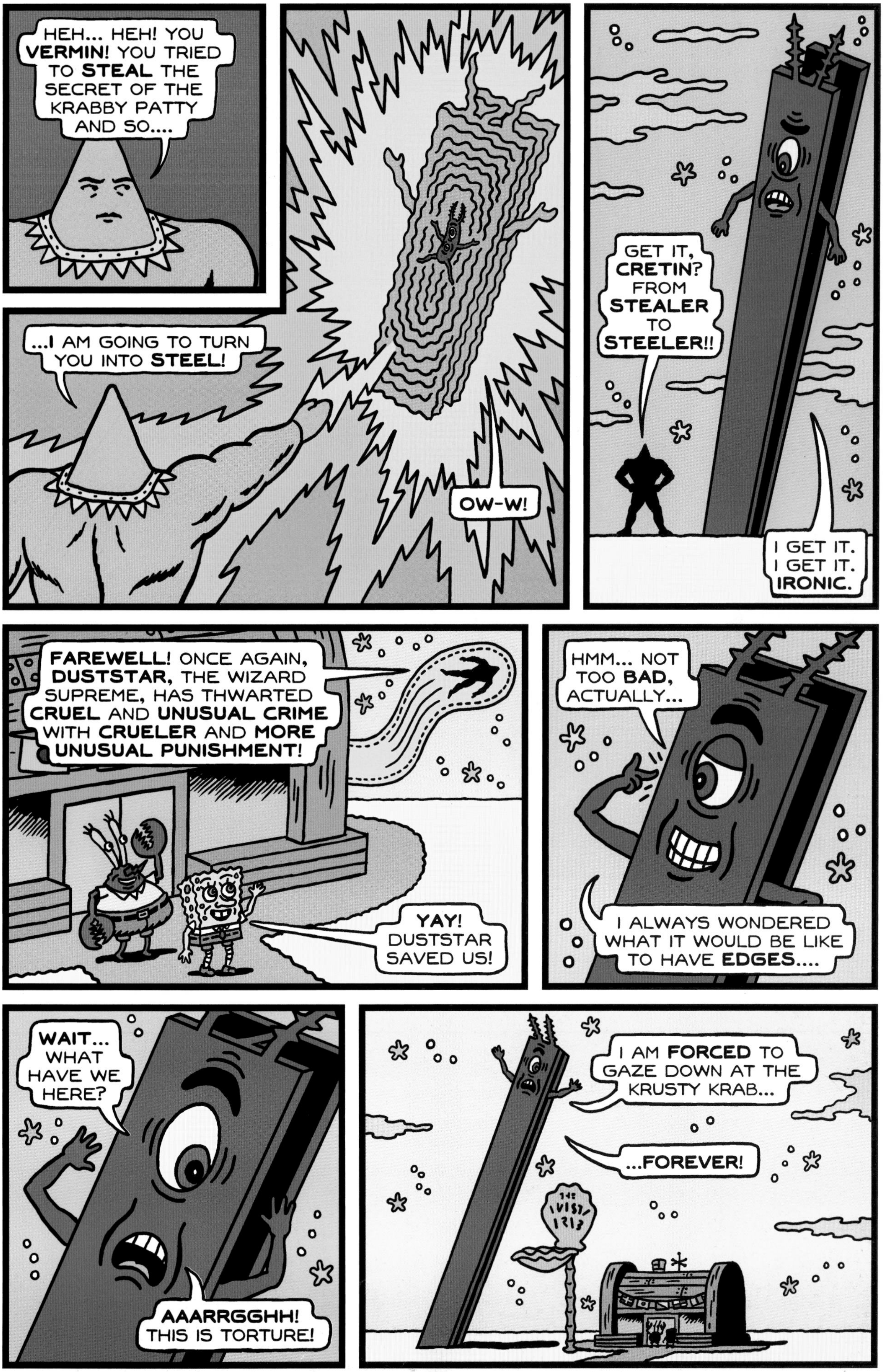
HEH... HEH! YOU VERMIN! YOU TRIED TO STEAL THE SECRET OF THE KRABBY PATTY AND SO....
...I AM GOING TO TURN YOU INTO STEEL!
OW-W!
GET IT, CRETIN? FROM STEALER TO STEELER!!
I GET IT. I GET IT. IRONIC.
FAREWELL! ONCE AGAIN, DUSTSTAR, THE WIZARD SUPREME, HAS THWARTED CRUEL AND UNUSUAL CRIME WITH CRUELER AND MORE UNUSUAL PUNISHMENT!
YAY! DUSTSTAR SAVED US!
HMM... NOT TOO BAD, ACTUALLY...
I ALWAYS WONDERED WHAT IT WOULD BE LIKE TO HAVE EDGES....
WAIT... WHAT HAVE WE HERE?
AAARRGGHH! THIS IS TORTURE!
I AM FORCED TO GAZE DOWN AT THE KRUSTY KRAB...
...FOREVER!

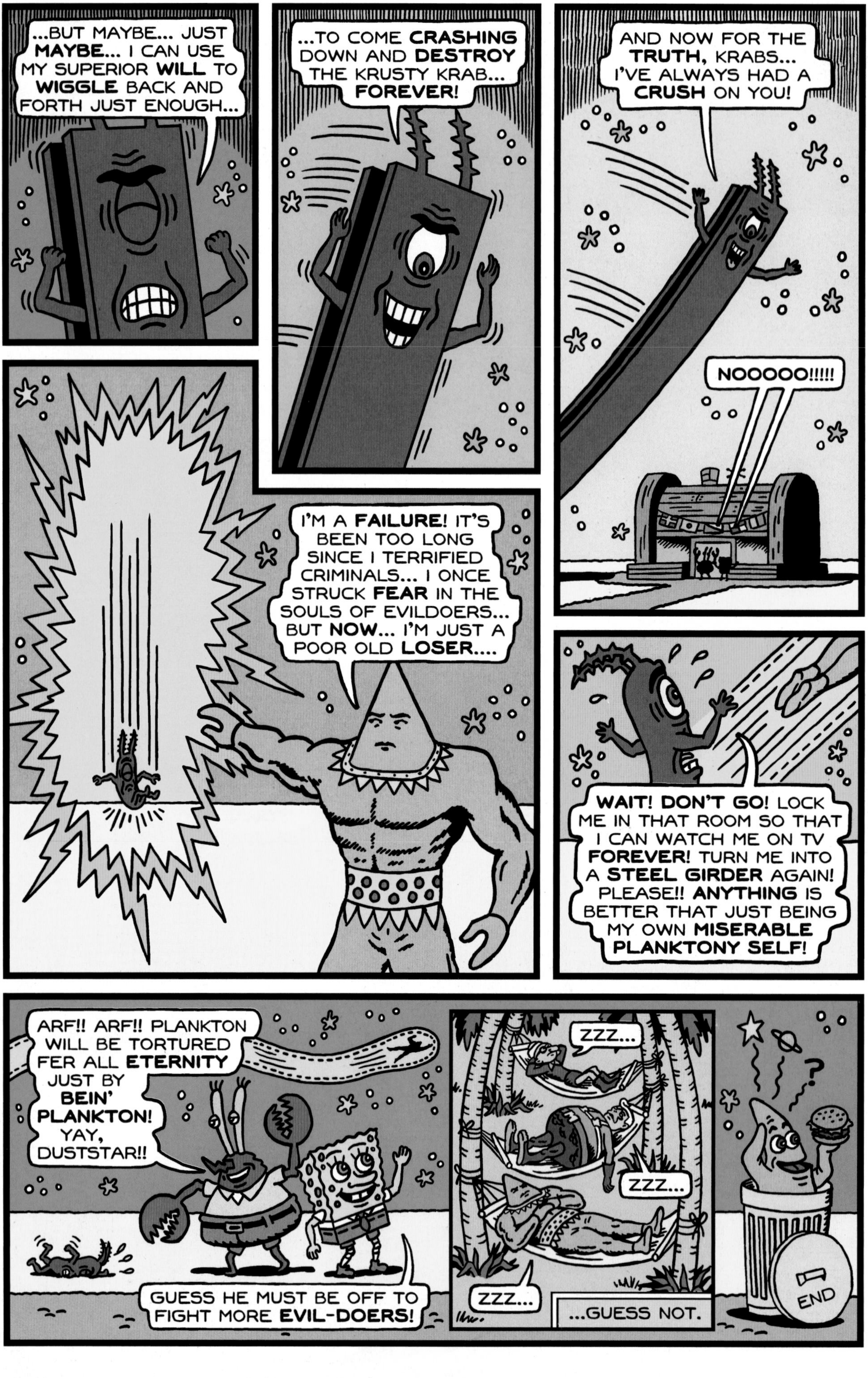
...BUT MAYBE... JUST MAYBE... I CAN USE MY SUPERIOR WILL TO WIGGLE BACK AND FORTH JUST ENOUGH...
...TO COME CRASHING DOWN AND DESTROY THE KRUSTY KRAB... FOREVER!
AND NOW FOR THE TRUTH, KRABS... I'VE ALWAYS HAD A CRUSH ON YOU!
NOOOOO!!!!!
I'M A FAILURE! IT'S BEEN TOO LONG SINCE I TERRIFIED CRIMINALS... I ONCE STRUCK FEAR IN THE SOULS OF EVILDOERS... BUT NOW... I'M JUST A POOR OLD LOSER....
WAIT! DON'T GO! LOCK ME IN THAT ROOM SO THAT I CAN WATCH ME ON TV FOREVER! TURN ME INTO A STEEL GIRDER AGAIN! PLEASE!! ANYTHING IS BETTER THAT JUST BEING MY OWN MISERABLE PLANKTONY SELF!
ARF!! ARF!! PLANKTON WILL BE TORTURED FER ALL ETERNITY JUST BY BEIN' PLANKTON! YAY, DUSTSTAR!!
GUESS HE MUST BE OFF TO FIGHT MORE EVIL-DOERS!
ZZZ...
ZZZ...
ZZZ...
...GUESS NOT.
END

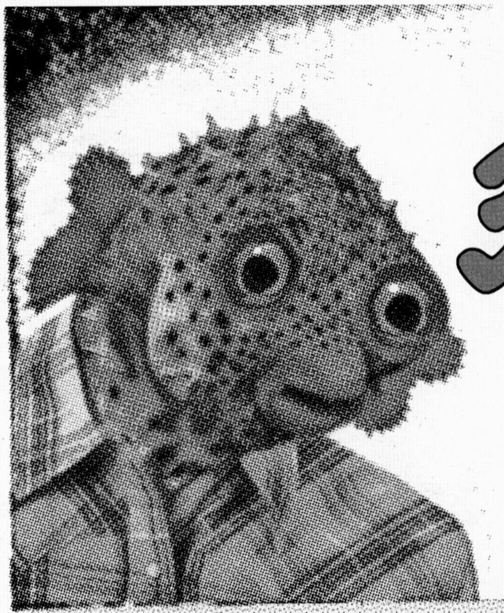

only $1.98

350,000 pc. PLANKTON SET

Shipped straight to you in a heavy-duty drum barrel!

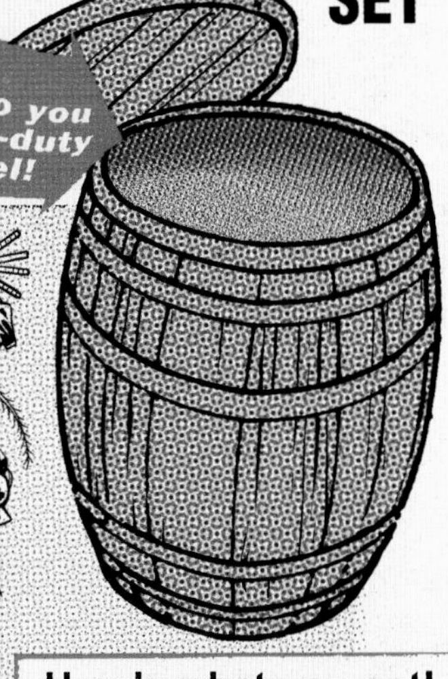

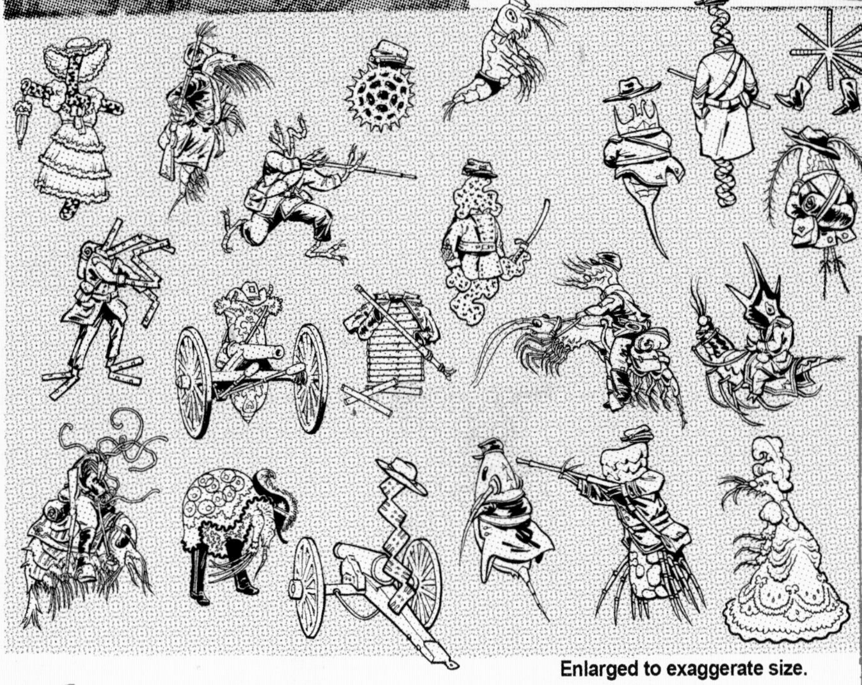

Robert Leighton & Mark Martin

Enlarged to exaggerate size.

Here's what you get!

120,000 Phytoplankton
114,960 Zooplankton
61,175 Flagellates
44,000 Antarctic krill
9000 Brine shrimp
824 Pacific krill
40 Marine viruses
1 Pair tweezers

Hey, Kids!

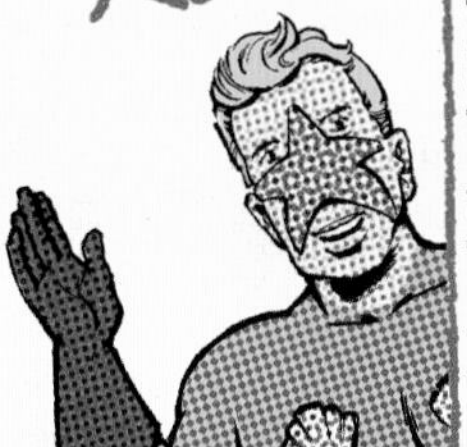

Have you ever wanted to know how the Civil War would have turned out if it had been fought by microscopic organisms of the deep? Well, now you can! Armies of Phytoplankton and Zooplankton battle it out in handcrafted, lifelike details that are far too small to see! Your set also comes with over 100,000 additional plankton townspeople, riding animals, and viruses!

Plus a SPECIAL BONUS! Two pieces of Pacific Krill specially designed to look like ME—Mermaid Man—and my faithful sidekick, Barnacle Boy! Keep looking—they're in there somewhere, GUARANTEED!

Each piece is stamped from pure molded plastic and provides hours of eye-straining fun! Set up dioramas! Move around your regiments! Sift them through your fingers like grains of sand!

Cut and send this coupon today!

You must be completely satisfied in order to avoid hefty return charges!

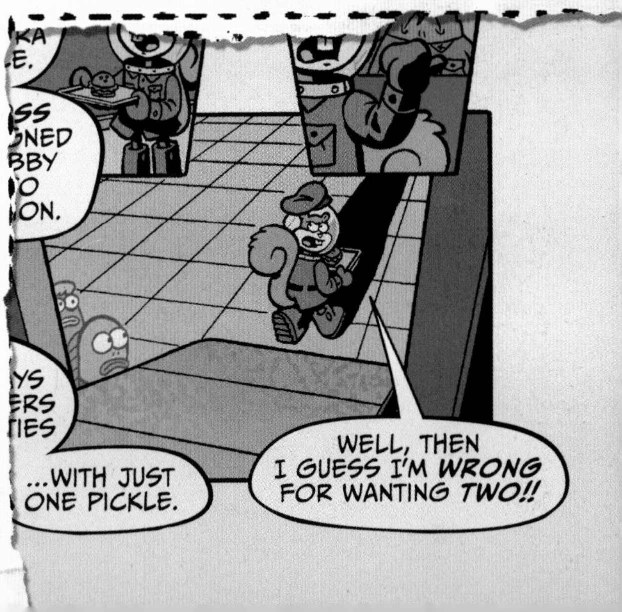
...WITH JUST ONE PICKLE.
WELL, THEN I GUESS I'M *WRONG* FOR WANTING *TWO!!*

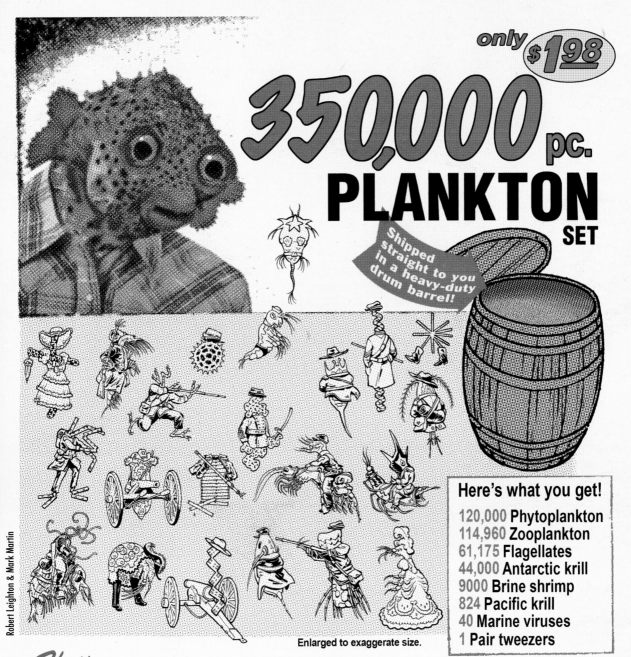

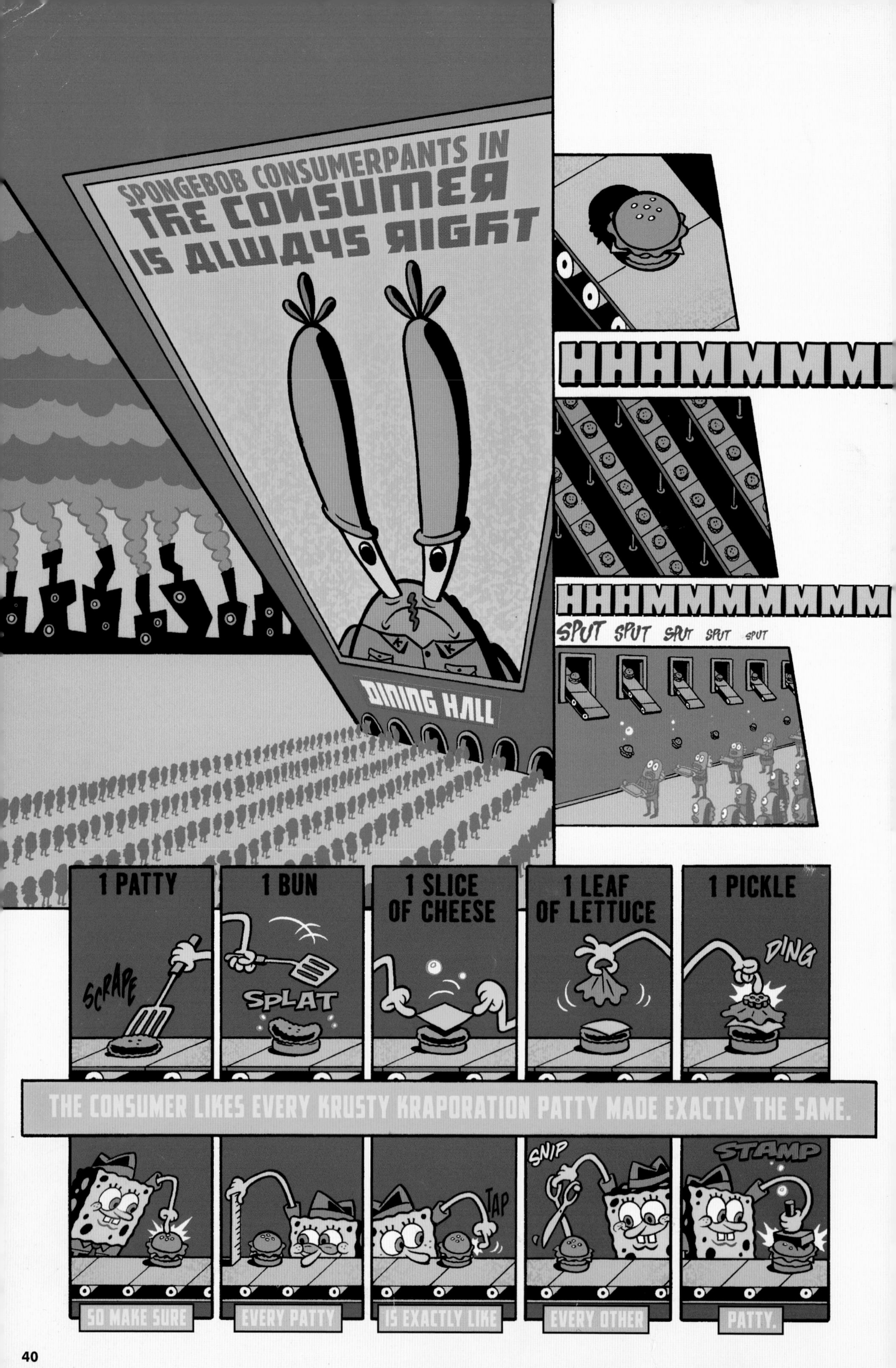

SPONGEBOB CONSUMERPANTS IN
THE CONSUMER IS ALWAYS RIGHT
DINING HALL
HHHMMMMMM
HHHMMMMMMMMM
SPUT SPUT SPUT SPUT SPUT
1 PATTY
SCRAPE
1 BUN
SPLAT
1 SLICE OF CHEESE
1 LEAF OF LETTUCE
1 PICKLE
DING
THE CONSUMER LIKES EVERY KRUSTY KRAPORATION PATTY MADE EXACTLY THE SAME.
TAP
SNIP
STAMP
SO MAKE SURE
EVERY PATTY
IS EXACTLY LIKE
EVERY OTHER
PATTY.

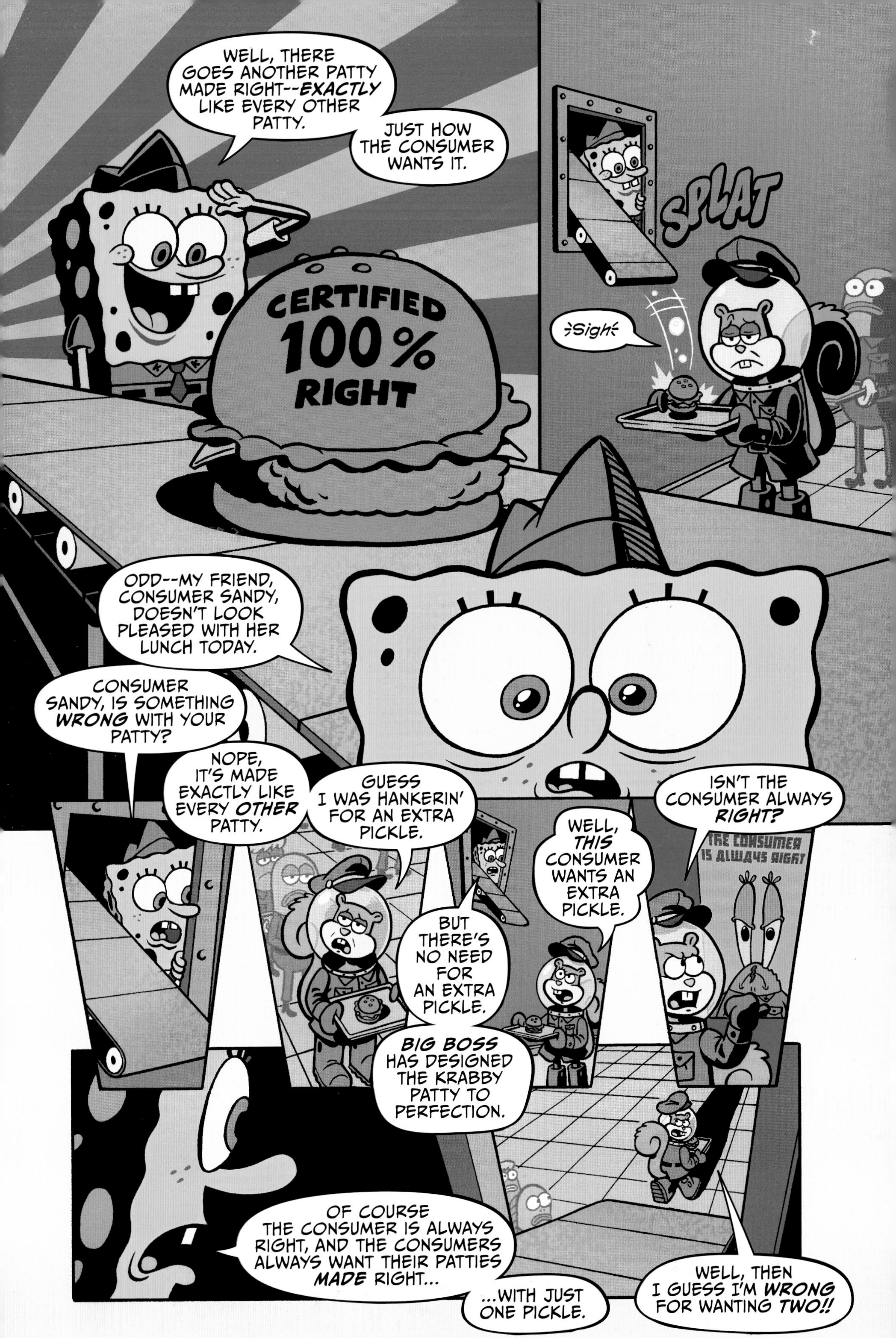
WELL, THERE GOES ANOTHER PATTY MADE RIGHT--EXACTLY LIKE EVERY OTHER PATTY.
JUST HOW THE CONSUMER WANTS IT.
CERTIFIED 100% RIGHT
SPLAT
Sigh
ODD--MY FRIEND, CONSUMER SANDY, DOESN'T LOOK PLEASED WITH HER LUNCH TODAY.
CONSUMER SANDY, IS SOMETHING WRONG WITH YOUR PATTY?
NOPE, IT'S MADE EXACTLY LIKE EVERY OTHER PATTY.
GUESS I WAS HANKERIN' FOR AN EXTRA PICKLE.
BUT THERE'S NO NEED FOR AN EXTRA PICKLE.
BIG BOSS HAS DESIGNED THE KRABBY PATTY TO PERFECTION.
WELL, THIS CONSUMER WANTS AN EXTRA PICKLE.
ISN'T THE CONSUMER ALWAYS RIGHT?
THE CONSUMER IS ALWAYS RIGHT
OF COURSE THE CONSUMER IS ALWAYS RIGHT, AND THE CONSUMERS ALWAYS WANT THEIR PATTIES MADE RIGHT...
...WITH JUST ONE PICKLE.
WELL, THEN I GUESS I'M WRONG FOR WANTING TWO!!

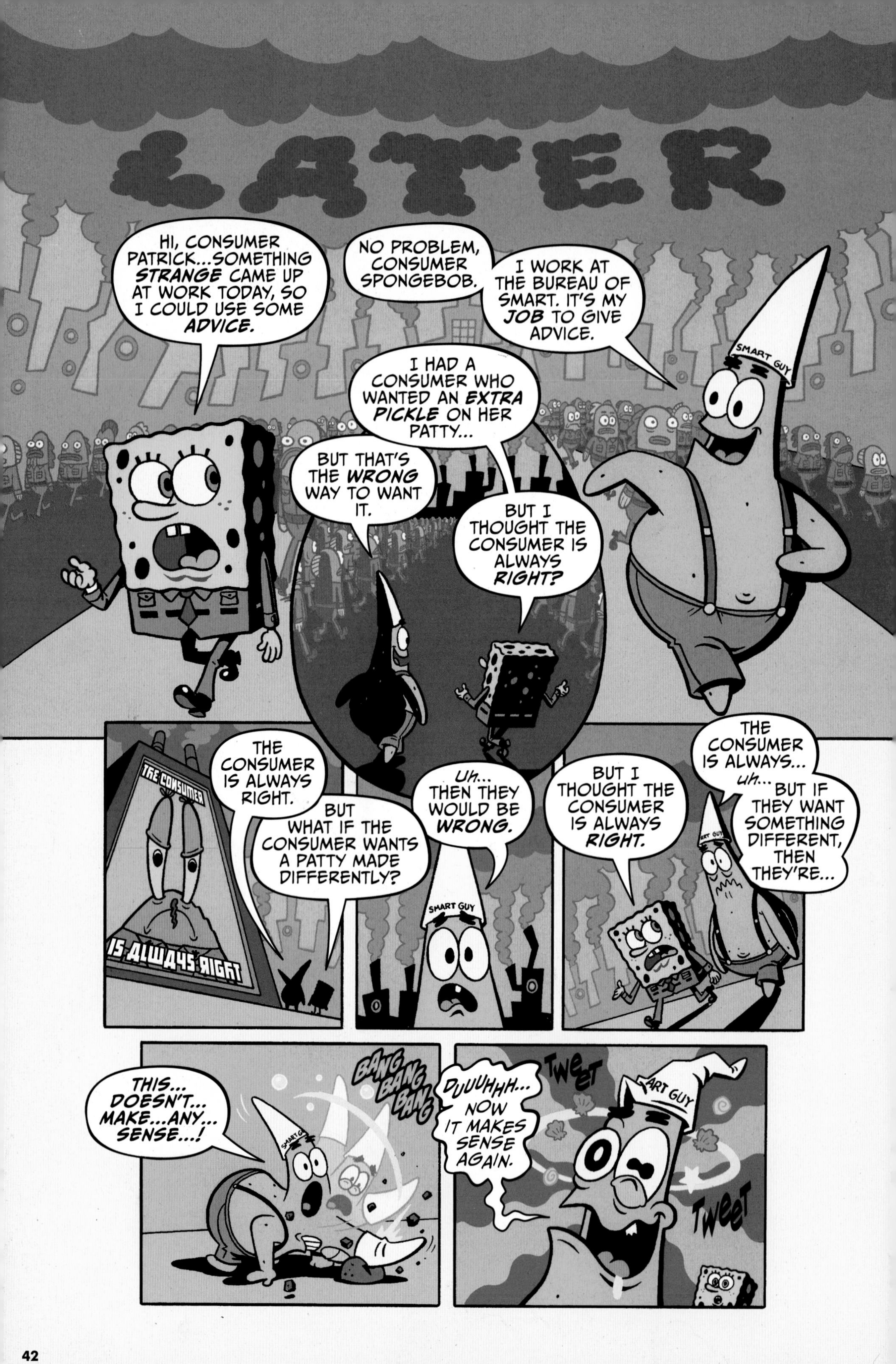
LATER
HI, CONSUMER PATRICK...SOMETHING STRANGE CAME UP AT WORK TODAY, SO I COULD USE SOME ADVICE.
NO PROBLEM, CONSUMER SPONGEBOB.
I WORK AT THE BUREAU OF SMART. IT'S MY JOB TO GIVE ADVICE.
SMART GUY
I HAD A CONSUMER WHO WANTED AN EXTRA PICKLE ON HER PATTY...
BUT THAT'S THE WRONG WAY TO WANT IT.
BUT I THOUGHT THE CONSUMER IS ALWAYS RIGHT?
THE CONSUMER IS ALWAYS RIGHT
THE CONSUMER IS ALWAYS RIGHT.
BUT WHAT IF THE CONSUMER WANTS A PATTY MADE DIFFERENTLY?
UH... THEN THEY WOULD BE WRONG.
SMART GUY
BUT I THOUGHT THE CONSUMER IS ALWAYS RIGHT.
THE CONSUMER IS ALWAYS... UH...
BUT IF THEY WANT SOMETHING DIFFERENT, THEN THEY'RE...
THIS... DOESN'T... MAKE...ANY... SENSE...!
BANG BANG BANG
DUUUHHH... NOW IT MAKES SENSE AGAIN.
TWEET
TWEET

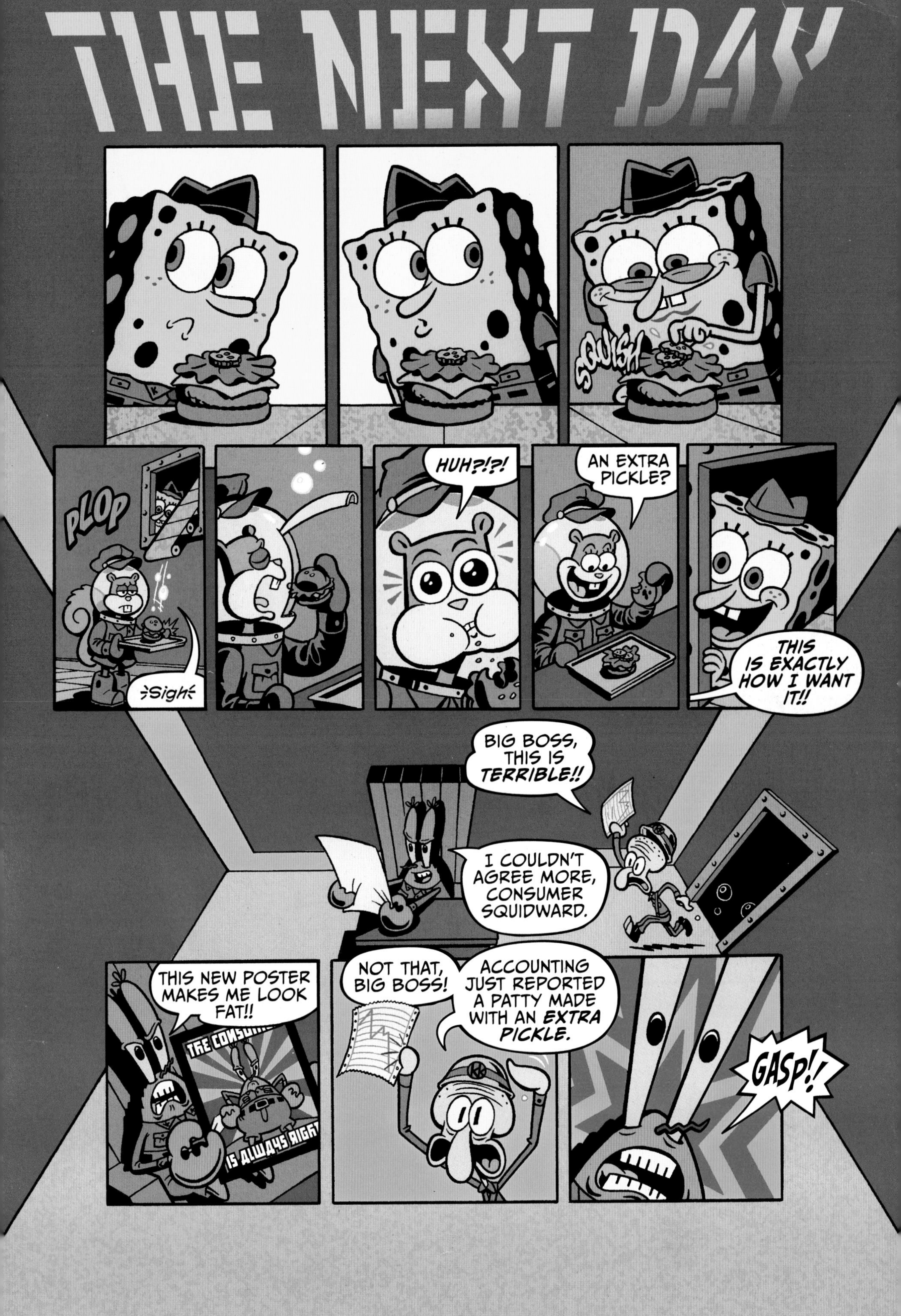
THE NEXT DAY
SQUISH
PLOP
Sigh
HUH?!?!
AN EXTRA PICKLE?
THIS IS EXACTLY HOW I WANT IT!!
BIG BOSS, THIS IS TERRIBLE!!
I COULDN'T AGREE MORE, CONSUMER SQUIDWARD.
THIS NEW POSTER MAKES ME LOOK FAT!!
IS ALWAYS RIGHT
NOT THAT, BIG BOSS!
ACCOUNTING JUST REPORTED A PATTY MADE WITH AN EXTRA PICKLE.
GASP!!

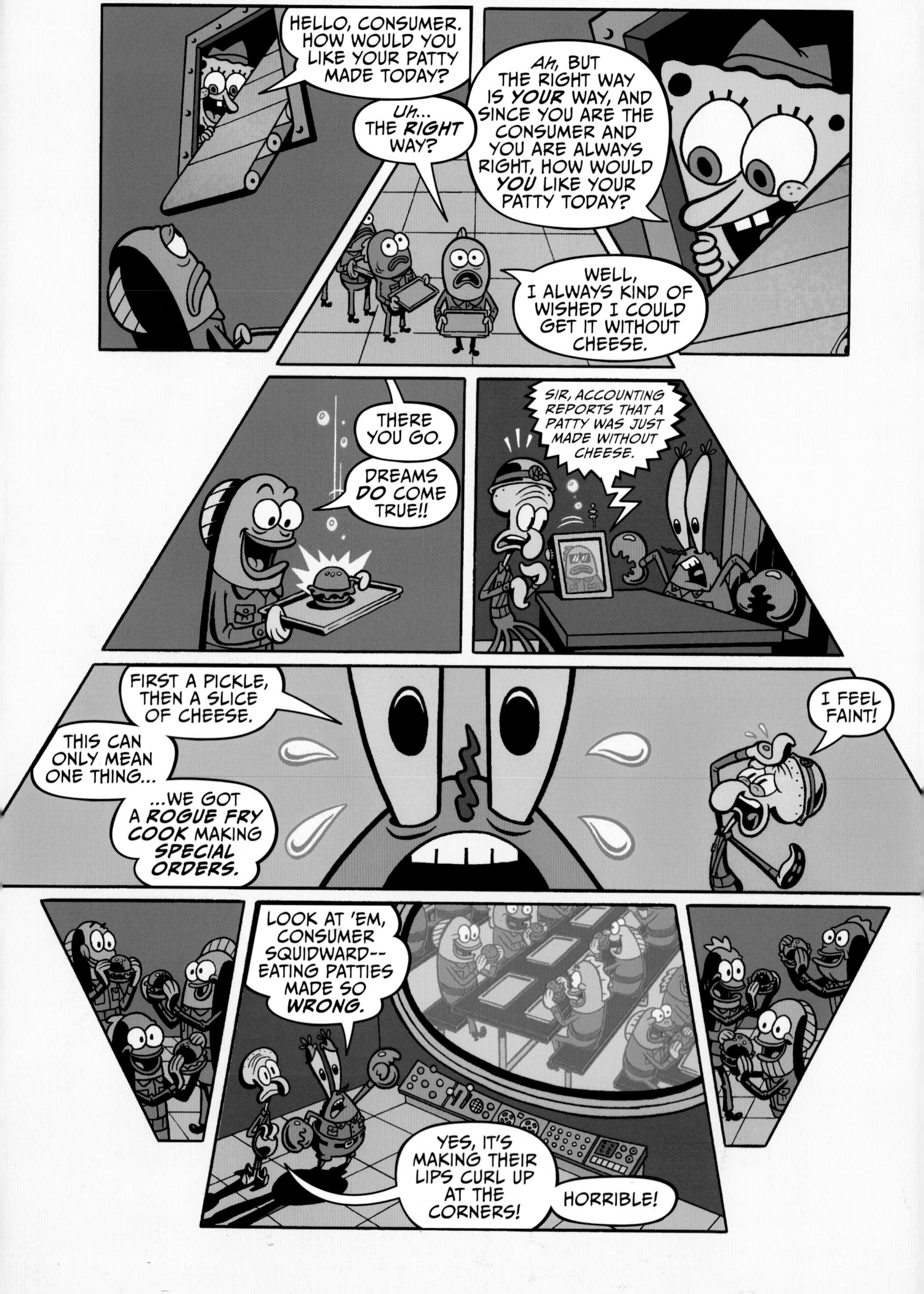
HELLO, CONSUMER. HOW WOULD YOU LIKE YOUR PATTY MADE TODAY?
Uh... THE RIGHT WAY?
Ah, BUT THE RIGHT WAY IS YOUR WAY, AND SINCE YOU ARE THE CONSUMER AND YOU ARE ALWAYS RIGHT, HOW WOULD YOU LIKE YOUR PATTY TODAY?
WELL, I ALWAYS KIND OF WISHED I COULD GET IT WITHOUT CHEESE.
THERE YOU GO.
DREAMS DO COME TRUE!!
SIR, ACCOUNTING REPORTS THAT A PATTY WAS JUST MADE WITHOUT CHEESE.
FIRST A PICKLE, THEN A SLICE OF CHEESE.
THIS CAN ONLY MEAN ONE THING...
...WE GOT A ROGUE FRY COOK MAKING SPECIAL ORDERS.
I FEEL FAINT!
LOOK AT 'EM, CONSUMER SQUIDWARD-- EATING PATTIES MADE SO WRONG.
YES, IT'S MAKING THEIR LIPS CURL UP AT THE CORNERS!
HORRIBLE!

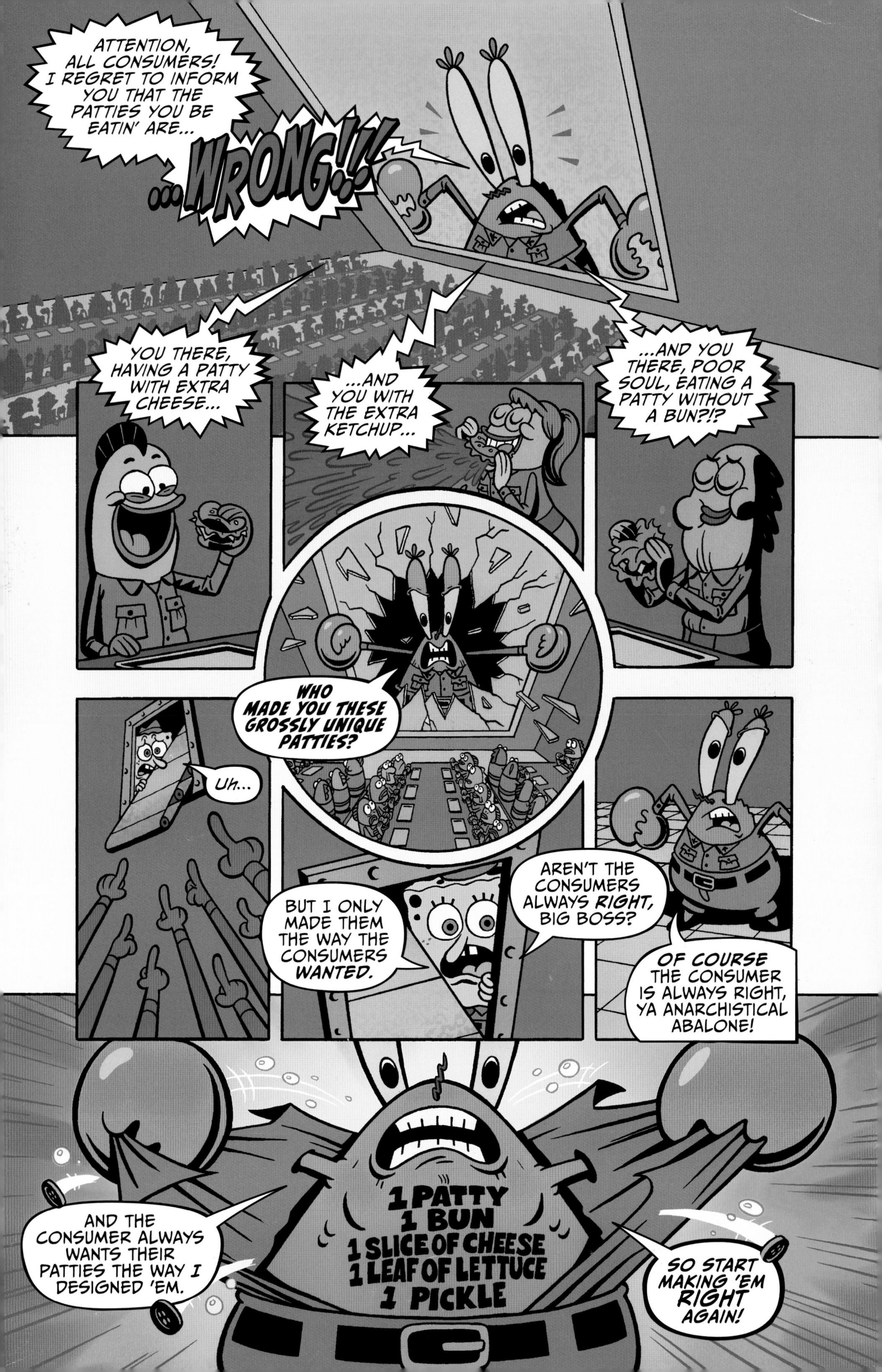
ATTENTION, ALL CONSUMERS! I REGRET TO INFORM YOU THAT THE PATTIES YOU BE EATIN' ARE...
...WRONG!!!
YOU THERE, HAVING A PATTY WITH EXTRA CHEESE...
...AND YOU WITH THE EXTRA KETCHUP...
...AND YOU THERE, POOR SOUL, EATING A PATTY WITHOUT A BUN?!?
WHO MADE YOU THESE GROSSLY UNIQUE PATTIES?
Uh...
BUT I ONLY MADE THEM THE WAY THE CONSUMERS WANTED.
AREN'T THE CONSUMERS ALWAYS RIGHT, BIG BOSS?
OF COURSE THE CONSUMER IS ALWAYS RIGHT, YA ANARCHISTICAL ABALONE!
AND THE CONSUMER ALWAYS WANTS THEIR PATTIES THE WAY I DESIGNED 'EM.
1 PATTY
1 BUN
1 SLICE OF CHEESE
1 LEAF OF LETTUCE
1 PICKLE
SO START MAKING 'EM RIGHT AGAIN!

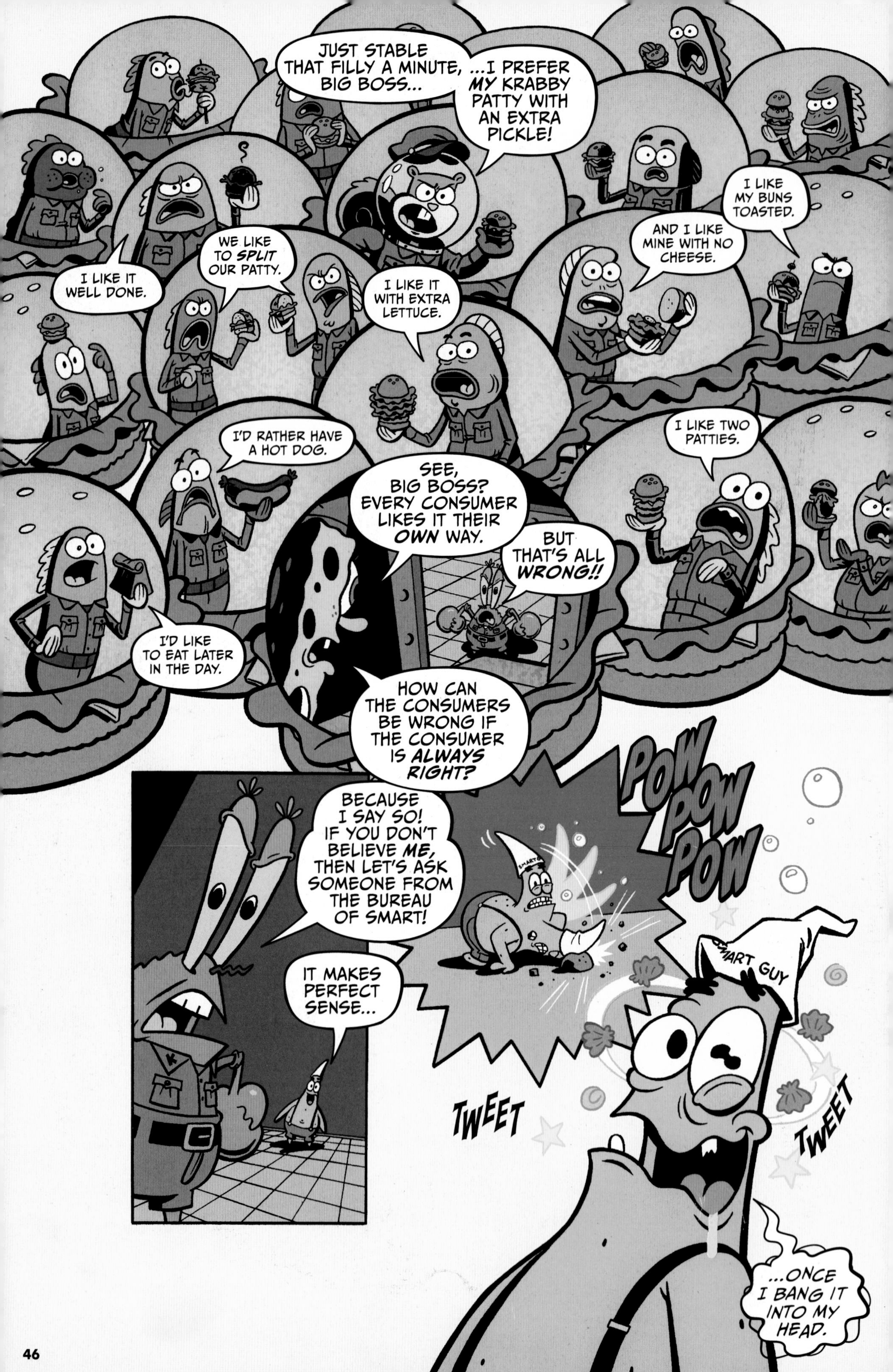
JUST STABLE THAT FILLY A MINUTE, BIG BOSS...
...I PREFER MY KRABBY PATTY WITH AN EXTRA PICKLE!
I LIKE MY BUNS TOASTED.
AND I LIKE MINE WITH NO CHEESE.
WE LIKE TO SPLIT OUR PATTY.
I LIKE IT WELL DONE.
I LIKE IT WITH EXTRA LETTUCE.
I'D RATHER HAVE A HOT DOG.
I LIKE TWO PATTIES.
SEE, BIG BOSS? EVERY CONSUMER LIKES IT THEIR OWN WAY.
BUT THAT'S ALL WRONG!!
I'D LIKE TO EAT LATER IN THE DAY.
HOW CAN THE CONSUMERS BE WRONG IF THE CONSUMER IS ALWAYS RIGHT?
BECAUSE I SAY SO! IF YOU DON'T BELIEVE ME, THEN LET'S ASK SOMEONE FROM THE BUREAU OF SMART!
IT MAKES PERFECT SENSE...
POW POW POW
SMART GUY
TWEET
TWEET
...ONCE I BANG IT INTO MY HEAD.

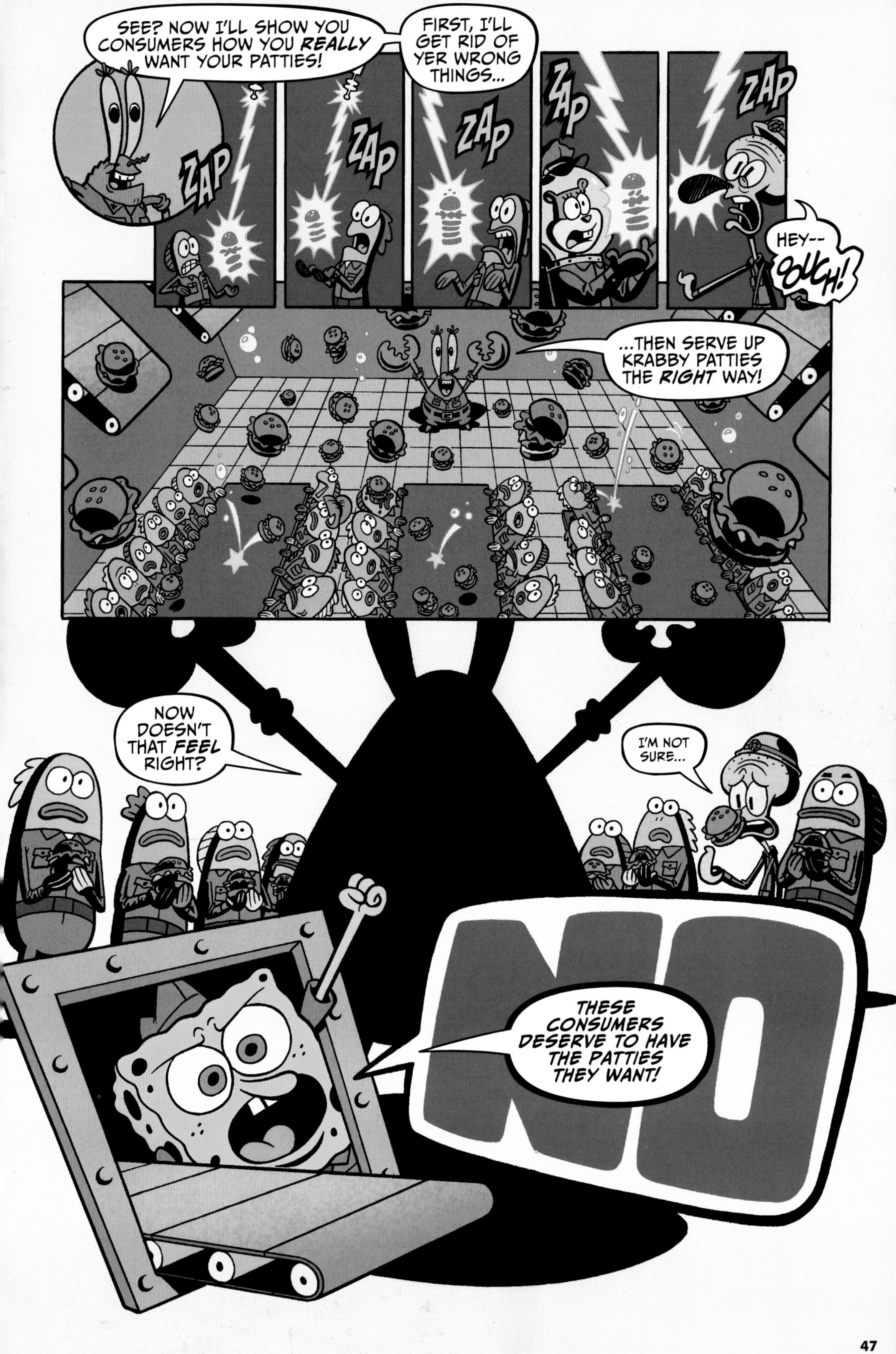
SEE? NOW I'LL SHOW YOU CONSUMERS HOW YOU REALLY WANT YOUR PATTIES!
FIRST, I'LL GET RID OF YER WRONG THINGS...
ZAP
ZAP
ZAP
ZAP
ZAP
HEY-- OUCH!
...THEN SERVE UP KRABBY PATTIES THE RIGHT WAY!
NOW DOESN'T THAT FEEL RIGHT?
I'M NOT SURE...
NO
THESE CONSUMERS DESERVE TO HAVE THE PATTIES THEY WANT!

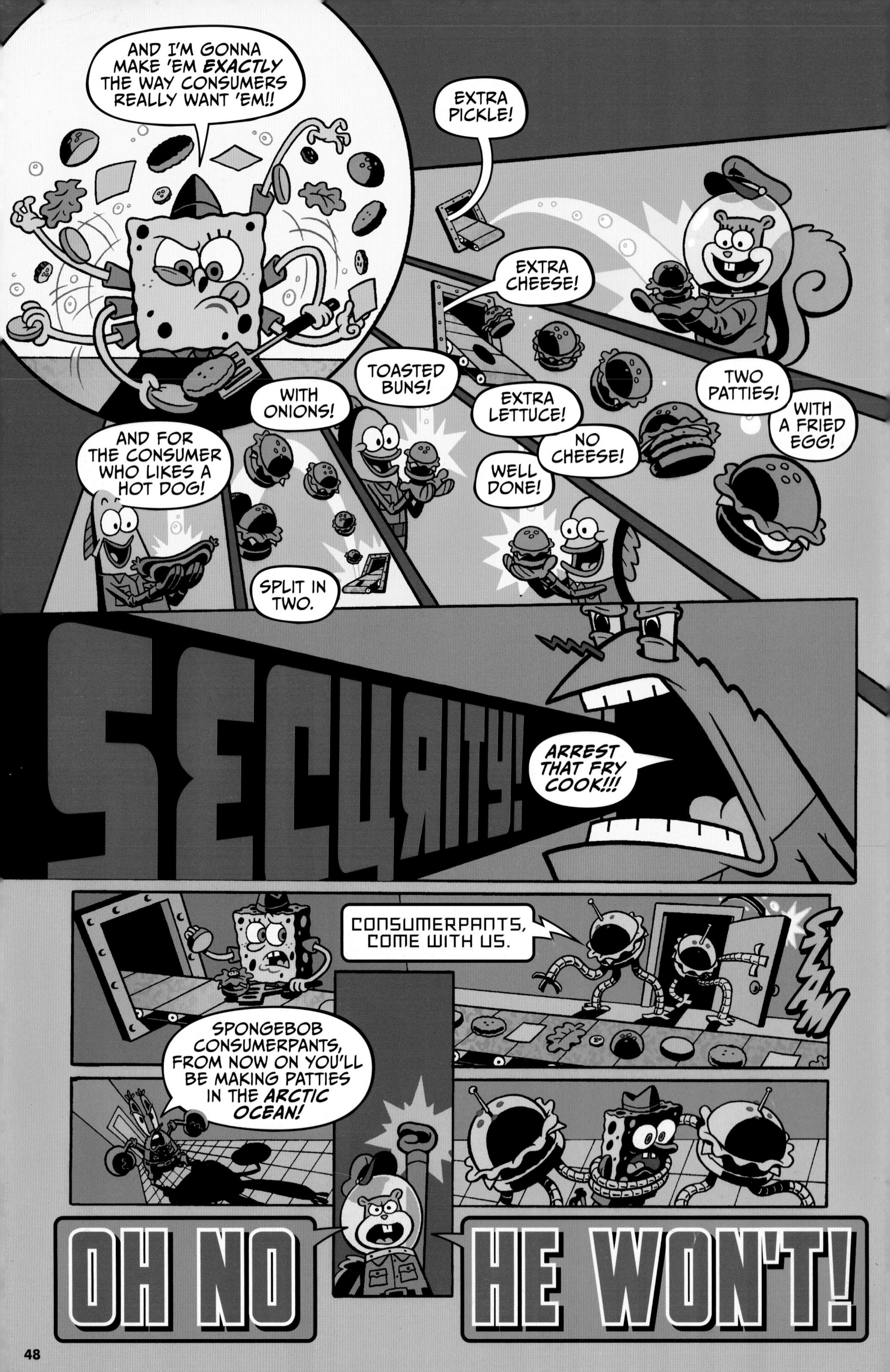
AND I'M GONNA MAKE 'EM EXACTLY THE WAY CONSUMERS REALLY WANT 'EM!!
EXTRA PICKLE!
EXTRA CHEESE!
TOASTED BUNS!
WITH ONIONS!
EXTRA LETTUCE!
TWO PATTIES!
WITH A FRIED EGG!
NO CHEESE!
WELL DONE!
AND FOR THE CONSUMER WHO LIKES A HOT DOG!
SPLIT IN TWO.
SECURITY!
ARREST THAT FRY COOK!!!
CONSUMERPANTS, COME WITH US.
SLAM
SPONGEBOB CONSUMERPANTS, FROM NOW ON YOU'LL BE MAKING PATTIES IN THE ARCTIC OCEAN!
OH NO
HE WON'T!

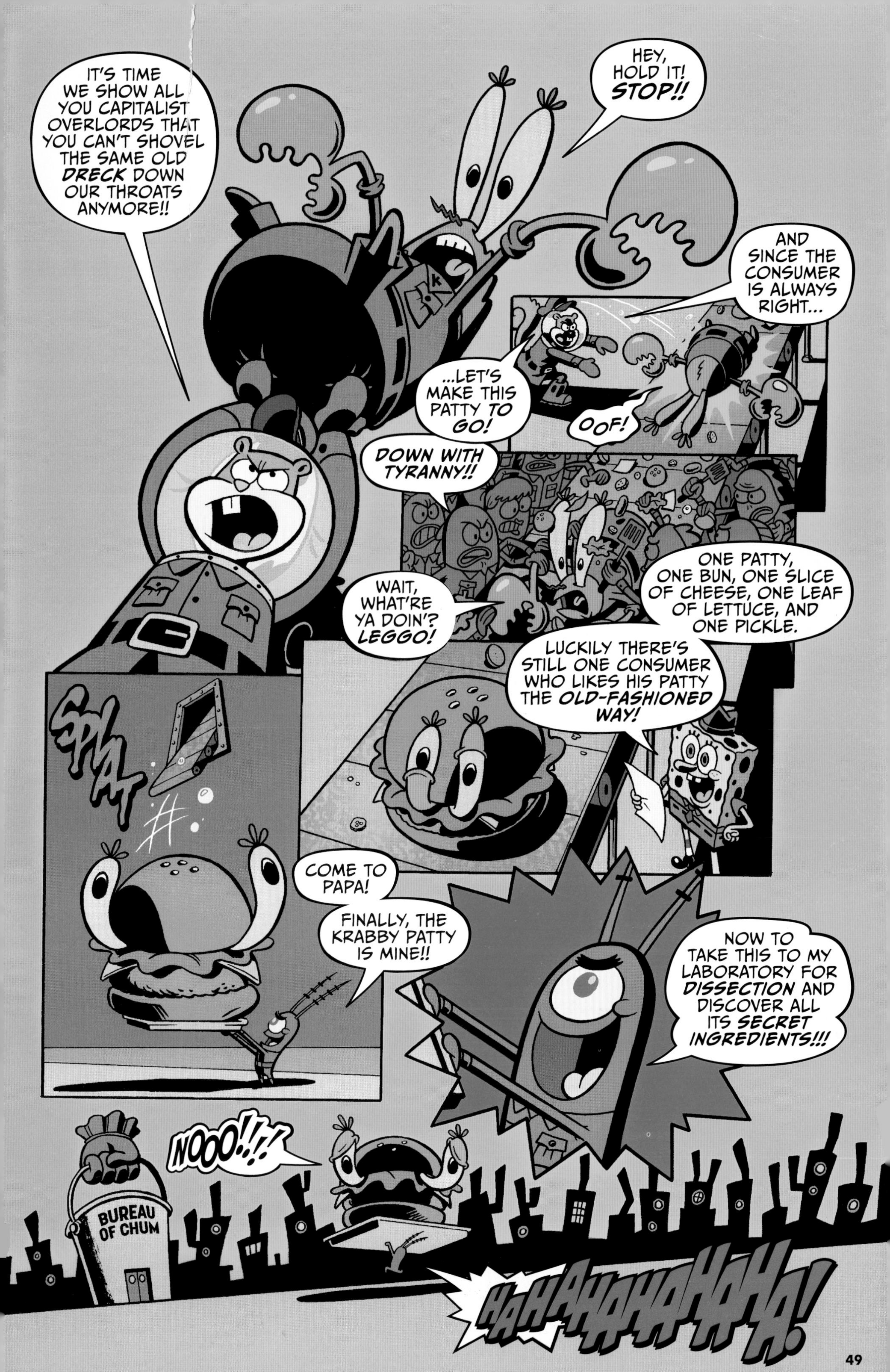

IT'S TIME WE SHOW ALL YOU CAPITALIST OVERLORDS THAT YOU CAN'T SHOVEL THE SAME OLD DRECK DOWN OUR THROATS ANYMORE!!
HEY, HOLD IT! STOP!!
AND SINCE THE CONSUMER IS ALWAYS RIGHT...
...LET'S MAKE THIS PATTY TO GO!
OOF!
DOWN WITH TYRANNY!!
WAIT, WHAT'RE YA DOIN'? LEGGO!
ONE PATTY, ONE BUN, ONE SLICE OF CHEESE, ONE LEAF OF LETTUCE, AND ONE PICKLE.
LUCKILY THERE'S STILL ONE CONSUMER WHO LIKES HIS PATTY THE OLD-FASHIONED WAY!
SPLAK
COME TO PAPA!
FINALLY, THE KRABBY PATTY IS MINE!!
NOW TO TAKE THIS TO MY LABORATORY FOR DISSECTION AND DISCOVER ALL ITS SECRET INGREDIENTS!!!
NOOO!!?!
BUREAU OF CHUM
HAHAHAHAHAHAHAHA!

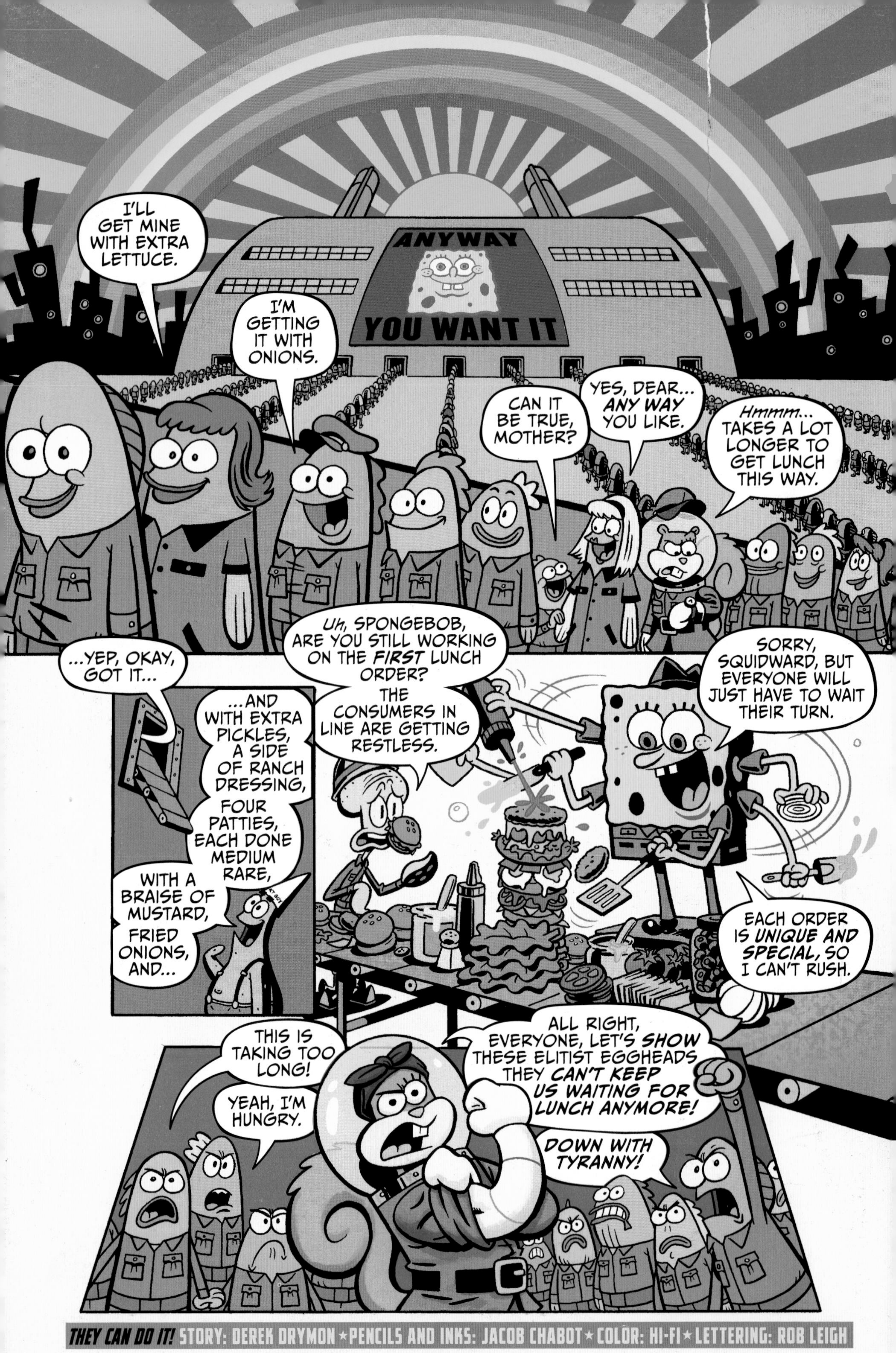

ANYWAY
YOU WANT IT
I'LL GET MINE WITH EXTRA LETTUCE.
I'M GETTING IT WITH ONIONS.
CAN IT BE TRUE, MOTHER?
YES, DEAR... *ANY WAY* YOU LIKE.
Hmmm... TAKES A LOT LONGER TO GET LUNCH THIS WAY.
...YEP, OKAY, GOT IT...
...AND WITH EXTRA PICKLES, A SIDE OF RANCH DRESSING,
FOUR PATTIES, EACH DONE MEDIUM RARE,
WITH A BRAISE OF MUSTARD,
FRIED ONIONS, AND...
Uh, SPONGEBOB, ARE YOU STILL WORKING ON THE *FIRST* LUNCH ORDER?
THE CONSUMERS IN LINE ARE GETTING RESTLESS.
SORRY, SQUIDWARD, BUT EVERYONE WILL JUST HAVE TO WAIT THEIR TURN.
EACH ORDER IS *UNIQUE AND SPECIAL*, SO I CAN'T RUSH.
THIS IS TAKING TOO LONG!
YEAH, I'M HUNGRY.
ALL RIGHT, EVERYONE, LET'S *SHOW* THESE ELITIST EGGHEADS THEY *CAN'T KEEP US WAITING FOR LUNCH ANYMORE!*
DOWN WITH TYRANNY!

THEY CAN DO IT! STORY: DEREK DRYMON ★ PENCILS AND INKS: JACOB CHABOT ★ COLOR: HI-FI ★ LETTERING: ROB LEIGH

Grandma's Cookies

STORY AND ART: BOB FLYNN
LETTERING: COMICRAFT

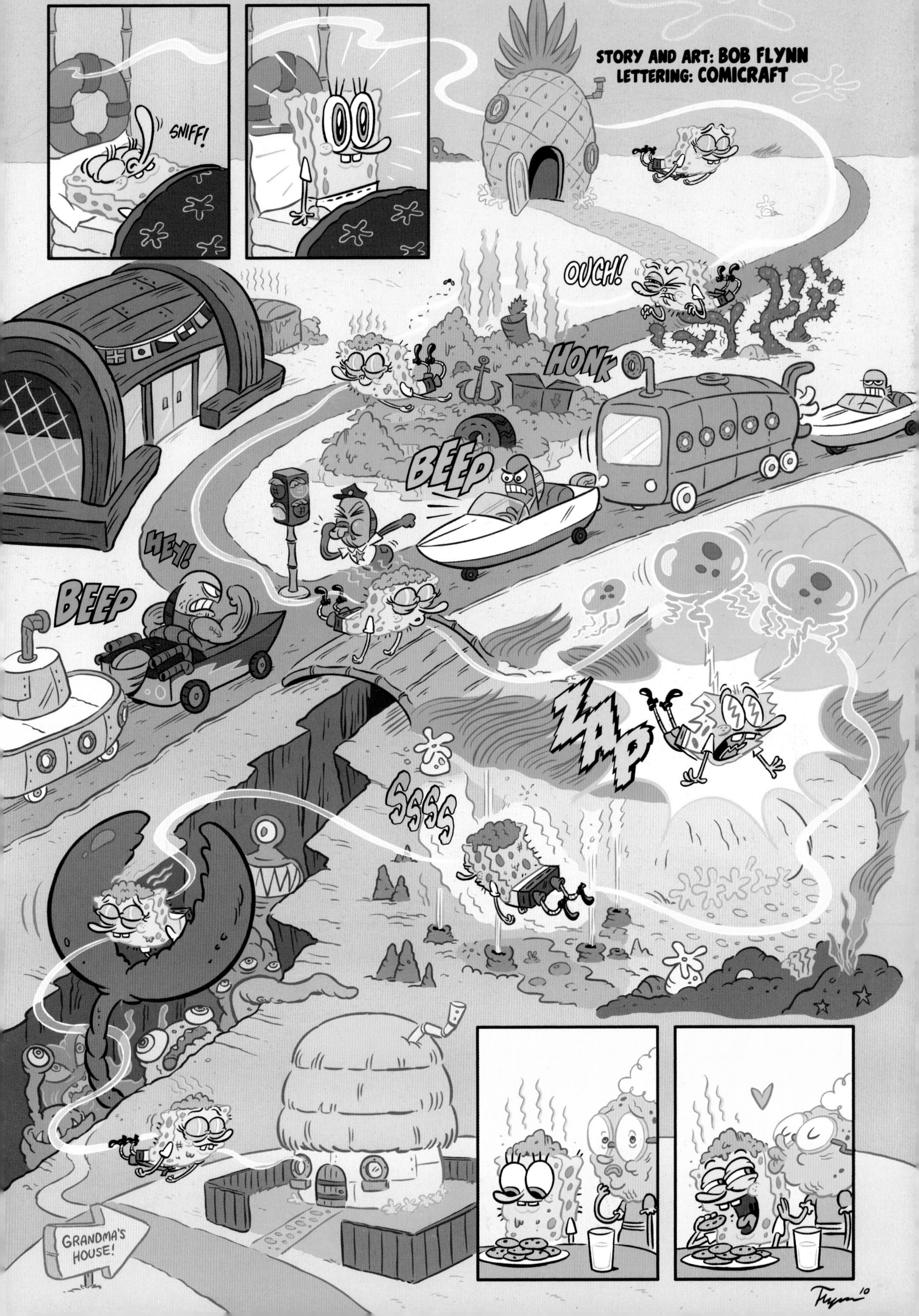
SNIFF!
OUCH!
HONK
BEEP
HEY!
BEEP
ZAP
SSSS
GRANDMA'S HOUSE!

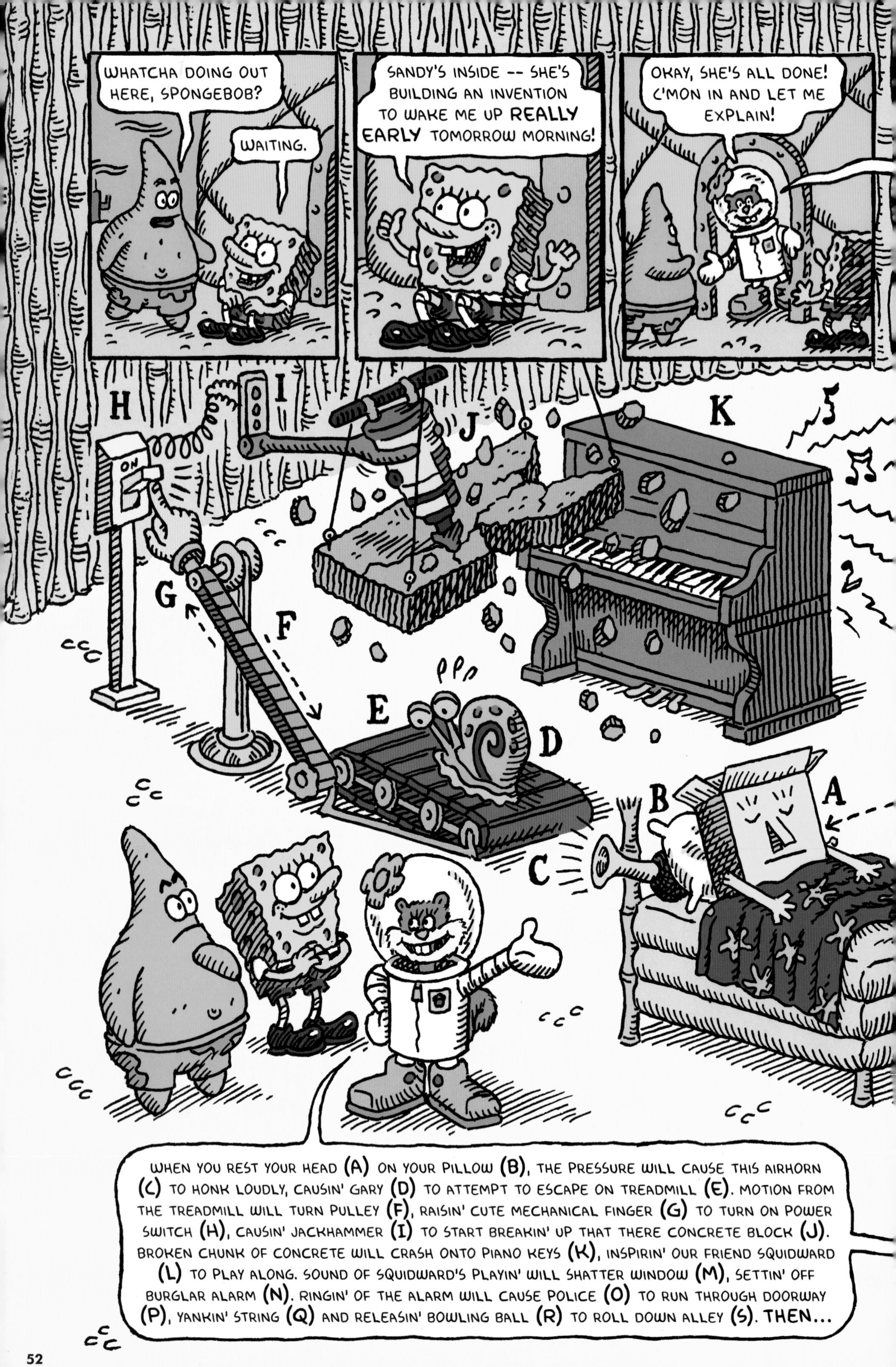
WHATCHA DOING OUT HERE, SPONGEBOB?
WAITING.
SANDY'S INSIDE -- SHE'S BUILDING AN INVENTION TO WAKE ME UP REALLY EARLY TOMORROW MORNING!
OKAY, SHE'S ALL DONE! C'MON IN AND LET ME EXPLAIN!
H
I
J
K
ON
G
F
E
D
C
B
A
WHEN YOU REST YOUR HEAD (A) ON YOUR PILLOW (B), THE PRESSURE WILL CAUSE THIS AIRHORN (C) TO HONK LOUDLY, CAUSIN' GARY (D) TO ATTEMPT TO ESCAPE ON TREADMILL (E). MOTION FROM THE TREADMILL WILL TURN PULLEY (F), RAISIN' CUTE MECHANICAL FINGER (G) TO TURN ON POWER SWITCH (H), CAUSIN' JACKHAMMER (I) TO START BREAKIN' UP THAT THERE CONCRETE BLOCK (J). BROKEN CHUNK OF CONCRETE WILL CRASH ONTO PIANO KEYS (K), INSPIRIN' OUR FRIEND SQUIDWARD (L) TO PLAY ALONG. SOUND OF SQUIDWARD'S PLAYIN' WILL SHATTER WINDOW (M), SETTIN' OFF BURGLAR ALARM (N). RINGIN' OF THE ALARM WILL CAUSE POLICE (O) TO RUN THROUGH DOORWAY (P), YANKIN' STRING (Q) AND RELEASIN' BOWLING BALL (R) TO ROLL DOWN ALLEY (S). THEN...

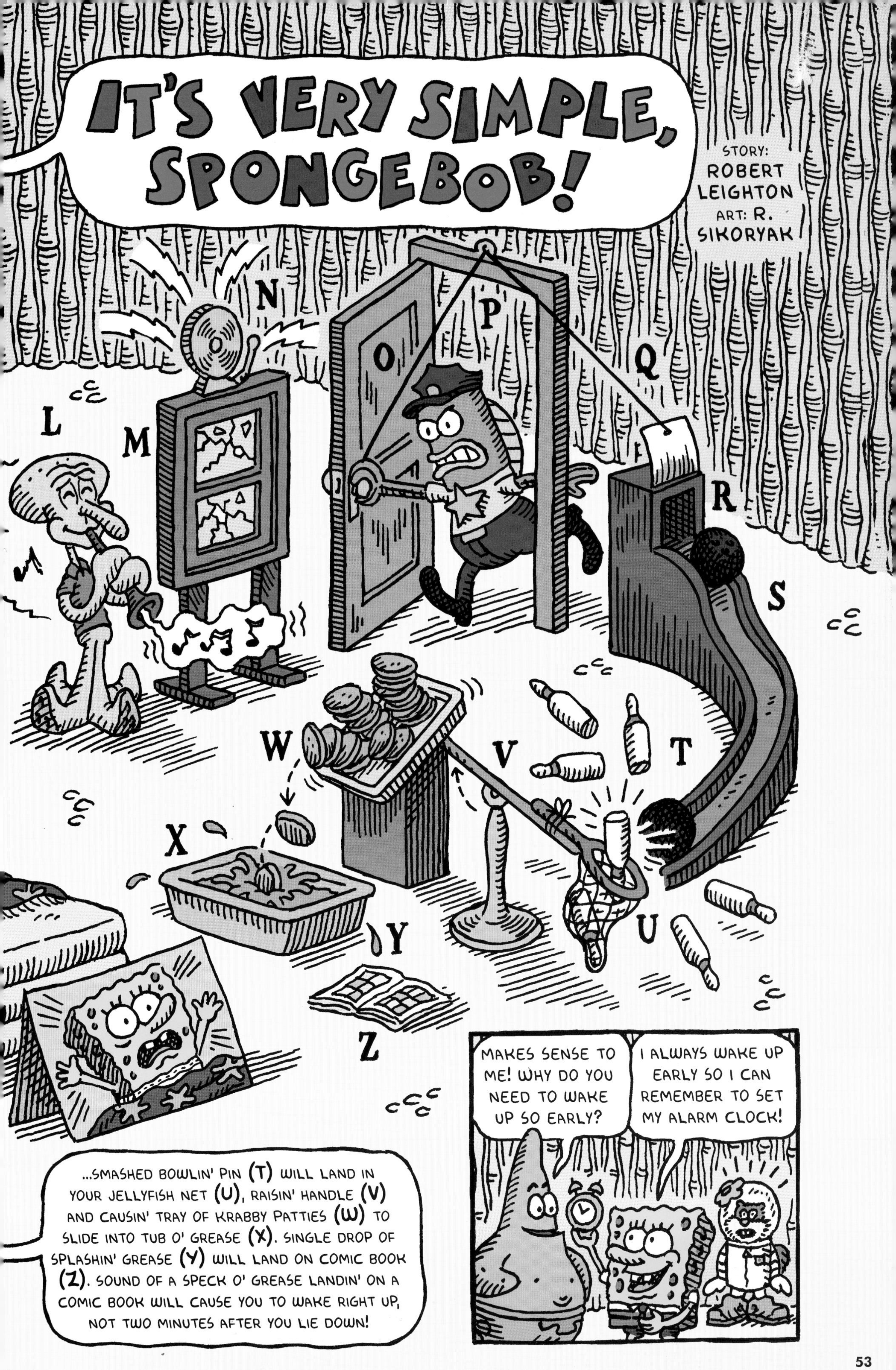

IT'S VERY SIMPLE, SPONGEBOB!
STORY: ROBERT LEIGHTON
ART: R. SIKORYAK
N
O
P
Q
L
M
R
S
T
V
W
X
U
Y
Z
...SMASHED BOWLIN' PIN (T) WILL LAND IN YOUR JELLYFISH NET (U), RAISIN' HANDLE (V) AND CAUSIN' TRAY OF KRABBY PATTIES (W) TO SLIDE INTO TUB O' GREASE (X). SINGLE DROP OF SPLASHIN' GREASE (Y) WILL LAND ON COMIC BOOK (Z). SOUND OF A SPECK O' GREASE LANDIN' ON A COMIC BOOK WILL CAUSE YOU TO WAKE RIGHT UP, NOT TWO MINUTES AFTER YOU LIE DOWN!
MAKES SENSE TO ME! WHY DO YOU NEED TO WAKE UP SO EARLY?
I ALWAYS WAKE UP EARLY SO I CAN REMEMBER TO SET MY ALARM CLOCK!

PLANKTON'S LAST LAFF

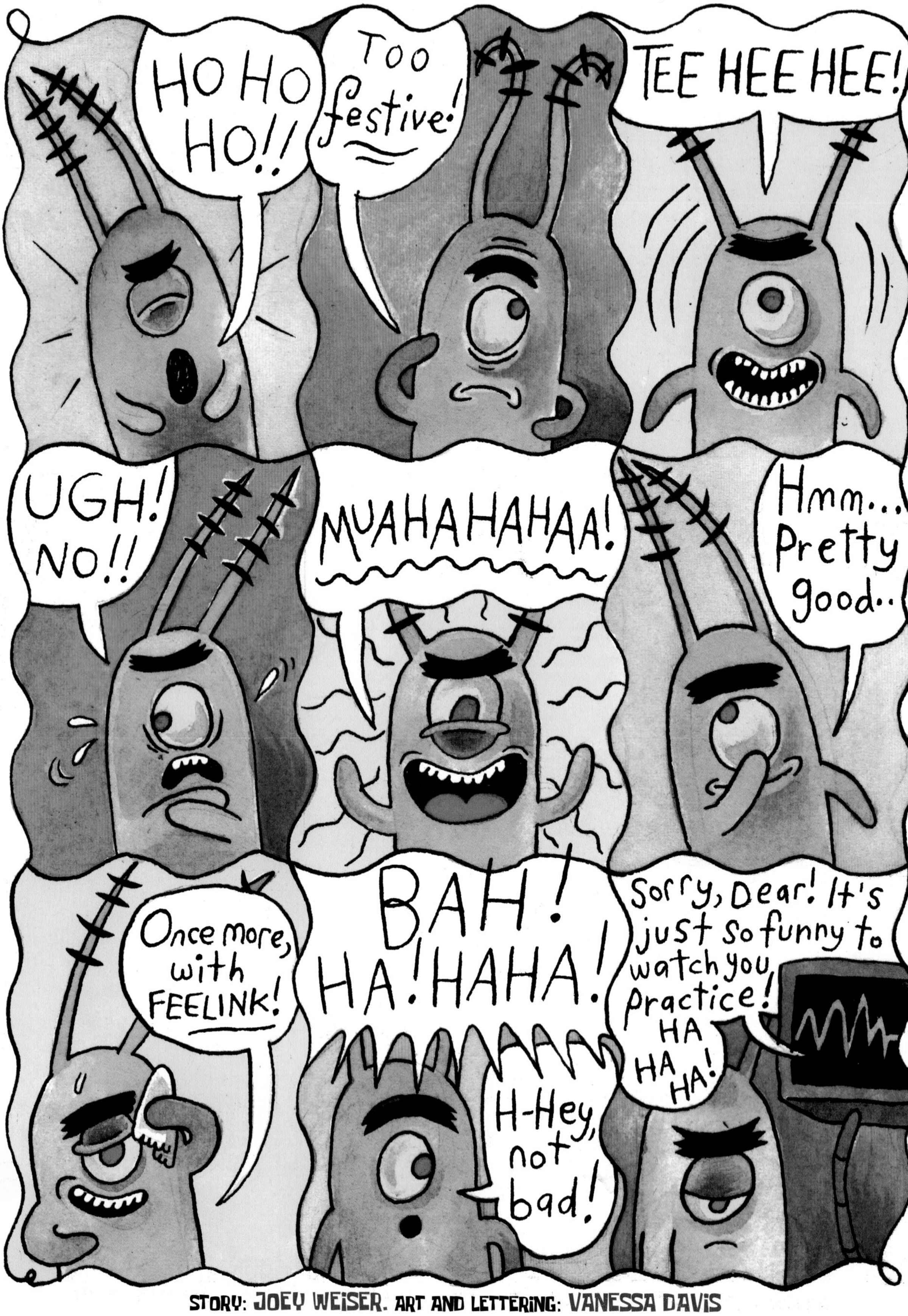

HO HO HO!!
Too festive!
TEE HEE HEE!
UGH! NO!!
MUAHAHAHAA!
Hmm... Pretty good..
Once more, with FEELINK!
BAH! HA! HAHA!
H-Hey, not bad!
Sorry, Dear! It's just so funny to watch you practice! HA HA HA!

STORY: JOEY WEISER. ART AND LETTERING: VANESSA DAVIS

SPONGEFUNNIES by KOCHALKA

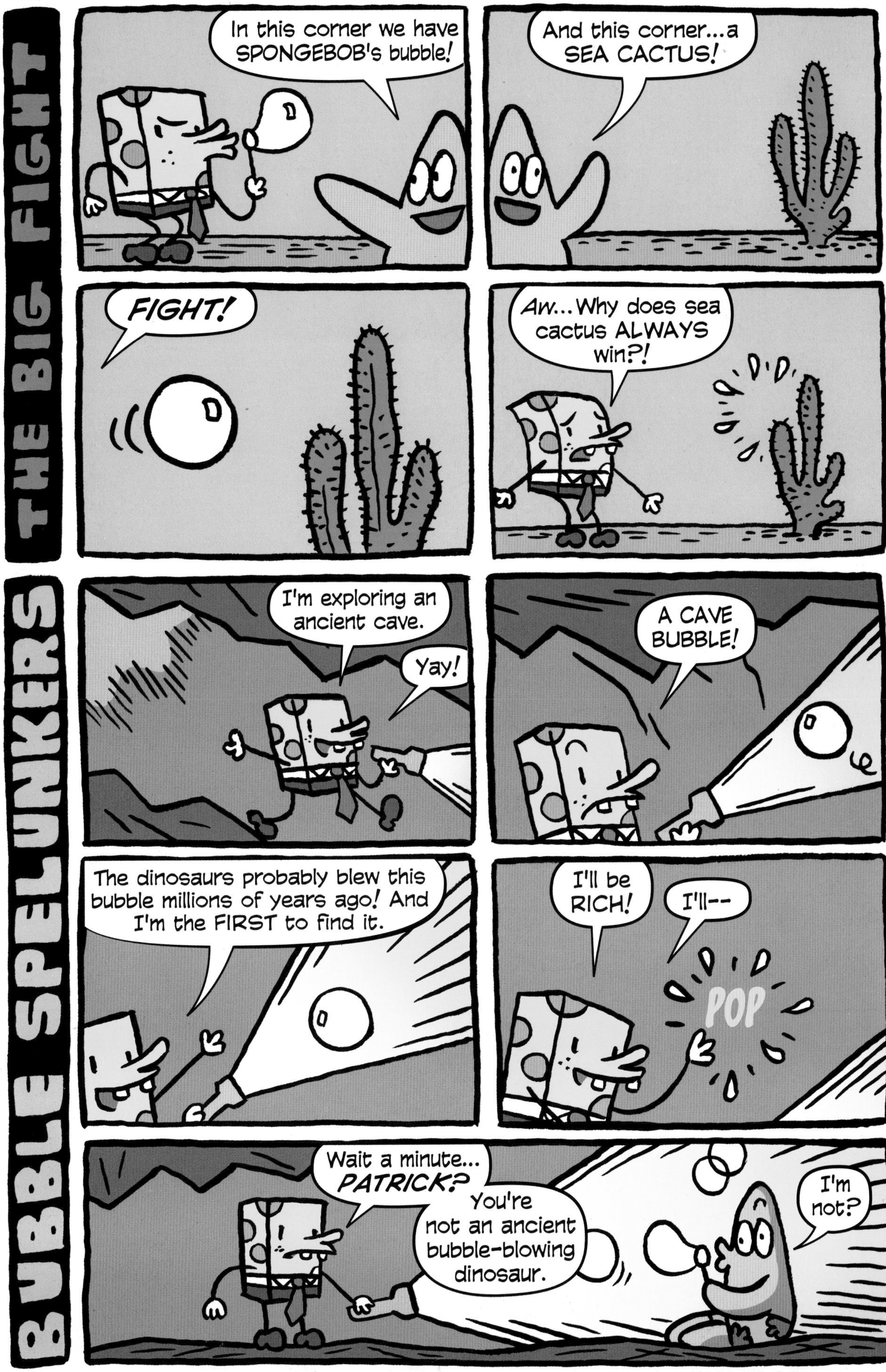
THE BIG FIGHT
In this corner we have SPONGEBOB's bubble!
And this corner...a SEA CACTUS!
FIGHT!
Aw...Why does sea cactus ALWAYS win?!
BUBBLE SPELUNKERS
I'm exploring an ancient cave.
Yay!
A CAVE BUBBLE!
The dinosaurs probably blew this bubble millions of years ago! And I'm the FIRST to find it.
I'll be RICH!
I'll--
POP
Wait a minute... PATRICK?
You're not an ancient bubble-blowing dinosaur.
I'm not?

STORY AND ART: JAMES KOCHALKA LETTERING: COMICRAFT

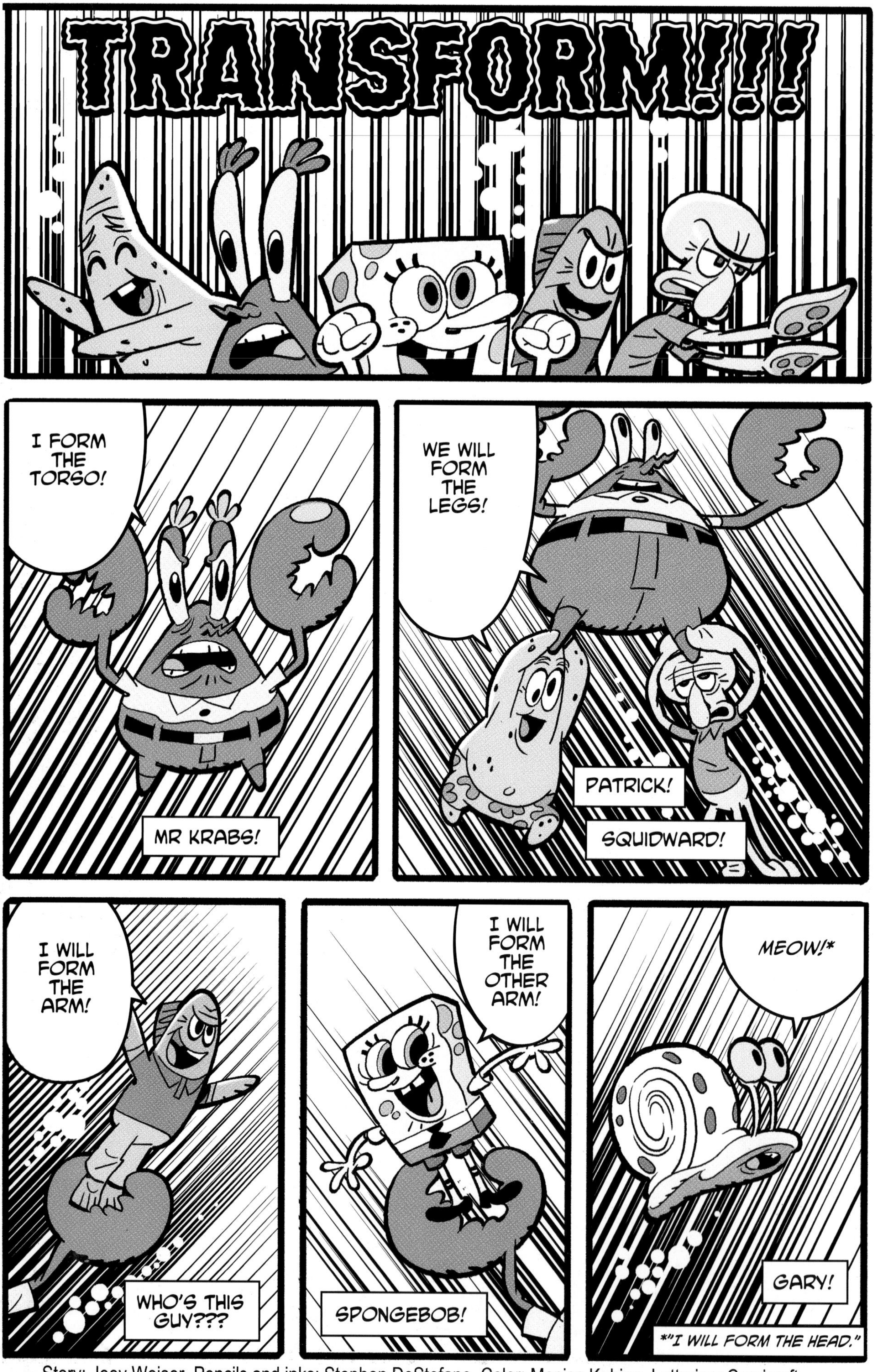
TRANSFORM!!!
I FORM THE TORSO!
MR KRABS!
WE WILL FORM THE LEGS!
PATRICK!
SQUIDWARD!
I WILL FORM THE ARM!
WHO'S THIS GUY???
I WILL FORM THE OTHER ARM!
SPONGEBOB!
MEOW!*
GARY!
*"I WILL FORM THE HEAD."

Story: Joey Weiser Pencils and inks: Stephen DeStefano Color: Monica Kubina Lettering: Comicraft

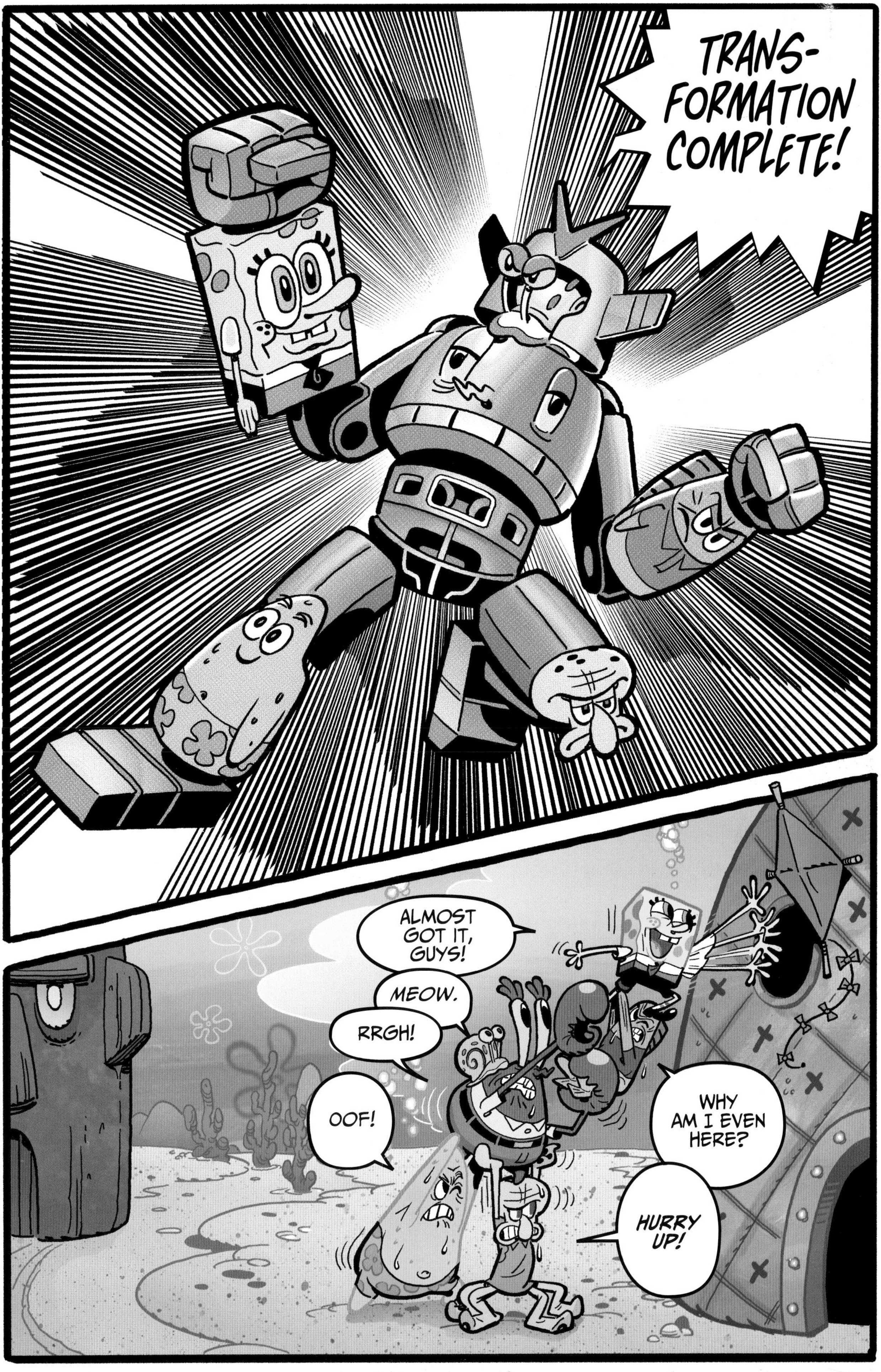
TRANS-
FORMATION
COMPLETE!
ALMOST GOT IT, GUYS!
MEOW.
RRGH!
OOF!
WHY AM I EVEN HERE?
HURRY UP!

END

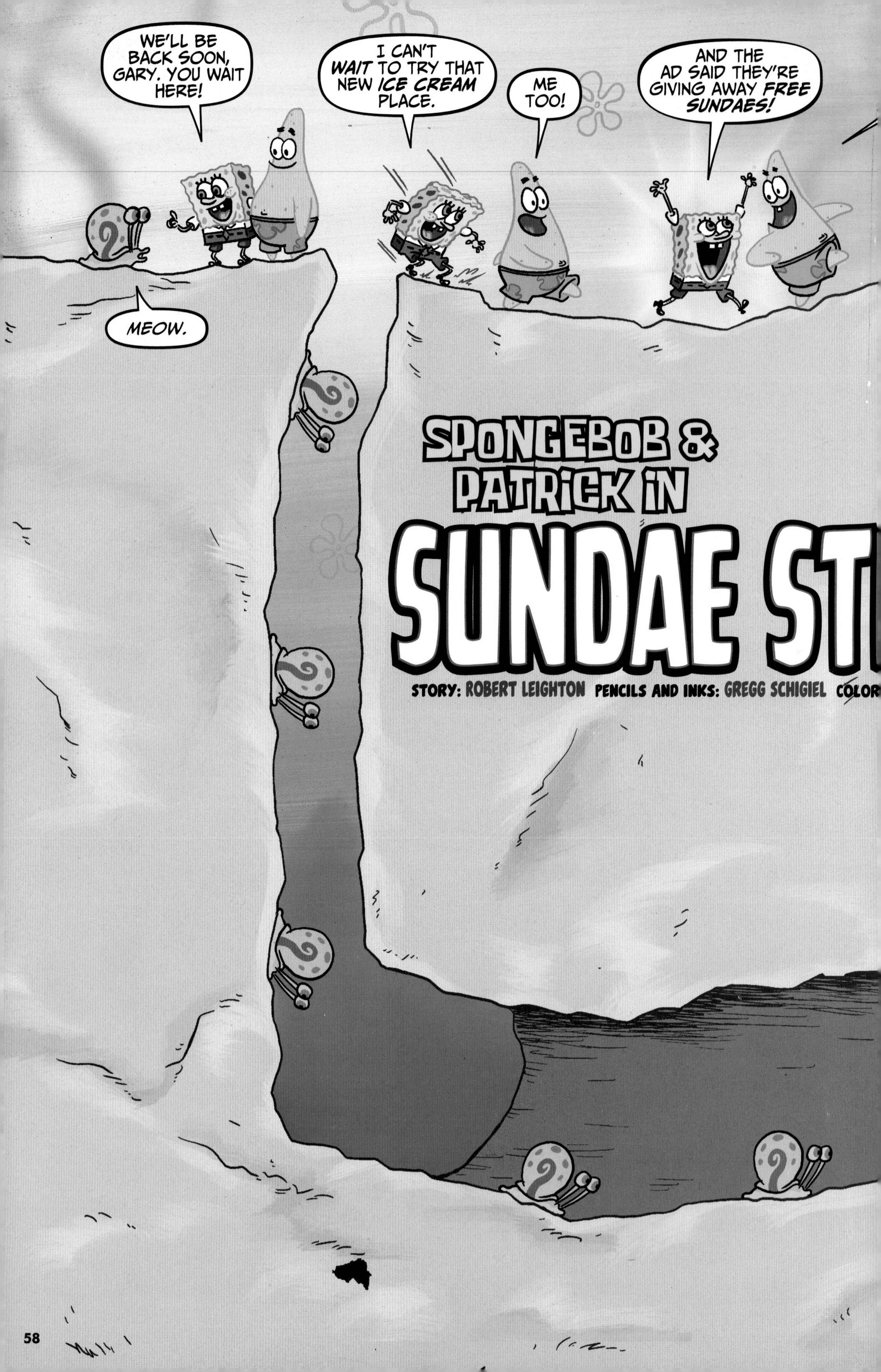

WE'LL BE BACK SOON, GARY. YOU WAIT HERE!
MEOW.
I CAN'T WAIT TO TRY THAT NEW ICE CREAM PLACE.
ME TOO!
AND THE AD SAID THEY'RE GIVING AWAY FREE SUNDAES!
SPONGEBOB & PATRICK IN
SUNDAE ST
STORY: ROBERT LEIGHTON PENCILS AND INKS: GREGG SCHIGIEL COLOR

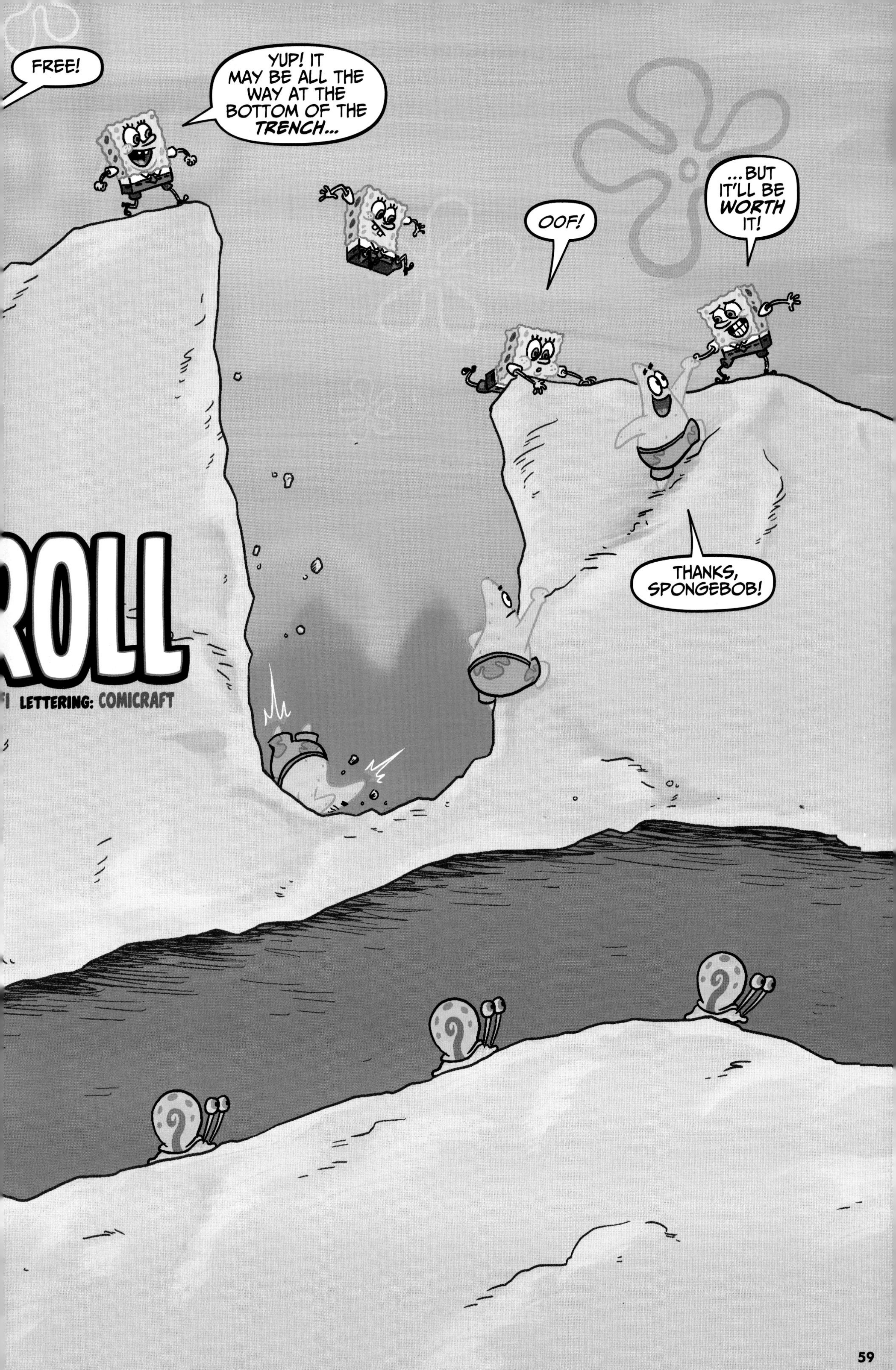
FREE!
YUP! IT MAY BE ALL THE WAY AT THE BOTTOM OF THE TRENCH...
OOF!
...BUT IT'LL BE WORTH IT!
THANKS, SPONGEBOB!
ROLL
LETTERING: COMICRAFT

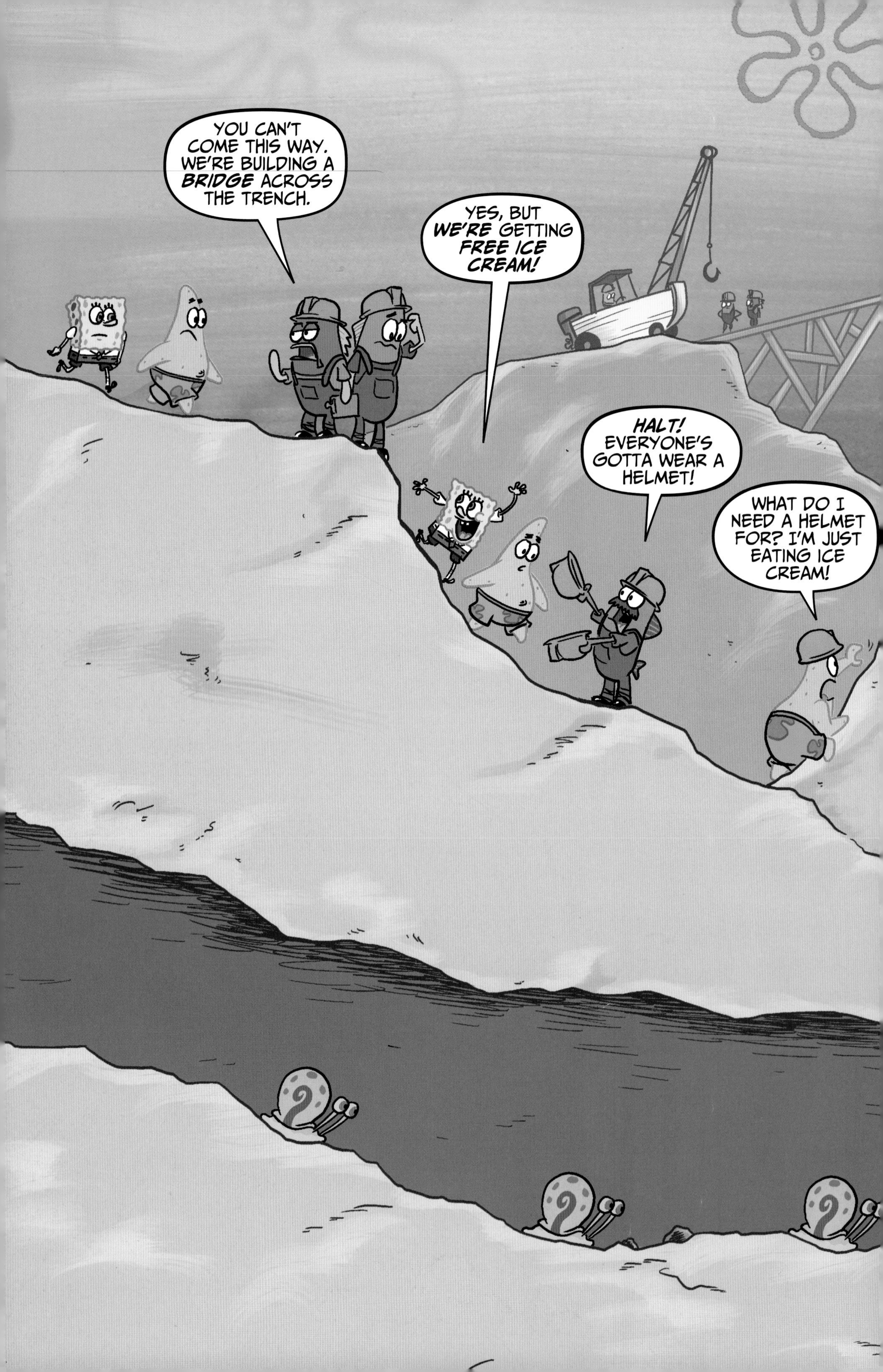
YOU CAN'T COME THIS WAY. WE'RE BUILDING A *BRIDGE* ACROSS THE TRENCH.
YES, BUT *WE'RE* GETTING *FREE ICE CREAM!*
HALT! EVERYONE'S GOTTA WEAR A HELMET!
WHAT DO I NEED A HELMET FOR? I'M JUST EATING ICE CREAM!

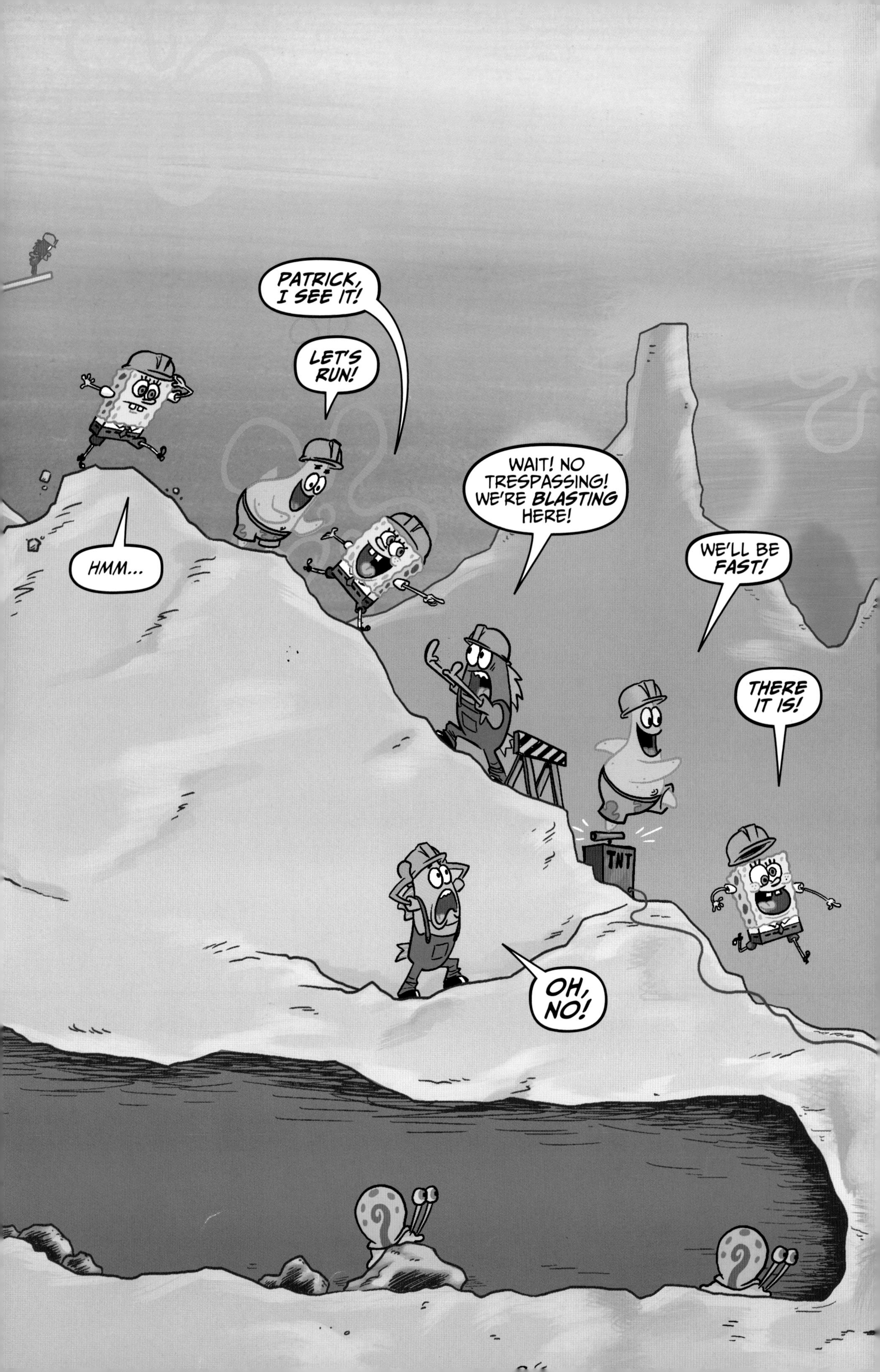
HMM...
PATRICK, I SEE IT!
LET'S RUN!
WAIT! NO TRESPASSING! WE'RE BLASTING HERE!
WE'LL BE FAST!
THERE IT IS!
TNT
OH, NO!

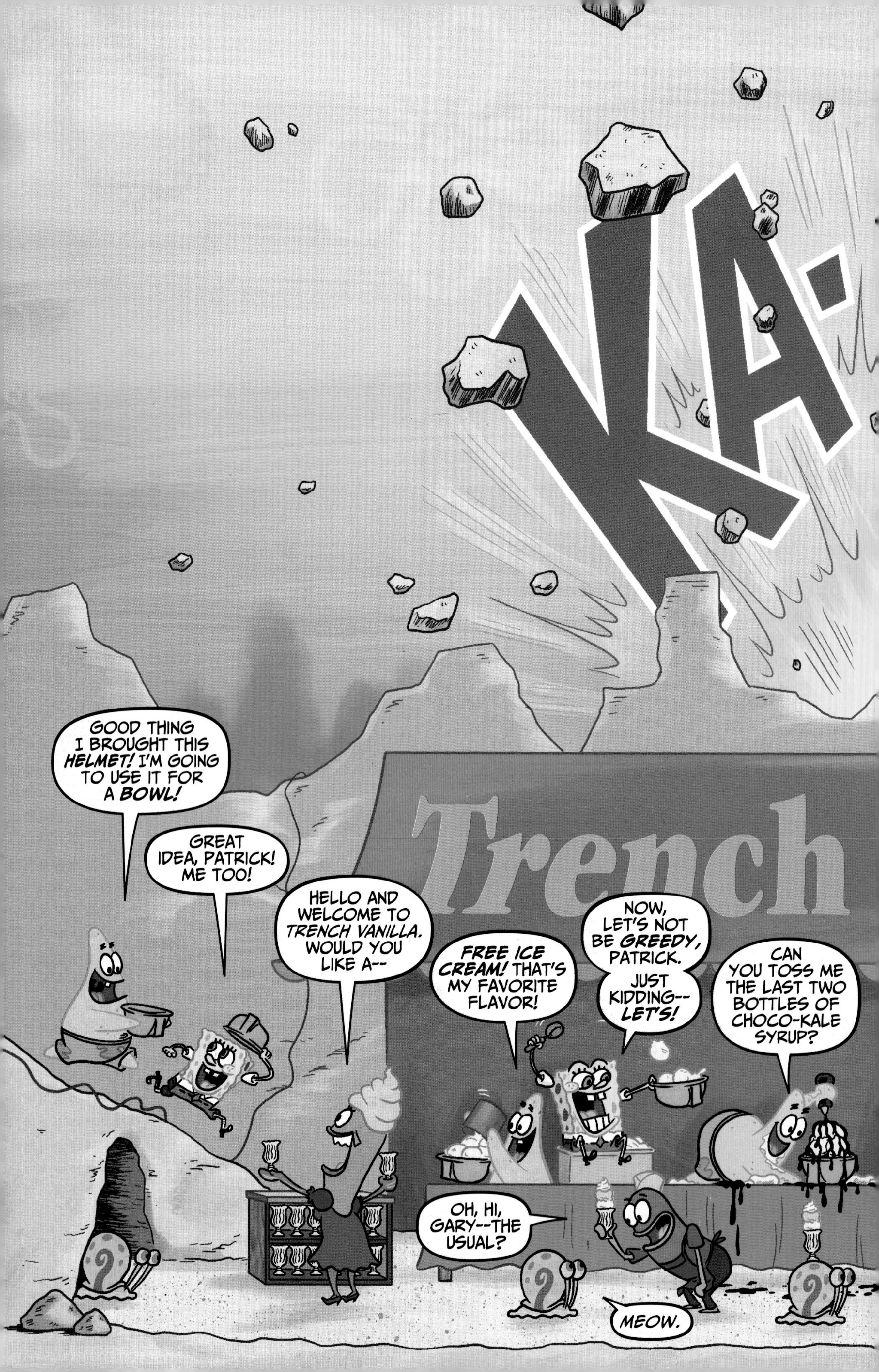
KA-
GOOD THING I BROUGHT THIS HELMET! I'M GOING TO USE IT FOR A BOWL!
GREAT IDEA, PATRICK! ME TOO!
HELLO AND WELCOME TO TRENCH VANILLA. WOULD YOU LIKE A--
Trench
FREE ICE CREAM! THAT'S MY FAVORITE FLAVOR!
NOW, LET'S NOT BE GREEDY, PATRICK.
JUST KIDDING-- LET'S!
CAN YOU TOSS ME THE LAST TWO BOTTLES OF CHOCO-KALE SYRUP?
OH, HI, GARY--THE USUAL?
MEOW.

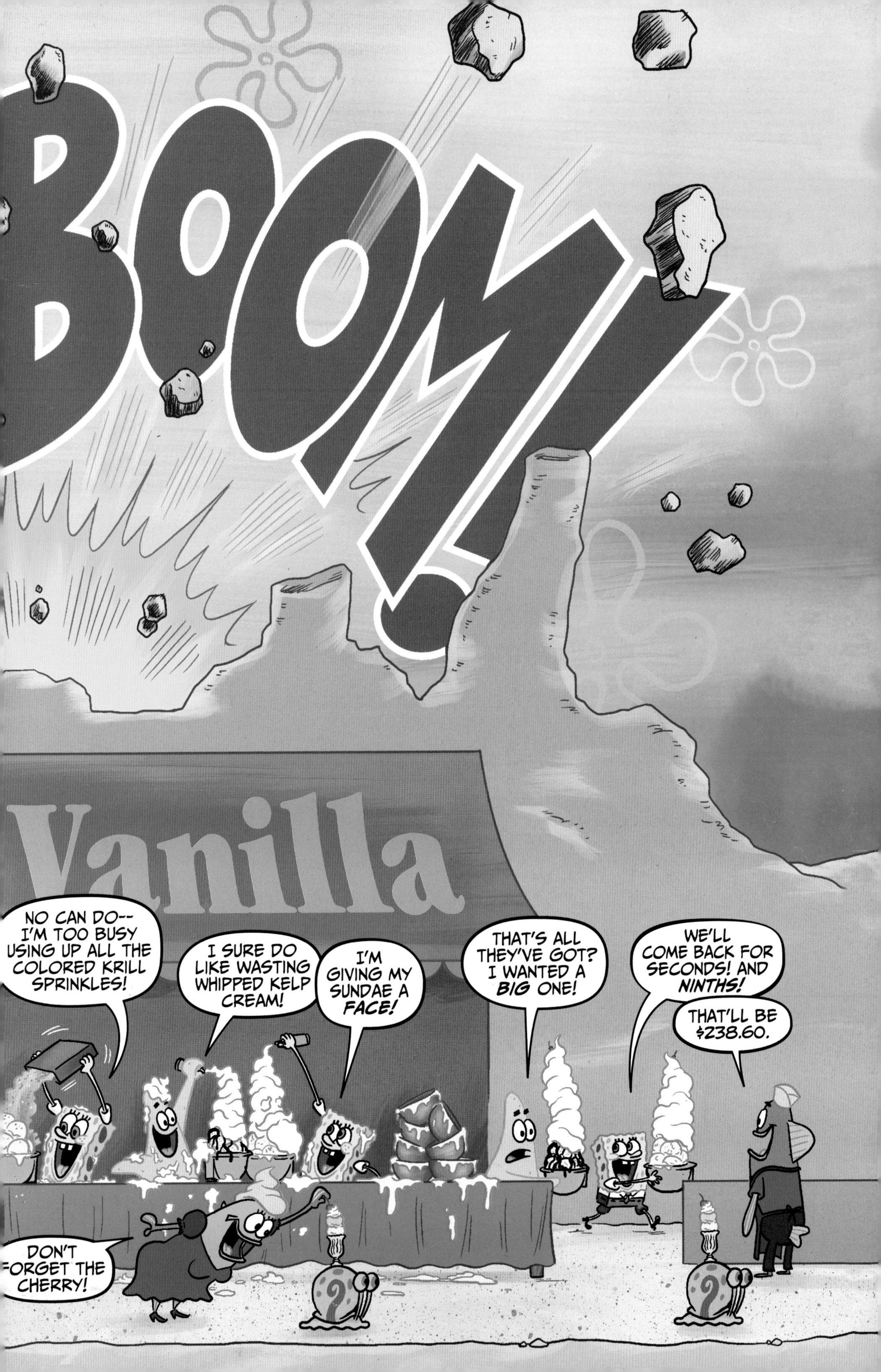
BOOM!
Vanilla
NO CAN DO-- I'M TOO BUSY USING UP ALL THE COLORED KRILL SPRINKLES!
I SURE DO LIKE WASTING WHIPPED KELP CREAM!
I'M GIVING MY SUNDAE A *FACE!*
THAT'S ALL THEY'VE GOT? I WANTED A *BIG* ONE!
WE'LL COME BACK FOR SECONDS! AND *NINTHS!*
THAT'LL BE $238.60.
DON'T FORGET THE CHERRY!

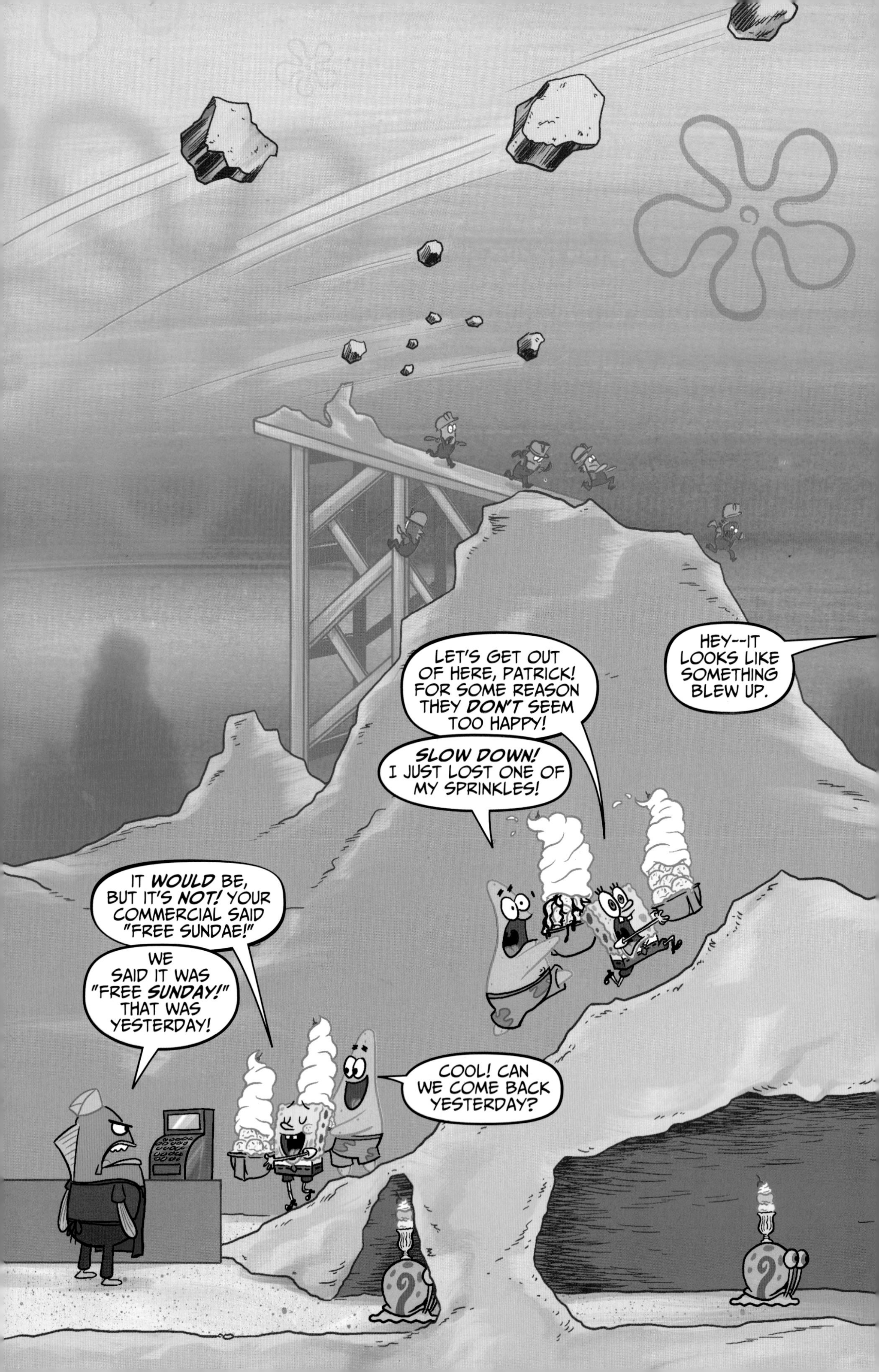
HEY--IT LOOKS LIKE SOMETHING BLEW UP.
LET'S GET OUT OF HERE, PATRICK! FOR SOME REASON THEY DON'T SEEM TOO HAPPY!
SLOW DOWN! I JUST LOST ONE OF MY SPRINKLES!
IT WOULD BE, BUT IT'S NOT! YOUR COMMERCIAL SAID "FREE SUNDAE!"
WE SAID IT WAS "FREE SUNDAY!" THAT WAS YESTERDAY!
COOL! CAN WE COME BACK YESTERDAY?

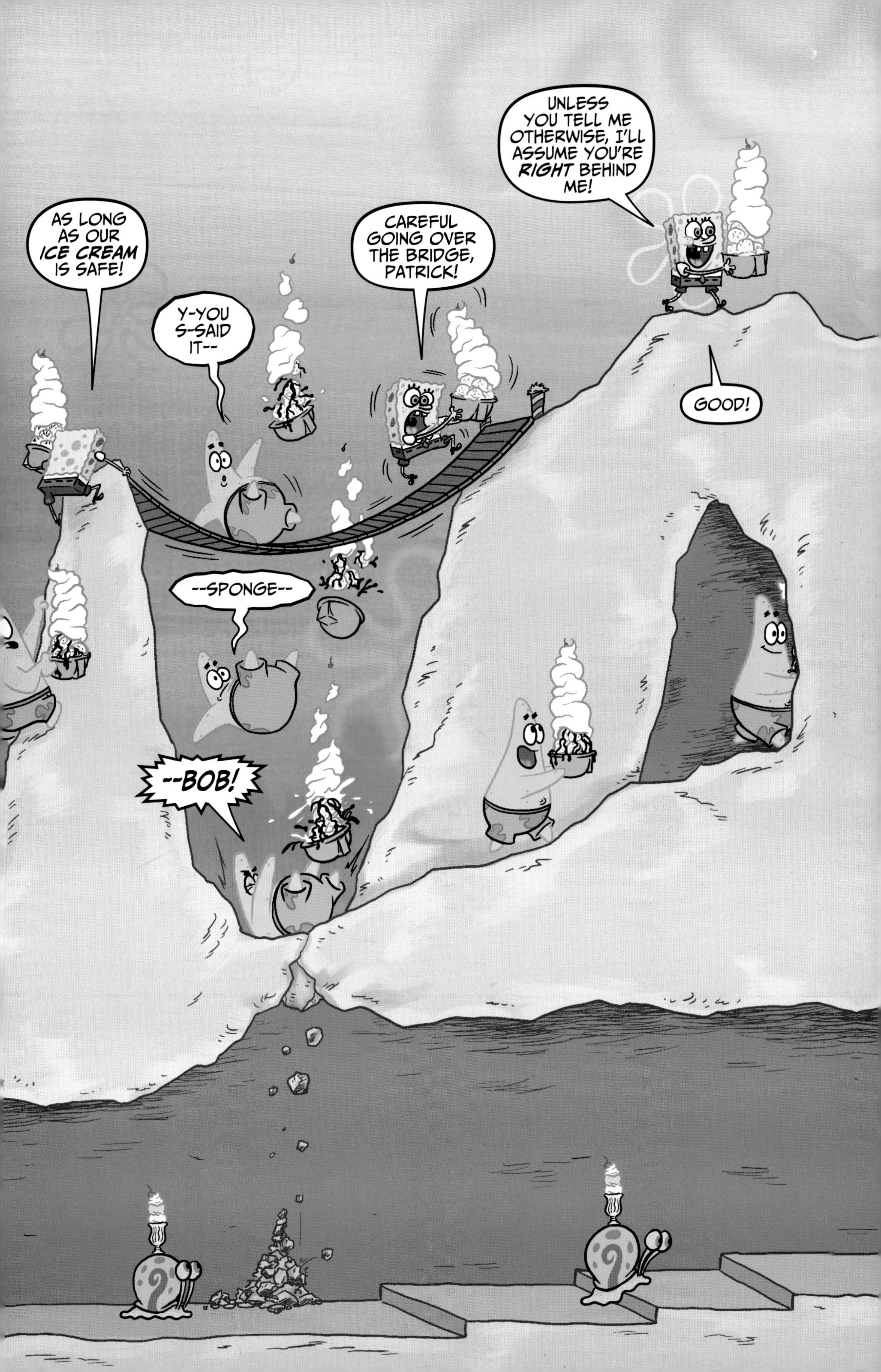

AS LONG AS OUR ICE CREAM IS SAFE!
Y-YOU S-SAID IT--
CAREFUL GOING OVER THE BRIDGE, PATRICK!
UNLESS YOU TELL ME OTHERWISE, I'LL ASSUME YOU'RE RIGHT BEHIND ME!
GOOD!
--SPONGE--
--BOB!

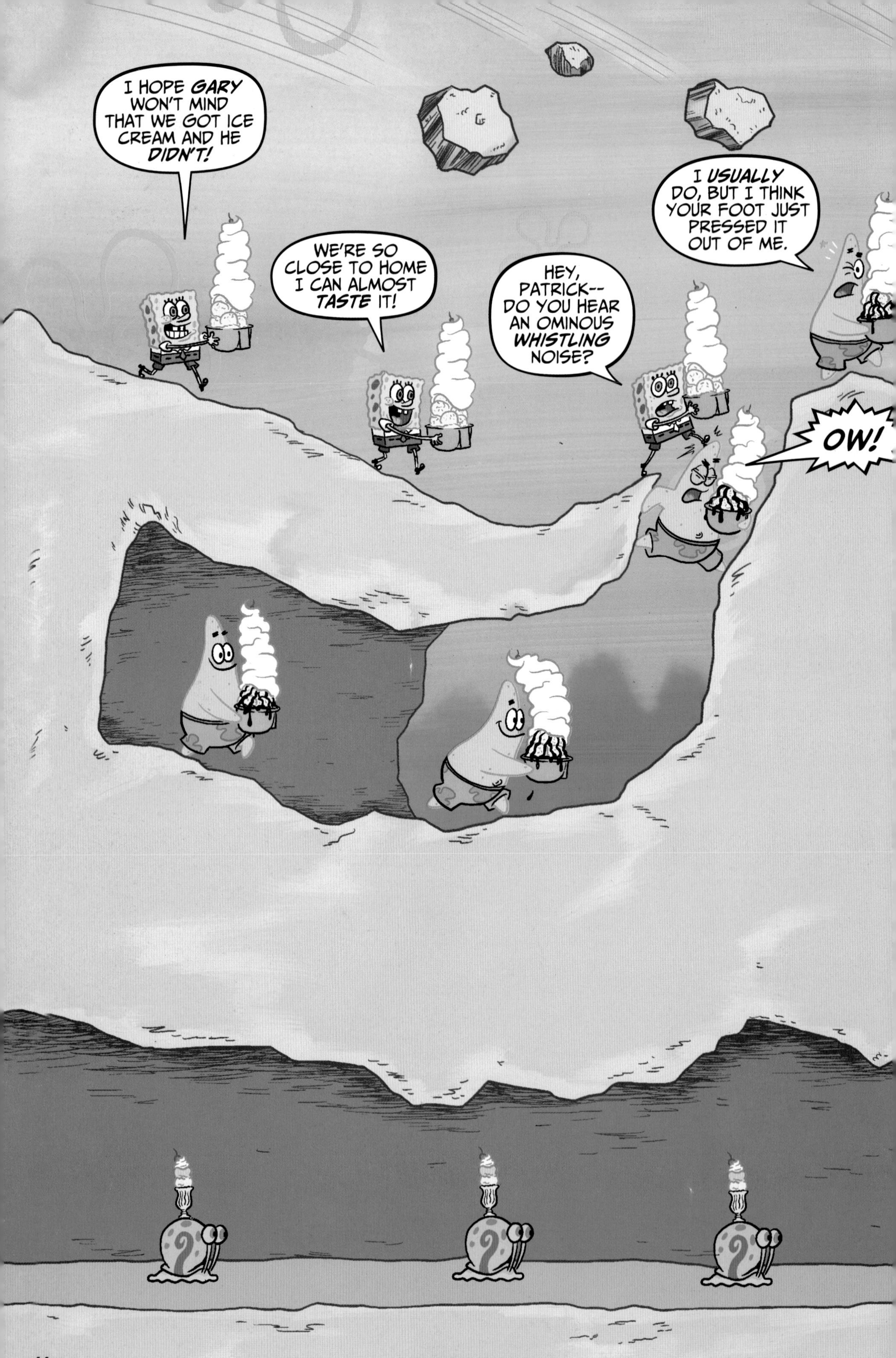
I HOPE GARY WON'T MIND THAT WE GOT ICE CREAM AND HE DIDN'T!
WE'RE SO CLOSE TO HOME I CAN ALMOST TASTE IT!
HEY, PATRICK-- DO YOU HEAR AN OMINOUS WHISTLING NOISE?
I USUALLY DO, BUT I THINK YOUR FOOT JUST PRESSED IT OUT OF ME.
OW!

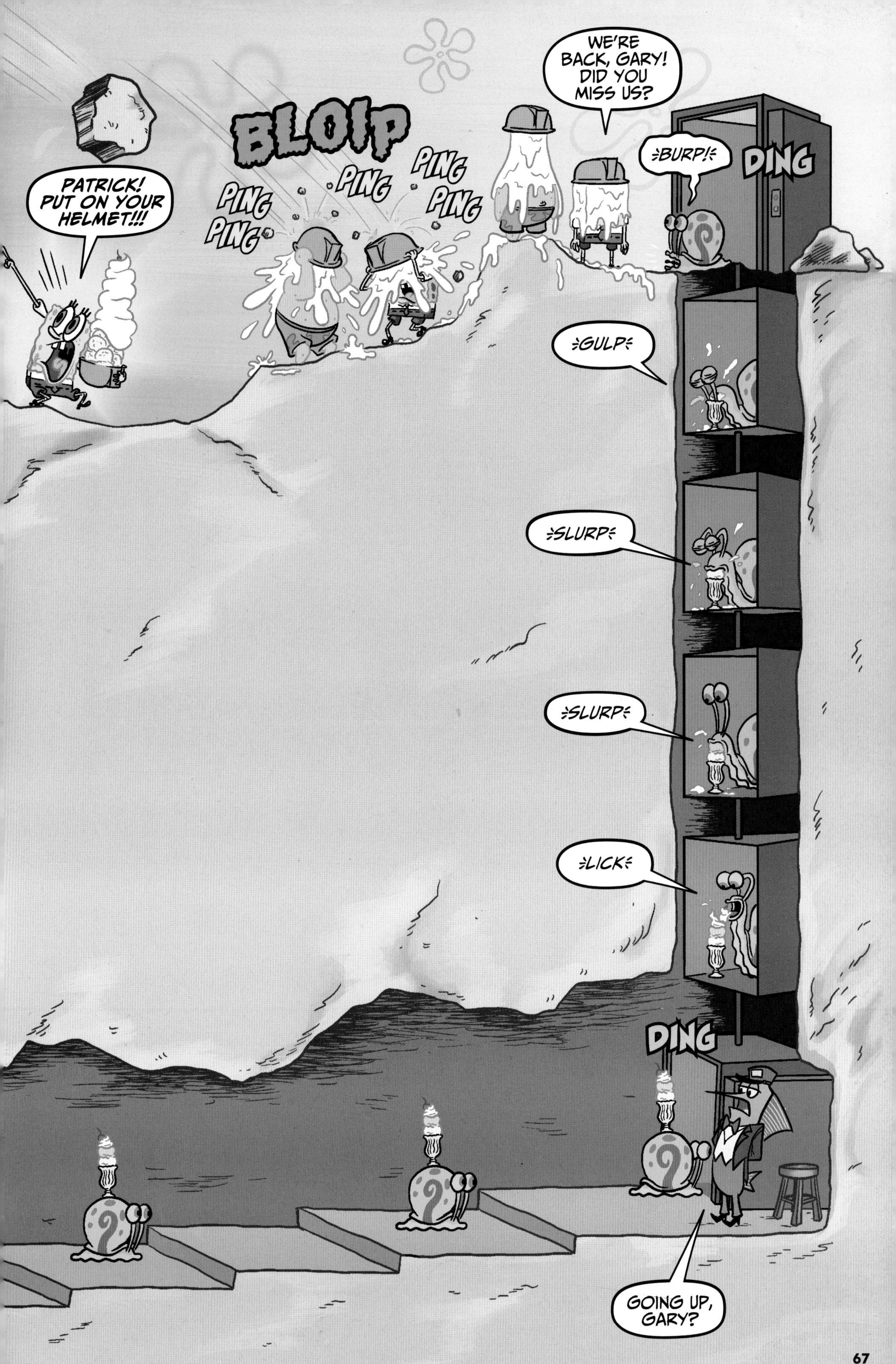
PATRICK! PUT ON YOUR HELMET!!!
BLOIP
PING PING
PING
PING PING
WE'RE BACK, GARY! DID YOU MISS US?
BURP!
DING
GULP
SLURP
SLURP
LICK
DING
GOING UP, GARY?

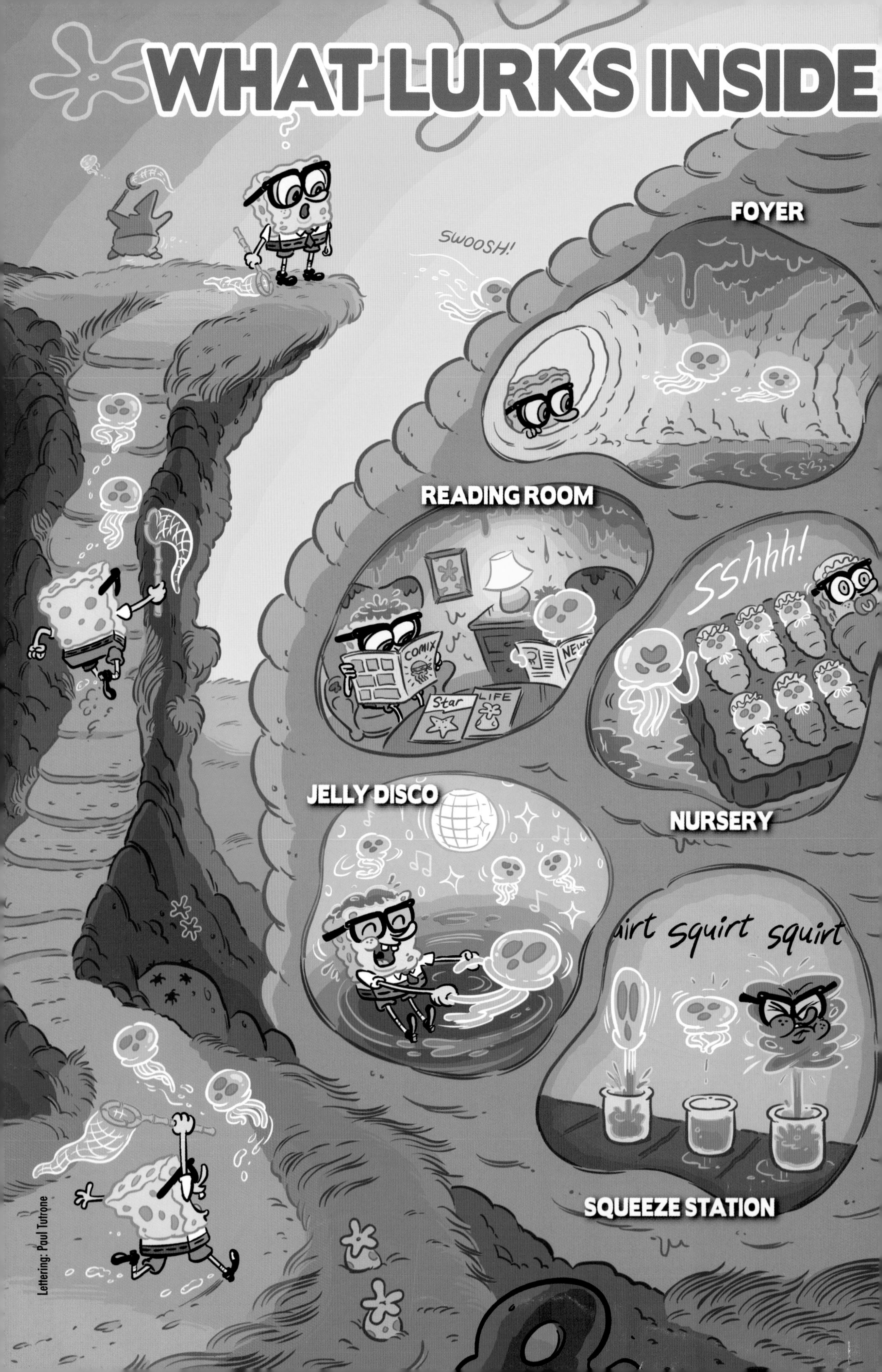
WHAT LURKS INSIDE
SWOOSH!
FOYER
READING ROOM
COMIX
NEWS
Star
LIFE
Sshhh!
NURSERY
JELLY DISCO
irt squirt squirt
SQUEEZE STATION
Lettering: Paul Tutrone

THE JELLY HIVE? by Bob Flynn

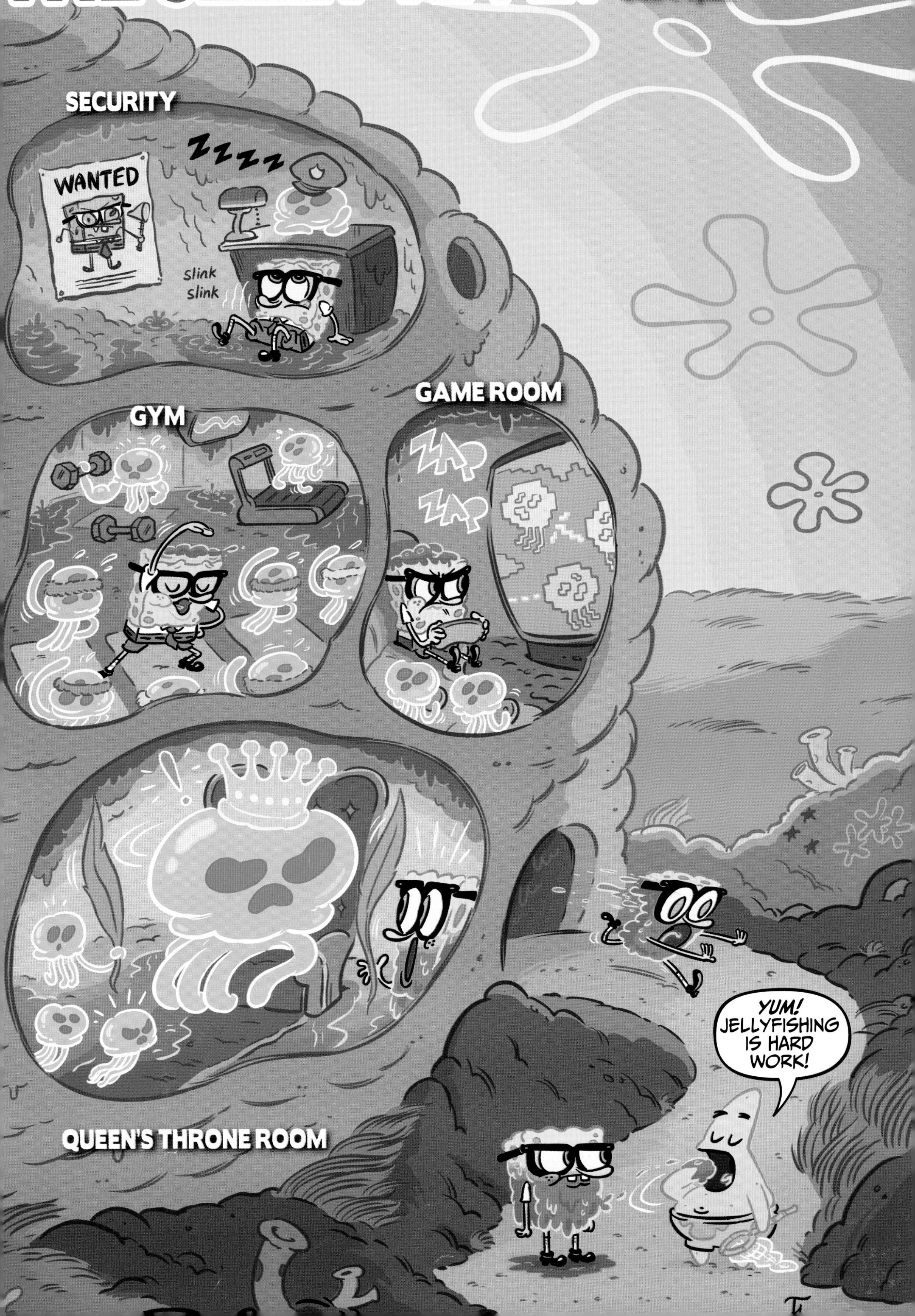
SECURITY
WANTED
ZZZZ
slink slink
GYM
GAME ROOM
ZAP
ZAP
QUEEN'S THRONE ROOM
YUM! JELLYFISHING IS HARD WORK!

Attend ye now a tale o' comic-collectin' corsairs 'n buccaneers!

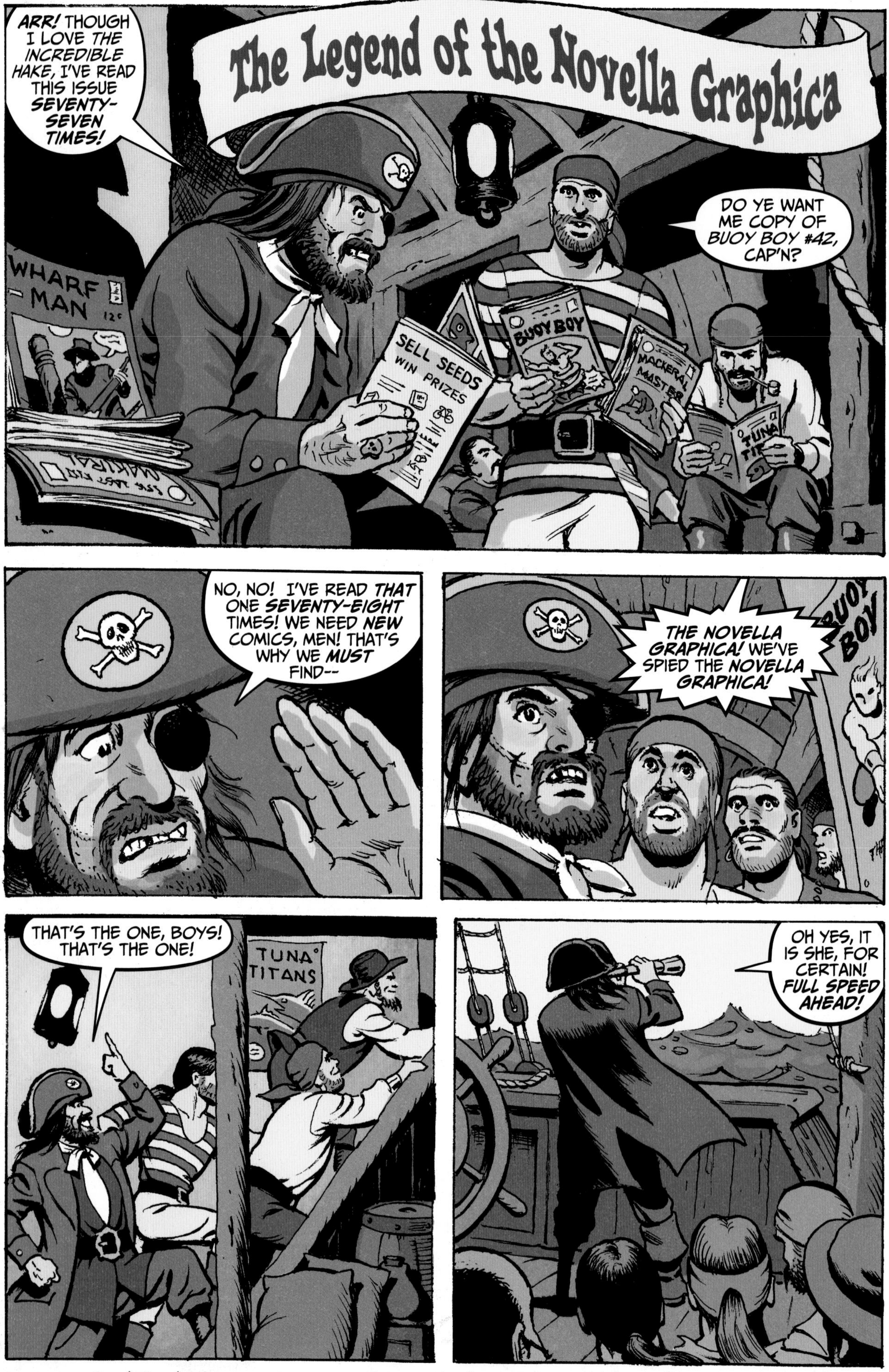

The Legend of the Novella Graphica
ARR! THOUGH I LOVE THE INCREDIBLE HAKE, I'VE READ THIS ISSUE SEVENTY-SEVEN TIMES!
WHARF-MAN 12¢
SELL SEEDS WIN PRIZES
BUOY BOY
MACKERAL MASTER
DO YE WANT ME COPY OF BUOY BOY #42, CAP'N?
NO, NO! I'VE READ THAT ONE SEVENTY-EIGHT TIMES! WE NEED NEW COMICS, MEN! THAT'S WHY WE MUST FIND--
THE NOVELLA GRAPHICA! WE'VE SPIED THE NOVELLA GRAPHICA!
BUOY BOY
THAT'S THE ONE, BOYS! THAT'S THE ONE!
TUNA TITANS
OH YES, IT IS SHE, FOR CERTAIN! FULL SPEED AHEAD!

Story: Jacob Lambert Pencils And Inks: Ramona Fradon Lettering: Comicraft Color: Jim Campbell

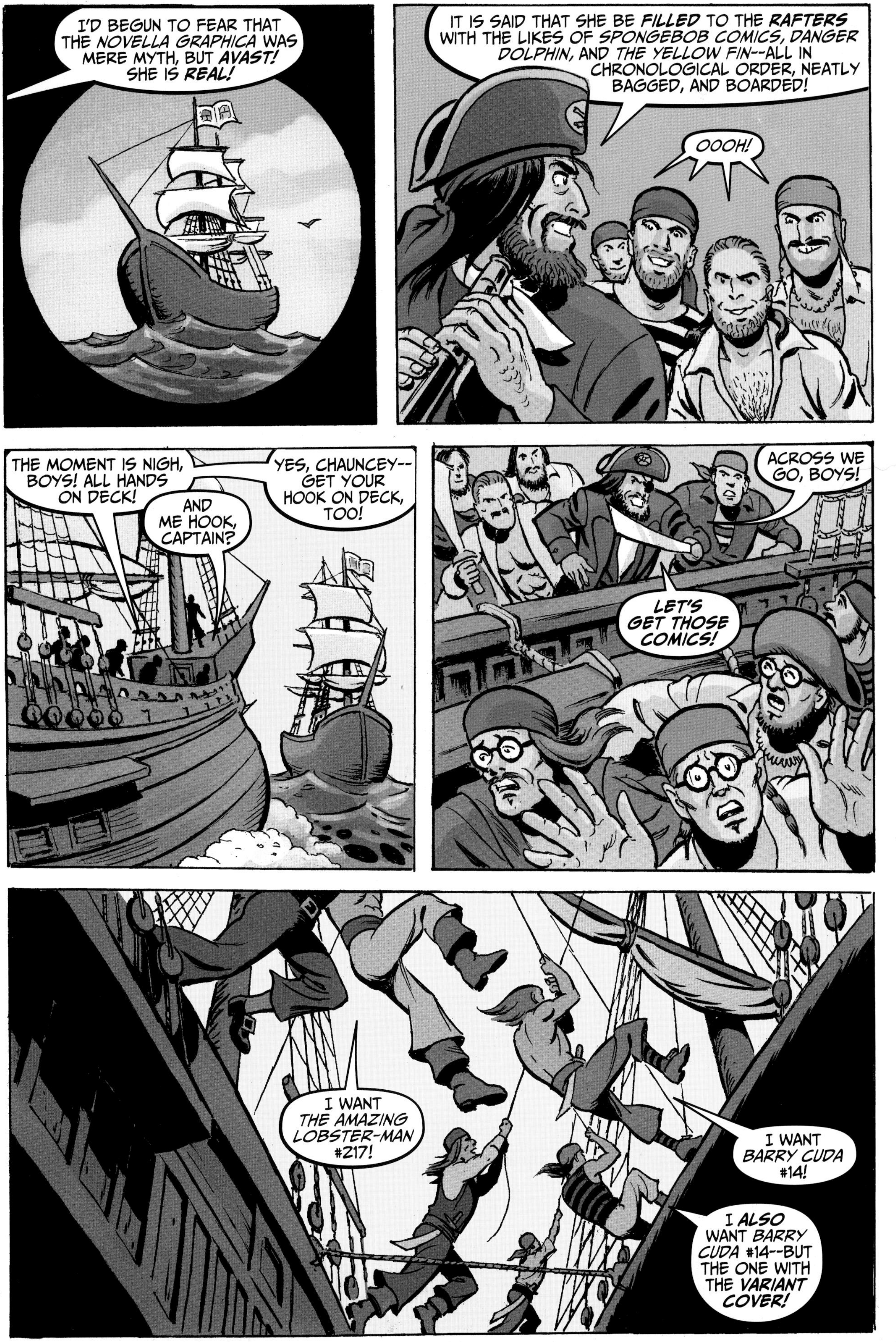
I'D BEGUN TO FEAR THAT THE *NOVELLA GRAPHICA* WAS MERE MYTH, BUT ***AVAST!*** SHE IS ***REAL!***
IT IS SAID THAT SHE BE ***FILLED*** TO THE ***RAFTERS*** WITH THE LIKES OF *SPONGEBOB COMICS, DANGER DOLPHIN,* AND *THE YELLOW FIN*--ALL IN CHRONOLOGICAL ORDER, NEATLY BAGGED, AND BOARDED!
OOOH!
THE MOMENT IS NIGH, BOYS! ALL HANDS ON DECK!
AND ME HOOK, CAPTAIN?
YES, CHAUNCEY--GET YOUR HOOK ON DECK, TOO!
ACROSS WE GO, BOYS!
LET'S GET THOSE COMICS!
I WANT *THE AMAZING LOBSTER-MAN* #217!
I WANT *BARRY CUDA* #14!
I ***ALSO*** WANT *BARRY CUDA* #14--BUT THE ONE WITH THE ***VARIANT COVER!***

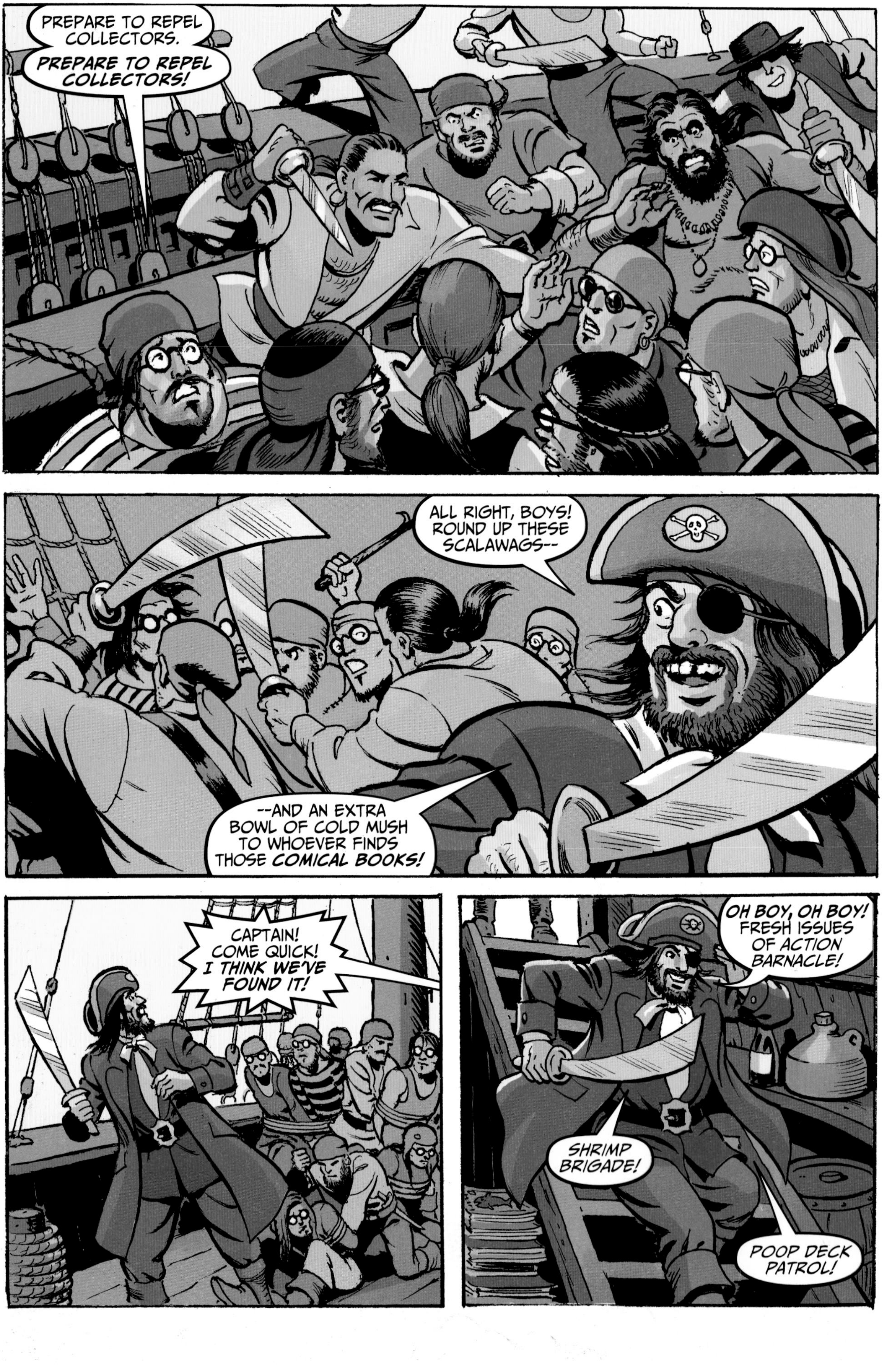
PREPARE TO REPEL COLLECTORS.
PREPARE TO REPEL COLLECTORS!
ALL RIGHT, BOYS! ROUND UP THESE SCALAWAGS--
--AND AN EXTRA BOWL OF COLD MUSH TO WHOEVER FINDS THOSE COMICAL BOOKS!
CAPTAIN! COME QUICK! I THINK WE'VE FOUND IT!
OH BOY, OH BOY! FRESH ISSUES OF ACTION BARNACLE!
SHRIMP BRIGADE!
POOP DECK PATROL!

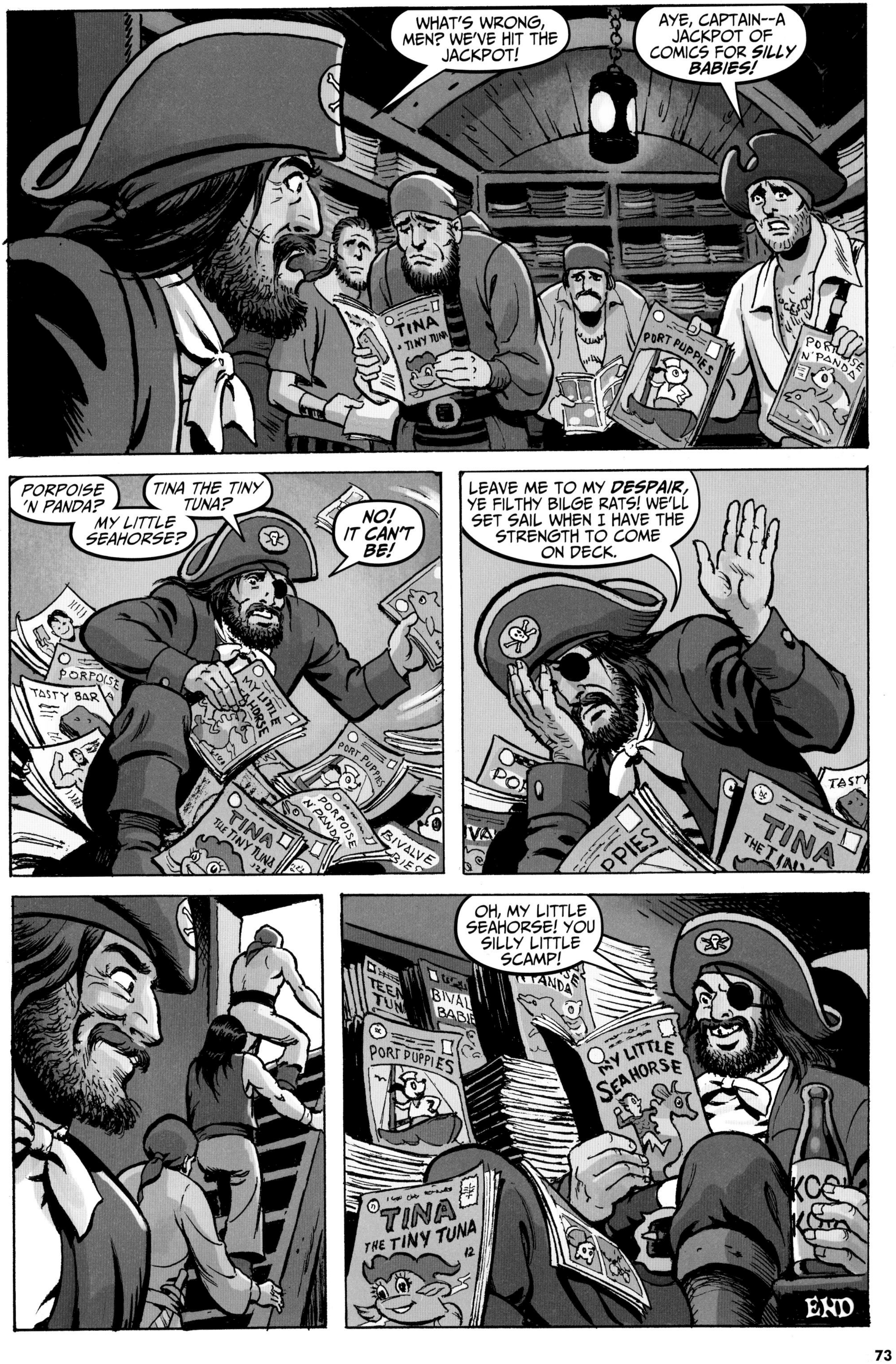

WHAT'S WRONG, MEN? WE'VE HIT THE JACKPOT!
AYE, CAPTAIN--A JACKPOT OF COMICS FOR SILLY BABIES!
PORPOISE 'N PANDA?
MY LITTLE SEAHORSE?
TINA THE TINY TUNA?
NO! IT CAN'T BE!
LEAVE ME TO MY DESPAIR, YE FILTHY BILGE RATS! WE'LL SET SAIL WHEN I HAVE THE STRENGTH TO COME ON DECK.
OH, MY LITTLE SEAHORSE! YOU SILLY LITTLE SCAMP!
END

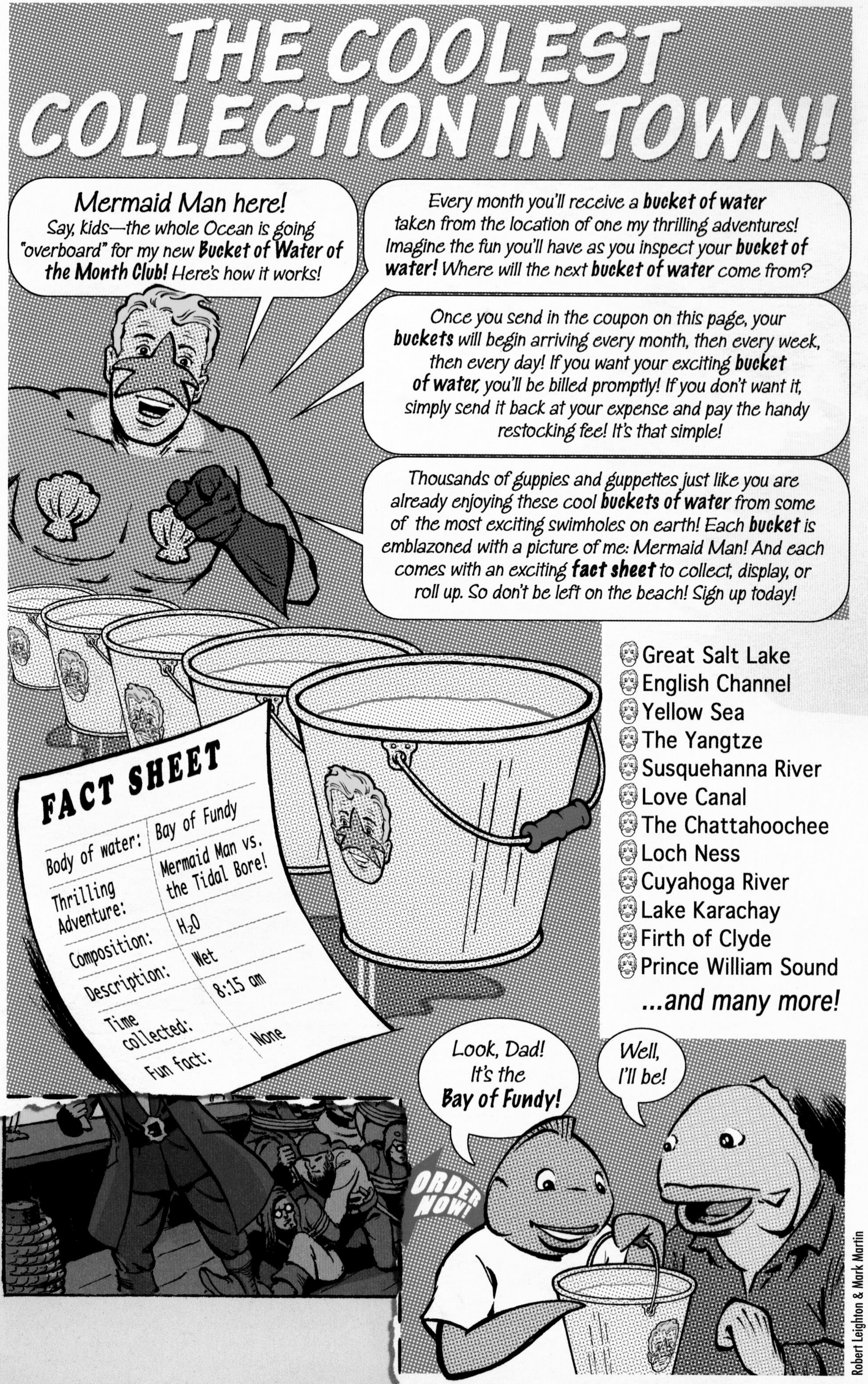

THE COOLEST COLLECTION IN TOWN!
Mermaid Man here! Say, kids—the whole Ocean is going "overboard" for my new Bucket of Water of the Month Club! Here's how it works!
Every month you'll receive a bucket of water taken from the location of one my thrilling adventures! Imagine the fun you'll have as you inspect your bucket of water! Where will the next bucket of water come from?
Once you send in the coupon on this page, your buckets will begin arriving every month, then every week, then every day! If you want your exciting bucket of water, you'll be billed promptly! If you don't want it, simply send it back at your expense and pay the handy restocking fee! It's that simple!
Thousands of guppies and guppettes just like you are already enjoying these cool buckets of water from some of the most exciting swimholes on earth! Each bucket is emblazoned with a picture of me: Mermaid Man! And each comes with an exciting fact sheet to collect, display, or roll up. So don't be left on the beach! Sign up today!
Great Salt Lake
English Channel
Yellow Sea
The Yangtze
Susquehanna River
Love Canal
The Chattahoochee
Loch Ness
Cuyahoga River
Lake Karachay
Firth of Clyde
Prince William Sound
...and many more!
FACT SHEET
Body of water: Bay of Fundy
Thrilling Adventure: Mermaid Man vs. the Tidal Bore!
Composition: H2O
Description: Wet
Time collected: 8:15 am
Fun fact: None
Look, Dad! It's the Bay of Fundy!
Well, I'll be!
ORDER NOW!
Robert Leighton & Mark Martin

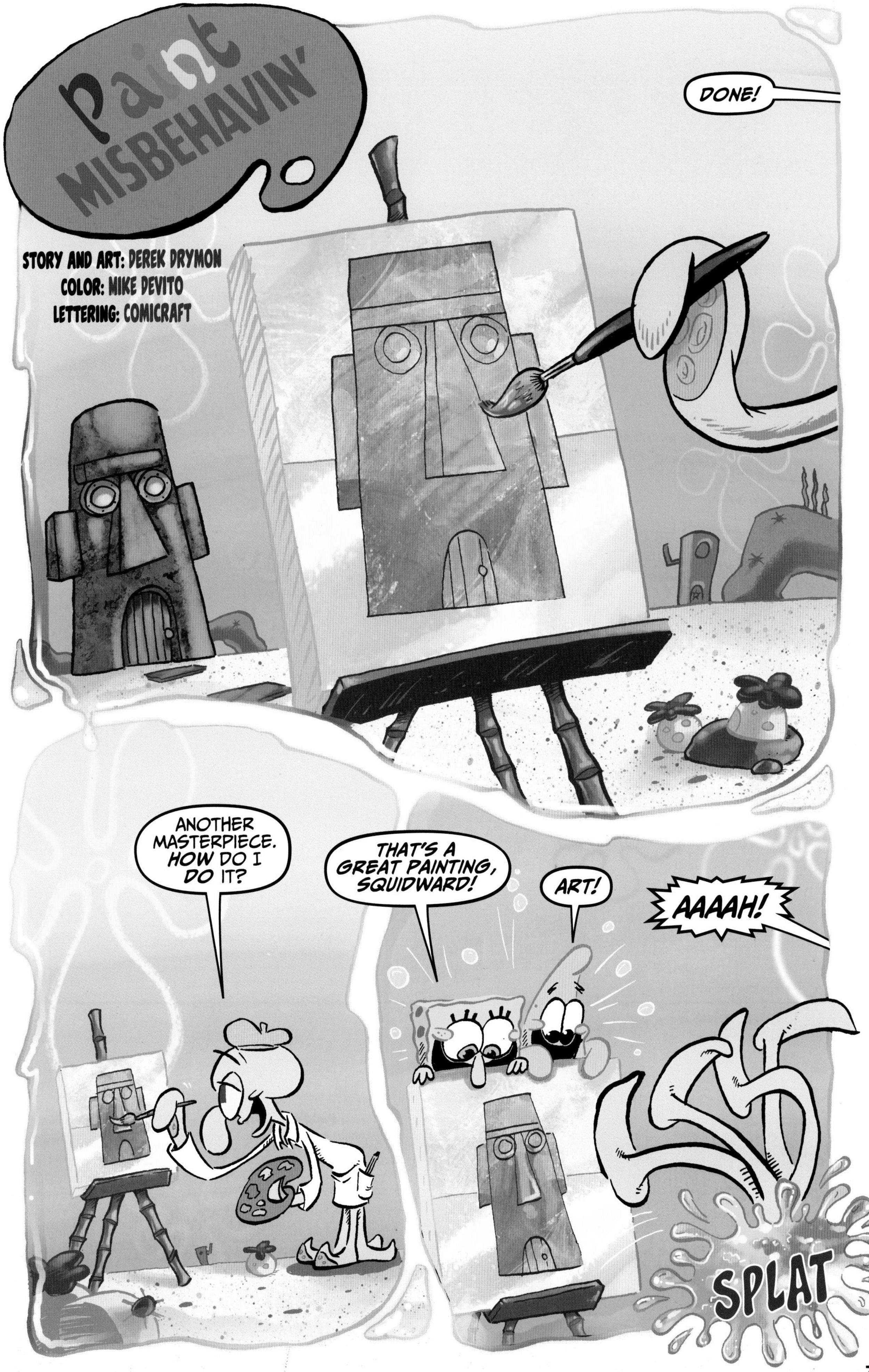
Paint MISBEHAVIN'
STORY AND ART: DEREK DRYMON
COLOR: MIKE DEVITO
LETTERING: COMICRAFT
DONE!
ANOTHER MASTERPIECE. HOW DO I DO IT?
THAT'S A GREAT PAINTING, SQUIDWARD!
ART!
AAAAH!
SPLAT

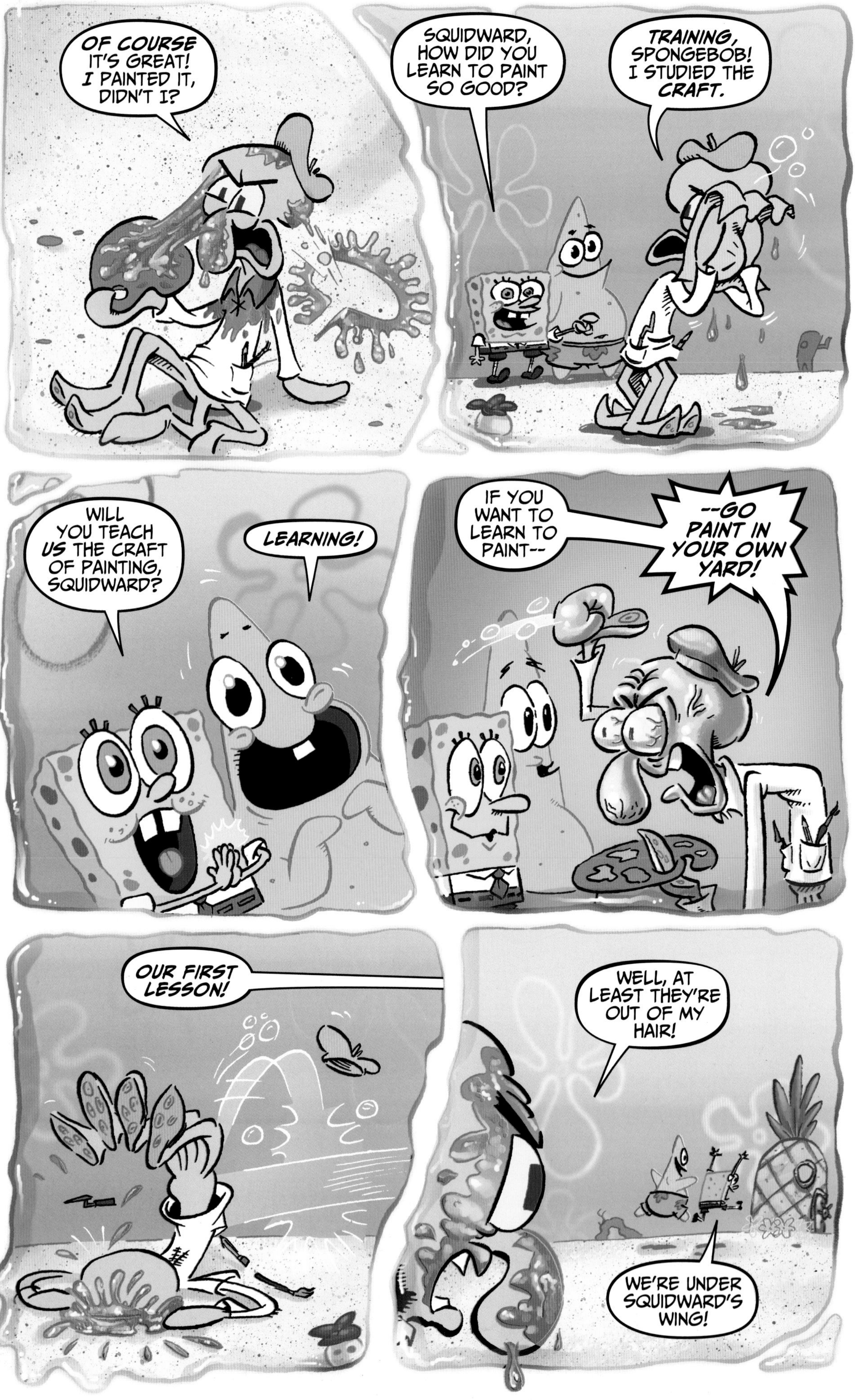
OF COURSE IT'S GREAT! I PAINTED IT, DIDN'T I?
SQUIDWARD, HOW DID YOU LEARN TO PAINT SO GOOD?
TRAINING, SPONGEBOB! I STUDIED THE CRAFT.
WILL YOU TEACH US THE CRAFT OF PAINTING, SQUIDWARD?
LEARNING!
IF YOU WANT TO LEARN TO PAINT--
--GO PAINT IN YOUR OWN YARD!
OUR FIRST LESSON!
WELL, AT LEAST THEY'RE OUT OF MY HAIR!
WE'RE UNDER SQUIDWARD'S WING!

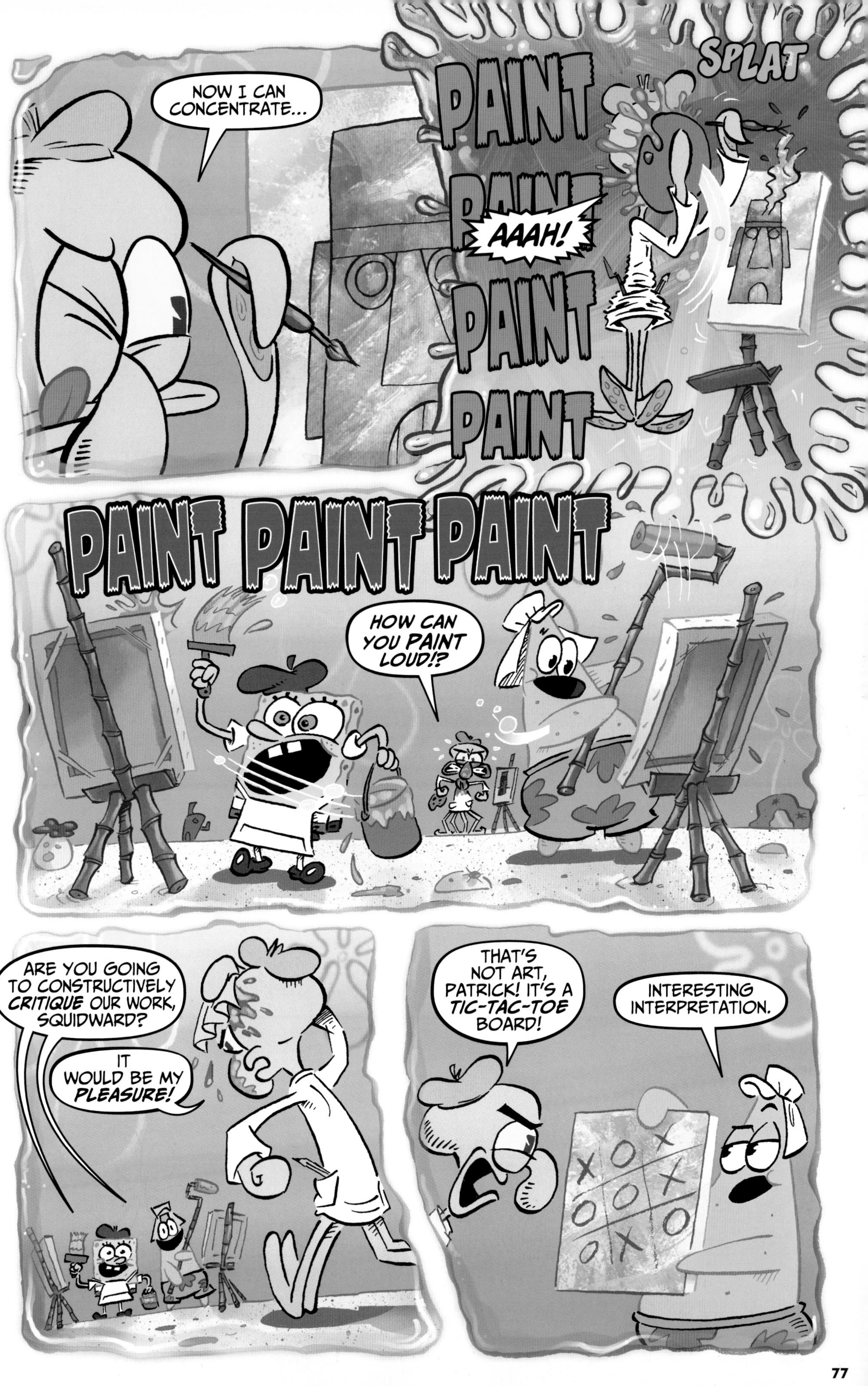
NOW I CAN CONCENTRATE...
PAINT
PAINT
AAAH!
PAINT
PAINT
SPLAT
PAINT PAINT PAINT
HOW CAN YOU PAINT LOUD!?
ARE YOU GOING TO CONSTRUCTIVELY CRITIQUE OUR WORK, SQUIDWARD?
IT WOULD BE MY PLEASURE!
THAT'S NOT ART, PATRICK! IT'S A TIC-TAC-TOE BOARD!
INTERESTING INTERPRETATION.

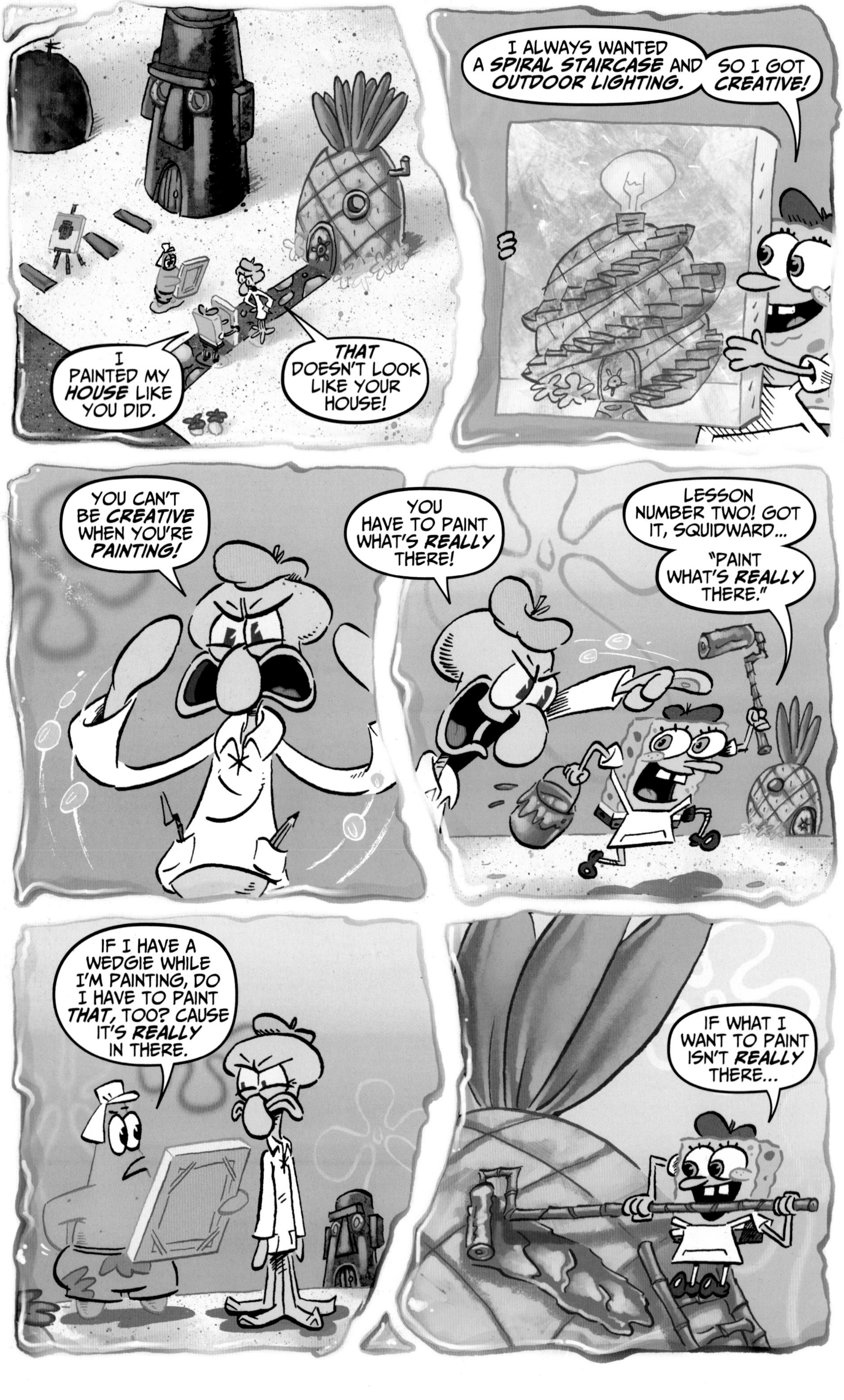
I PAINTED MY HOUSE LIKE YOU DID.
THAT DOESN'T LOOK LIKE YOUR HOUSE!
I ALWAYS WANTED A SPIRAL STAIRCASE AND OUTDOOR LIGHTING.
SO I GOT CREATIVE!
YOU CAN'T BE CREATIVE WHEN YOU'RE PAINTING!
YOU HAVE TO PAINT WHAT'S REALLY THERE!
LESSON NUMBER TWO! GOT IT, SQUIDWARD...
"PAINT WHAT'S REALLY THERE."
IF I HAVE A WEDGIE WHILE I'M PAINTING, DO I HAVE TO PAINT THAT, TOO? CAUSE IT'S REALLY IN THERE.
IF WHAT I WANT TO PAINT ISN'T REALLY THERE...

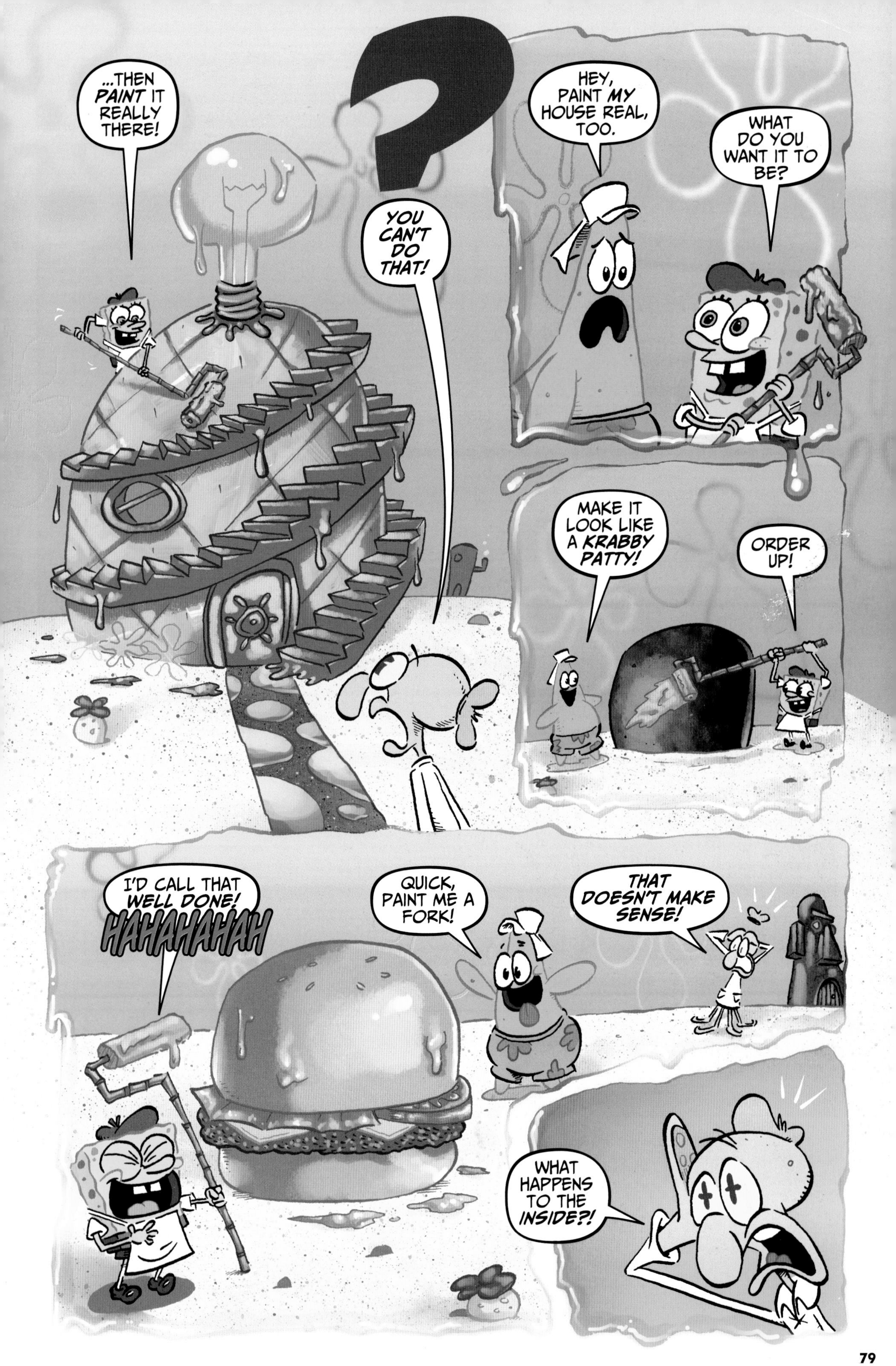
...THEN *PAINT* IT REALLY THERE!
YOU CAN'T DO THAT!
HEY, PAINT *MY* HOUSE REAL, TOO.
WHAT DO YOU WANT IT TO BE?
MAKE IT LOOK LIKE A *KRABBY PATTY!*
ORDER UP!
I'D CALL THAT *WELL DONE!*
HAHAHAHAH
QUICK, PAINT ME A FORK!
THAT DOESN'T MAKE SENSE!
WHAT HAPPENS TO THE *INSIDE?!*

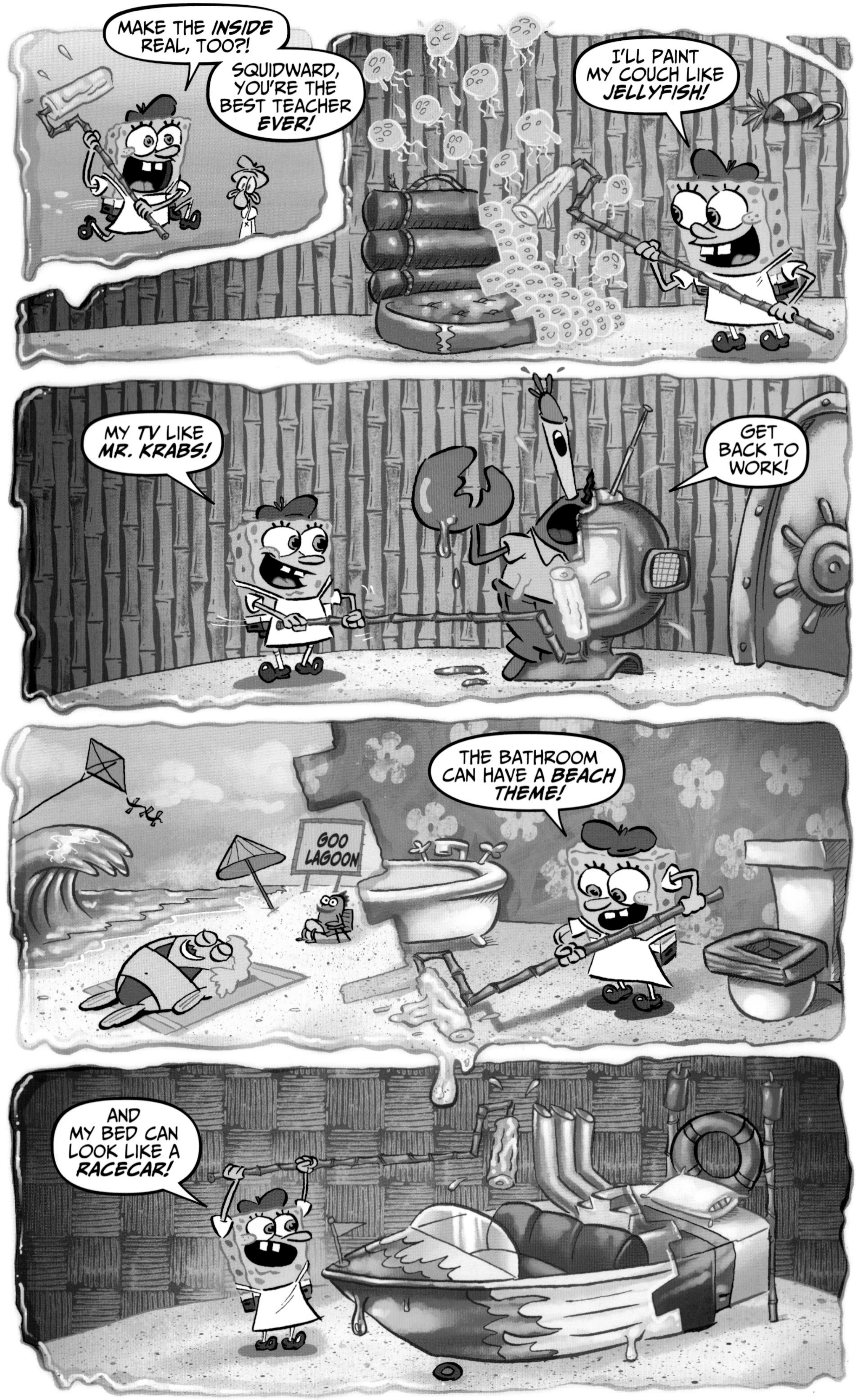
MAKE THE INSIDE REAL, TOO?!
SQUIDWARD, YOU'RE THE BEST TEACHER EVER!
I'LL PAINT MY COUCH LIKE JELLYFISH!
MY TV LIKE MR. KRABS!
GET BACK TO WORK!
GOO LAGOON
THE BATHROOM CAN HAVE A BEACH THEME!
AND MY BED CAN LOOK LIKE A RACECAR!

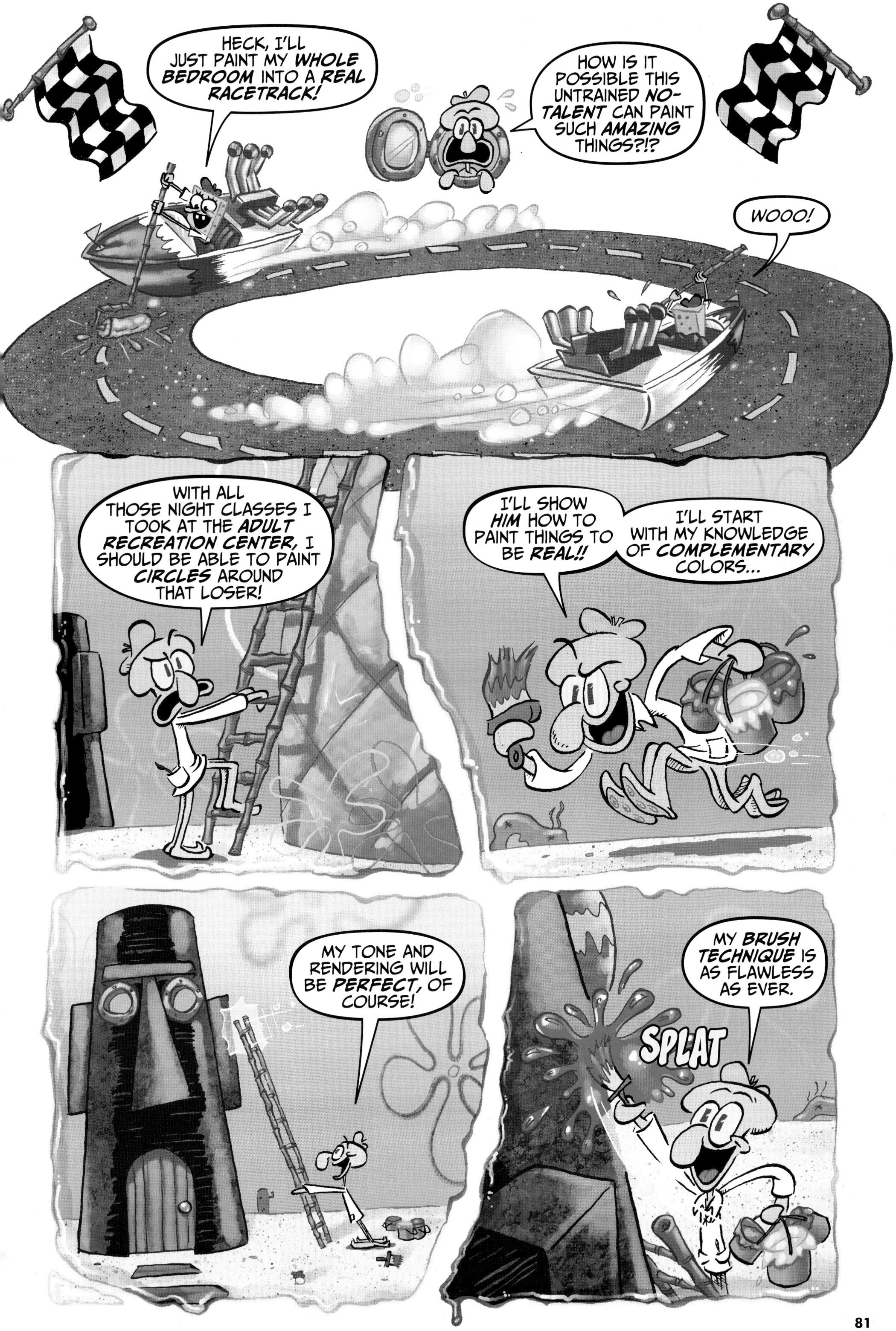
HECK, I'LL JUST PAINT MY WHOLE BEDROOM INTO A REAL RACETRACK!
HOW IS IT POSSIBLE THIS UNTRAINED NO-TALENT CAN PAINT SUCH AMAZING THINGS?!?
WOOO!
WITH ALL THOSE NIGHT CLASSES I TOOK AT THE ADULT RECREATION CENTER, I SHOULD BE ABLE TO PAINT CIRCLES AROUND THAT LOSER!
I'LL SHOW HIM HOW TO PAINT THINGS TO BE REAL!!
I'LL START WITH MY KNOWLEDGE OF COMPLEMENTARY COLORS...
MY TONE AND RENDERING WILL BE PERFECT, OF COURSE!
MY BRUSH TECHNIQUE IS AS FLAWLESS AS EVER.
SPLAT

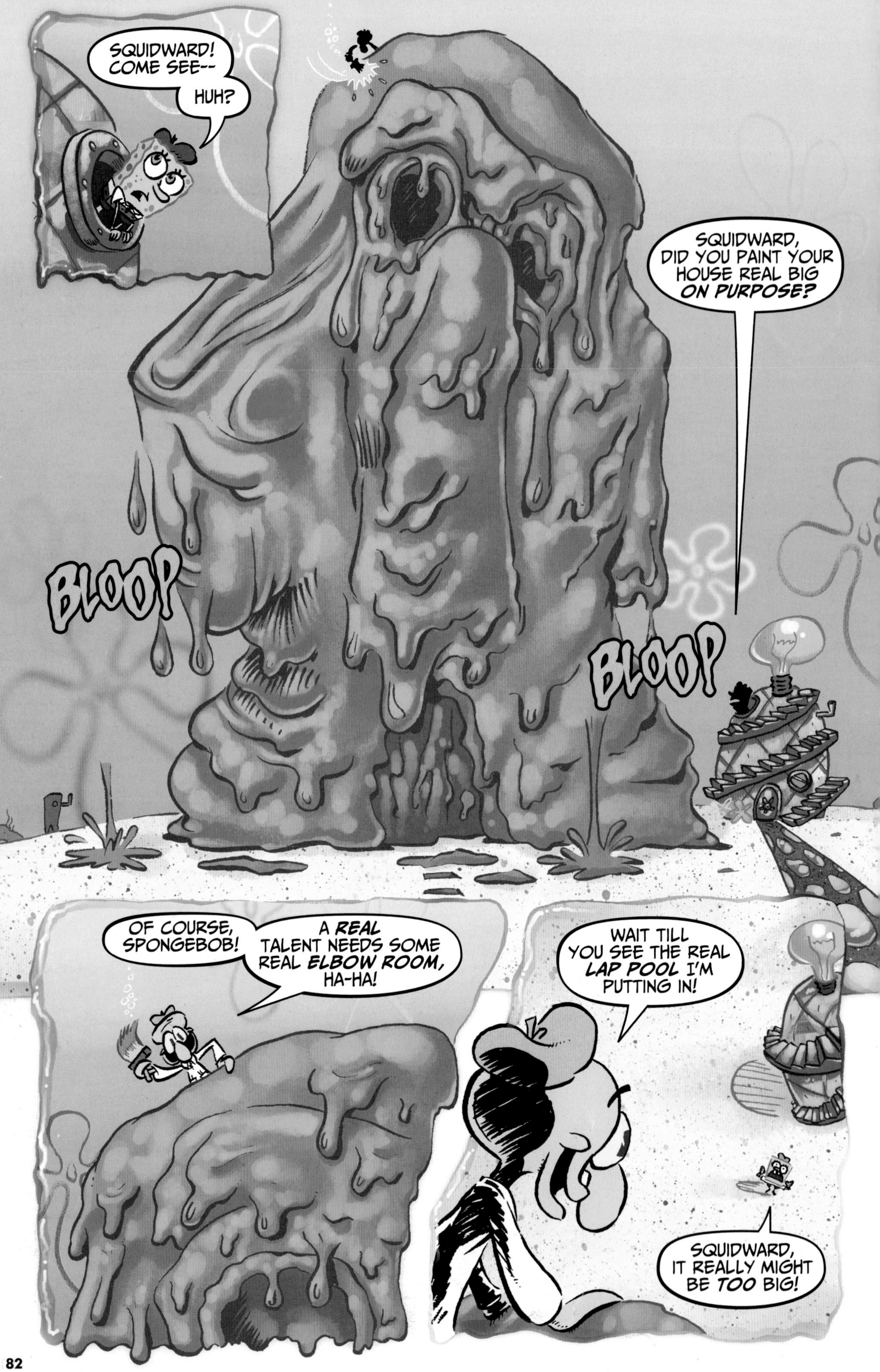
SQUIDWARD! COME SEE--
HUH?
SQUIDWARD, DID YOU PAINT YOUR HOUSE REAL BIG ON PURPOSE?
BLOOP
BLOOP
OF COURSE, SPONGEBOB!
A REAL TALENT NEEDS SOME REAL ELBOW ROOM, HA-HA!
WAIT TILL YOU SEE THE REAL LAP POOL I'M PUTTING IN!
SQUIDWARD, IT REALLY MIGHT BE TOO BIG!

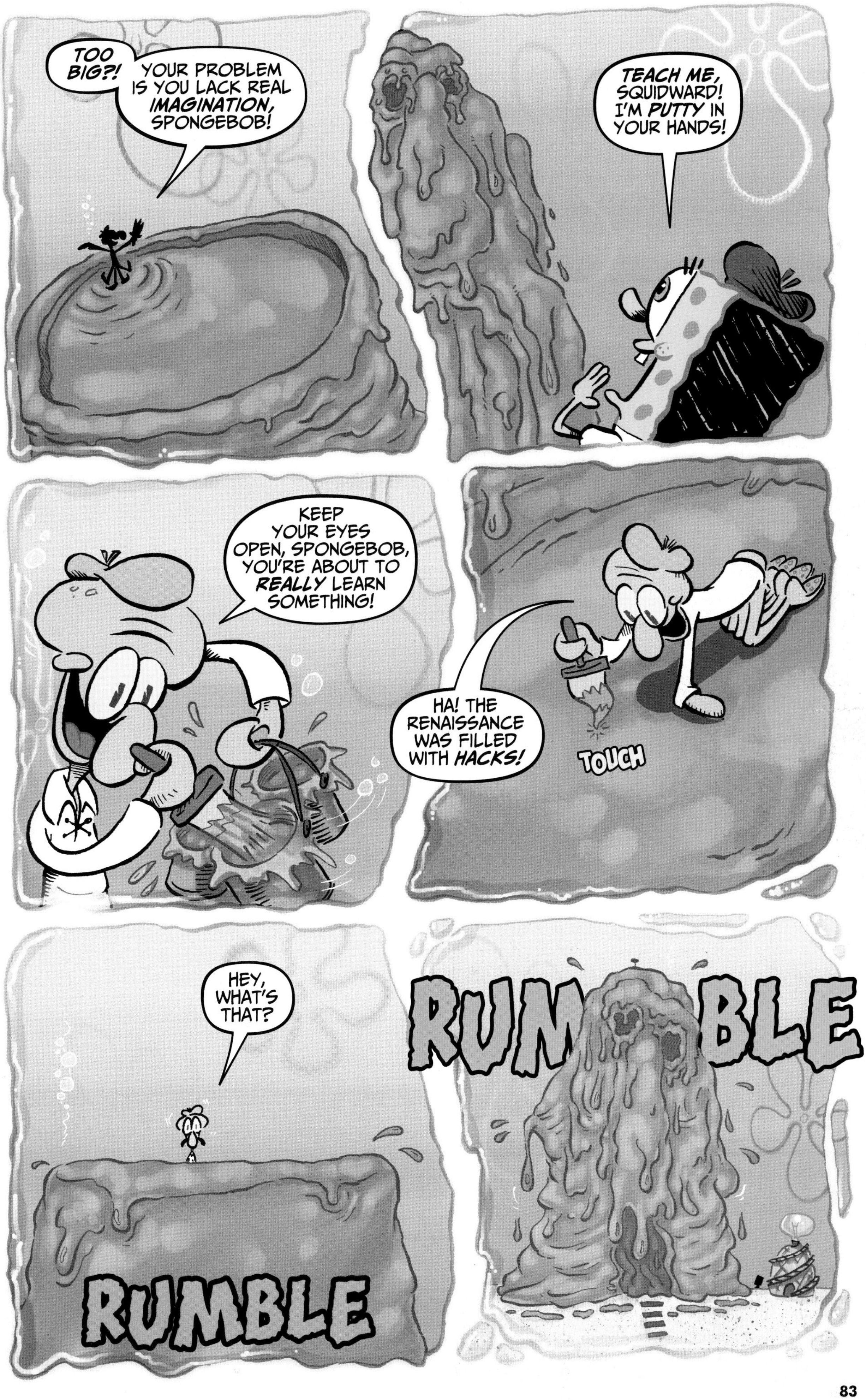
TOO BIG?!
YOUR PROBLEM IS YOU LACK REAL IMAGINATION, SPONGEBOB!
TEACH ME, SQUIDWARD! I'M PUTTY IN YOUR HANDS!
KEEP YOUR EYES OPEN, SPONGEBOB, YOU'RE ABOUT TO REALLY LEARN SOMETHING!
HA! THE RENAISSANCE WAS FILLED WITH HACKS!
TOUCH
HEY, WHAT'S THAT?
RUMBLE
RUMBLE

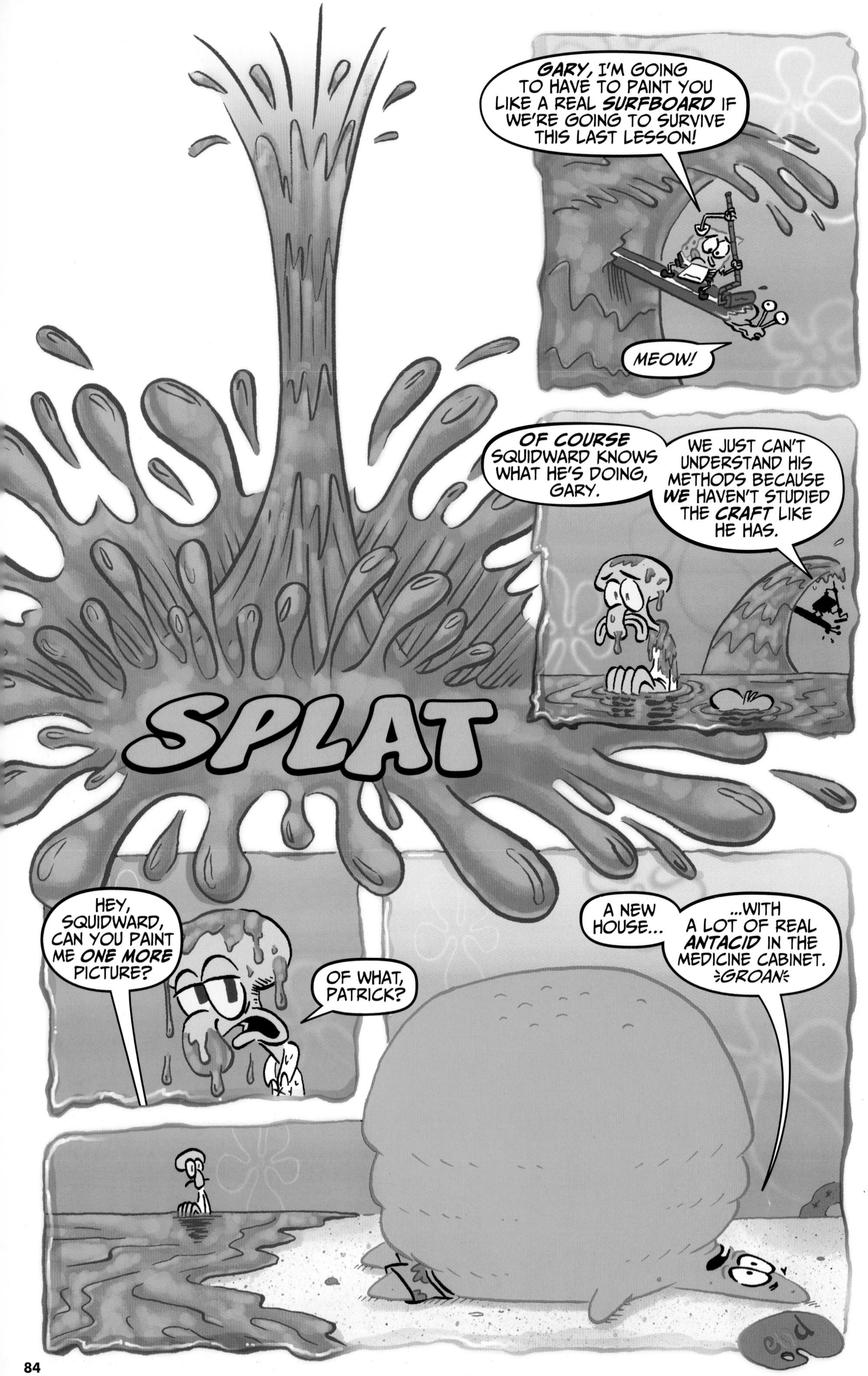

GARY, I'M GOING TO HAVE TO PAINT YOU LIKE A REAL SURFBOARD IF WE'RE GOING TO SURVIVE THIS LAST LESSON!
MEOW!
OF COURSE SQUIDWARD KNOWS WHAT HE'S DOING, GARY.
WE JUST CAN'T UNDERSTAND HIS METHODS BECAUSE WE HAVEN'T STUDIED THE CRAFT LIKE HE HAS.
SPLAT
HEY, SQUIDWARD, CAN YOU PAINT ME ONE MORE PICTURE?
OF WHAT, PATRICK?
A NEW HOUSE...
...WITH A LOT OF REAL ANTACID IN THE MEDICINE CABINET.
GROAN
end

COMICS BARGAIN BONANZA!

COMPLETE YOUR COLLECTION WITH THESE THRILLING EDUCATIONAL COMICS!

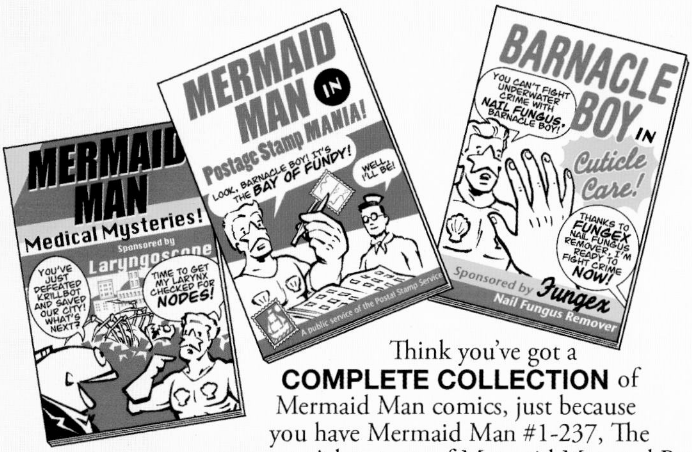
MERMAID MAN
Medical Mysteries!
Sponsored by Laryngoscope
YOU'VE JUST DEFEATED KRILLBOT AND SAVED OUR CITY! WHAT'S NEXT?
TIME TO GET MY LARYNX CHECKED FOR NODES!
MERMAID MAN IN
Postage Stamp MANIA!
LOOK, BARNACLE BOY! IT'S THE BAY OF FUNDY!
WELL, I'LL BE!
A public service of the Postal Stamp Service
BARNACLE BOY IN
Cuticle Care!
YOU CAN'T FIGHT UNDERWATER CRIME WITH NAIL FUNGUS, BARNACLE BOY!
THANKS TO FUNGEX NAIL FUNGUS REMOVER, I'M READY TO FIGHT CRIME NOW!
Sponsored by Fungex
Nail Fungus Remover

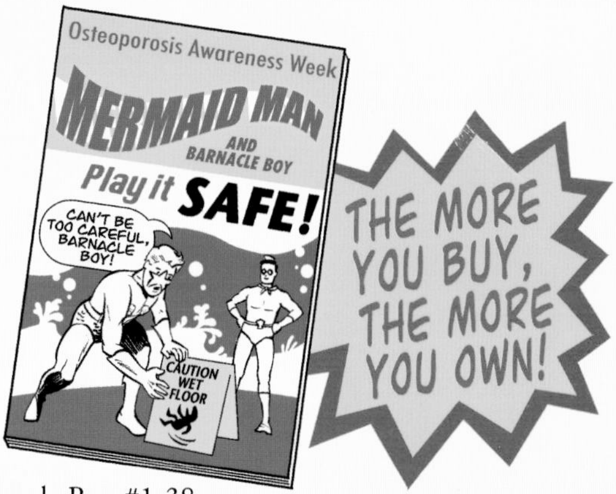
Osteoporosis Awareness Week
MERMAID MAN AND BARNACLE BOY
Play it SAFE!
CAN'T BE TOO CAREFUL, BARNACLE BOY!
CAUTION WET FLOOR
THE MORE YOU BUY, THE MORE YOU OWN!

Think you've got a **COMPLETE COLLECTION** of Mermaid Man comics, just because you have Mermaid Man #1-237, The Adventures of Mermaid Man and Barnacle Boy #1-38, Mermaid Man: Defender of the Deep #1-77, Barnacle Boy Comics #1-6, The Monumental Mermaid Man #78-79, Young Mermaid Man and Barnacle Boy #7-41, and Mermaid Man and Barnacle Boy Thrilling Undersea Adventures #39-114? Your collection still contains embarrassing gaps as long as you are missing all the **THRILLING** and **EDUCATIONAL** comics starring ME – Mermaid Man, and my trusty sidekick Barnacle Boy! You'll **THRILL** to the **EDUCATION** packed in every issue! WOW! Isn't **EDUCATION** a **THRILL?** Wait till your friends see the **EDUCATION** on each and every page in these **THRILLING EDUCATIONAL COMICS,** produced in cooperation with some of our most **THRILLING EDUCATIONAL** corporate sponsors!

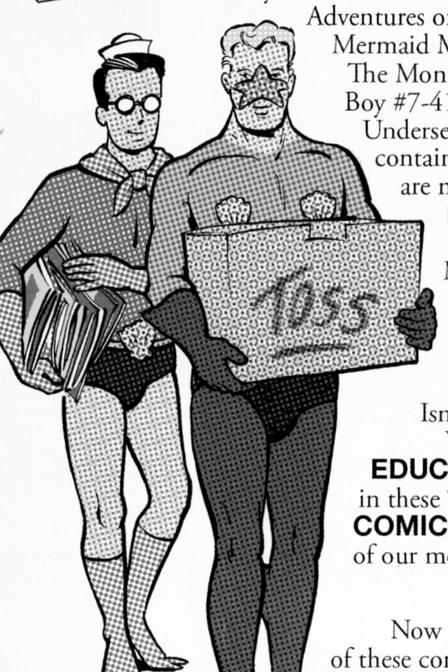
TOSS

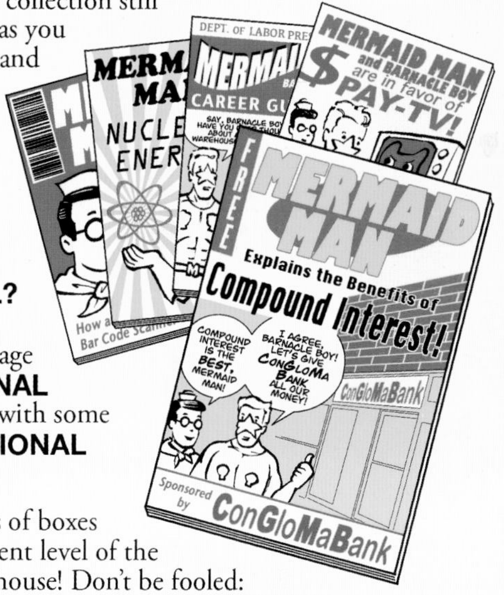
DEPT. OF LABOR PRE
MERMAID CAREER GU
SAY, BARNACLE BOY! HAVE YOU
MERMAID MAN NUCLEAR ENERGY
How a Bar Code Scanner
MERMAID MAN and BARNACLE BOY are in favor of PAY-TV!
FREE
MERMAID MAN Explains the Benefits of Compound Interest!
COMPOUND INTEREST IS THE BEST, MERMAID MAN!
I AGREE, BARNACLE BOY! LET'S GIVE CONGLOMA BANK ALL OUR MONEY!
ConGloMaBank
Sponsored by ConGloMaBank

Now we've just released thousands of boxes of these comics from the bargain basement level of the Mermaid Man Undersea Warehouse! Don't be fooled: The covers say *"FREE"* but the comics are *PRICELESS!**

Robert Leighton & Mark Martin

TITLE	QTY
Mermaid Man's Story of Creosote!	
Mermaid Man and Barnacle Boy in Let's Eat Margarine!	
Mermaid Man's Multiplication Table Comics!	
Mermaid Man Explains How a Bill is Vetoed!	
Barnacle Boy Learns to Read a Food Label!	
Mermaid Man and Barnacle Boy Organize Their Closets!	
Mermaid Man and Barnacle Boy in Floss Your Cares Away!	
Barnacle Boy Seaweed Identification Guide!	
Mermaid Man's Career Guide Comics!	
Barnacle Boy in How a Bar Code Scanner Works!	
Mermaid Man Loves Nuclear Energy!	
Mermaid Man and Barnacle Boy Are in Favor of Pay-TV!	
Mermaid Man Explains the Benefits of Compound Interest!	
Mermaid Man and Barnacle Boy Play It Safe!	
Barnacle Boy in Cuticle Care!	
Mermaid Man and Barnacle Boy in Postage Stamp MANIA!	
Mermaid Man Medical Mysteries!	

Order now! Supplies are Unlimited!

*Note that each comic costs $4.95 plus Shipping and Handling.–Ed.

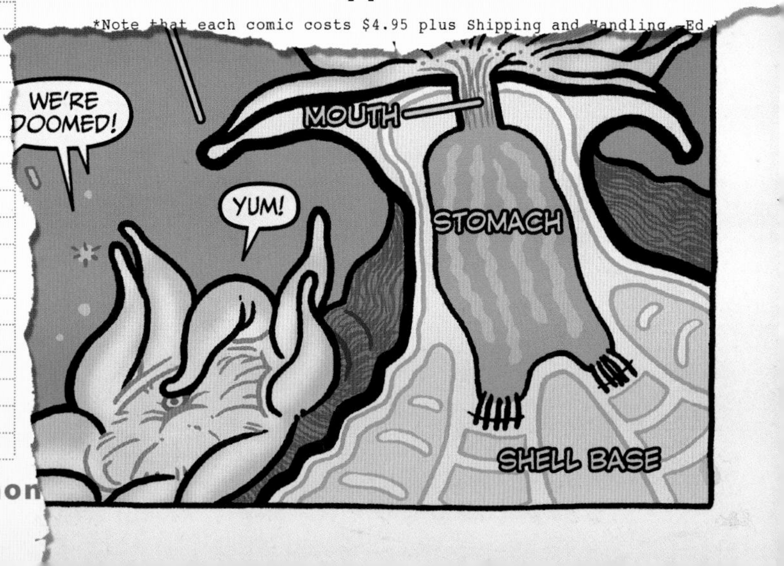
WE'RE DOOMED!
MOUTH
YUM!
STOMACH
SHELL BASE

Please allow 6-8 mon

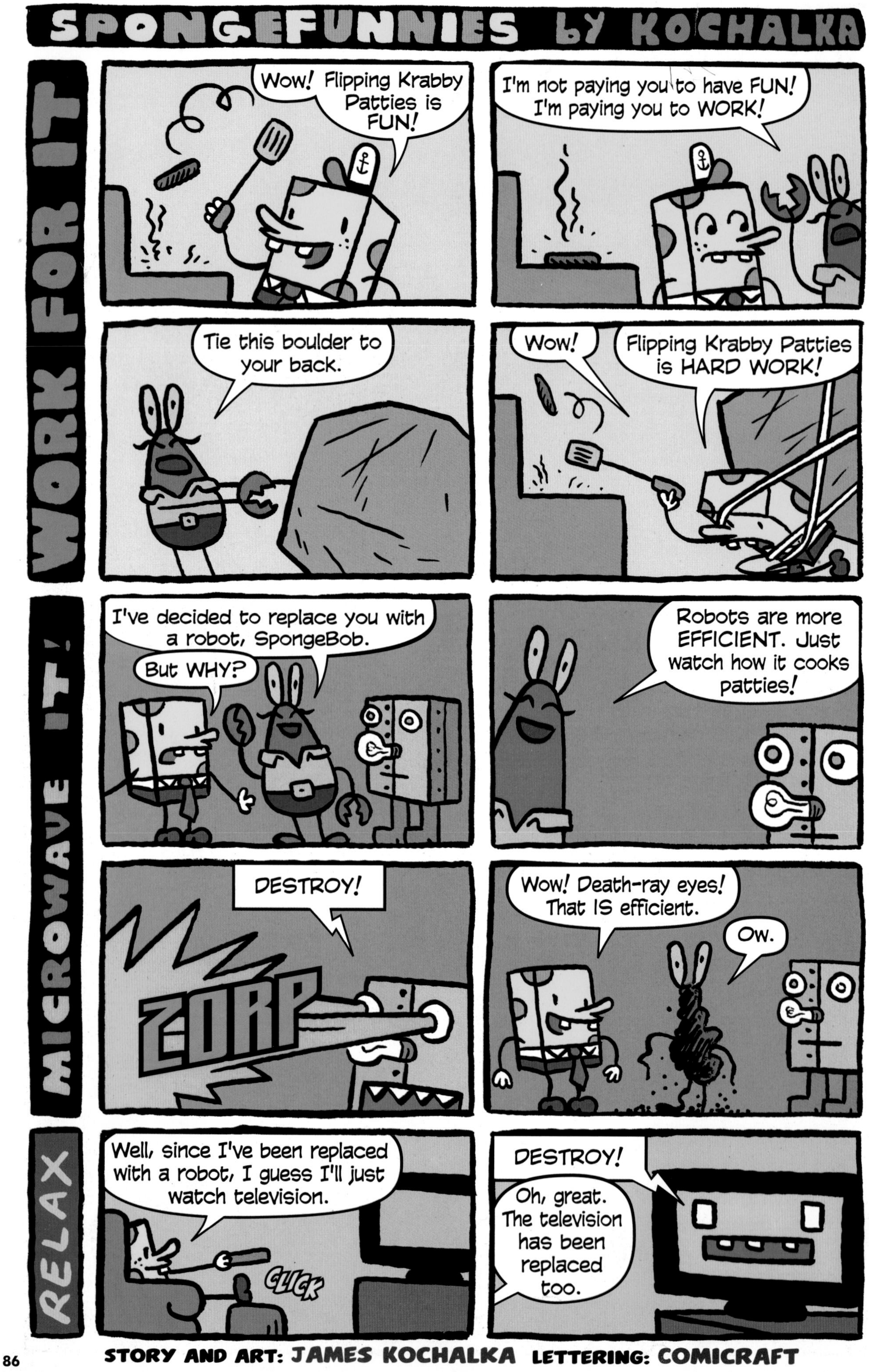

SPONGEFUNNIES by KOCHALKA
WORK FOR IT
Wow! Flipping Krabby Patties is FUN!
I'm not paying you to have FUN! I'm paying you to WORK!
Tie this boulder to your back.
Wow!
Flipping Krabby Patties is HARD WORK!
MICROWAVE IT!
I've decided to replace you with a robot, SpongeBob.
But WHY?
Robots are more EFFICIENT. Just watch how it cooks patties!
DESTROY!
ZORP
Wow! Death-ray eyes! That IS efficient.
Ow.
RELAX
Well, since I've been replaced with a robot, I guess I'll just watch television.
CLICK
DESTROY!
Oh, great. The television has been replaced too.

STORY AND ART: JAMES KOCHALKA LETTERING: COMICRAFT

CORAL

BY MARIS WICKS

OCEAN FACTS

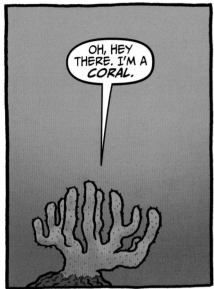

OH, HEY THERE. I'M A *CORAL.*

AND THESE ARE MY *BUDDIES;* THIS IS A *CORAL REEF.*

OOH, LOOK AT ALL THE PRETTY COLORED ROCKS!

UGH, WE'RE *NOT* ROCKS...

...WE ARE *ANIMALS!*

ALL OF US HERE BELONG TO A GROUP OF ANIMALS CALLED *CNIDARIA.*

YEAH!

THAT'S RIGHT! AND IT'S PRONOUNCED "NIE-DAREEUH."

HELLO CORAL

HELLO jellyfish

HELLO anemone

Now, I'm not just ONE coral...I'm a *colony* of thousands of tiny *coral polyps!*

Let's look closer:

HERE WE ARE!!

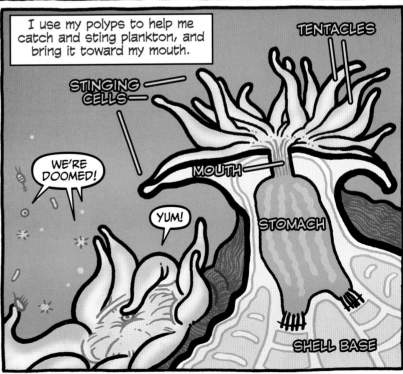

I use my polyps to help me catch and sting plankton, and bring it toward my mouth.

TENTACLES

STINGING CELLS

WE'RE DOOMED!

MOUTH

YUM!

STOMACH

SHELL BASE

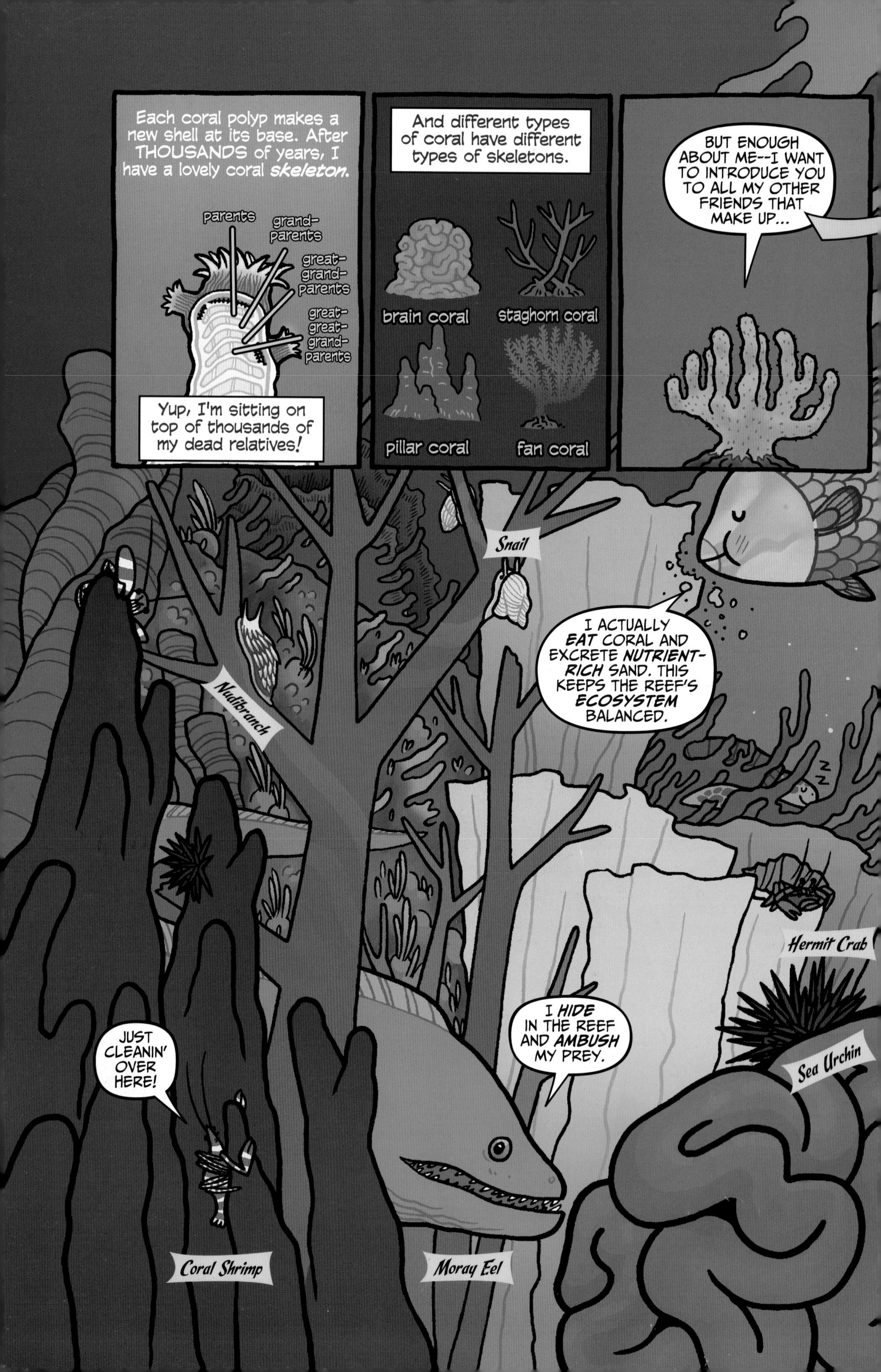
Each coral polyp makes a new shell at its base. After THOUSANDS of years, I have a lovely coral *skeleton*.
parents
grand-parents
great-grand-parents
great-great-grand-parents
Yup, I'm sitting on top of thousands of my dead relatives!
And different types of coral have different types of skeletons.
brain coral
staghorn coral
pillar coral
fan coral
BUT ENOUGH ABOUT ME--I WANT TO INTRODUCE YOU TO ALL MY OTHER FRIENDS THAT MAKE UP...
Snail
I ACTUALLY *EAT* CORAL AND EXCRETE *NUTRIENT-RICH* SAND. THIS KEEPS THE REEF'S *ECOSYSTEM* BALANCED.
Nudibranch
Hermit Crab
I *HIDE* IN THE REEF AND *AMBUSH* MY PREY.
Sea Urchin
JUST CLEANIN' OVER HERE!
Coral Shrimp
Moray Eel

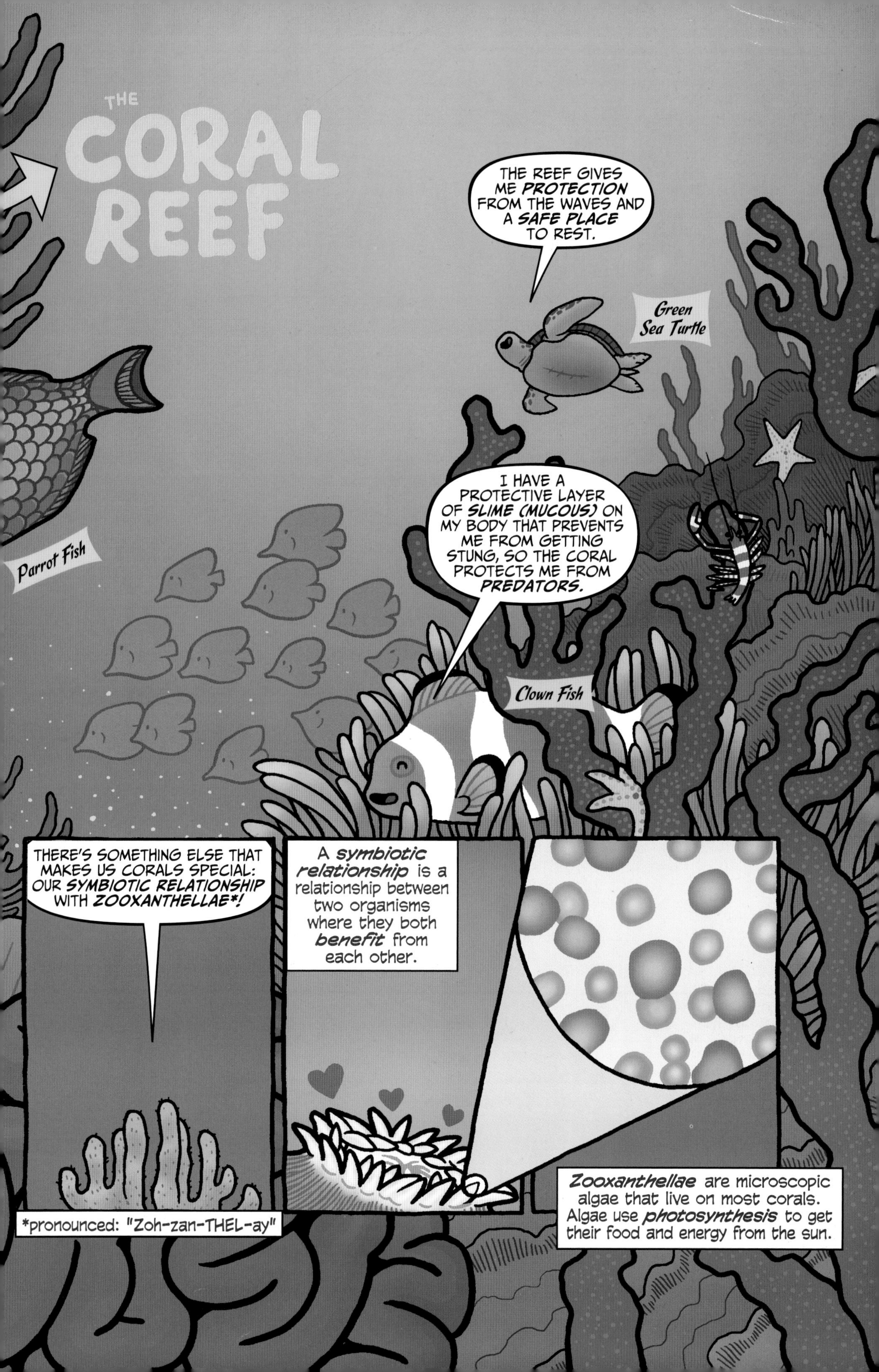

THE CORAL REEF
THE REEF GIVES ME PROTECTION FROM THE WAVES AND A SAFE PLACE TO REST.
Green Sea Turtle
Parrot Fish
I HAVE A PROTECTIVE LAYER OF SLIME (MUCOUS) ON MY BODY THAT PREVENTS ME FROM GETTING STUNG, SO THE CORAL PROTECTS ME FROM PREDATORS.
Clown Fish
THERE'S SOMETHING ELSE THAT MAKES US CORALS SPECIAL: OUR SYMBIOTIC RELATIONSHIP WITH ZOOXANTHELLAE*!
*pronounced: "Zoh-zan-THEL-ay"
A symbiotic relationship is a relationship between two organisms where they both benefit from each other.
Zooxanthellae are microscopic algae that live on most corals. Algae use photosynthesis to get their food and energy from the sun.

Coral provides the zooxanthellae with a protective habitat close to the sun, and the zooxanthellae provide the coral with nutrients and oxygen.
HOW'RE YOU DOIN' IN THERE, ZOO-IE?
GREAT!!
DUDE, IT'S A LIKE MAGIC RAINBOW...
Zooxanthellae also give corals their vibrant colors.
Coral reefs are home to 25% of the animals in the ocean.
That's why it's a big deal when people talk about coral reefs being ENDANGERED.
It's true! Let's look at where coral reefs are found:
Notice that coral reefs are found only in water that is *close to land* and *close to the equator?*
Well, people are found in those areas there, too. And that means pollution...
Coral reefs are threatened by something else: *climate change.*
IS IT GETTING HOT IN HERE?
If the water gets too warm, too cold, or too polluted, the zooxanthellae leave, and the coral can not get enough nutrients and oxygen.
EW! WHO PUT *THIS* HERE?
NO! DON'T LEAVE!
This is called *coral bleaching,* because the coral loses its color as well.
If the conditions get worse or don't change, the coral will eventually die.
So how can you help coral reefs?
Saving energy, recycling, buying local goods...
...all of these things put less strain on the the world's resources and oceans. To learn more: check out this site: coralreef.noaa.gov/
I'M SURE YOU CAN THINK OF MORE WAYS TO KEEP THE OCEAN CLEAN... AND DON'T WORRY IF YOU DON'T LIVE NEAR A CORAL REEF. THINGS THAT KEEP YOUR ENVIRONMENT HEALTHY ALSO KEEP THE OCEAN HEALTHY.
THANK YOU, FROM THE BOTTOM OF MY *POLYPS!*

A section of a coral reef the size of this page could be home to thousands of animals.

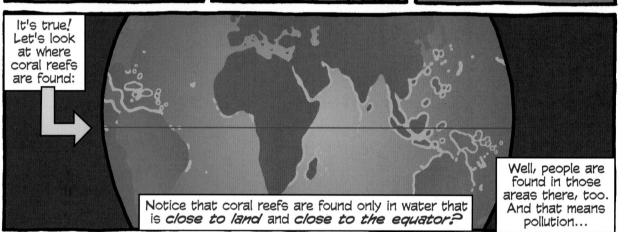

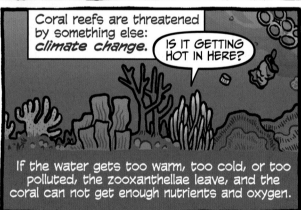

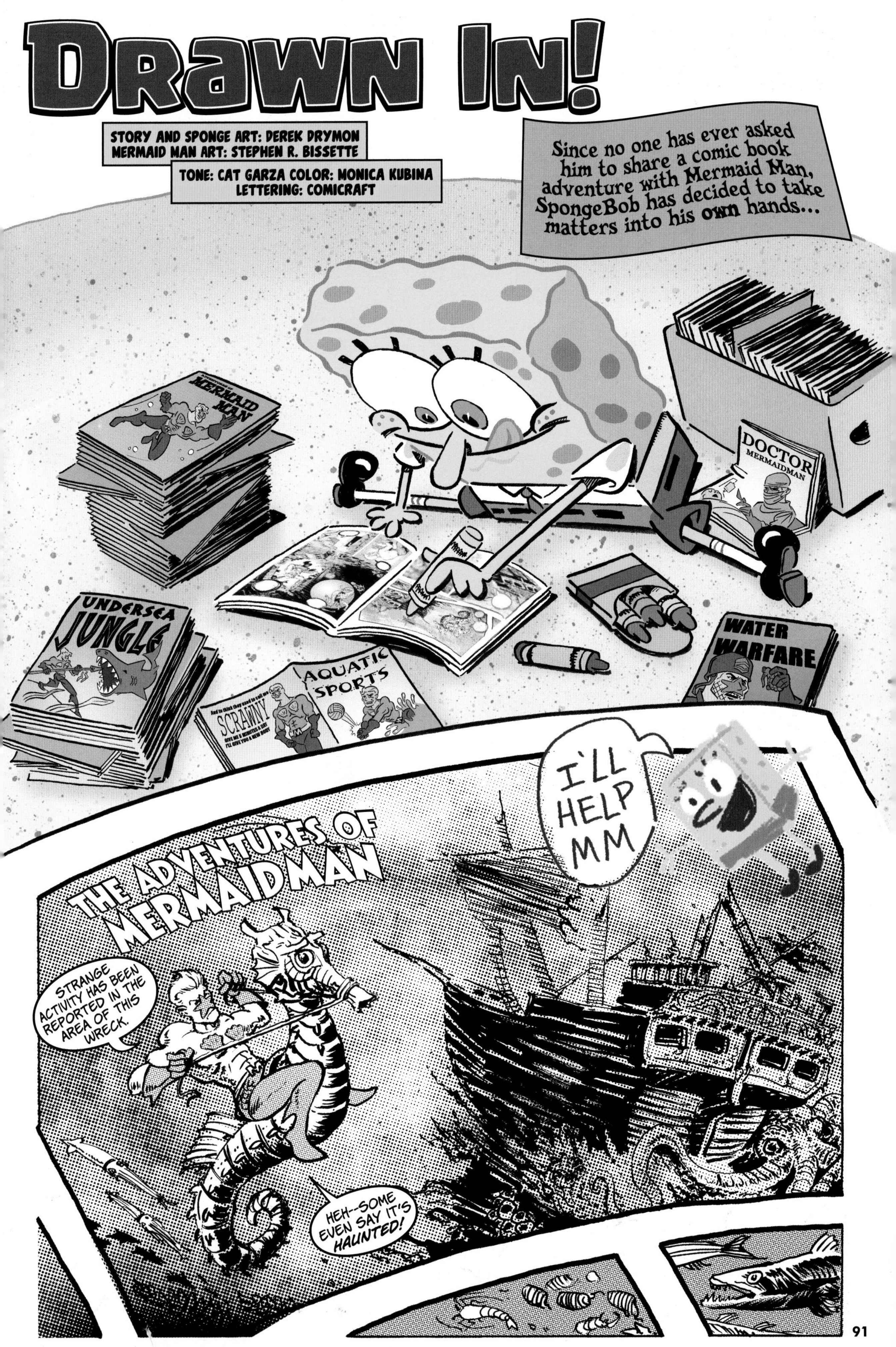
DRAWN IN!
STORY AND SPONGE ART: DEREK DRYMON
MERMAID MAN ART: STEPHEN R. BISSETTE
TONE: CAT GARZA COLOR: MONICA KUBINA
LETTERING: COMICRAFT
Since no one has ever asked him to share a comic book adventure with Mermaid Man, SpongeBob has decided to take matters into his own hands...
MERMAID MAN
DOCTOR MERMAIDMAN
UNDERSEA JUNGLE
WATER WARFARE
AQUATIC SPORTS
SCRAWNY
THE ADVENTURES OF MERMAIDMAN
I'LL HELP MM
STRANGE ACTIVITY HAS BEEN REPORTED IN THE AREA OF THIS WRECK.
HEH--SOME EVEN SAY IT'S HAUNTED!

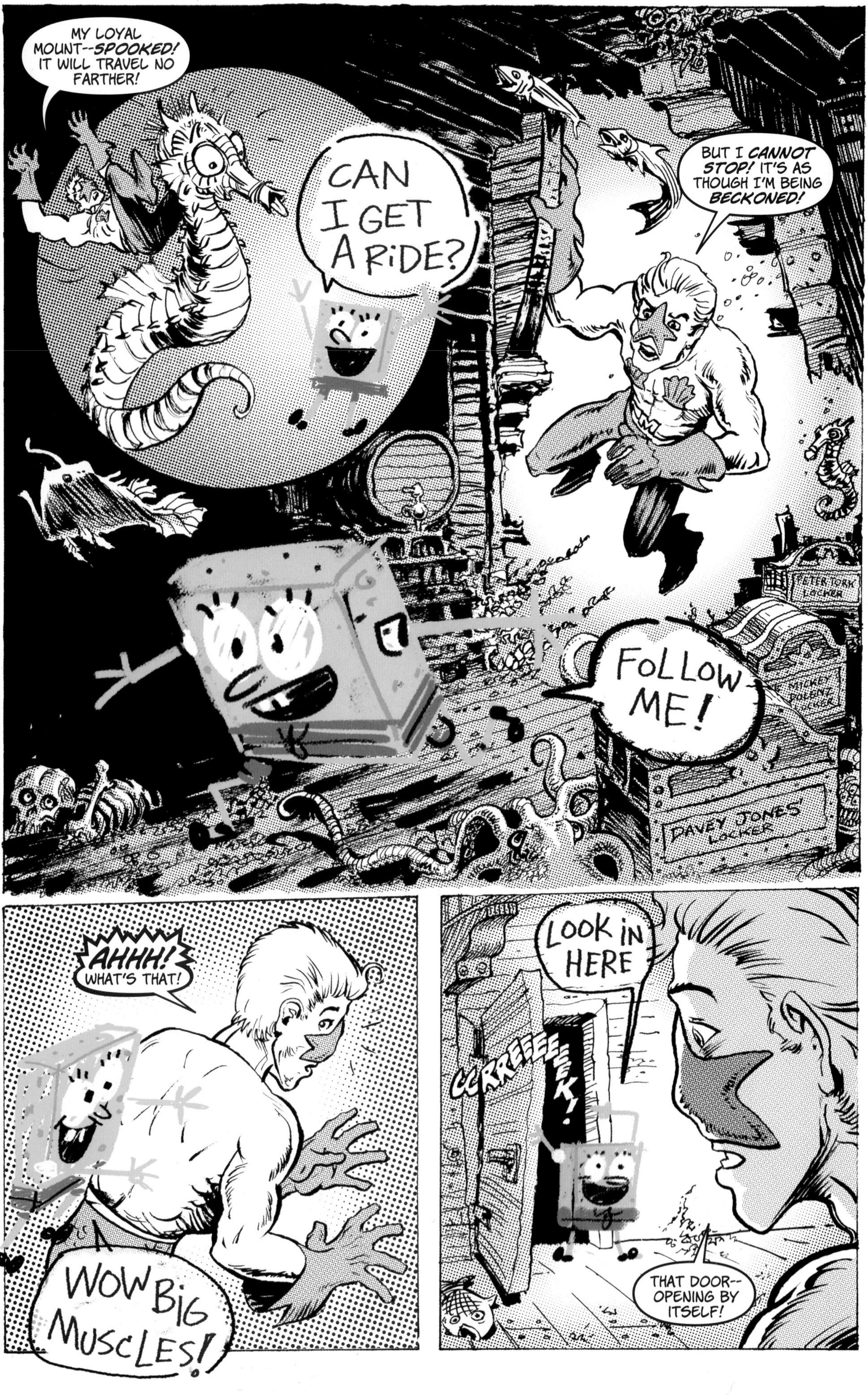

MY LOYAL MOUNT--SPOOKED! IT WILL TRAVEL NO FARTHER!
CAN I GET A RIDE?
BUT I CANNOT STOP! IT'S AS THOUGH I'M BEING BECKONED!
PETER TORK LOCKER
FOLLOW ME!
DAVEY JONES' LOCKER
AHHH! WHAT'S THAT!
WOW BIG MUSCLES!
LOOK IN HERE
THAT DOOR-- OPENING BY ITSELF!

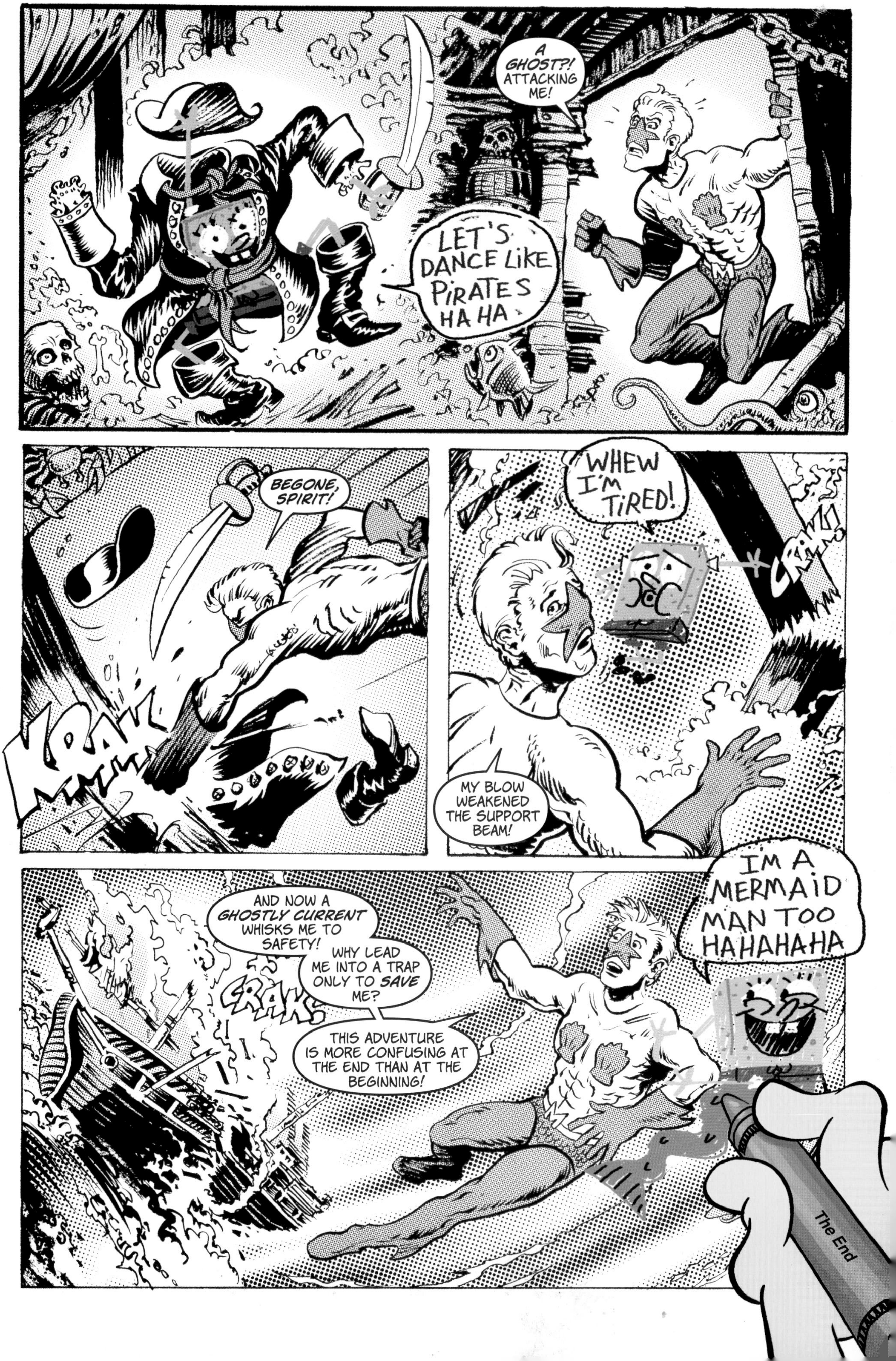
A GHOST?! ATTACKING ME!
LET'S DANCE LIKE PIRATES HA HA
BEGONE, SPIRIT!
KRAK
WHEW I'M TIRED!
MY BLOW WEAKENED THE SUPPORT BEAM!
AND NOW A GHOSTLY CURRENT WHISKS ME TO SAFETY!
WHY LEAD ME INTO A TRAP ONLY TO SAVE ME?
THIS ADVENTURE IS MORE CONFUSING AT THE END THAN AT THE BEGINNING!
CRAK
I'M A MERMAID MAN TOO HAHAHAHA
The End

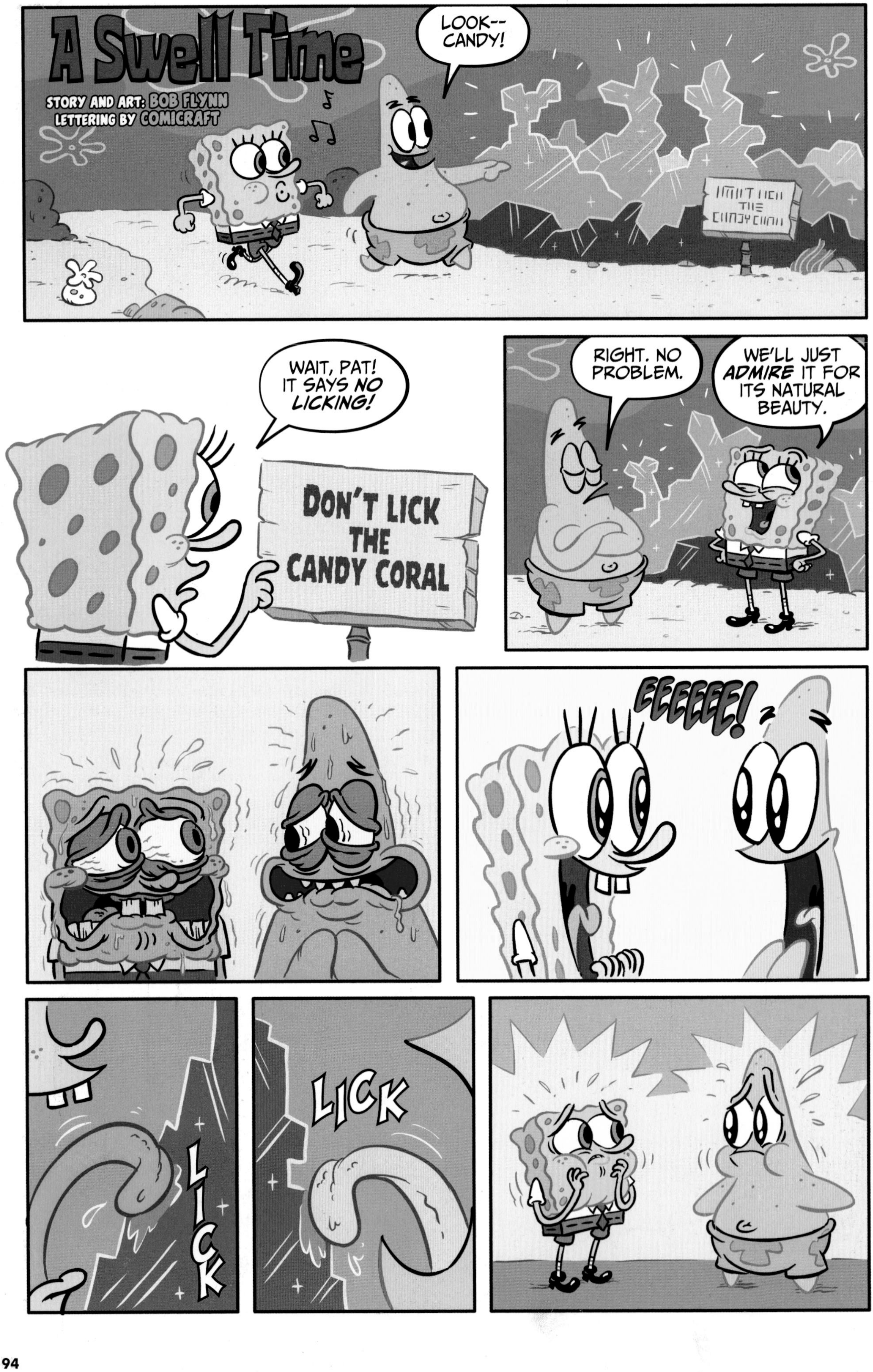
A Swell Time
STORY AND ART: BOB FLYNN
LETTERING BY COMICRAFT
LOOK-- CANDY!
WAIT, PAT! IT SAYS NO LICKING!
DON'T LICK THE CANDY CORAL
RIGHT. NO PROBLEM.
WE'LL JUST ADMIRE IT FOR ITS NATURAL BEAUTY.
EEEEEE!
LICK
LICK

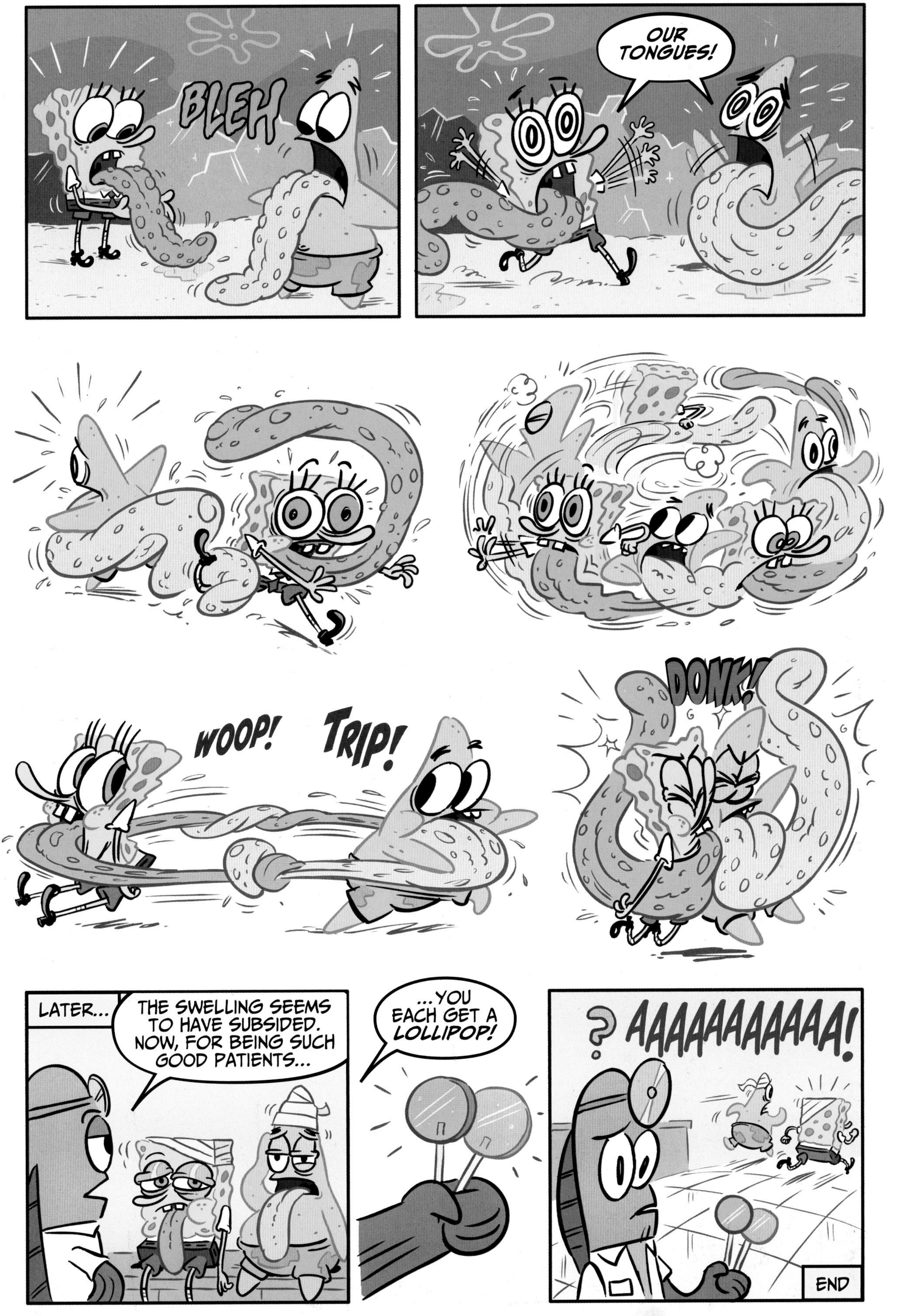
BLEH
OUR TONGUES!
WOOP!
TRIP!
DONK!
LATER...
THE SWELLING SEEMS TO HAVE SUBSIDED. NOW, FOR BEING SUCH GOOD PATIENTS...
...YOU EACH GET A LOLLIPOP!
?
AAAAAAAAAA!
END

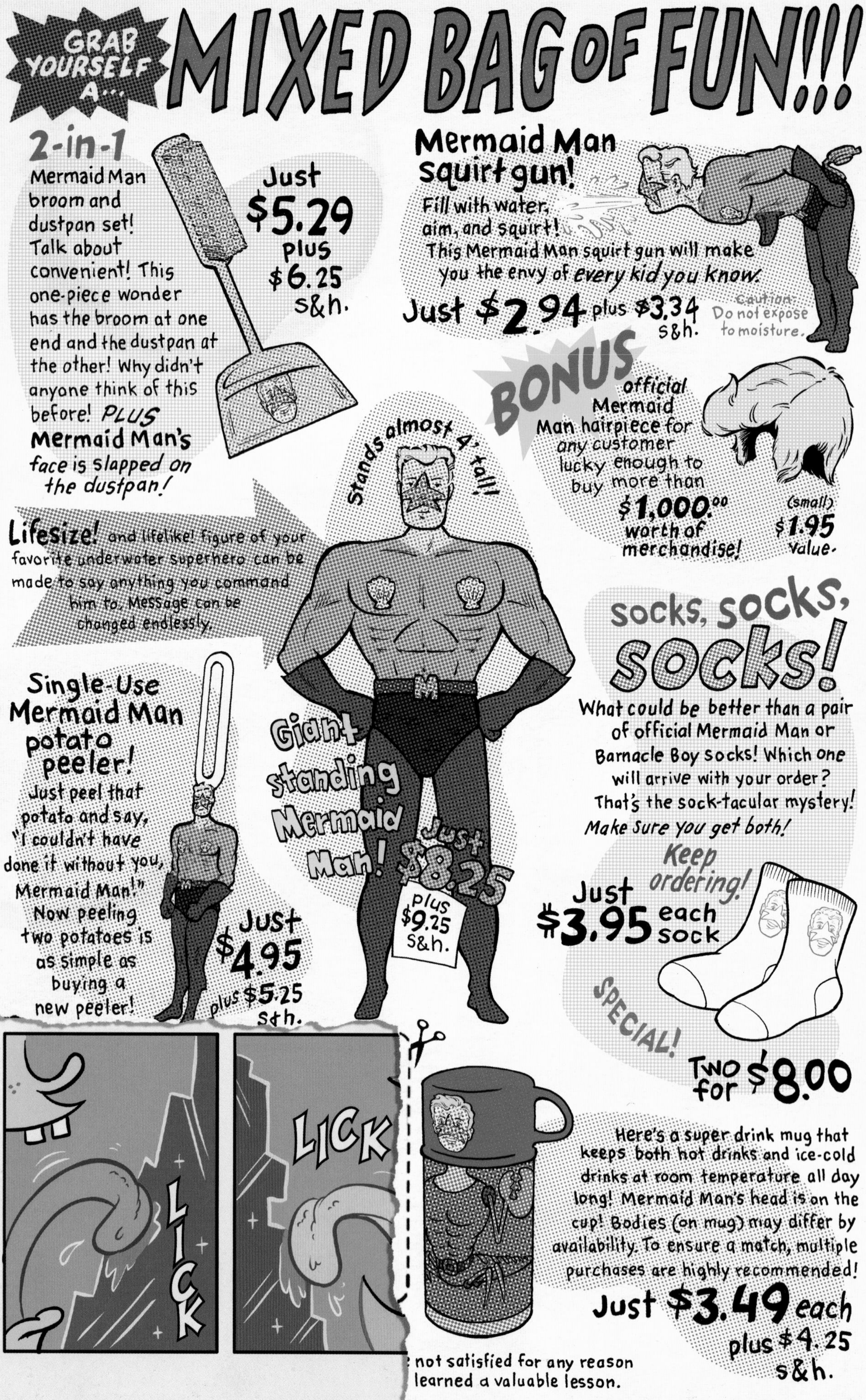
GRAB YOURSELF A...
MIXED BAG OF FUN!!!
2-in-1
Mermaid Man broom and dustpan set! Talk about convenient! This one-piece wonder has the broom at one end and the dustpan at the other! Why didn't anyone think of this before! PLUS Mermaid Man's face is slapped on the dustpan!
Just $5.29 plus $6.25 s&h.
Mermaid Man squirt gun!
Fill with water, aim, and squirt!
This Mermaid Man squirt gun will make you the envy of every kid you know.
Just $2.94 plus $3.34 s&h.
Caution: Do not expose to moisture.
BONUS
official Mermaid Man hairpiece for any customer lucky enough to buy more than $1,000.00 worth of merchandise!
(small) $1.95 value.
Stands almost 4' tall!
Lifesize! and lifelike! figure of your favorite underwater superhero can be made to say anything you command him to. Message can be changed endlessly.
Giant standing Mermaid Man!
Just $8.25
plus $9.25 s&h.
Single-Use Mermaid Man potato peeler!
Just peel that potato and say, "I couldn't have done it without you, Mermaid Man!" Now peeling two potatoes is as simple as buying a new peeler!
Just $4.95 plus $5.25 s&h.
Socks, socks, socks!
What could be better than a pair of official Mermaid Man or Barnacle Boy socks! Which one will arrive with your order? That's the sock-tacular mystery! Make sure you get both!
Keep ordering!
Just $3.95 each sock
SPECIAL!
Two for $8.00
Here's a super drink mug that keeps both hot drinks and ice-cold drinks at room temperature all day long! Mermaid Man's head is on the cup! Bodies (on mug) may differ by availability. To ensure a match, multiple purchases are highly recommended!
Just $3.49 each plus $4.25 s&h.
LICK
LICK
not satisfied for any reason
learned a valuable lesson.

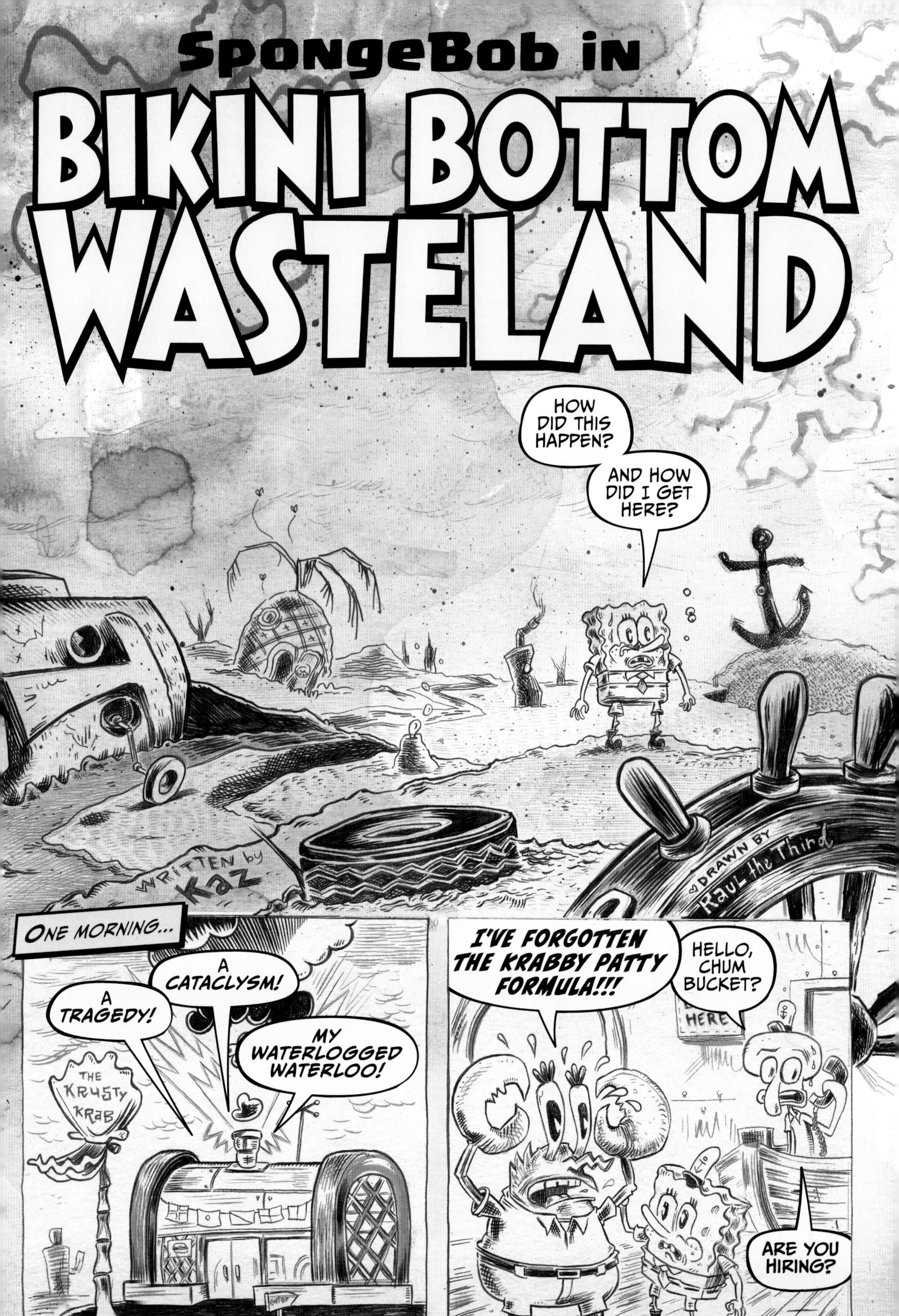
SpongeBob in
BIKINI BOTTOM WASTELAND
HOW DID THIS HAPPEN?
AND HOW DID I GET HERE?
WRITTEN by Kaz
DRAWN BY Raul the Third
ONE MORNING...
A TRAGEDY!
A CATACLYSM!
MY WATERLOGGED WATERLOO!
THE KRUSTY KRAB
I'VE FORGOTTEN THE KRABBY PATTY FORMULA!!!
HELLO, CHUM BUCKET?
ARE YOU HIRING?

SPECIAL THANKS TO ELAINE BAY

LETTERING BY ROB LEIGH

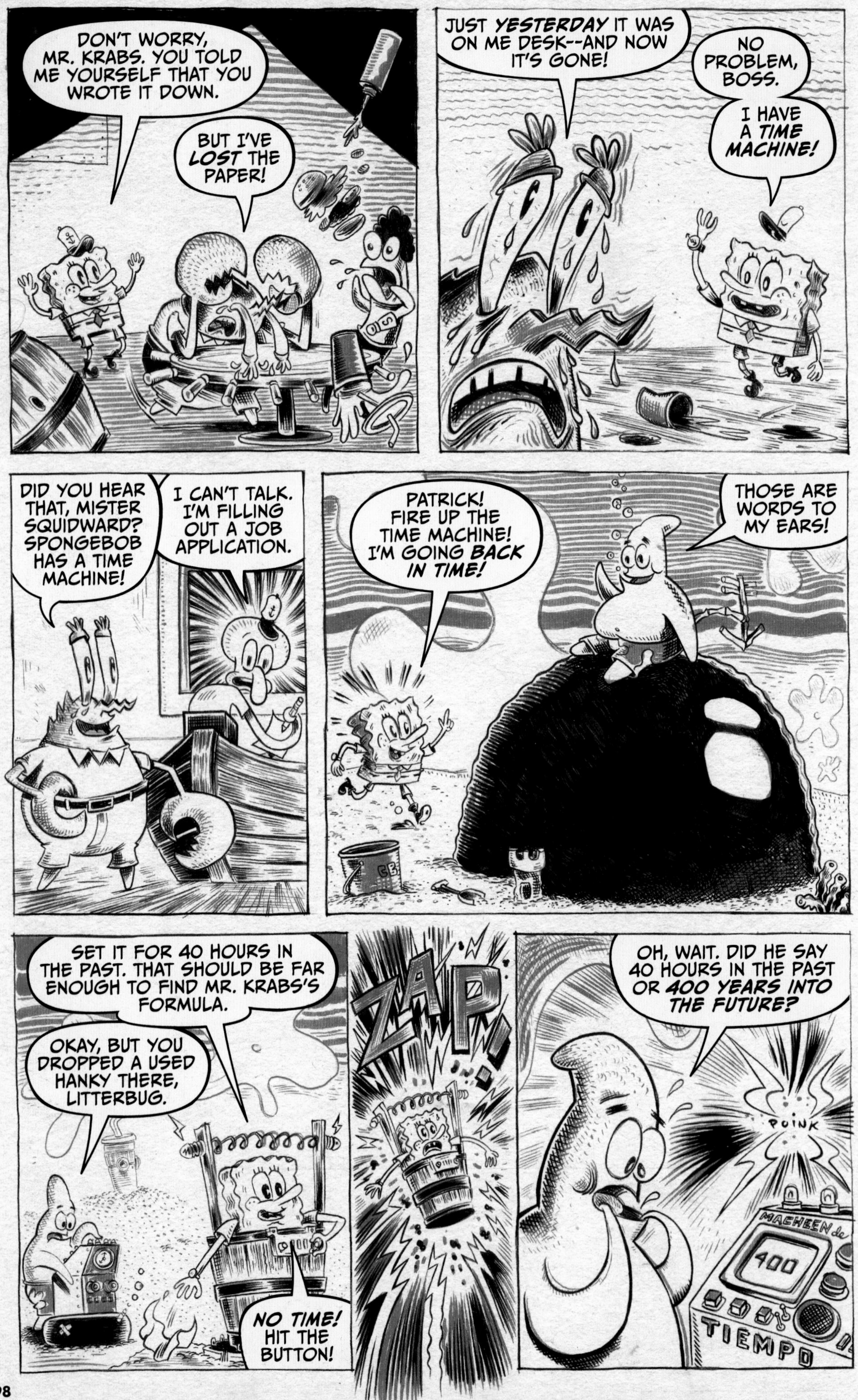
DON'T WORRY, MR. KRABS. YOU TOLD ME YOURSELF THAT YOU WROTE IT DOWN.
BUT I'VE *LOST* THE PAPER!
JUST *YESTERDAY* IT WAS ON ME DESK--AND NOW IT'S GONE!
NO PROBLEM, BOSS.
I HAVE A *TIME MACHINE!*
DID YOU HEAR THAT, MISTER SQUIDWARD? SPONGEBOB HAS A TIME MACHINE!
I CAN'T TALK. I'M FILLING OUT A JOB APPLICATION.
PATRICK! FIRE UP THE TIME MACHINE! I'M GOING *BACK IN TIME!*
THOSE ARE WORDS TO MY EARS!
SET IT FOR 40 HOURS IN THE PAST. THAT SHOULD BE FAR ENOUGH TO FIND MR. KRABS'S FORMULA.
OKAY, BUT YOU DROPPED A USED HANKY THERE, LITTERBUG.
NO TIME! HIT THE BUTTON!
ZAP!
OH, WAIT. DID HE SAY 40 HOURS IN THE PAST OR *400 YEARS INTO THE FUTURE?*
POINK
400
TIEMPO

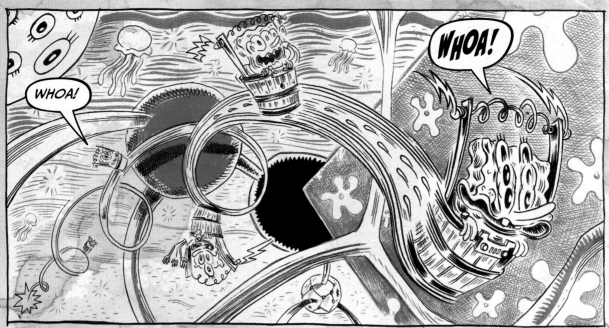

WHOA!

WHOA!

HARD LANDING!

CRASH!

WHAT HAPPENED? BIKINI BOTTOM IS IN RUINS!

A WASTELAND.

HAVE A GOOD DAY

MY WATCH SAYS 2415. I'M IN THE FUTURE.

COULD MY LITTERING IN THE PAST HAVE LED TO A CHAIN REACTION THAT DESTROYED EVERYTHING?

WAIT! THAT DUST ON THE HORIZON...IT'S VEHICLES. SOMEONE IS COMING THIS WAY.

RUMBLE RUMBLE

ALL IS LOST

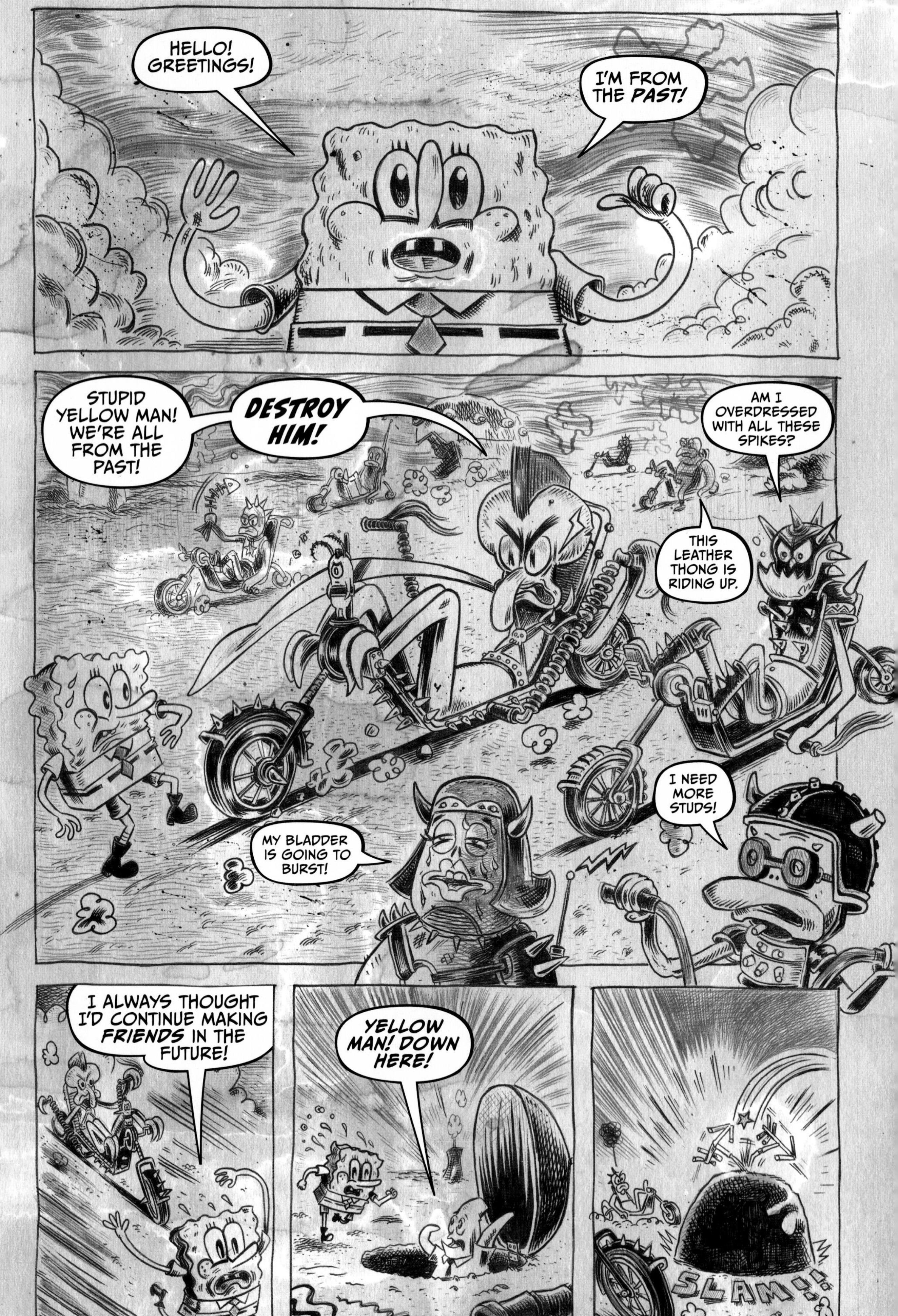
HELLO! GREETINGS!
I'M FROM THE *PAST!*
STUPID YELLOW MAN! WE'RE ALL FROM THE PAST!
DESTROY HIM!
AM I OVERDRESSED WITH ALL THESE SPIKES?
THIS LEATHER THONG IS RIDING UP.
I NEED MORE STUDS!
MY BLADDER IS GOING TO BURST!
I ALWAYS THOUGHT I'D CONTINUE MAKING *FRIENDS* IN THE FUTURE!
YELLOW MAN! DOWN HERE!
SLAM!!

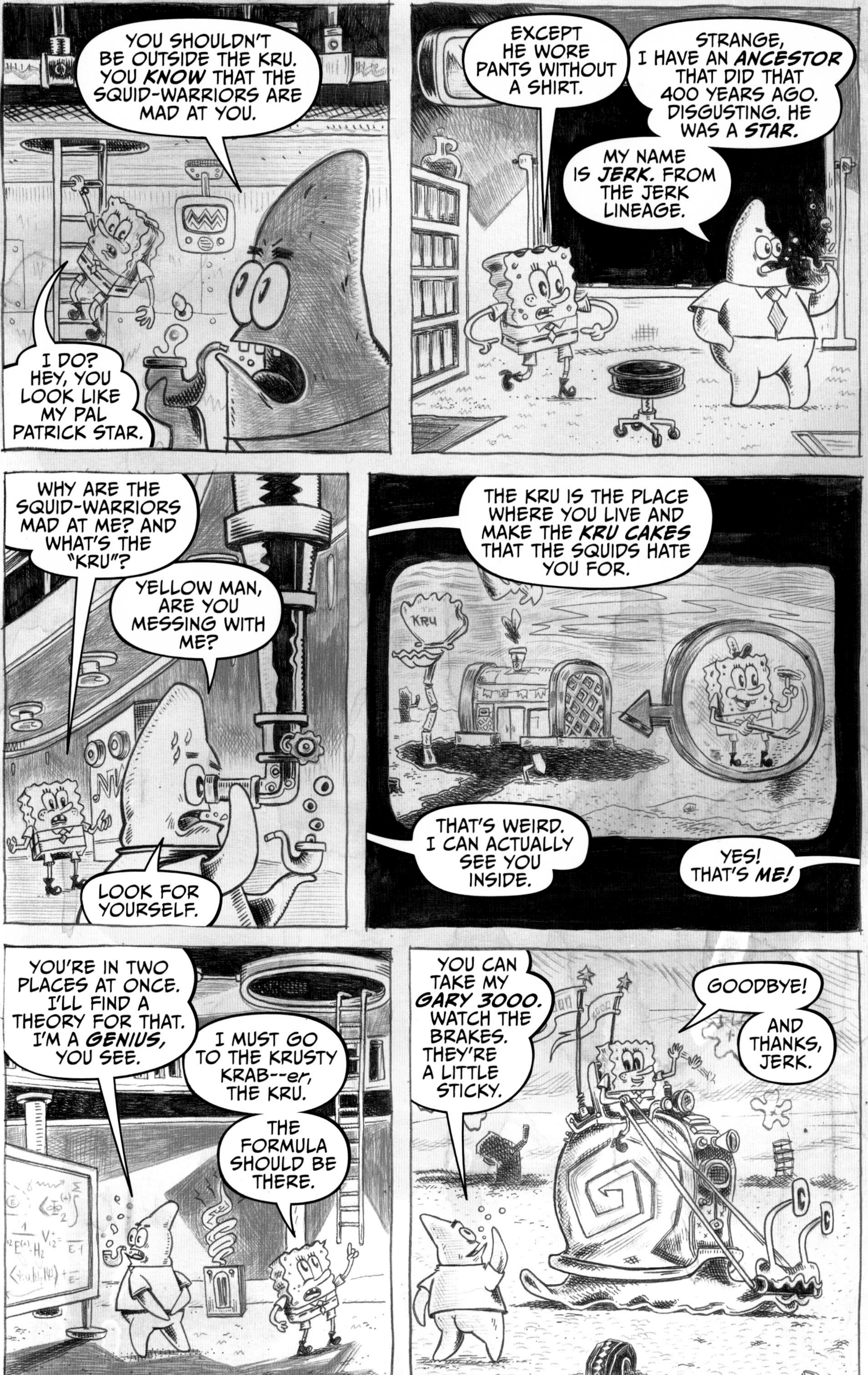
YOU SHOULDN'T BE OUTSIDE THE KRU. YOU KNOW THAT THE SQUID-WARRIORS ARE MAD AT YOU.
I DO? HEY, YOU LOOK LIKE MY PAL PATRICK STAR.
STRANGE, I HAVE AN ANCESTOR THAT DID THAT 400 YEARS AGO. DISGUSTING. HE WAS A STAR.
EXCEPT HE WORE PANTS WITHOUT A SHIRT.
MY NAME IS JERK. FROM THE JERK LINEAGE.
WHY ARE THE SQUID-WARRIORS MAD AT ME? AND WHAT'S THE "KRU"?
YELLOW MAN, ARE YOU MESSING WITH ME?
LOOK FOR YOURSELF.
THE KRU IS THE PLACE WHERE YOU LIVE AND MAKE THE KRU CAKES THAT THE SQUIDS HATE YOU FOR.
KRU
THAT'S WEIRD. I CAN ACTUALLY SEE YOU INSIDE.
YES! THAT'S ME!
YOU'RE IN TWO PLACES AT ONCE. I'LL FIND A THEORY FOR THAT. I'M A GENIUS, YOU SEE.
I MUST GO TO THE KRUSTY KRAB--er, THE KRU.
THE FORMULA SHOULD BE THERE.
YOU CAN TAKE MY GARY 3000. WATCH THE BRAKES. THEY'RE A LITTLE STICKY.
GOODBYE!
AND THANKS, JERK.

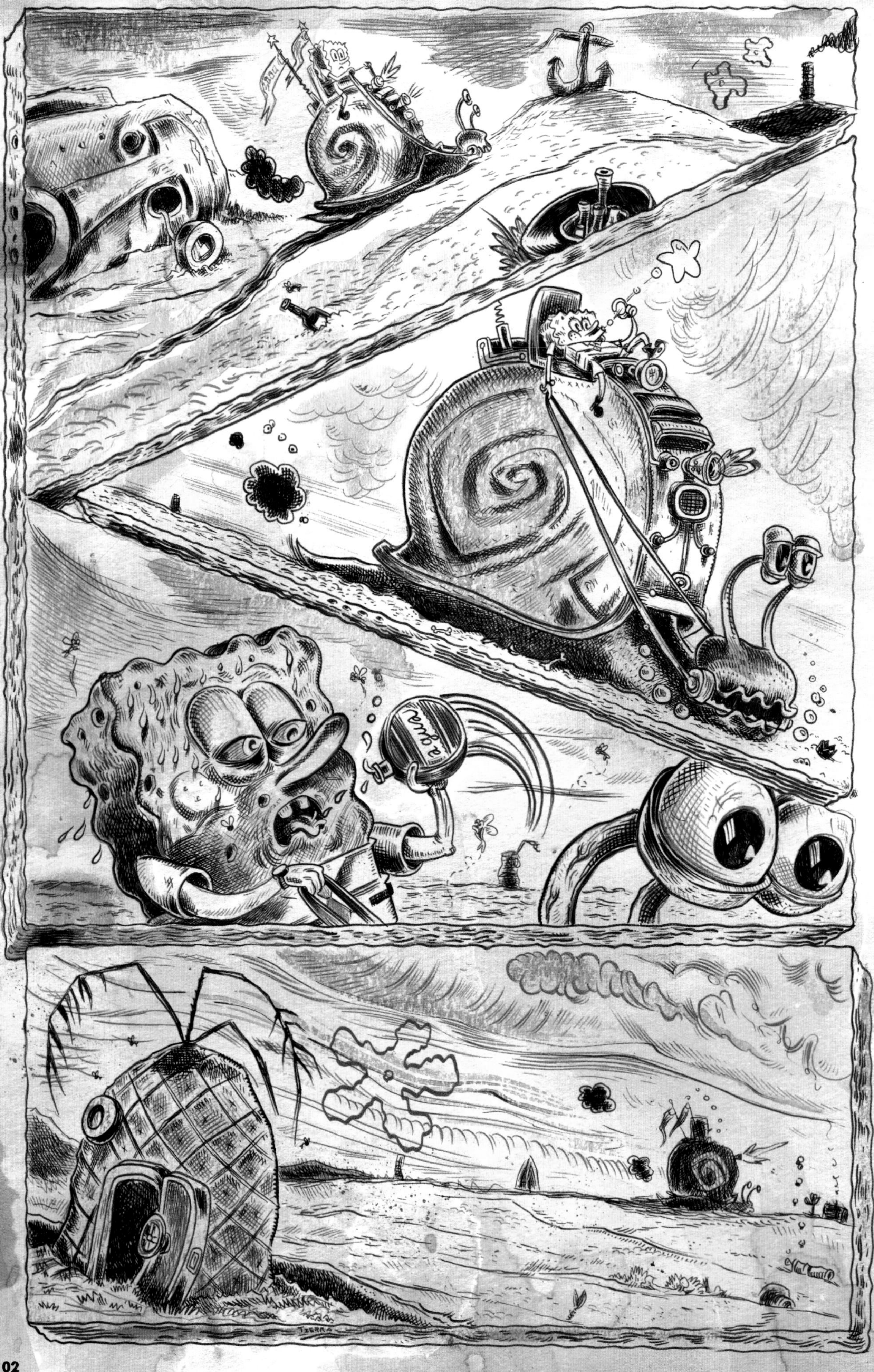
agua
TIERRA

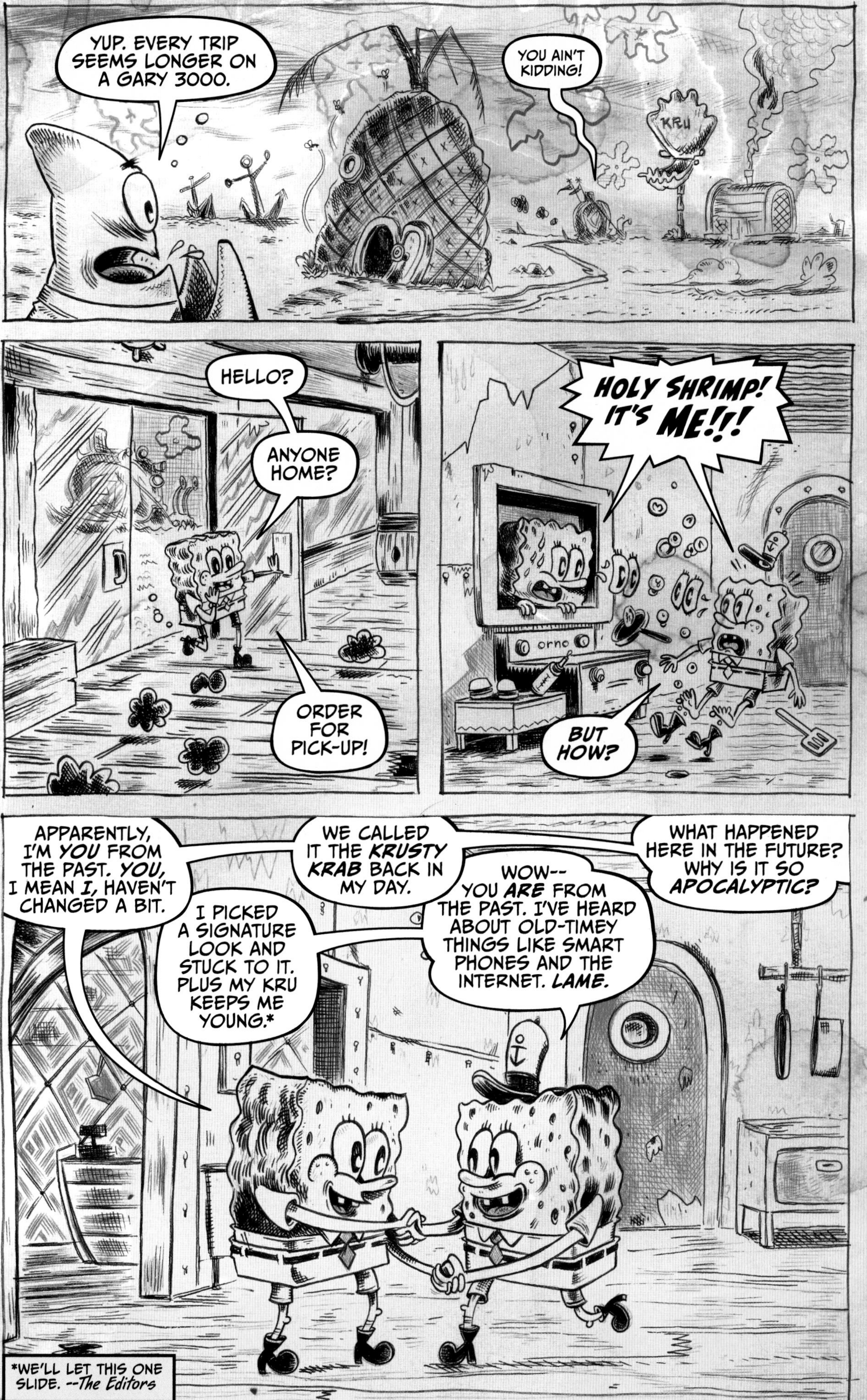
YUP. EVERY TRIP SEEMS LONGER ON A GARY 3000.
YOU AIN'T KIDDING!
KRU
HELLO?
ANYONE HOME?
ORDER FOR PICK-UP!
HOLY SHRIMP! IT'S ME!?!
BUT HOW?
APPARENTLY, I'M YOU FROM THE PAST. YOU, I MEAN I, HAVEN'T CHANGED A BIT.
WE CALLED IT THE KRUSTY KRAB BACK IN MY DAY.
WHAT HAPPENED HERE IN THE FUTURE? WHY IS IT SO APOCALYPTIC?
I PICKED A SIGNATURE LOOK AND STUCK TO IT. PLUS MY KRU KEEPS ME YOUNG.*
WOW-- YOU ARE FROM THE PAST. I'VE HEARD ABOUT OLD-TIMEY THINGS LIKE SMART PHONES AND THE INTERNET. LAME.
*WE'LL LET THIS ONE SLIDE. --The Editors

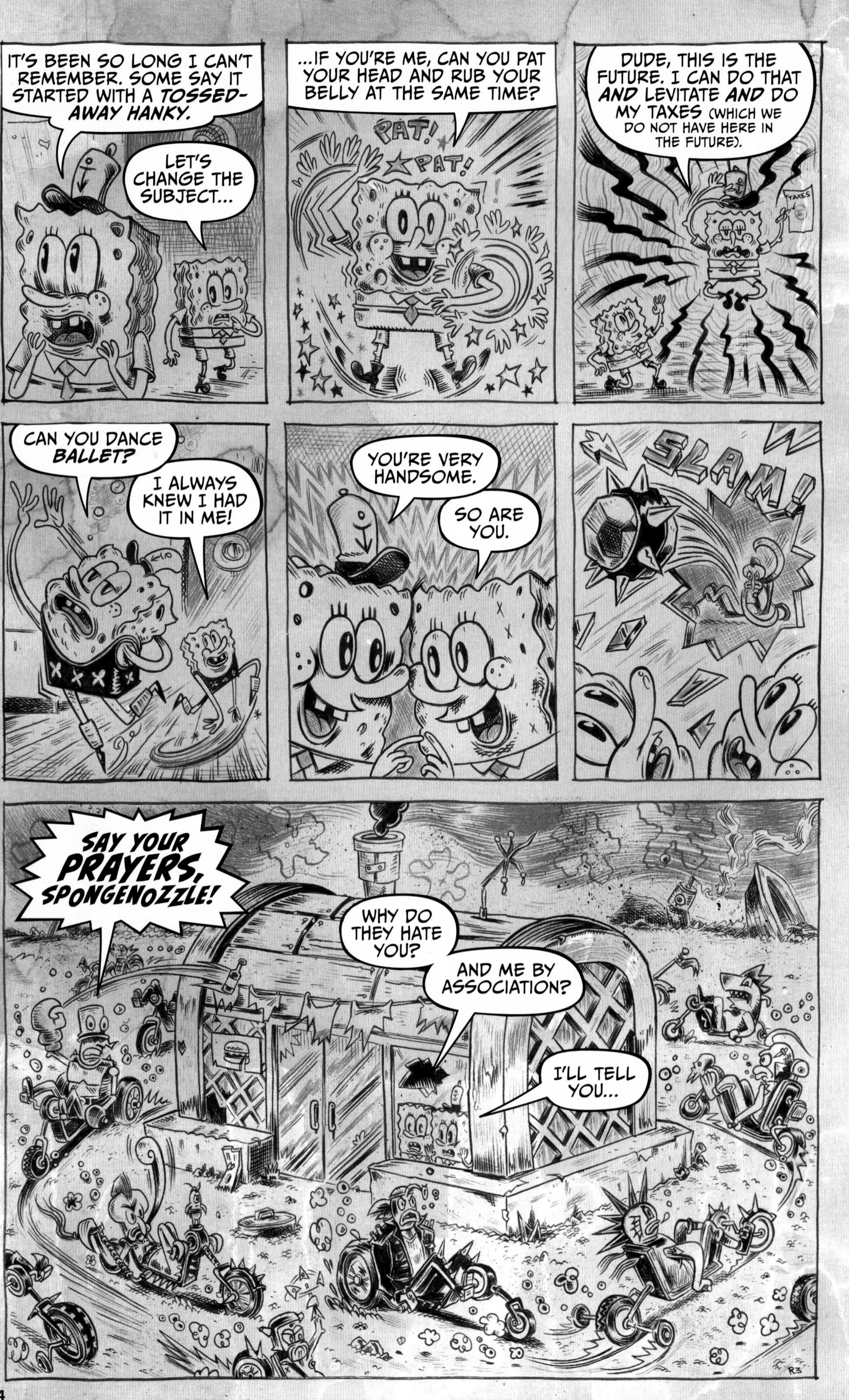
IT'S BEEN SO LONG I CAN'T REMEMBER. SOME SAY IT STARTED WITH A TOSSED-AWAY HANKY.
LET'S CHANGE THE SUBJECT...
...IF YOU'RE ME, CAN YOU PAT YOUR HEAD AND RUB YOUR BELLY AT THE SAME TIME?
PAT! PAT!
DUDE, THIS IS THE FUTURE. I CAN DO THAT AND LEVITATE AND DO MY TAXES (WHICH WE DO NOT HAVE HERE IN THE FUTURE).
TAXES
CAN YOU DANCE BALLET?
I ALWAYS KNEW I HAD IT IN ME!
YOU'RE VERY HANDSOME.
SO ARE YOU.
SLAM!
SAY YOUR PRAYERS, SPONGENOZZLE!
WHY DO THEY HATE YOU?
AND ME BY ASSOCIATION?
I'LL TELL YOU...

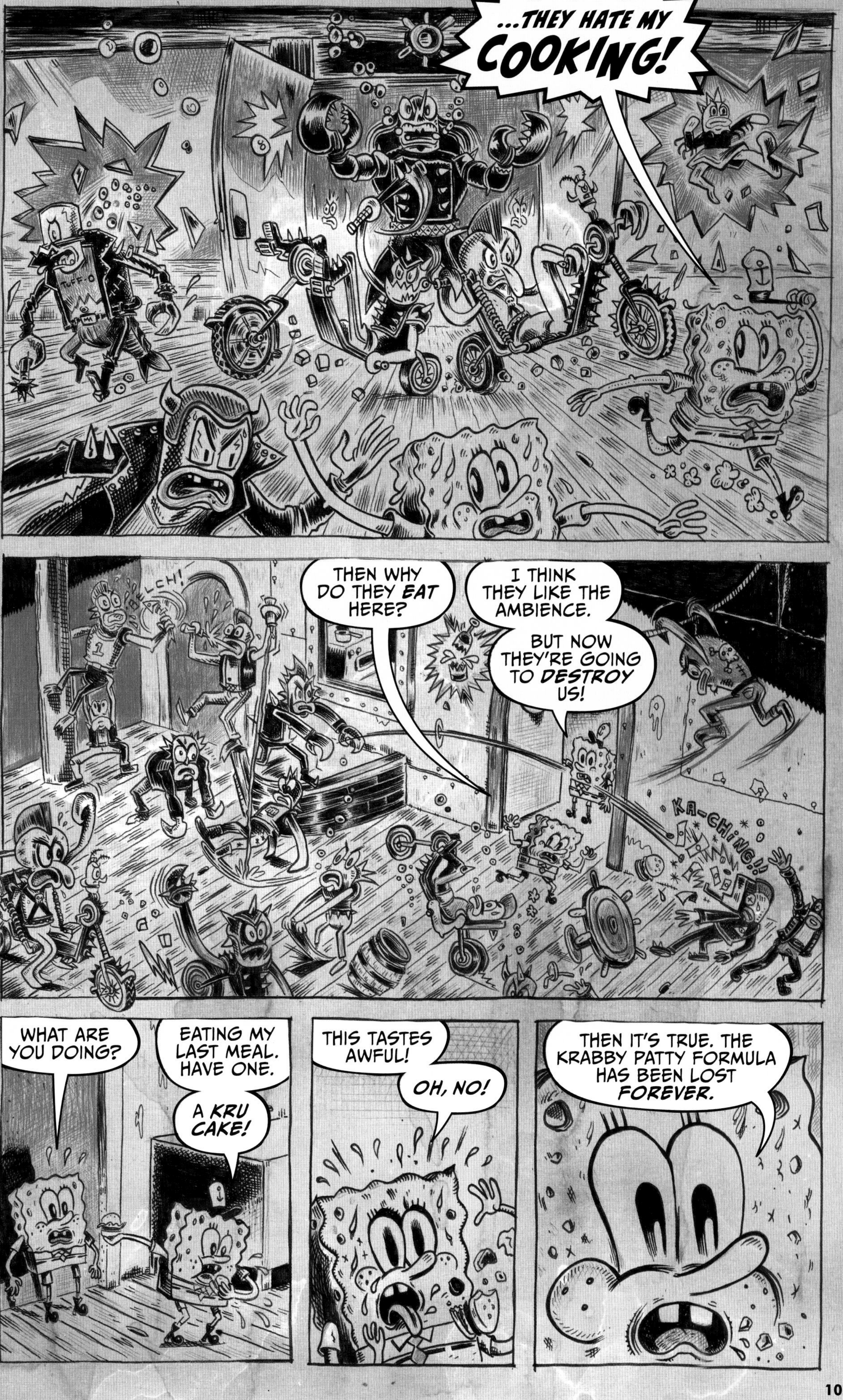
...THEY HATE MY COOKING!
THEN WHY DO THEY EAT HERE?
I THINK THEY LIKE THE AMBIENCE.
BUT NOW THEY'RE GOING TO DESTROY US!
KA-CHING!!
WHAT ARE YOU DOING?
EATING MY LAST MEAL. HAVE ONE.
A KRU CAKE!
THIS TASTES AWFUL!
OH, NO!
THEN IT'S TRUE. THE KRABBY PATTY FORMULA HAS BEEN LOST FOREVER.

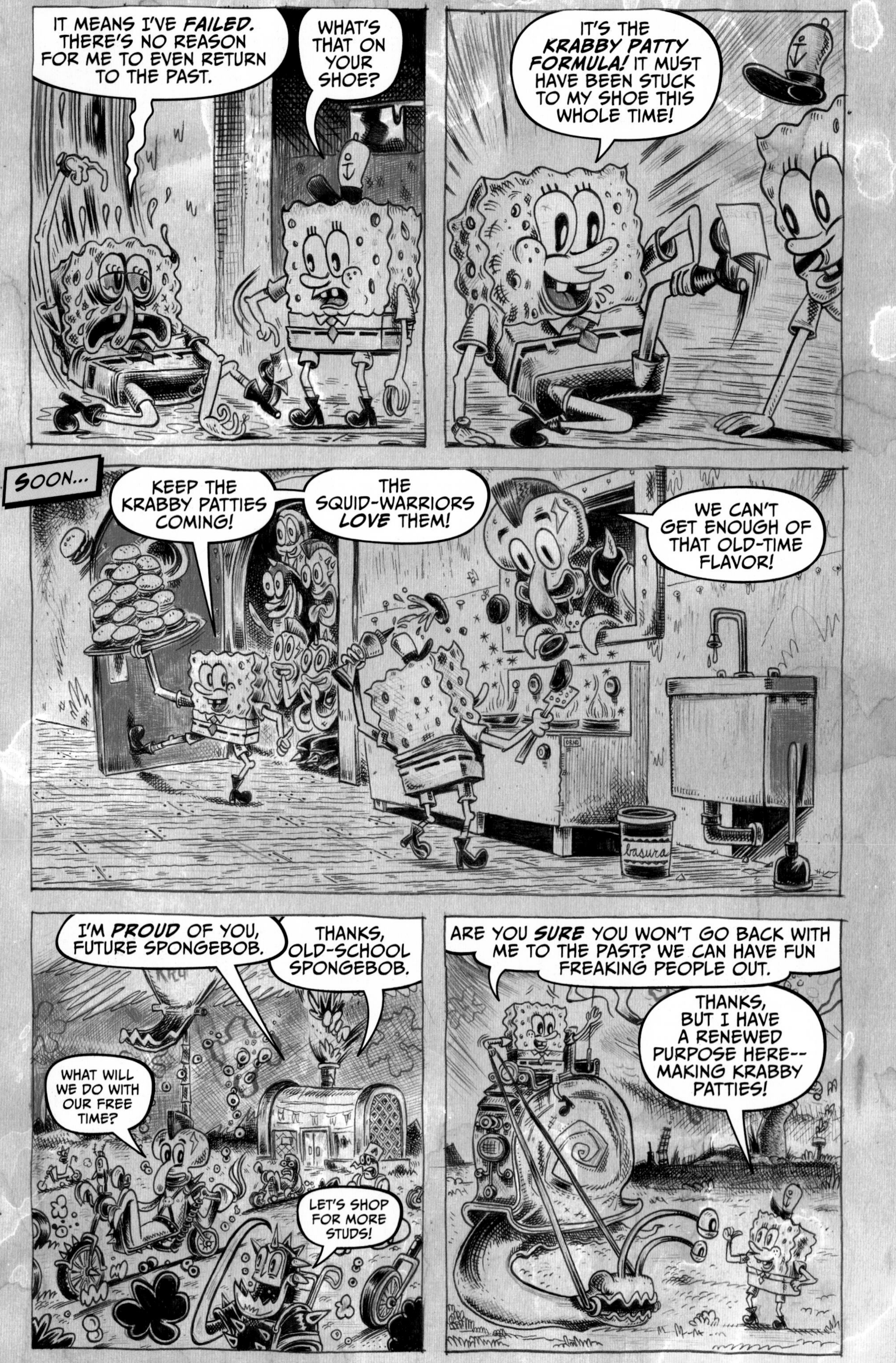
IT MEANS I'VE FAILED. THERE'S NO REASON FOR ME TO EVEN RETURN TO THE PAST.
WHAT'S THAT ON YOUR SHOE?
IT'S THE KRABBY PATTY FORMULA! IT MUST HAVE BEEN STUCK TO MY SHOE THIS WHOLE TIME!
SOON...
KEEP THE KRABBY PATTIES COMING!
THE SQUID-WARRIORS LOVE THEM!
WE CAN'T GET ENOUGH OF THAT OLD-TIME FLAVOR!
basura
I'M PROUD OF YOU, FUTURE SPONGEBOB.
THANKS, OLD-SCHOOL SPONGEBOB.
WHAT WILL WE DO WITH OUR FREE TIME?
LET'S SHOP FOR MORE STUDS!
ARE YOU SURE YOU WON'T GO BACK WITH ME TO THE PAST? WE CAN HAVE FUN FREAKING PEOPLE OUT.
THANKS, BUT I HAVE A RENEWED PURPOSE HERE-- MAKING KRABBY PATTIES!

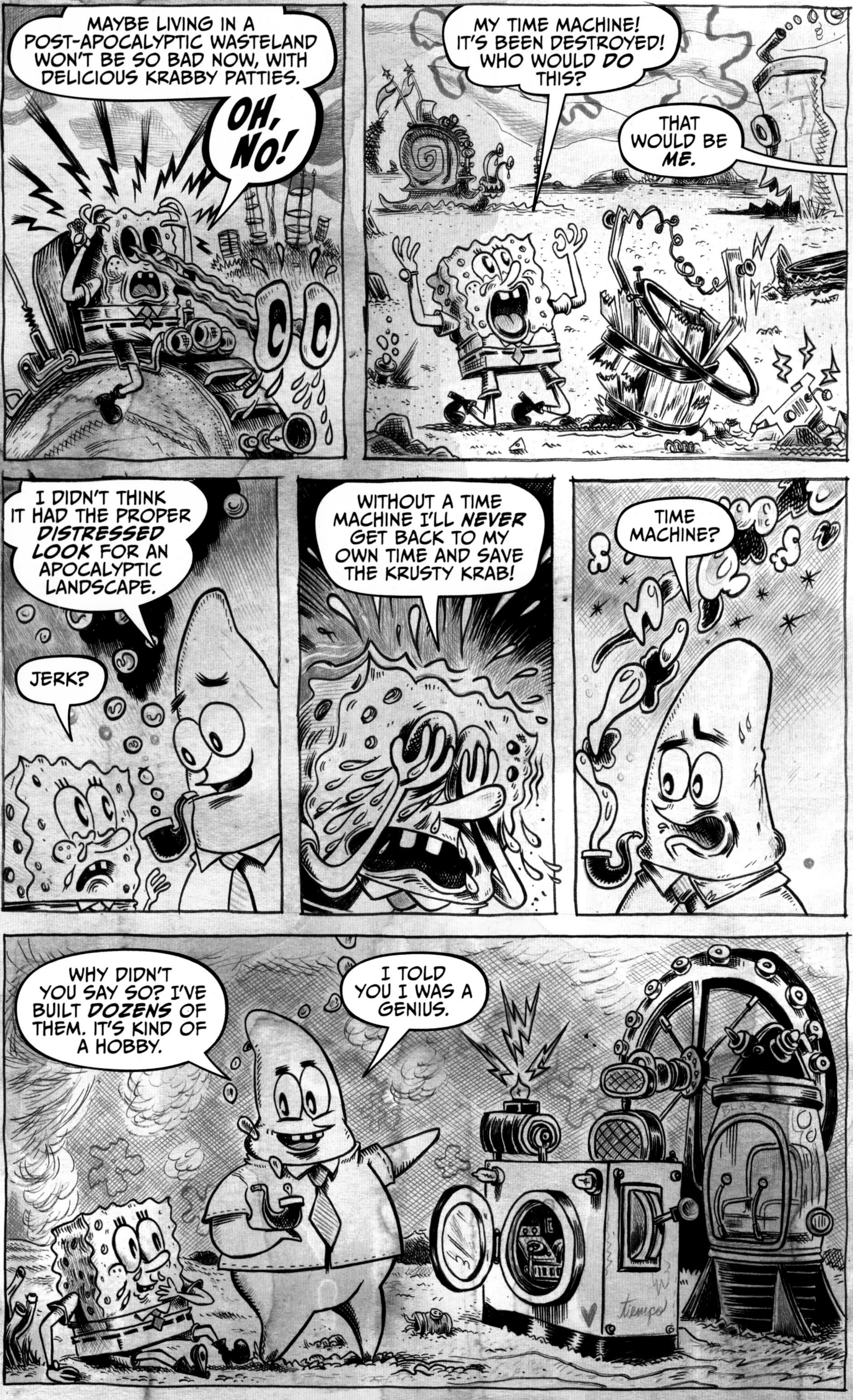
MAYBE LIVING IN A POST-APOCALYPTIC WASTELAND WON'T BE SO BAD NOW, WITH DELICIOUS KRABBY PATTIES.
OH, NO!
MY TIME MACHINE! IT'S BEEN DESTROYED! WHO WOULD DO THIS?
THAT WOULD BE ME.
I DIDN'T THINK IT HAD THE PROPER DISTRESSED LOOK FOR AN APOCALYPTIC LANDSCAPE.
JERK?
WITHOUT A TIME MACHINE I'LL NEVER GET BACK TO MY OWN TIME AND SAVE THE KRUSTY KRAB!
TIME MACHINE?
WHY DIDN'T YOU SAY SO? I'VE BUILT DOZENS OF THEM. IT'S KIND OF A HOBBY.
I TOLD YOU I WAS A GENIUS.
tiempo

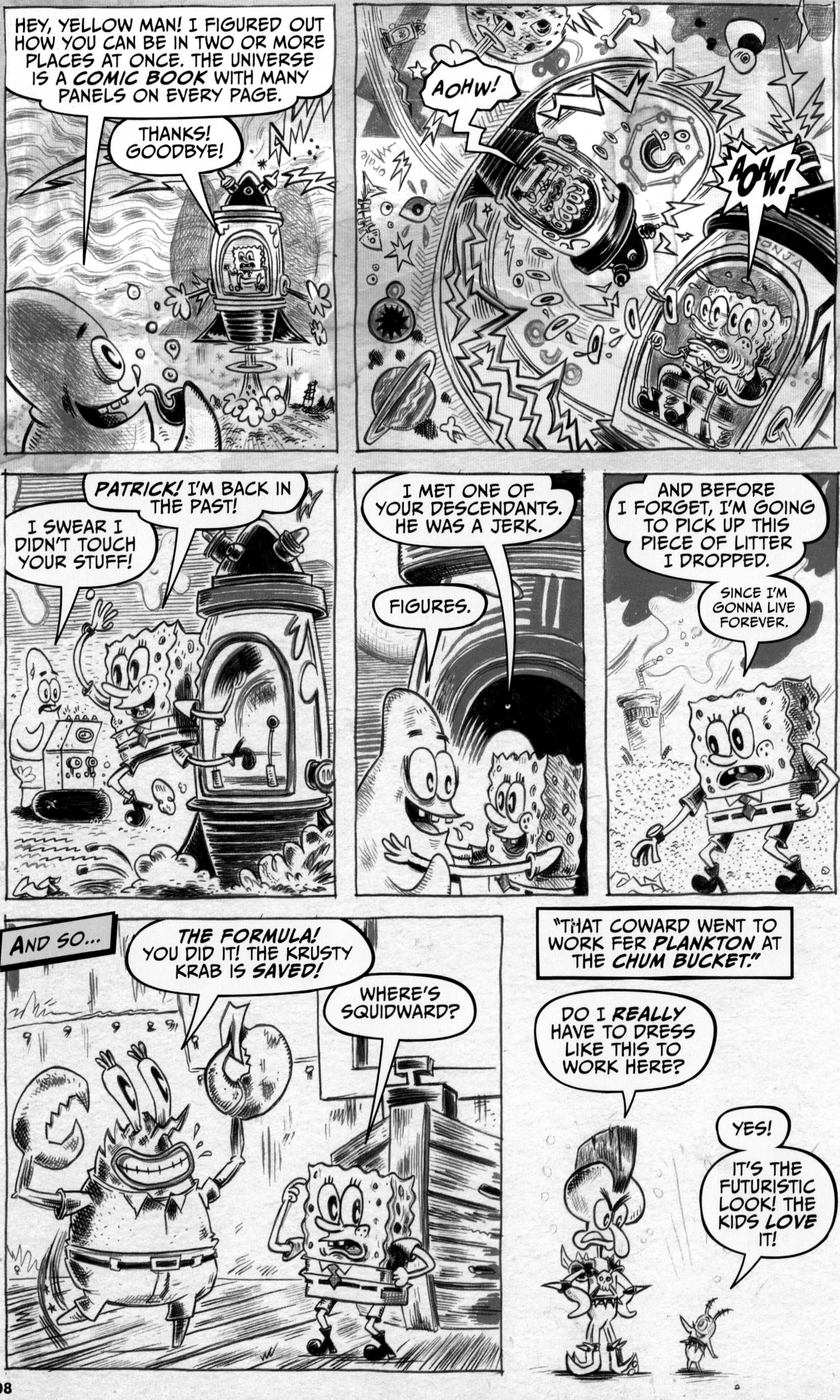
HEY, YELLOW MAN! I FIGURED OUT HOW YOU CAN BE IN TWO OR MORE PLACES AT ONCE. THE UNIVERSE IS A COMIC BOOK WITH MANY PANELS ON EVERY PAGE.
THANKS! GOODBYE!
AOHW!
AOHW!
PATRICK! I'M BACK IN THE PAST!
I SWEAR I DIDN'T TOUCH YOUR STUFF!
I MET ONE OF YOUR DESCENDANTS. HE WAS A JERK.
FIGURES.
AND BEFORE I FORGET, I'M GOING TO PICK UP THIS PIECE OF LITTER I DROPPED.
SINCE I'M GONNA LIVE FOREVER.
AND SO...
THE FORMULA! YOU DID IT! THE KRUSTY KRAB IS SAVED!
WHERE'S SQUIDWARD?
"THAT COWARD WENT TO WORK FER PLANKTON AT THE CHUM BUCKET."
DO I REALLY HAVE TO DRESS LIKE THIS TO WORK HERE?
YES!
IT'S THE FUTURISTIC LOOK! THE KIDS LOVE IT!

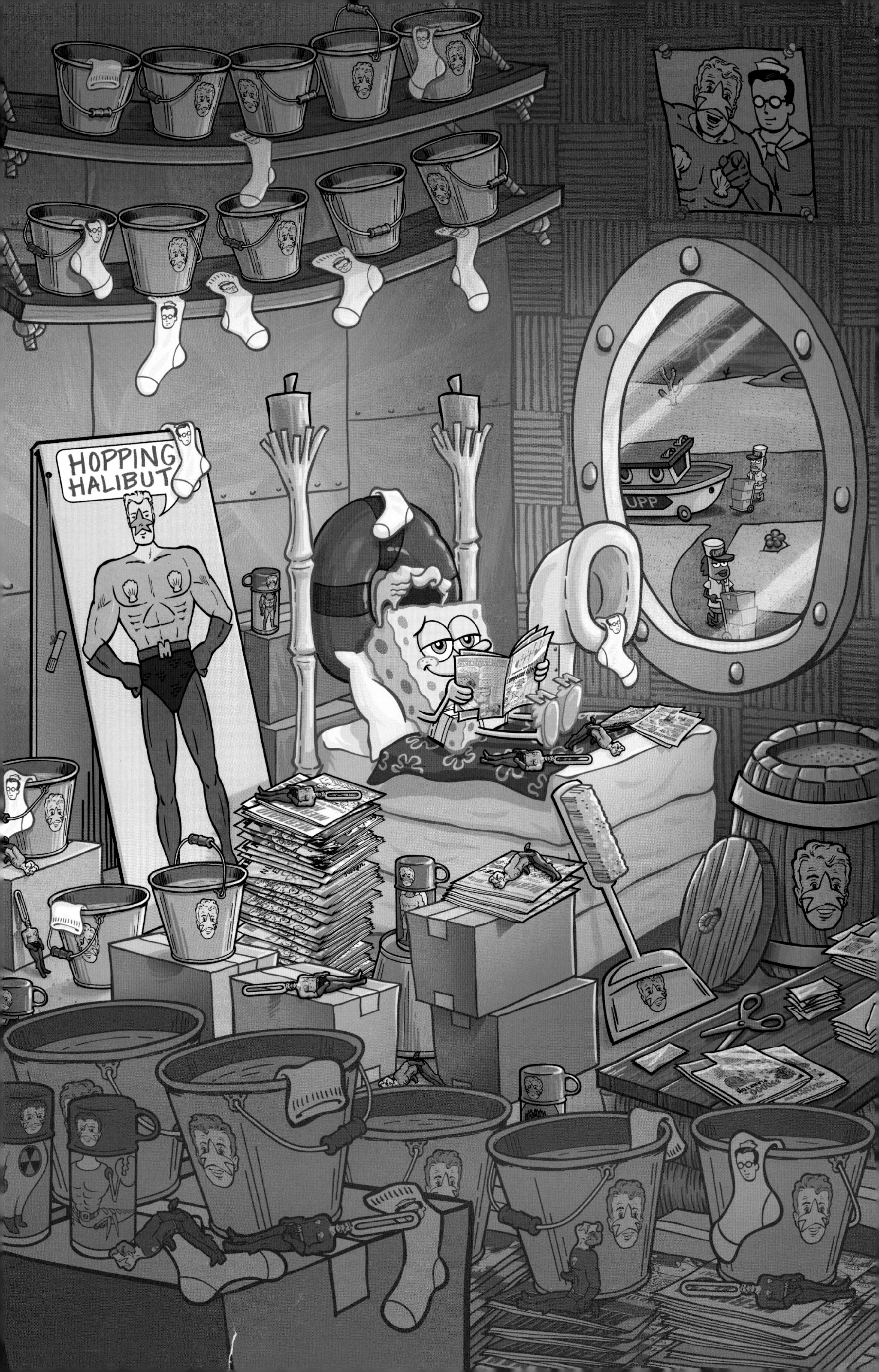
HOPPING
HALIBUT
UPP

What terrible thing terrifies the citizens of Bikini Bottom?

To find out, fold page so "A" meets "B"

A SpongeBob Comics

FINNY FOLD-OVER

by Al Jaffee

FOLD LIKE THIS:

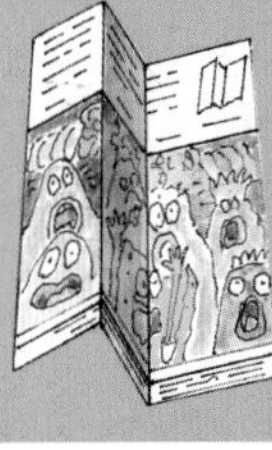

A► ◄B FOLD SO "A" MEETS "B"

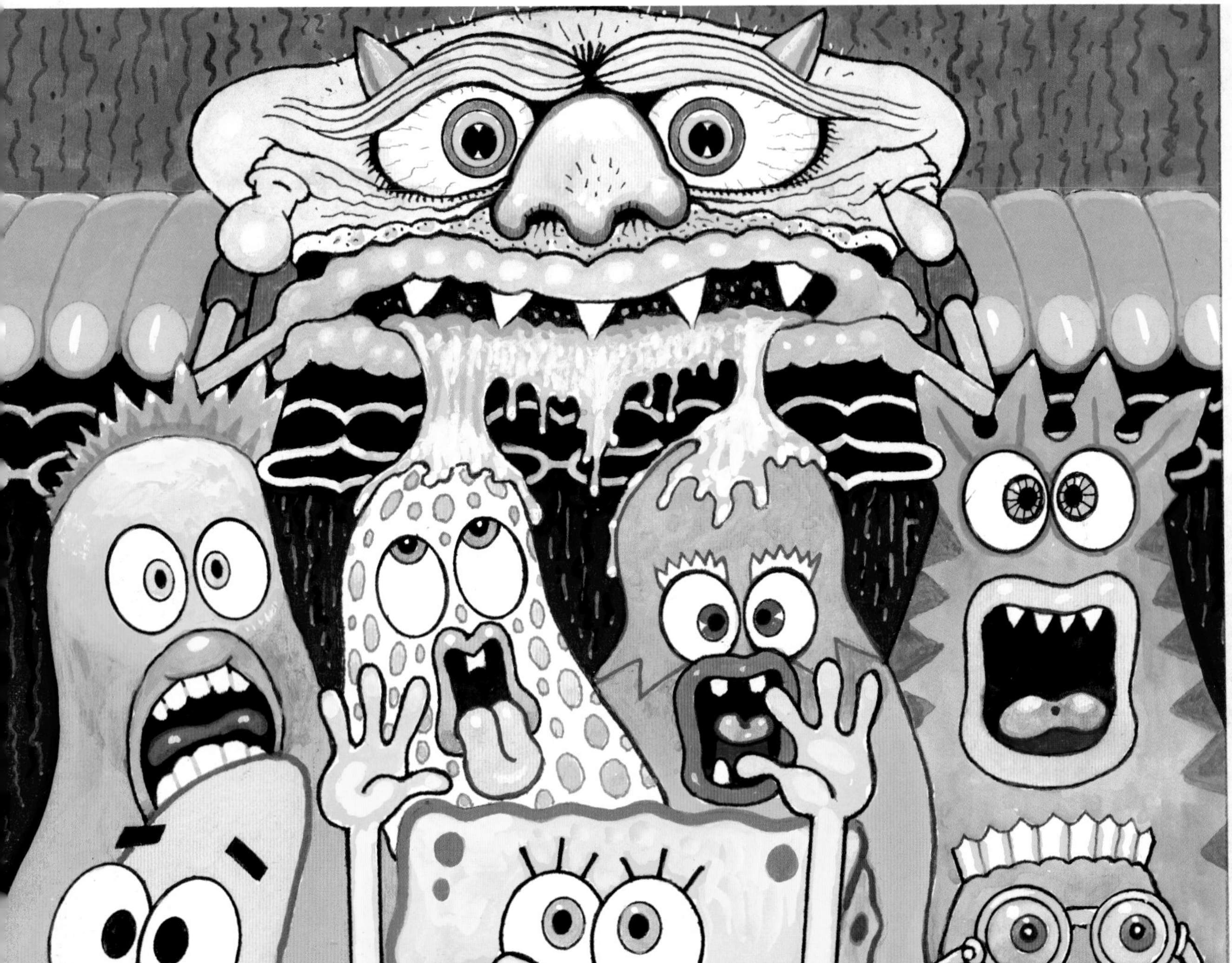

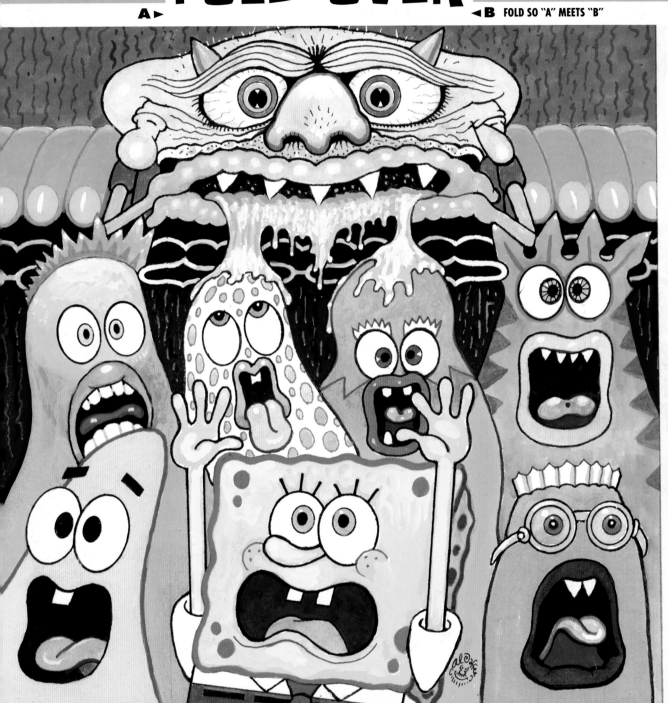

SQUATTING ON A BUILDING IS THIS HID-
EOUS MONSTER. HE MOVES FORWARD
ON HIS FAT BELLY, SNORTING AND DE-
CLARING HE WILL EAT ANYONE HE CAN GET

A► ◄B

Lettering by Rob Leigh

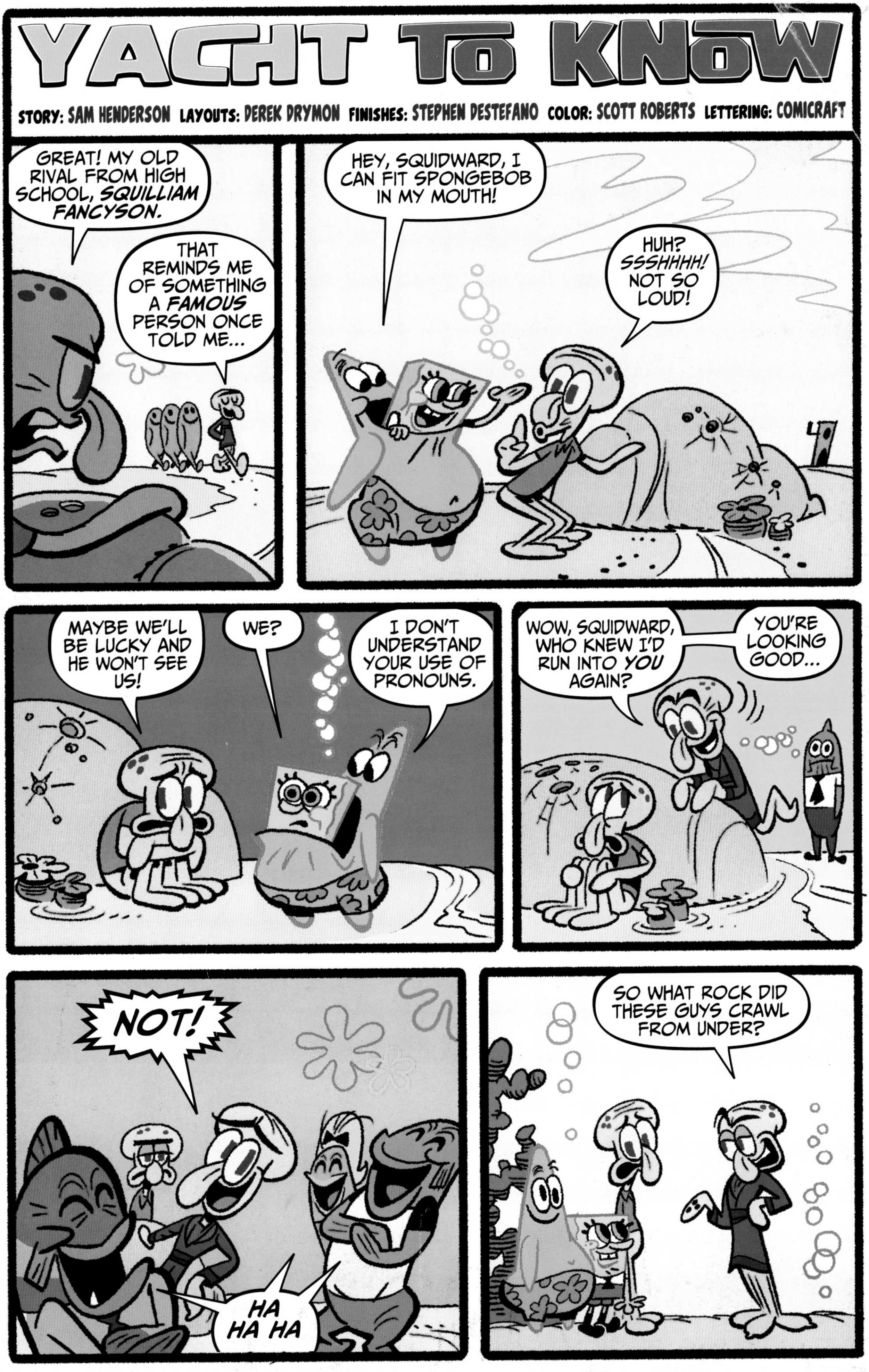
YACHT TO KNOW
STORY: SAM HENDERSON LAYOUTS: DEREK DRYMON FINISHES: STEPHEN DESTEFANO COLOR: SCOTT ROBERTS LETTERING: COMICRAFT
GREAT! MY OLD RIVAL FROM HIGH SCHOOL, SQUILLIAM FANCYSON.
THAT REMINDS ME OF SOMETHING A FAMOUS PERSON ONCE TOLD ME...
HEY, SQUIDWARD, I CAN FIT SPONGEBOB IN MY MOUTH!
HUH? SSSHHHH! NOT SO LOUD!
MAYBE WE'LL BE LUCKY AND HE WON'T SEE US!
WE?
I DON'T UNDERSTAND YOUR USE OF PRONOUNS.
WOW, SQUIDWARD, WHO KNEW I'D RUN INTO YOU AGAIN?
YOU'RE LOOKING GOOD...
NOT!
HA HA HA
SO WHAT ROCK DID THESE GUYS CRAWL FROM UNDER?

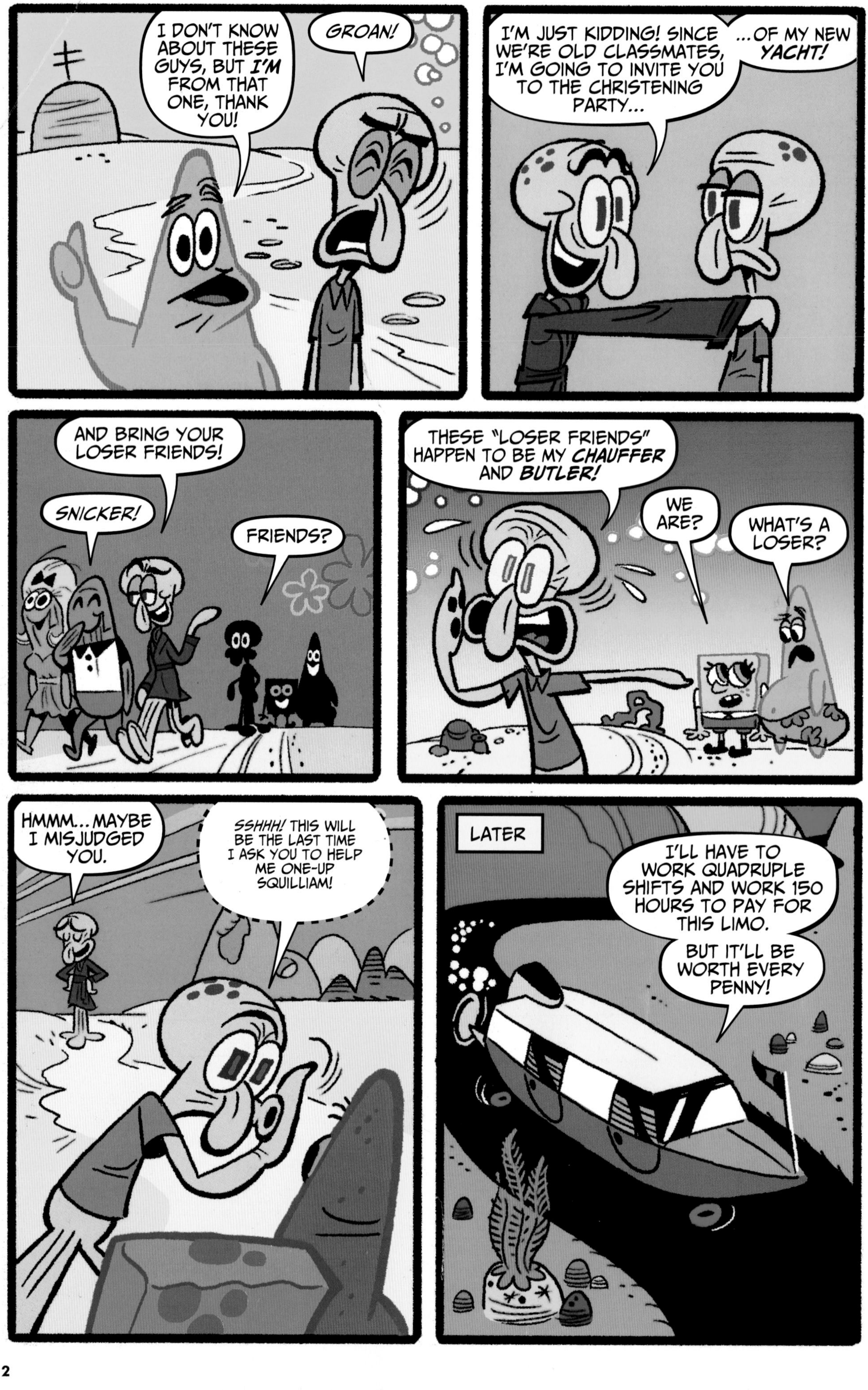
I DON'T KNOW ABOUT THESE GUYS, BUT I'M FROM THAT ONE, THANK YOU!
GROAN!
I'M JUST KIDDING! SINCE WE'RE OLD CLASSMATES, I'M GOING TO INVITE YOU TO THE CHRISTENING PARTY...
...OF MY NEW YACHT!
AND BRING YOUR LOSER FRIENDS!
SNICKER!
FRIENDS?
THESE "LOSER FRIENDS" HAPPEN TO BE MY CHAUFFER AND BUTLER!
WE ARE?
WHAT'S A LOSER?
HMMM... MAYBE I MISJUDGED YOU.
SSHHH! THIS WILL BE THE LAST TIME I ASK YOU TO HELP ME ONE-UP SQUILLIAM!
LATER
I'LL HAVE TO WORK QUADRUPLE SHIFTS AND WORK 150 HOURS TO PAY FOR THIS LIMO.
BUT IT'LL BE WORTH EVERY PENNY!

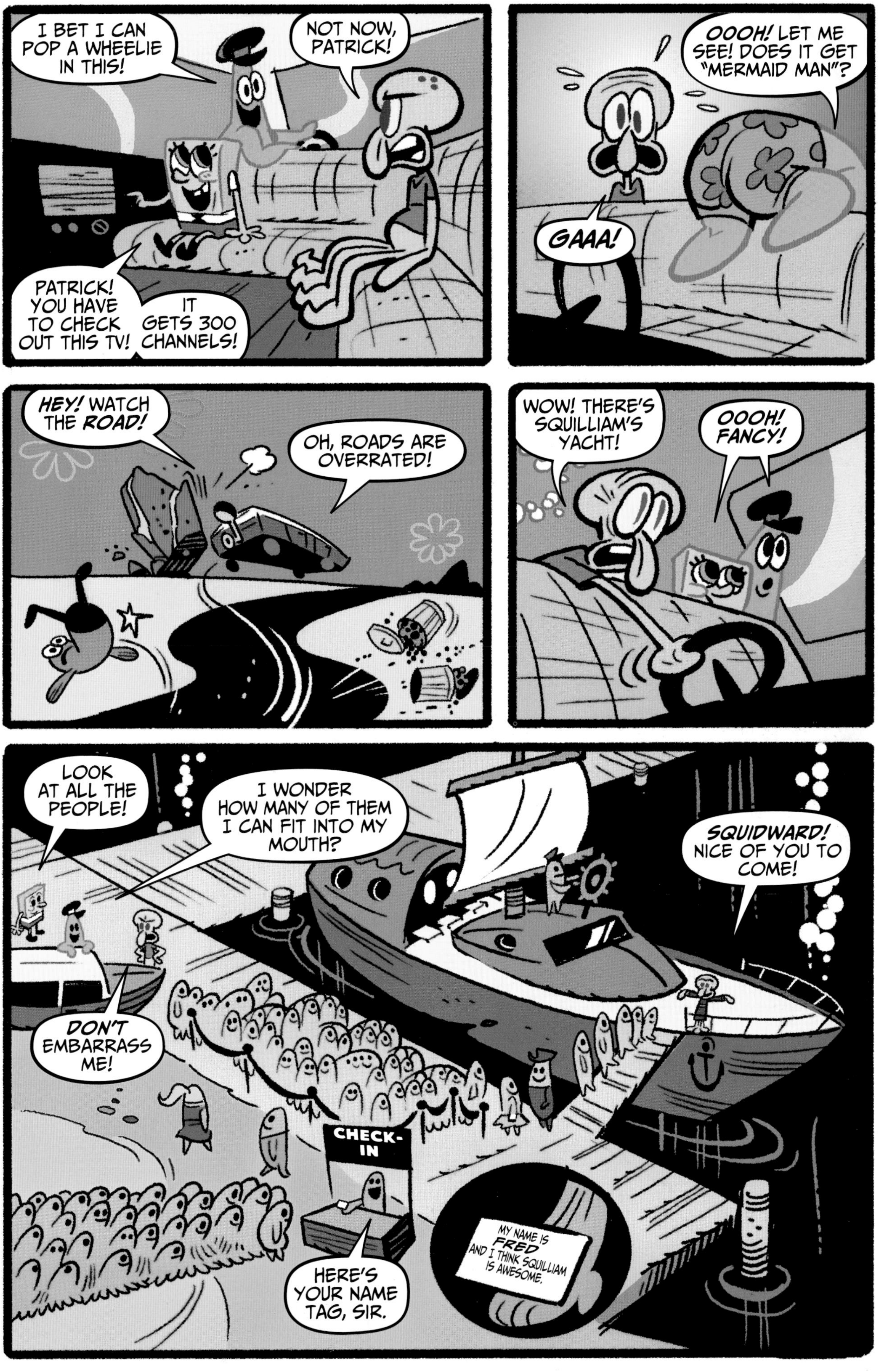
I BET I CAN POP A WHEELIE IN THIS!
NOT NOW, PATRICK!
PATRICK! YOU HAVE TO CHECK OUT THIS TV!
IT GETS 300 CHANNELS!
OOOH! LET ME SEE! DOES IT GET "MERMAID MAN"?
GAAA!
HEY! WATCH THE ROAD!
OH, ROADS ARE OVERRATED!
WOW! THERE'S SQUILLIAM'S YACHT!
OOOH! FANCY!
LOOK AT ALL THE PEOPLE!
I WONDER HOW MANY OF THEM I CAN FIT INTO MY MOUTH?
SQUIDWARD! NICE OF YOU TO COME!
DON'T EMBARRASS ME!
CHECK-IN
HERE'S YOUR NAME TAG, SIR.
MY NAME IS FRED AND I THINK SQUILLIAM IS AWESOME.

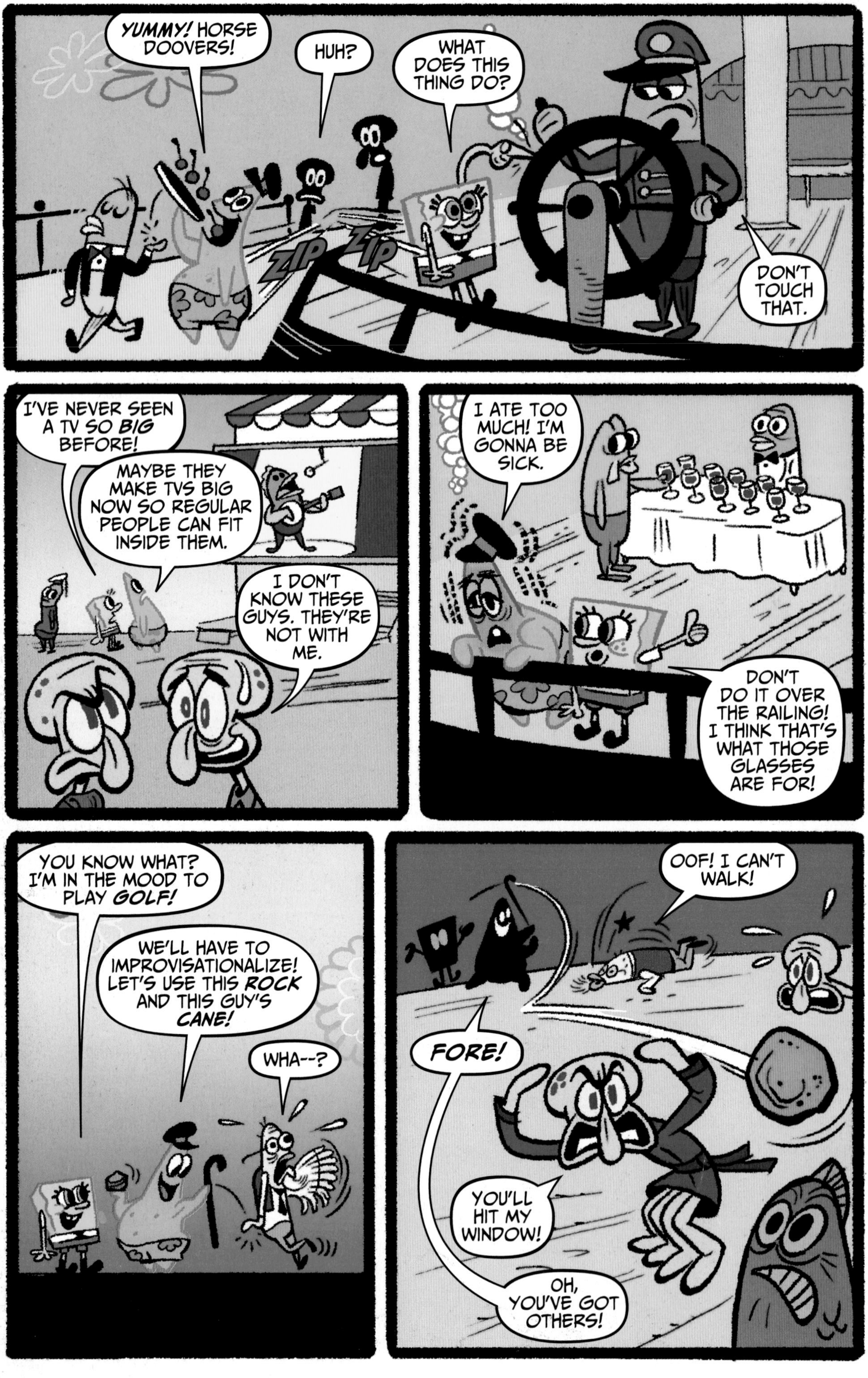
YUMMY! HORSE DOOVERS!
HUH?
WHAT DOES THIS THING DO?
ZIP ZIP
DON'T TOUCH THAT.
I'VE NEVER SEEN A TV SO BIG BEFORE!
MAYBE THEY MAKE TVS BIG NOW SO REGULAR PEOPLE CAN FIT INSIDE THEM.
I DON'T KNOW THESE GUYS. THEY'RE NOT WITH ME.
I ATE TOO MUCH! I'M GONNA BE SICK.
DON'T DO IT OVER THE RAILING! I THINK THAT'S WHAT THOSE GLASSES ARE FOR!
YOU KNOW WHAT? I'M IN THE MOOD TO PLAY GOLF!
WE'LL HAVE TO IMPROVISATIONALIZE! LET'S USE THIS ROCK AND THIS GUY'S CANE!
WHA--?
OOF! I CAN'T WALK!
FORE!
YOU'LL HIT MY WINDOW!
OH, YOU'VE GOT OTHERS!

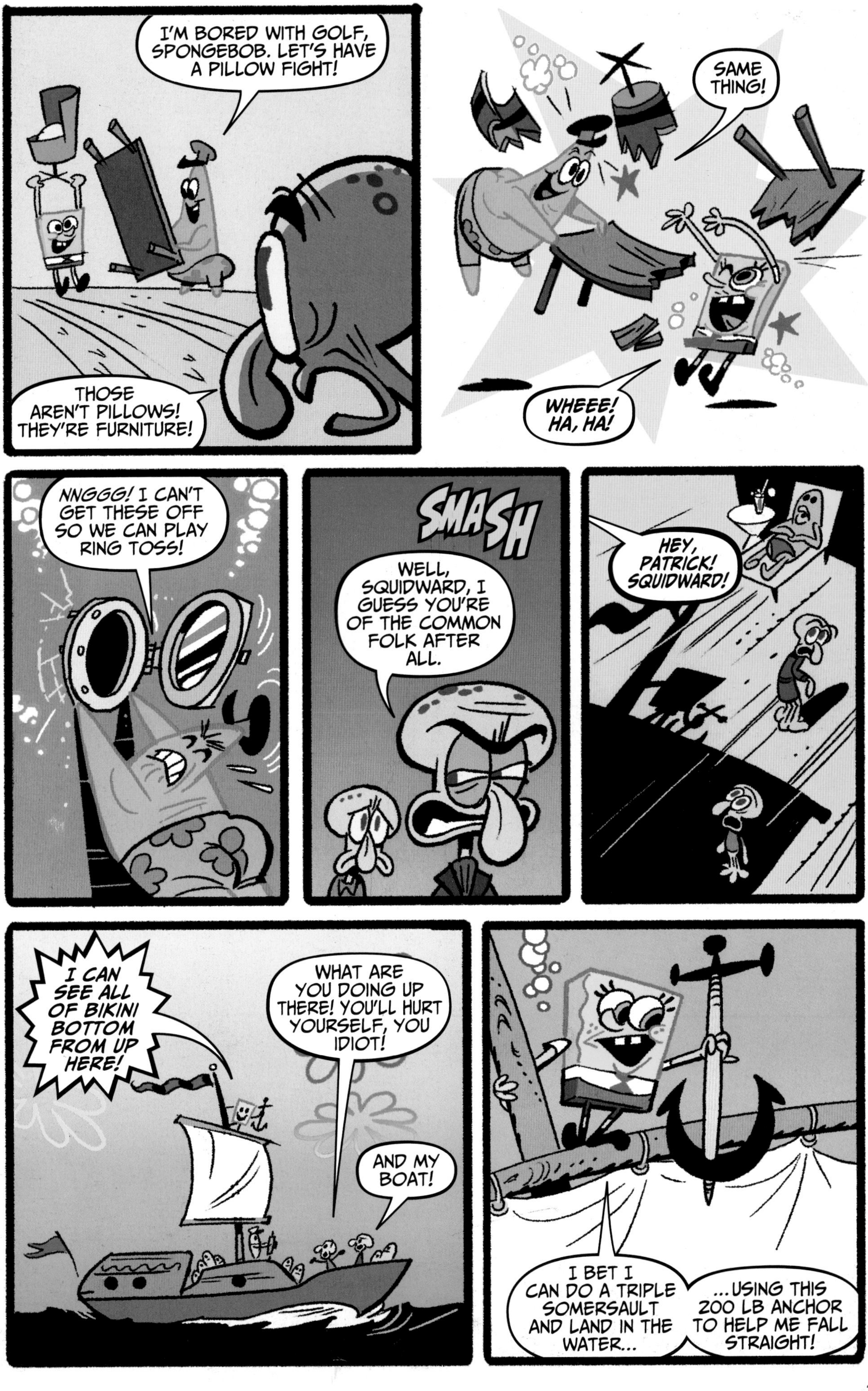

I'M BORED WITH GOLF, SPONGEBOB. LET'S HAVE A PILLOW FIGHT!
THOSE AREN'T PILLOWS! THEY'RE FURNITURE!
SAME THING!
WHEEE! HA, HA!
NNGGG! I CAN'T GET THESE OFF SO WE CAN PLAY RING TOSS!
SMASH
WELL, SQUIDWARD, I GUESS YOU'RE OF THE COMMON FOLK AFTER ALL.
HEY, PATRICK! SQUIDWARD!
I CAN SEE ALL OF BIKINI BOTTOM FROM UP HERE!
WHAT ARE YOU DOING UP THERE! YOU'LL HURT YOURSELF, YOU IDIOT!
AND MY BOAT!
I BET I CAN DO A TRIPLE SOMERSAULT AND LAND IN THE WATER...
...USING THIS 200 LB ANCHOR TO HELP ME FALL STRAIGHT!

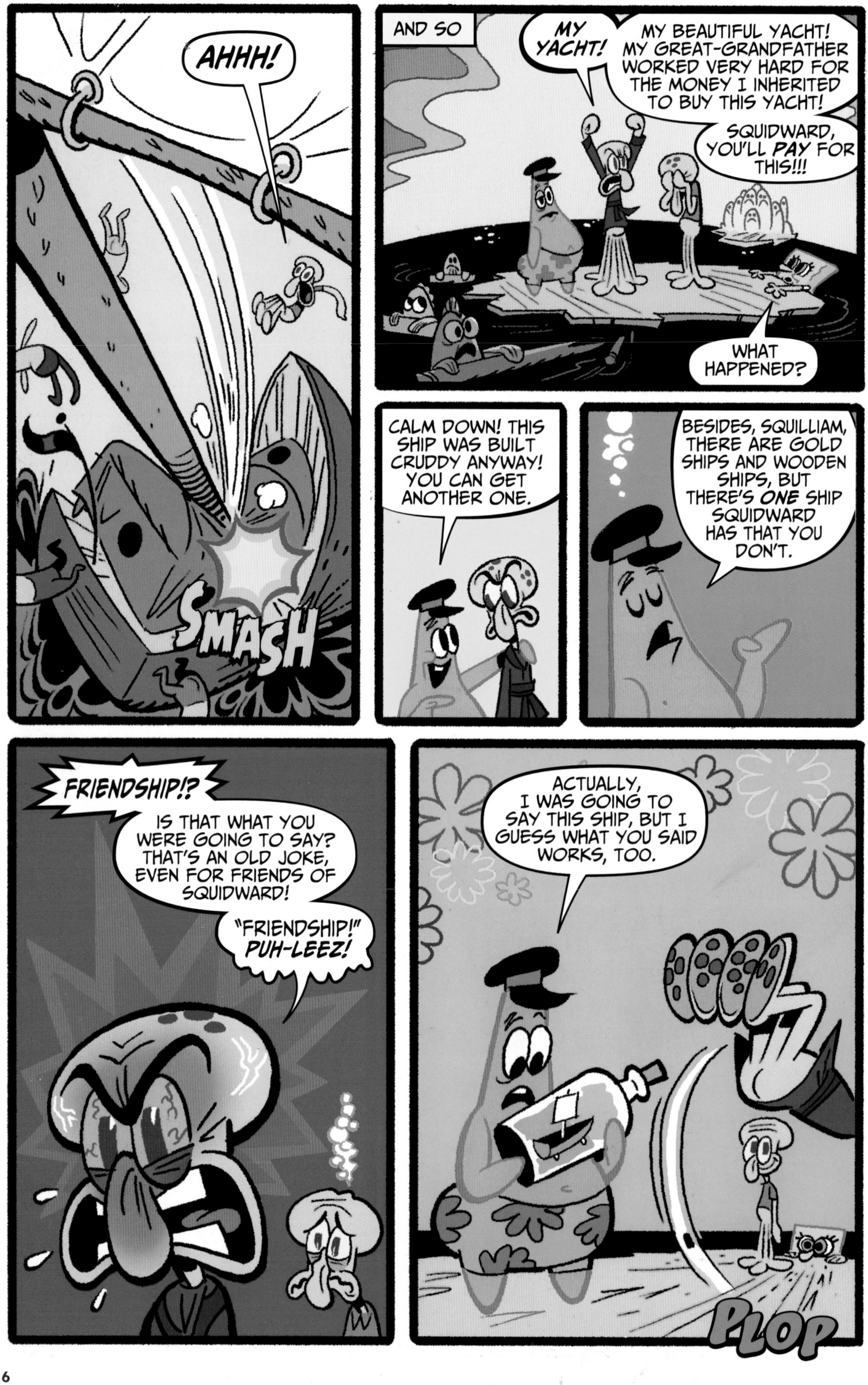
AHHH!
SMASH
AND SO
MY YACHT!
MY BEAUTIFUL YACHT! MY GREAT-GRANDFATHER WORKED VERY HARD FOR THE MONEY I INHERITED TO BUY THIS YACHT!
SQUIDWARD, YOU'LL PAY FOR THIS!!!
WHAT HAPPENED?
CALM DOWN! THIS SHIP WAS BUILT CRUDDY ANYWAY! YOU CAN GET ANOTHER ONE.
BESIDES, SQUILLIAM, THERE ARE GOLD SHIPS AND WOODEN SHIPS, BUT THERE'S ONE SHIP SQUIDWARD HAS THAT YOU DON'T.
FRIENDSHIP!?
IS THAT WHAT YOU WERE GOING TO SAY? THAT'S AN OLD JOKE, EVEN FOR FRIENDS OF SQUIDWARD!
"FRIENDSHIP!" PUH-LEEZ!
ACTUALLY, I WAS GOING TO SAY THIS SHIP, BUT I GUESS WHAT YOU SAID WORKS, TOO.
PLOP

Facial Hair Flair

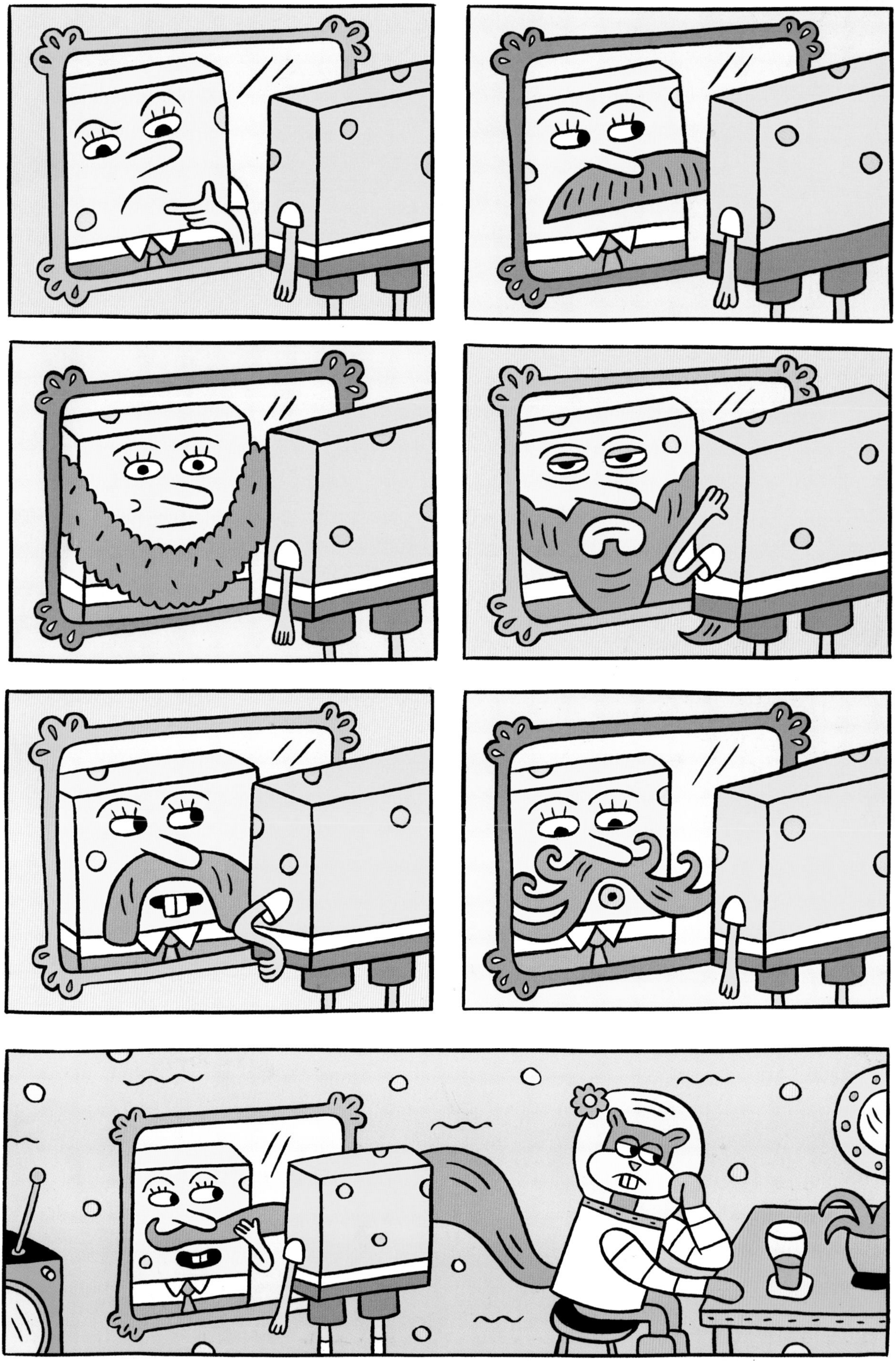

STORY: SHANE HOUGHTON   ART: ANDY REMENTER

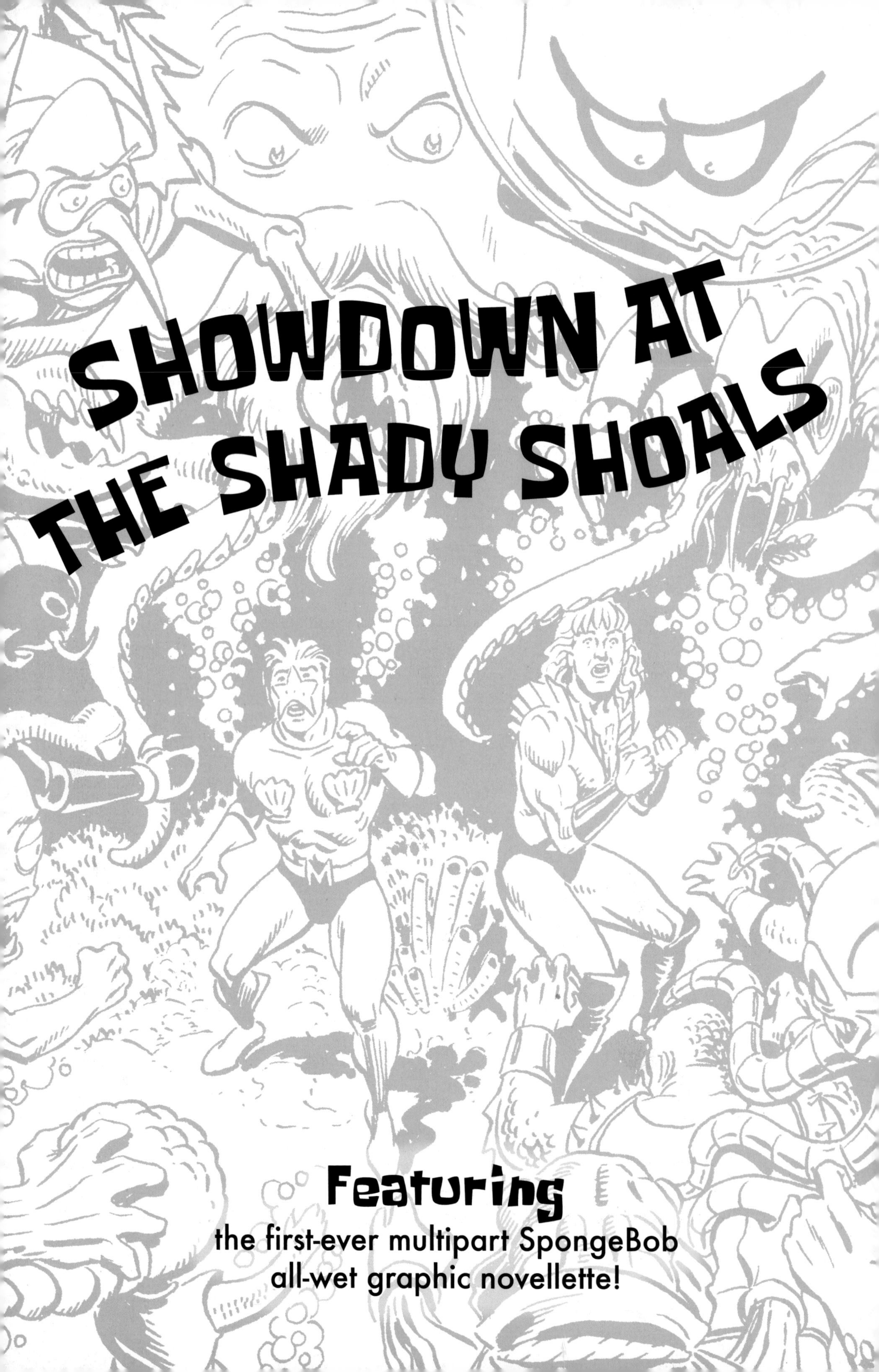

SHOWDOWN AT THE SHADY SHOALS

Featuring

the first-ever multipart SpongeBob all-wet graphic novellette!

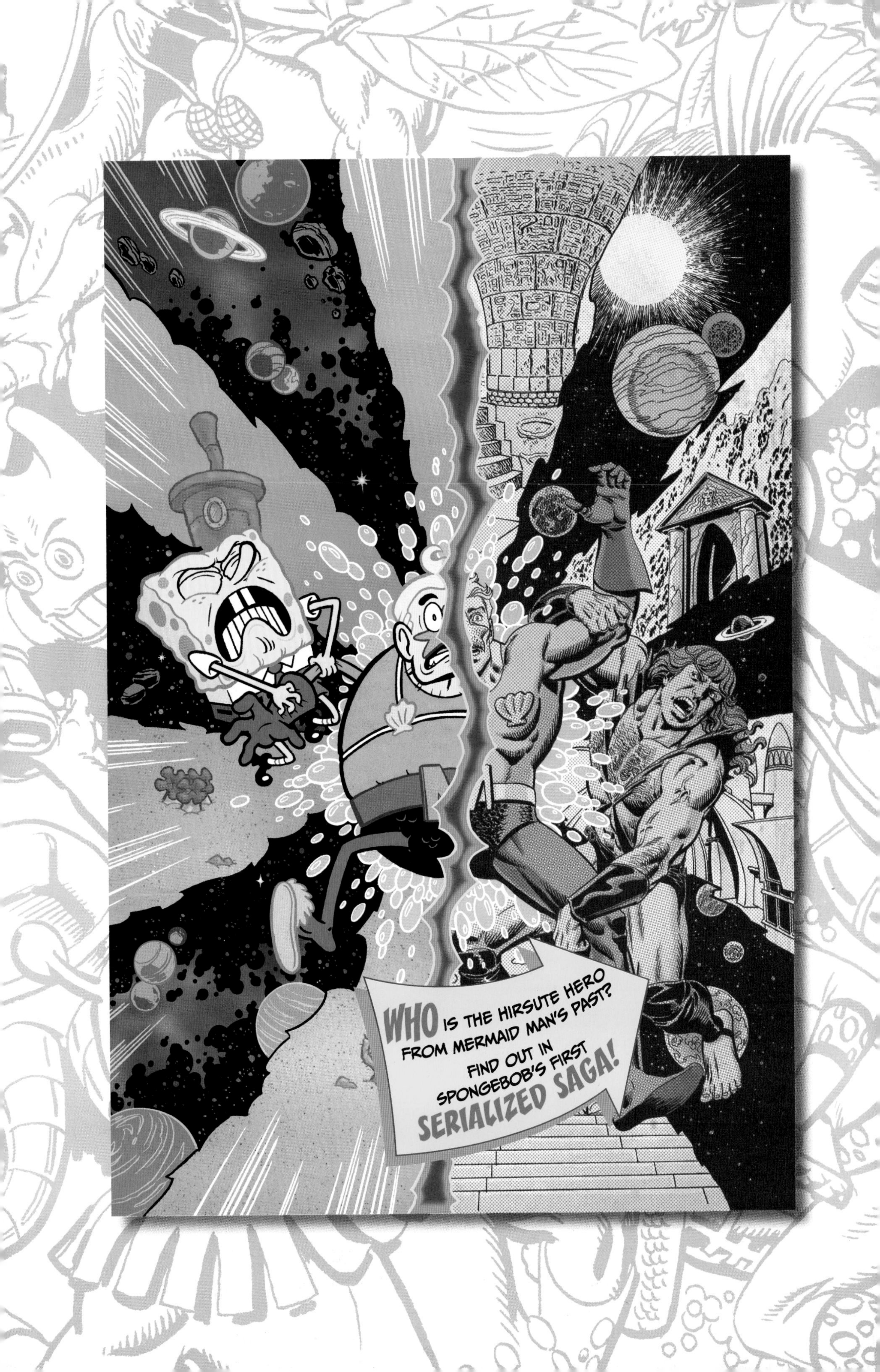
WHO IS THE HIRSUTE HERO FROM MERMAID MAN'S PAST?
FIND OUT IN SPONGEBOB'S FIRST
SERIALIZED SAGA!

UNITED PLANKTON PICTURES

PRESENTS

SPONGEBOB SQUAREPANTS

AND HIS AQUATIC FRIENDS

IN THEIR 1ST-EVER EPISODIC COMIC PERIODICAL SAGA!

(CONSISTING OF 5 PARTS)

And introducing that proud UNDERSEA POTENTATE and RIVAL to MERMAID MAN, the mysterious and muscular VIRO REGANTO!

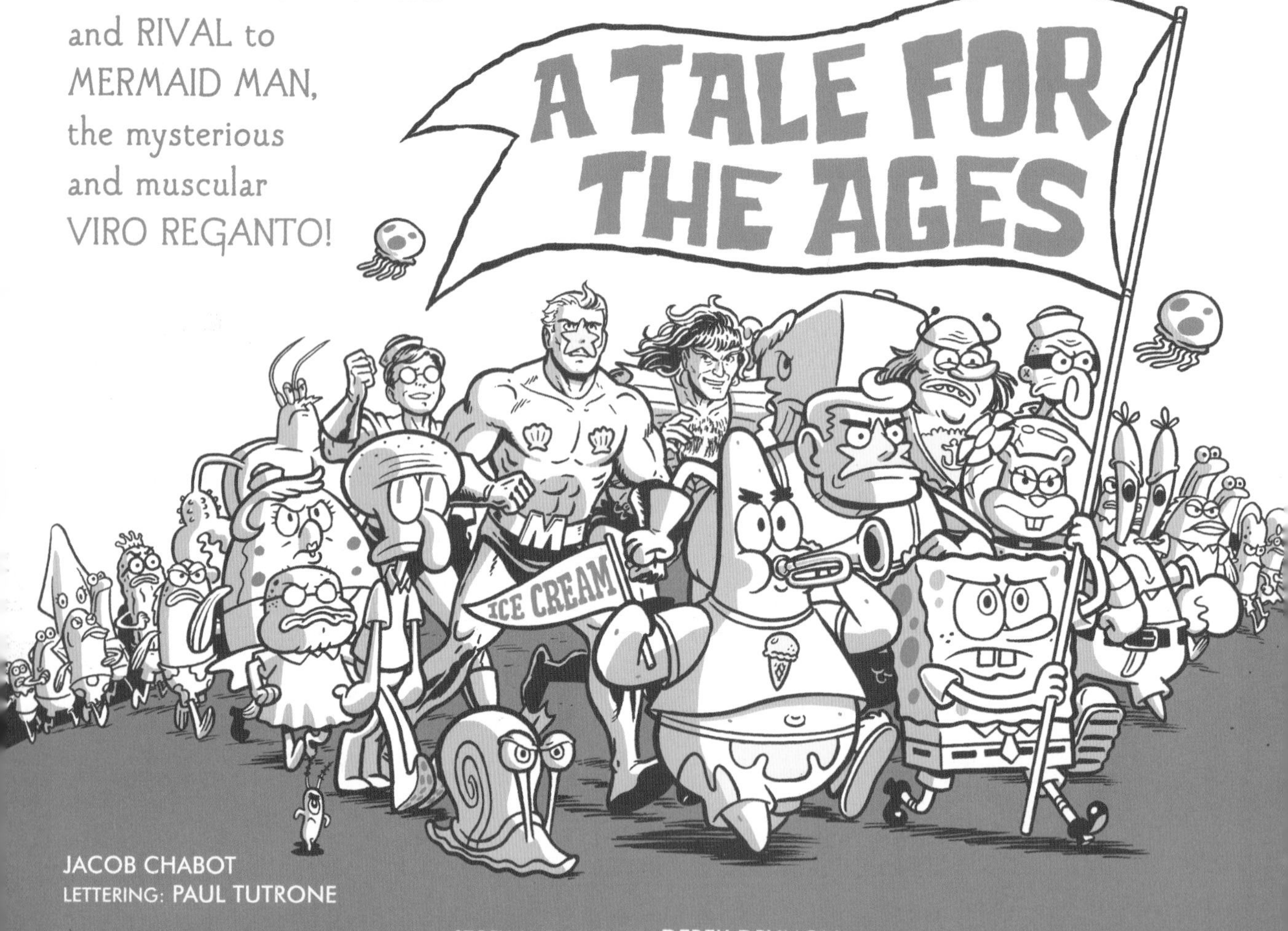
A TALE FOR THE AGES
ICE CREAM
M

JACOB CHABOT
LETTERING: PAUL TUTRONE

STORY AND LAYOUTS: DEREK DRYMON
PENCILS AND INKS, SPONGEPAGES: DEREK DRYMON
PENCILS AND INKS, CLASSIC MERMAID MAN, FLASHBACKS, AND SEA CUCUMBER: JERRY ORDWAY
COLOR: HIFI
LETTERING: COMICRAFT
ESPERANTO TRANSLATION PAGES BY BRIAN MURNANE (SCRIPT), JACOB CHABOT (ART), AND COMICRAFT (LETTERING)
VIRO REGANTO PINUP BY RAMONA FRADON (PENCILS AND INKS), AND JIM CAMPBELL (COLOR)

PREVIOUS PAGE: PENCILS AND INKS: JACOB CHABOT AND JERRY ORDWAY. COLOR: RICK NEILSEN

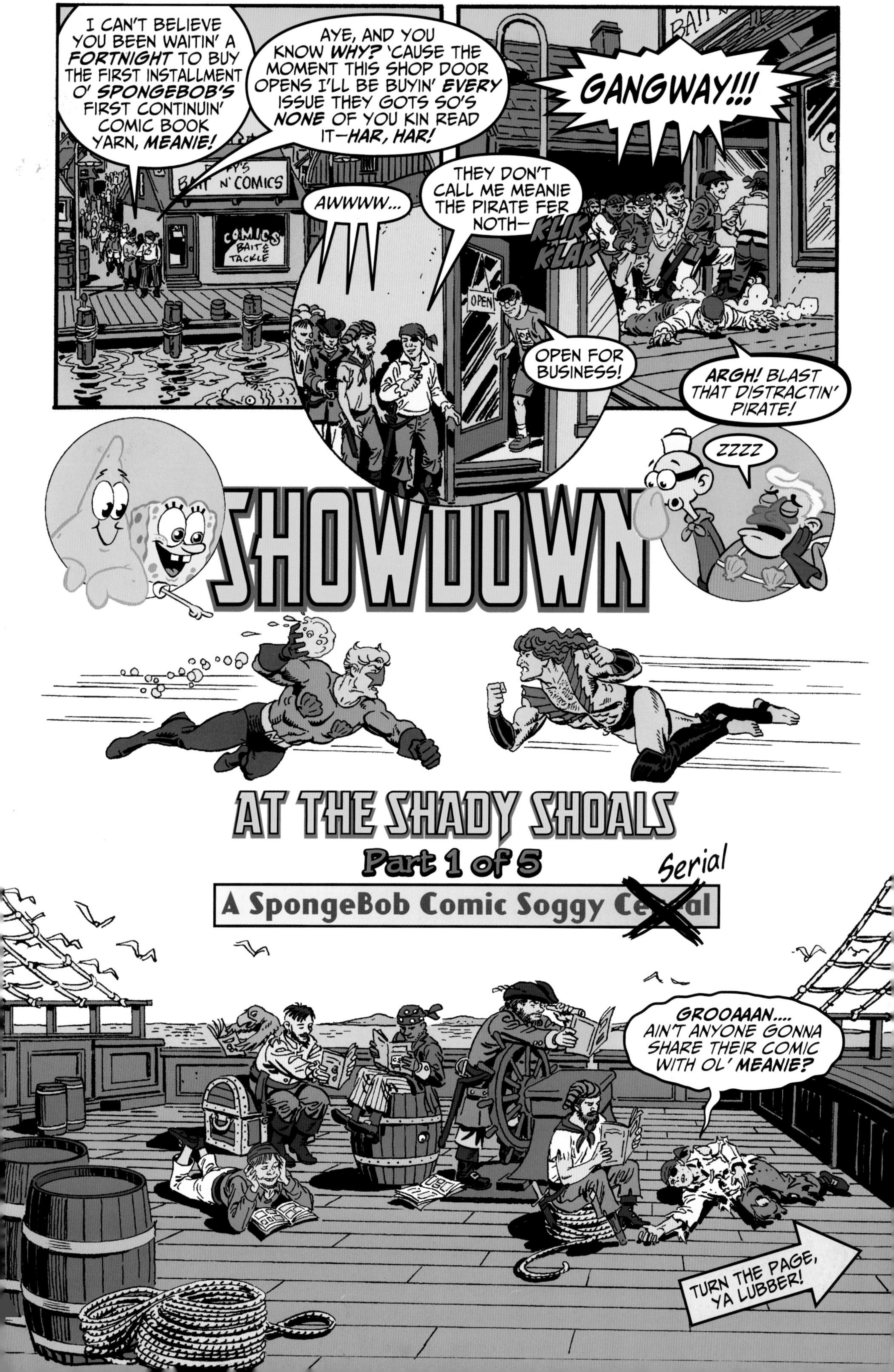
I CAN'T BELIEVE YOU BEEN WAITIN' A FORTNIGHT TO BUY THE FIRST INSTALLMENT O' SPONGEBOB'S FIRST CONTINUIN' COMIC BOOK YARN, MEANIE!
AYE, AND YOU KNOW WHY? 'CAUSE THE MOMENT THIS SHOP DOOR OPENS I'LL BE BUYIN' EVERY ISSUE THEY GOTS SO'S NONE OF YOU KIN READ IT—HAR, HAR!
BAIT N' COMICS
COMICS BAIT & TACKLE
AWWWW...
THEY DON'T CALL ME MEANIE THE PIRATE FER NOTH—
KLIK KLAK
OPEN
OPEN FOR BUSINESS!
GANGWAY!!!
ARGH! BLAST THAT DISTRACTIN' PIRATE!
ZZZZ
SHOWDOWN
AT THE SHADY SHOALS
Part 1 of 5
A SpongeBob Comic Soggy Cereal Serial
GROOAAAN.... AIN'T ANYONE GONNA SHARE THEIR COMIC WITH OL' MEANIE?
TURN THE PAGE, YA LUBBER!

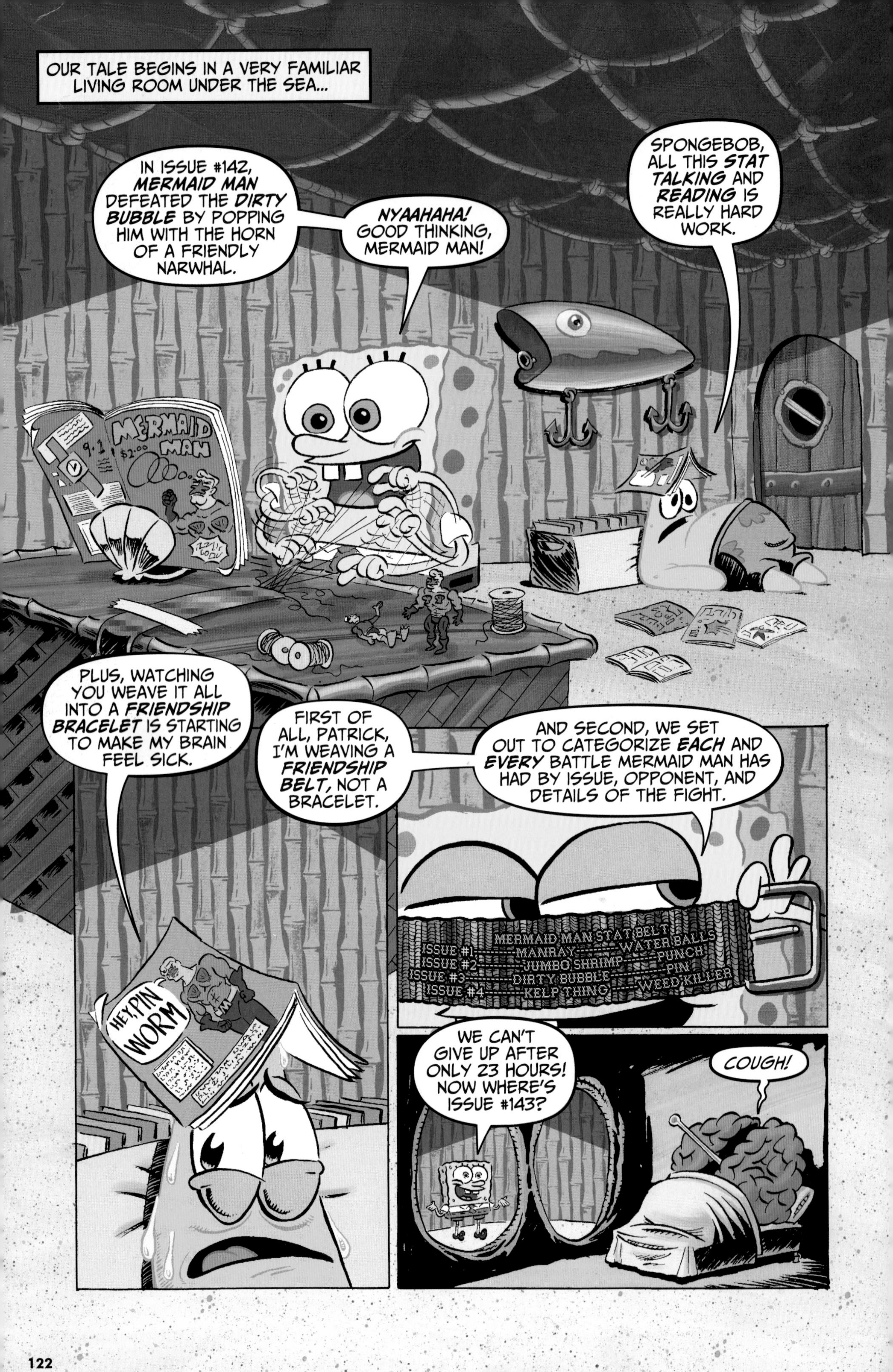
OUR TALE BEGINS IN A VERY FAMILIAR LIVING ROOM UNDER THE SEA...
IN ISSUE #142, MERMAID MAN DEFEATED THE DIRTY BUBBLE BY POPPING HIM WITH THE HORN OF A FRIENDLY NARWHAL.
NYAAHAHA! GOOD THINKING, MERMAID MAN!
SPONGEBOB, ALL THIS STAT TALKING AND READING IS REALLY HARD WORK.
MERMAID MAN
$2.00
PLUS, WATCHING YOU WEAVE IT ALL INTO A FRIENDSHIP BRACELET IS STARTING TO MAKE MY BRAIN FEEL SICK.
HEY, PIN WORM
FIRST OF ALL, PATRICK, I'M WEAVING A FRIENDSHIP BELT, NOT A BRACELET.
AND SECOND, WE SET OUT TO CATEGORIZE EACH AND EVERY BATTLE MERMAID MAN HAS HAD BY ISSUE, OPPONENT, AND DETAILS OF THE FIGHT.
MERMAID MAN STAT BELT
ISSUE #1 MANRAY WATER BALLS
ISSUE #2 JUMBO SHRIMP PUNCH
ISSUE #3 DIRTY BUBBLE PIN
ISSUE #4 KELP THING WEED KILLER
WE CAN'T GIVE UP AFTER ONLY 23 HOURS! NOW WHERE'S ISSUE #143?
COUGH!

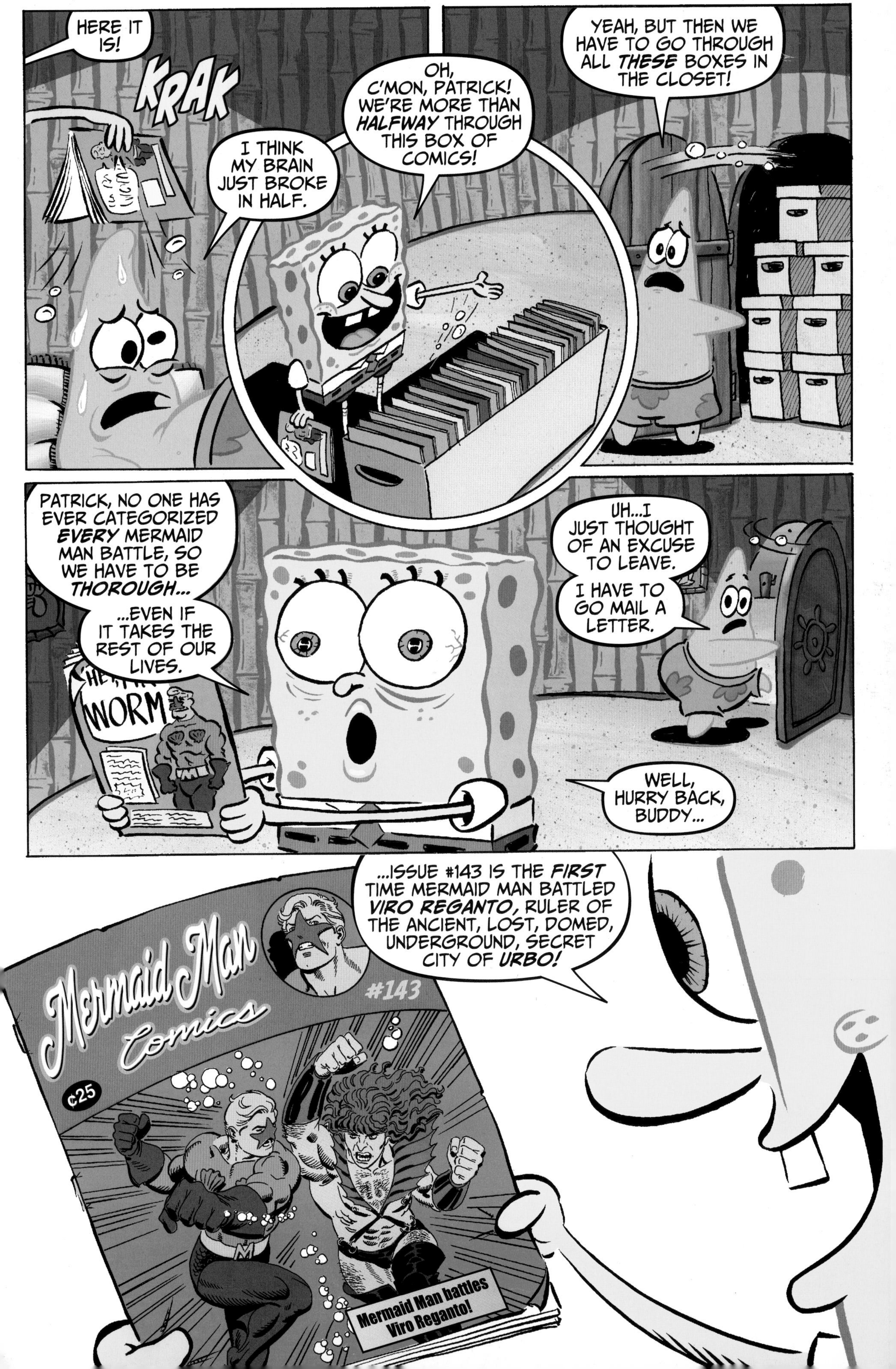
HERE IT IS!
KRAK
I THINK MY BRAIN JUST BROKE IN HALF.
OH, C'MON, PATRICK! WE'RE MORE THAN HALFWAY THROUGH THIS BOX OF COMICS!
YEAH, BUT THEN WE HAVE TO GO THROUGH ALL THESE BOXES IN THE CLOSET!
PATRICK, NO ONE HAS EVER CATEGORIZED EVERY MERMAID MAN BATTLE, SO WE HAVE TO BE THOROUGH...
...EVEN IF IT TAKES THE REST OF OUR LIVES.
WORM
UH...I JUST THOUGHT OF AN EXCUSE TO LEAVE.
I HAVE TO GO MAIL A LETTER.
WELL, HURRY BACK, BUDDY...
...ISSUE #143 IS THE FIRST TIME MERMAID MAN BATTLED VIRO REGANTO, RULER OF THE ANCIENT, LOST, DOMED, UNDERGROUND, SECRET CITY OF URBO!
Mermaid Man Comics
#143
¢25
Mermaid Man battles Viro Reganto!

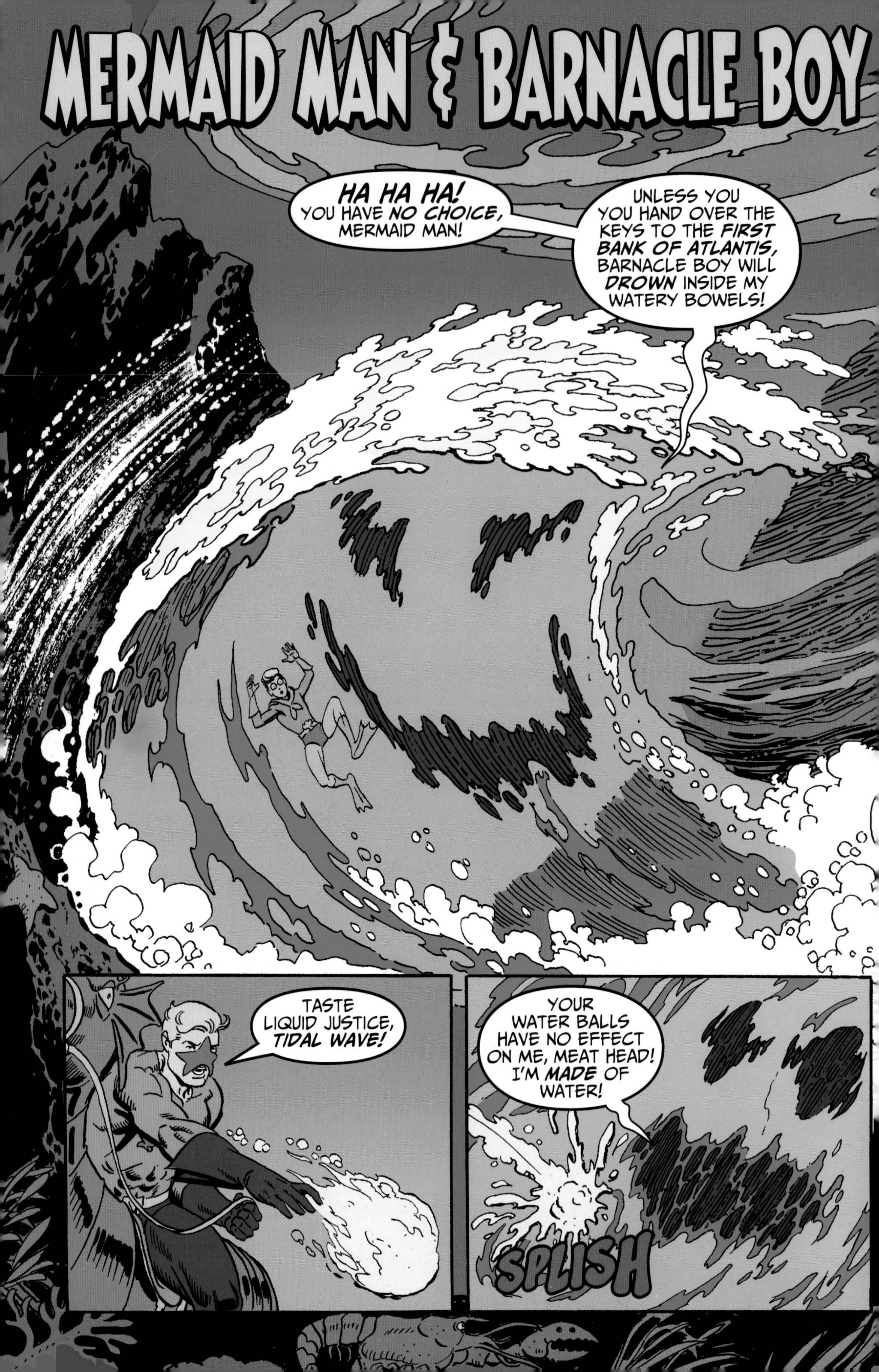
MERMAID MAN & BARNACLE BOY
HA HA HA! YOU HAVE NO CHOICE, MERMAID MAN!
UNLESS YOU YOU HAND OVER THE KEYS TO THE FIRST BANK OF ATLANTIS, BARNACLE BOY WILL DROWN INSIDE MY WATERY BOWELS!
TASTE LIQUID JUSTICE, TIDAL WAVE!
YOUR WATER BALLS HAVE NO EFFECT ON ME, MEAT HEAD! I'M MADE OF WATER!
SPLISH

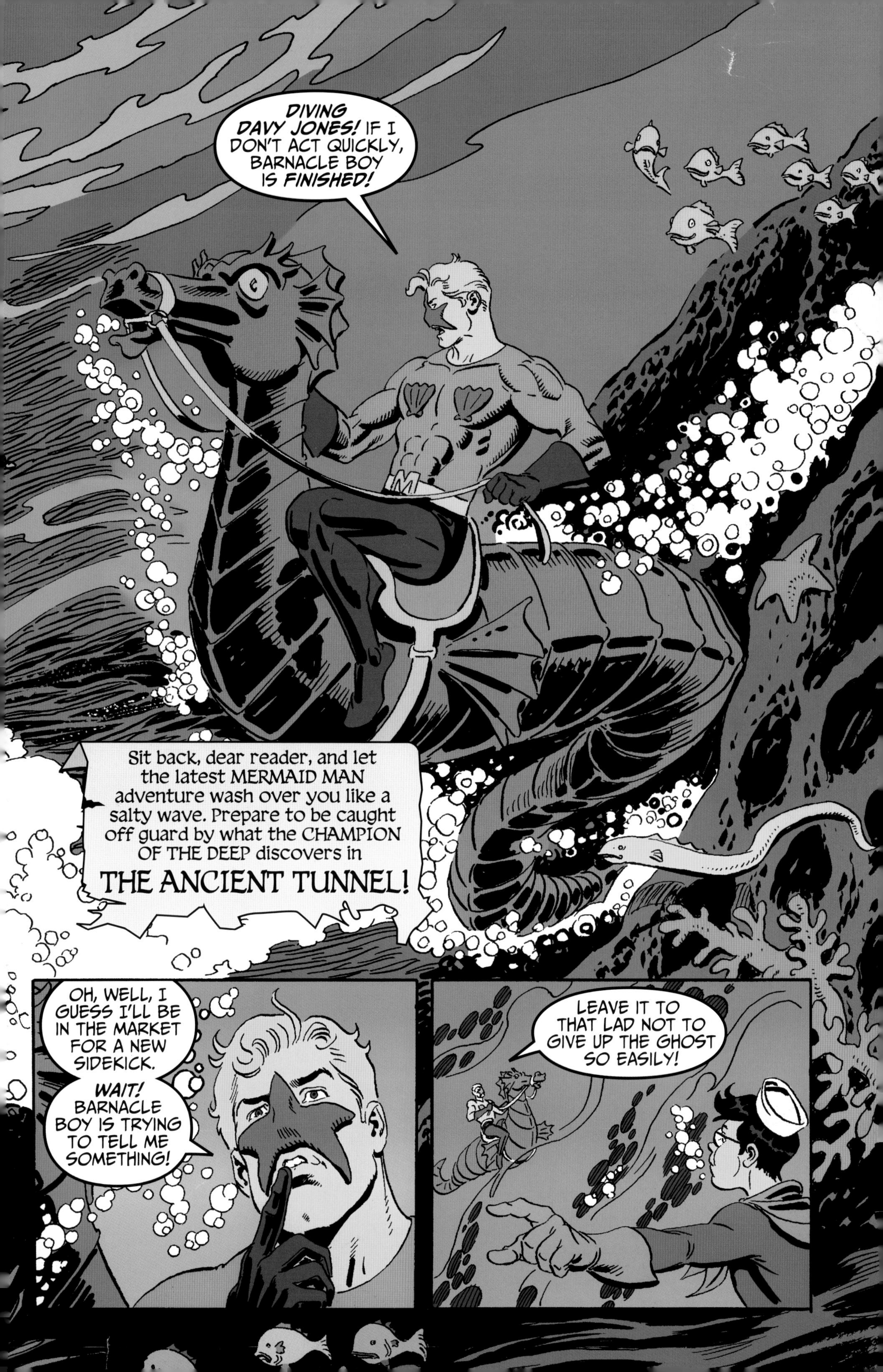
DIVING DAVY JONES! IF I DON'T ACT QUICKLY, BARNACLE BOY IS FINISHED!
Sit back, dear reader, and let the latest MERMAID MAN adventure wash over you like a salty wave. Prepare to be caught off guard by what the CHAMPION OF THE DEEP discovers in
THE ANCIENT TUNNEL!
OH, WELL, I GUESS I'LL BE IN THE MARKET FOR A NEW SIDEKICK.
WAIT! BARNACLE BOY IS TRYING TO TELL ME SOMETHING!
LEAVE IT TO THAT LAD NOT TO GIVE UP THE GHOST SO EASILY!

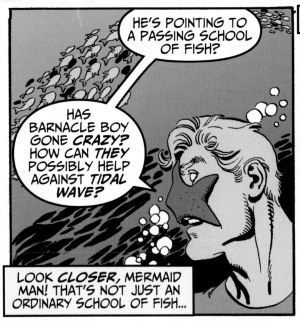

HE'S POINTING TO A PASSING SCHOOL OF FISH?

HAS BARNACLE BOY GONE *CRAZY?* HOW CAN *THEY* POSSIBLY HELP AGAINST *TIDAL WAVE?*

LOOK *CLOSER*, MERMAID MAN! THAT'S NOT JUST AN ORDINARY SCHOOL OF FISH...

...THEY'RE *PORCUPINE FISH!*

WAIT! NOW I KNOW WHAT BARNACLE BOY IS THINKING!

YOU'RE SENDING A BUNCH OF LITTLE *FISH* TO FIGHT ME? *HA HA HA!*

WHA--? THEY'RE *GULPING* SMALL BITS OF WATER FROM ME!?

GULP GULP GULP GULP GULP GULP

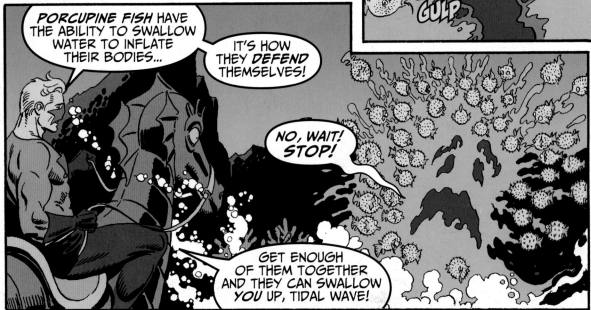

PORCUPINE FISH HAVE THE ABILITY TO SWALLOW WATER TO INFLATE THEIR BODIES...

IT'S HOW THEY *DEFEND* THEMSELVES!

NO, WAIT! STOP!

GET ENOUGH OF THEM TOGETHER AND THEY CAN SWALLOW *YOU* UP, TIDAL WAVE!

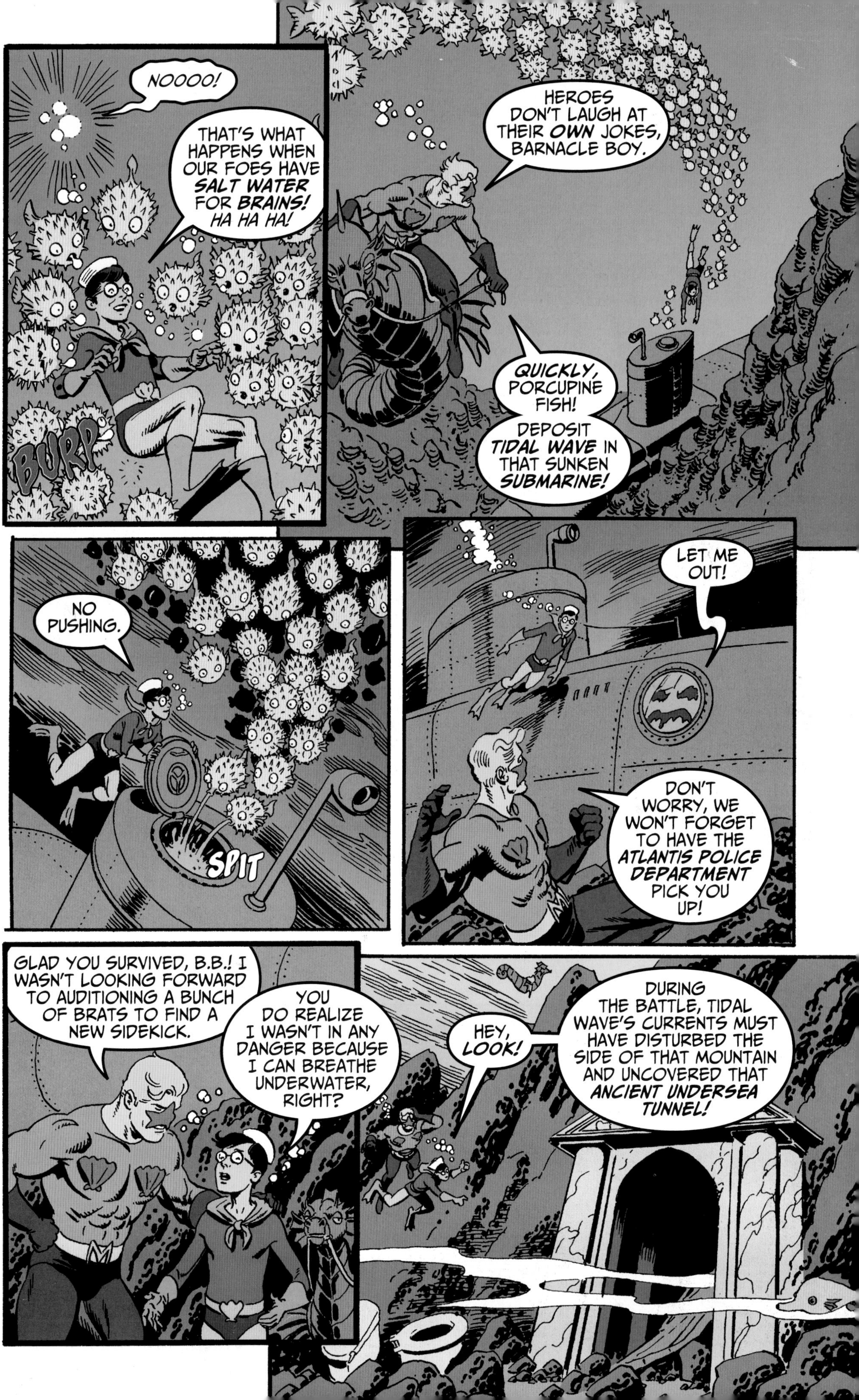
NOOOO!
THAT'S WHAT HAPPENS WHEN OUR FOES HAVE SALT WATER FOR BRAINS! HA HA HA!
BURP
HEROES DON'T LAUGH AT THEIR OWN JOKES, BARNACLE BOY.
QUICKLY, PORCUPINE FISH!
DEPOSIT TIDAL WAVE IN THAT SUNKEN SUBMARINE!
NO PUSHING.
SPIT
LET ME OUT!
DON'T WORRY, WE WON'T FORGET TO HAVE THE ATLANTIS POLICE DEPARTMENT PICK YOU UP!
GLAD YOU SURVIVED, B.B.! I WASN'T LOOKING FORWARD TO AUDITIONING A BUNCH OF BRATS TO FIND A NEW SIDEKICK.
YOU DO REALIZE I WASN'T IN ANY DANGER BECAUSE I CAN BREATHE UNDERWATER, RIGHT?
HEY, LOOK!
DURING THE BATTLE, TIDAL WAVE'S CURRENTS MUST HAVE DISTURBED THE SIDE OF THAT MOUNTAIN AND UNCOVERED THAT ANCIENT UNDERSEA TUNNEL!

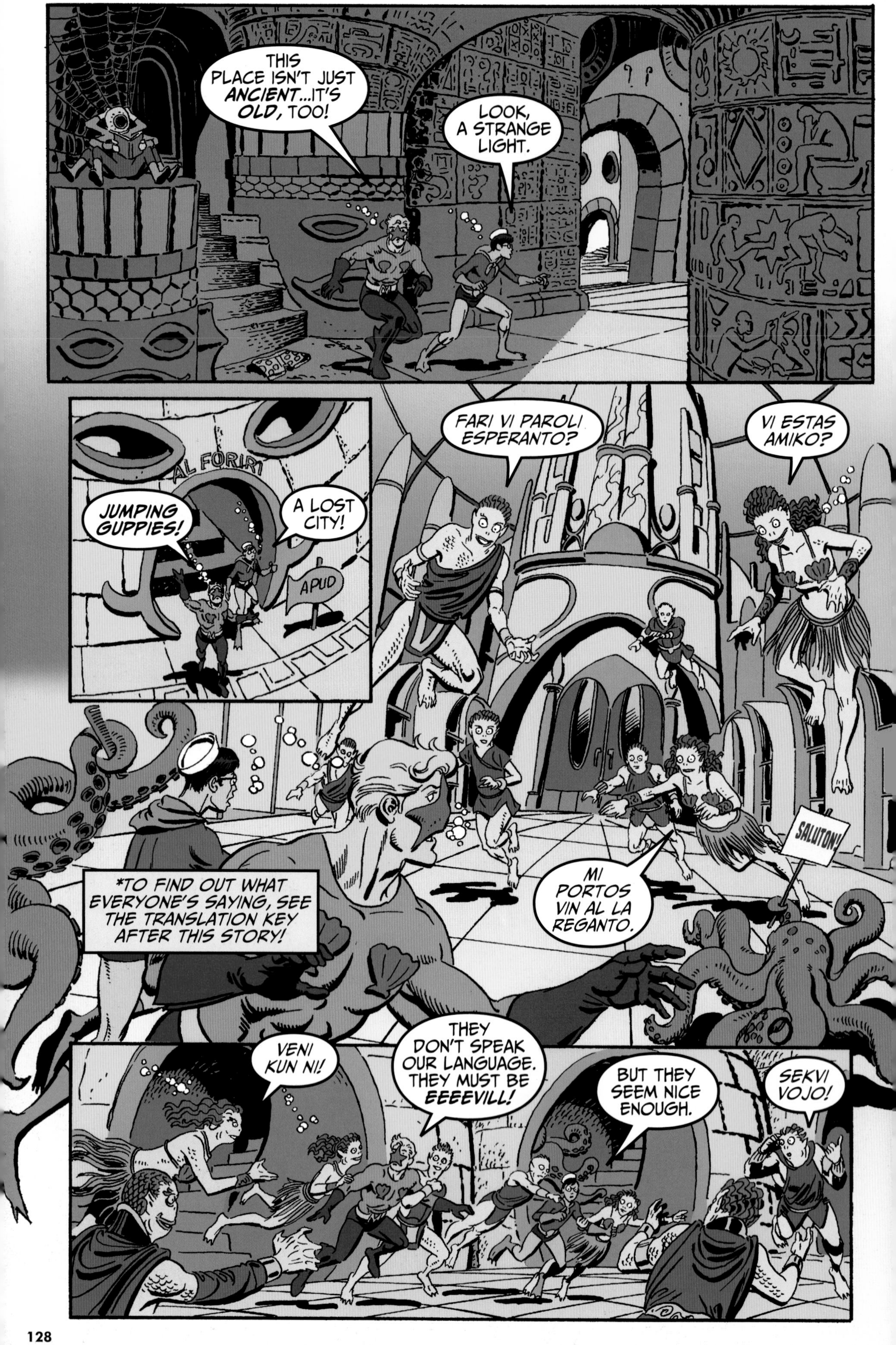

THIS PLACE ISN'T JUST ANCIENT...IT'S OLD, TOO!
LOOK, A STRANGE LIGHT.
AL FORIRI
JUMPING GUPPIES!
A LOST CITY!
APUD
FARI VI PAROLI ESPERANTO?
VI ESTAS AMIKO?
SALUTON!
MI PORTOS VIN AL LA REGANTO.
*TO FIND OUT WHAT EVERYONE'S SAYING, SEE THE TRANSLATION KEY AFTER THIS STORY!
VENI KUN NI!
THEY DON'T SPEAK OUR LANGUAGE. THEY MUST BE EEEEVILL!
BUT THEY SEEM NICE ENOUGH.
SEKVI VOJO!

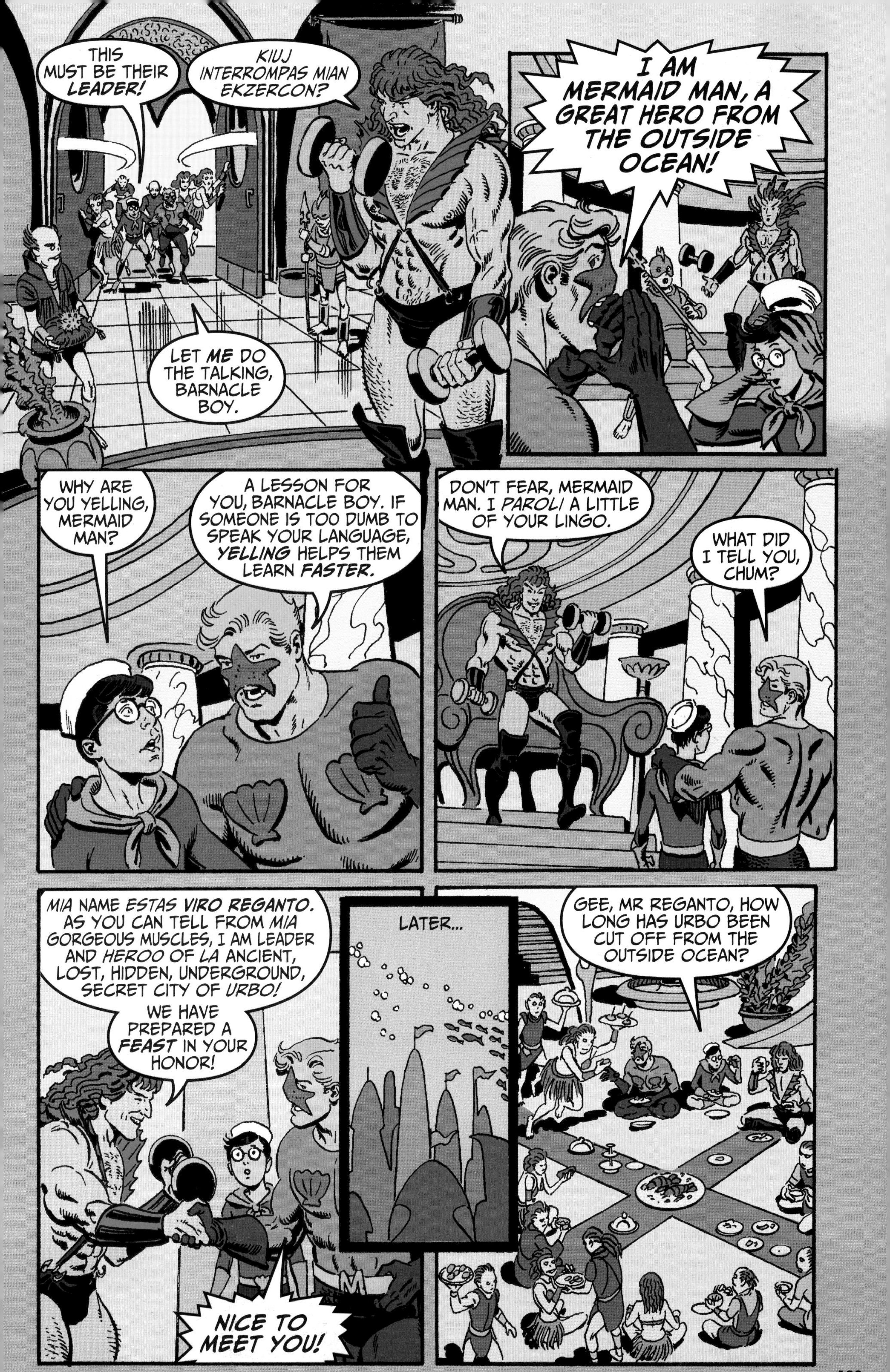
THIS MUST BE THEIR LEADER!
KIUJ INTERROMPAS MIAN EKZERCON?
LET ME DO THE TALKING, BARNACLE BOY.
I AM MERMAID MAN, A GREAT HERO FROM THE OUTSIDE OCEAN!
WHY ARE YOU YELLING, MERMAID MAN?
A LESSON FOR YOU, BARNACLE BOY. IF SOMEONE IS TOO DUMB TO SPEAK YOUR LANGUAGE, YELLING HELPS THEM LEARN FASTER.
DON'T FEAR, MERMAID MAN. I PAROLI A LITTLE OF YOUR LINGO.
WHAT DID I TELL YOU, CHUM?
MIA NAME ESTAS VIRO REGANTO. AS YOU CAN TELL FROM MIA GORGEOUS MUSCLES, I AM LEADER AND HEROO OF LA ANCIENT, LOST, HIDDEN, UNDERGROUND, SECRET CITY OF URBO!
WE HAVE PREPARED A FEAST IN YOUR HONOR!
NICE TO MEET YOU!
LATER...
GEE, MR REGANTO, HOW LONG HAS URBO BEEN CUT OFF FROM THE OUTSIDE OCEAN?

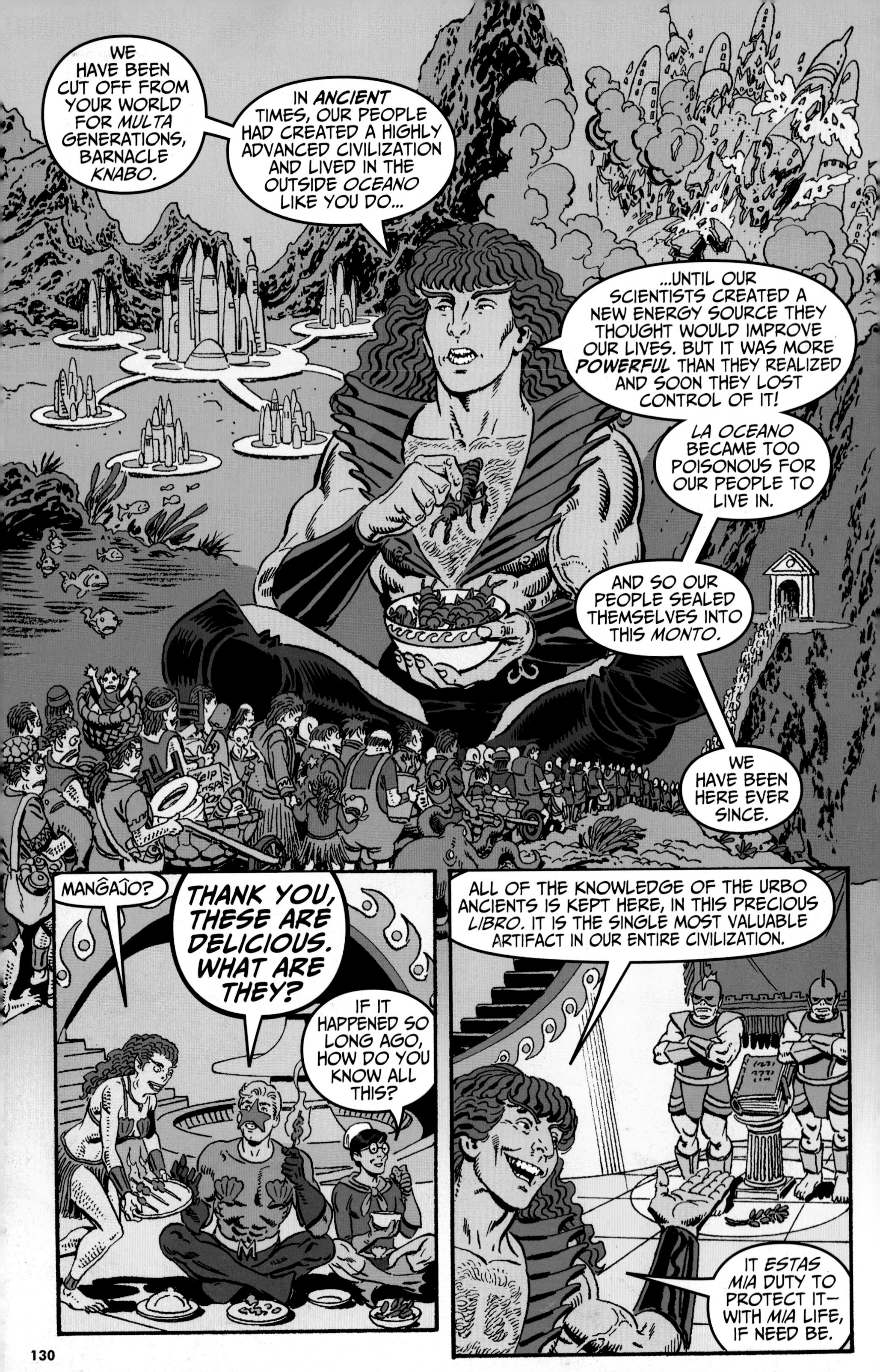
WE HAVE BEEN CUT OFF FROM YOUR WORLD FOR *MULTA* GENERATIONS, BARNACLE *KNABO*.
IN ***ANCIENT*** TIMES, OUR PEOPLE HAD CREATED A HIGHLY ADVANCED CIVILIZATION AND LIVED IN THE OUTSIDE *OCEANO* LIKE YOU DO...
...UNTIL OUR SCIENTISTS CREATED A NEW ENERGY SOURCE THEY THOUGHT WOULD IMPROVE OUR LIVES. BUT IT WAS MORE ***POWERFUL*** THAN THEY REALIZED AND SOON THEY LOST CONTROL OF IT!
LA OCEANO BECAME TOO POISONOUS FOR OUR PEOPLE TO LIVE IN.
AND SO OUR PEOPLE SEALED THEMSELVES INTO THIS *MONTO*.
WE HAVE BEEN HERE EVER SINCE.
MANĜAĴO?
THANK YOU, THESE ARE DELICIOUS. WHAT ARE THEY?
IF IT HAPPENED SO LONG AGO, HOW DO YOU KNOW ALL THIS?
ALL OF THE KNOWLEDGE OF THE URBO ANCIENTS IS KEPT HERE, IN THIS PRECIOUS *LIBRO*. IT IS THE SINGLE MOST VALUABLE ARTIFACT IN OUR ENTIRE CIVILIZATION.
IT *ESTAS MIA* DUTY TO PROTECT IT— WITH *MIA* LIFE, IF NEED BE.

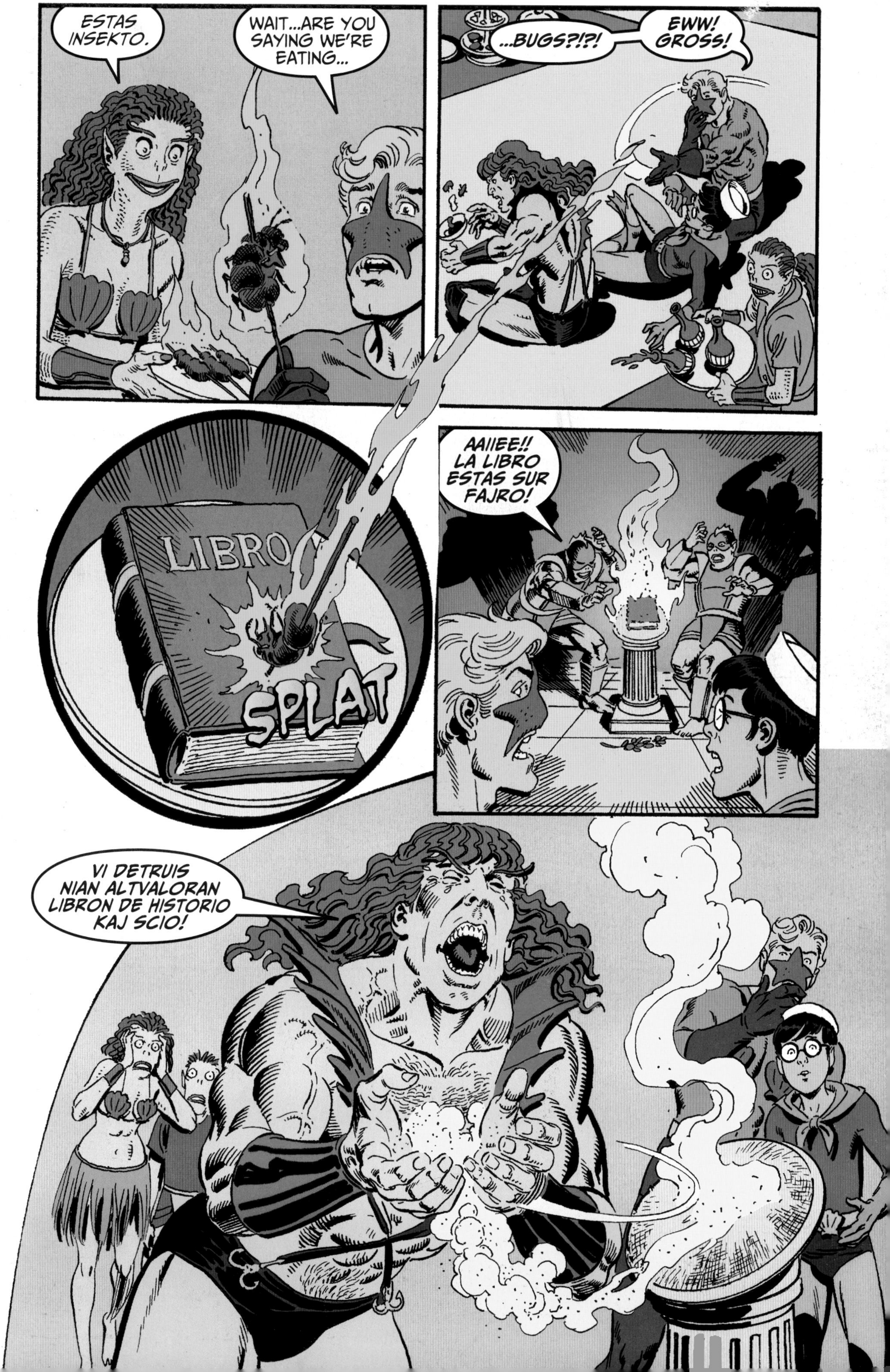
ESTAS INSEKTO.
WAIT...ARE YOU SAYING WE'RE EATING...
...BUGS?!?!
EWW! GROSS!
LIBRO
SPLAT
AAIIEE!! LA LIBRO ESTAS SUR FAJRO!
VI DETRUIS NIAN ALTVALORAN LIBRON DE HISTORIO KAJ SCIO!

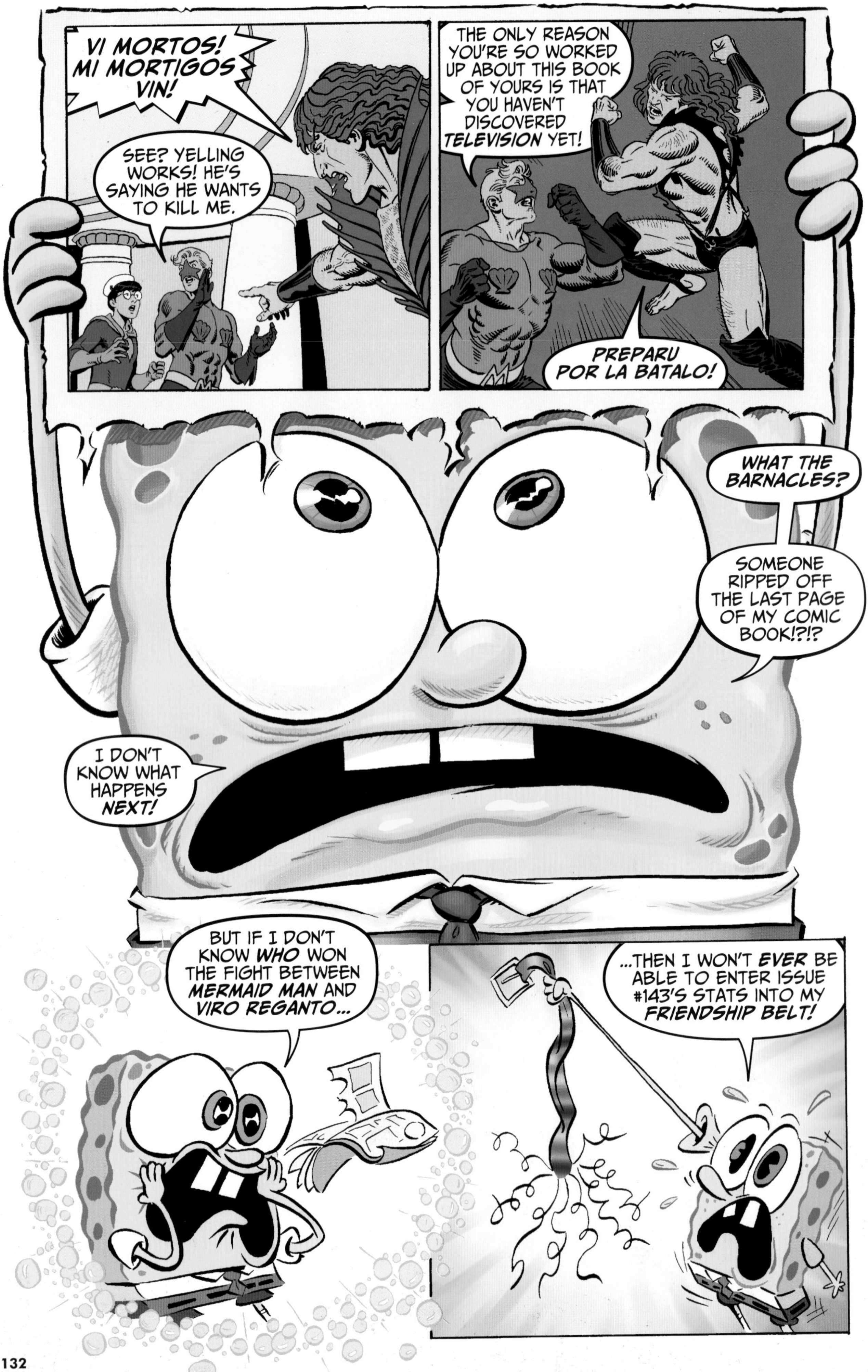
VI MORTOS! MI MORTIGOS VIN!
SEE? YELLING WORKS! HE'S SAYING HE WANTS TO KILL ME.
THE ONLY REASON YOU'RE SO WORKED UP ABOUT THIS BOOK OF YOURS IS THAT YOU HAVEN'T DISCOVERED TELEVISION YET!
PREPARU POR LA BATALO!
WHAT THE BARNACLES?
SOMEONE RIPPED OFF THE LAST PAGE OF MY COMIC BOOK!?!?
I DON'T KNOW WHAT HAPPENS NEXT!
BUT IF I DON'T KNOW WHO WON THE FIGHT BETWEEN MERMAID MAN AND VIRO REGANTO...
...THEN I WON'T EVER BE ABLE TO ENTER ISSUE #143'S STATS INTO MY FRIENDSHIP BELT!

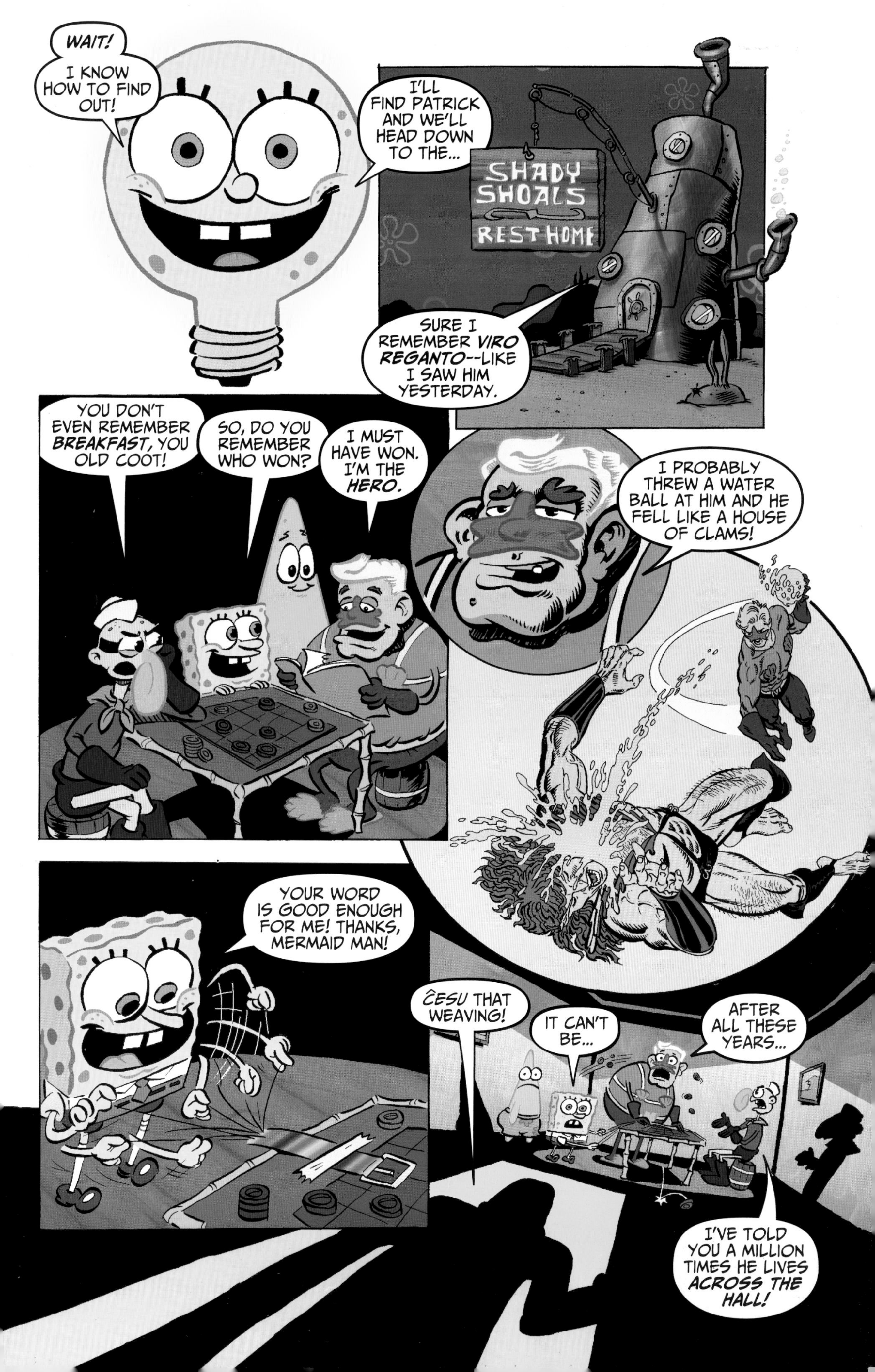
WAIT!
I KNOW HOW TO FIND OUT!
I'LL FIND PATRICK AND WE'LL HEAD DOWN TO THE...
SHADY SHOALS REST HOME
SURE I REMEMBER *VIRO REGANTO*--LIKE I SAW HIM YESTERDAY.
YOU DON'T EVEN REMEMBER *BREAKFAST*, YOU OLD COOT!
SO, DO YOU REMEMBER WHO WON?
I MUST HAVE WON. I'M THE *HERO.*
I PROBABLY THREW A WATER BALL AT HIM AND HE FELL LIKE A HOUSE OF CLAMS!
YOUR WORD IS GOOD ENOUGH FOR ME! THANKS, MERMAID MAN!
ĈESU THAT WEAVING!
IT CAN'T BE...
AFTER ALL THESE YEARS...
I'VE TOLD YOU A MILLION TIMES HE LIVES *ACROSS THE HALL!*

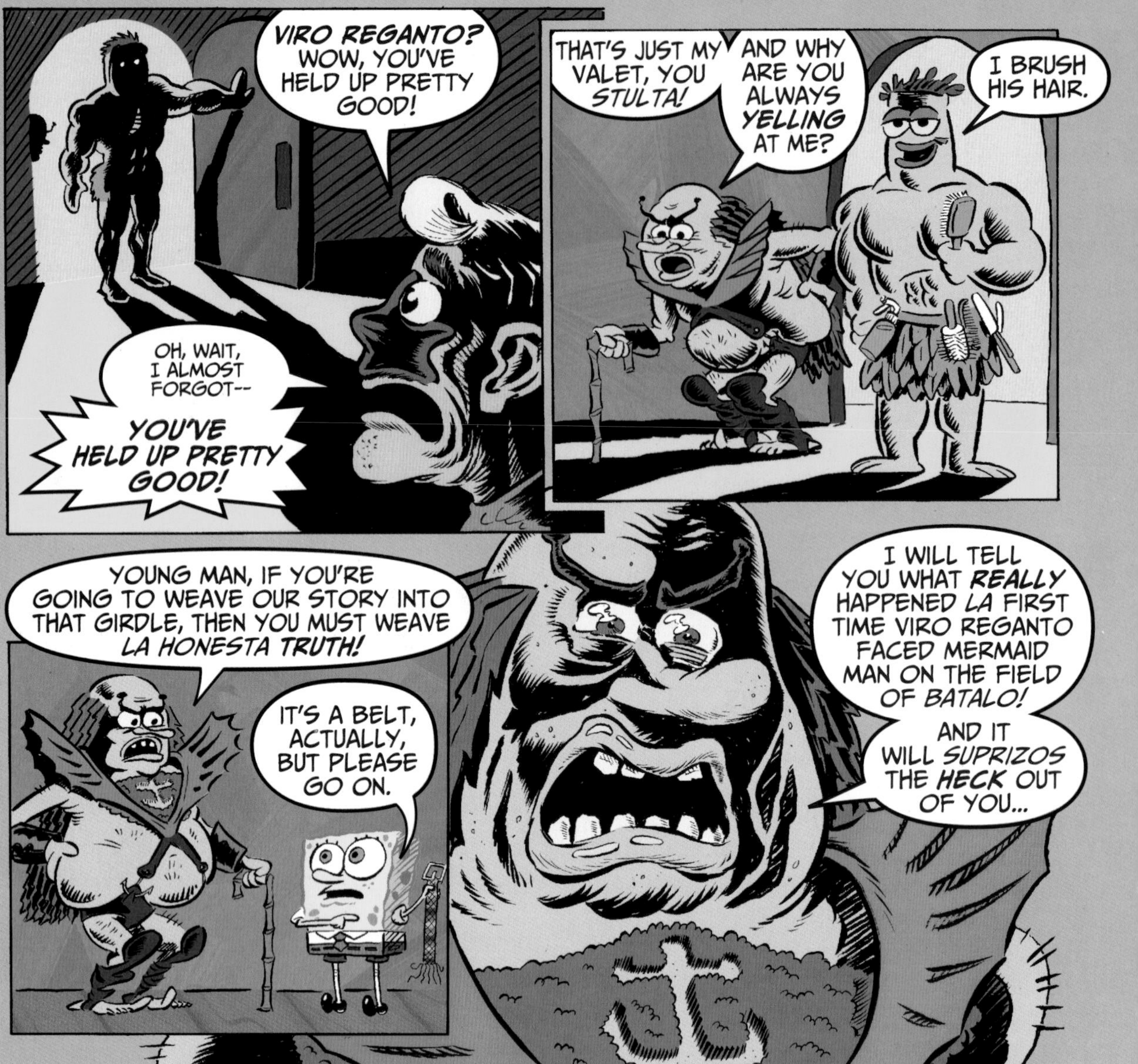
VIRO REGANTO? WOW, YOU'VE HELD UP PRETTY GOOD!
OH, WAIT, I ALMOST FORGOT--
YOU'VE HELD UP PRETTY GOOD!
THAT'S JUST MY VALET, YOU STULTA!
AND WHY ARE YOU ALWAYS YELLING AT ME?
I BRUSH HIS HAIR.
YOUNG MAN, IF YOU'RE GOING TO WEAVE OUR STORY INTO THAT GIRDLE, THEN YOU MUST WEAVE LA HONESTA TRUTH!
IT'S A BELT, ACTUALLY, BUT PLEASE GO ON.
I WILL TELL YOU WHAT REALLY HAPPENED LA FIRST TIME VIRO REGANTO FACED MERMAID MAN ON THE FIELD OF BATALO!
AND IT WILL SUPRIZOS THE HECK OUT OF YOU...

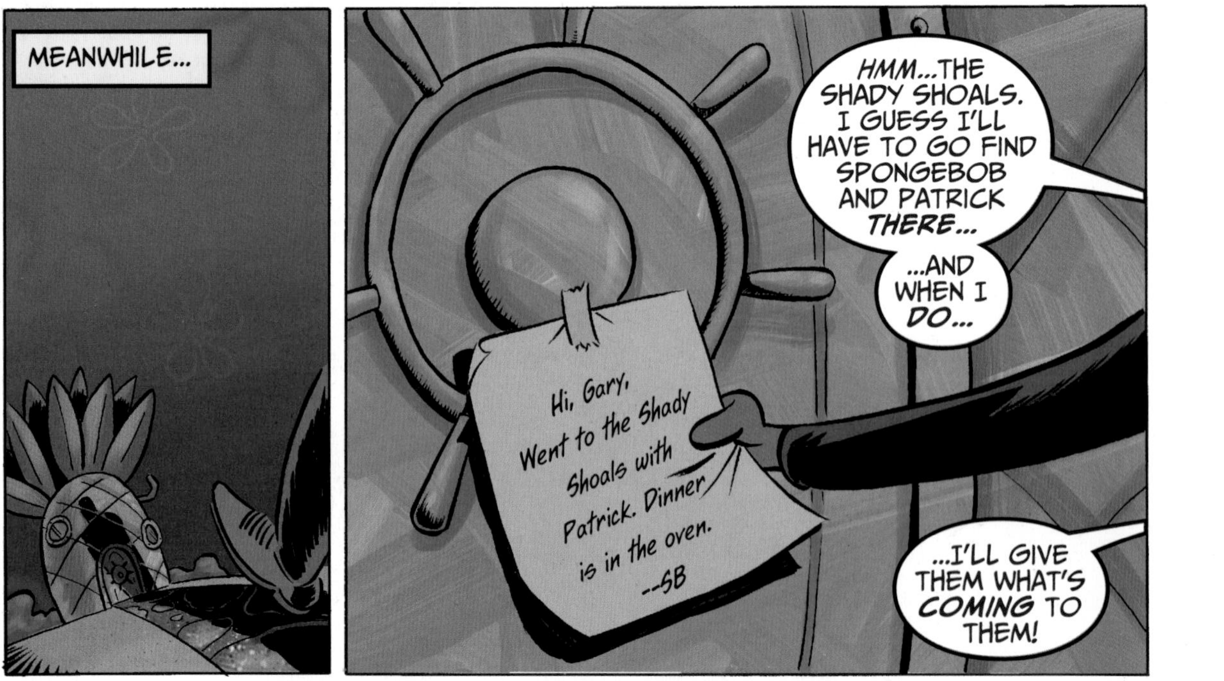
MEANWHILE...
Hi, Gary, Went to the Shady Shoals with Patrick. Dinner is in the oven. --SB
HMM...THE SHADY SHOALS. I GUESS I'LL HAVE TO GO FIND SPONGEBOB AND PATRICK THERE...
...AND WHEN I DO...
...I'LL GIVE THEM WHAT'S COMING TO THEM!

TO BE CONTINUED!!!

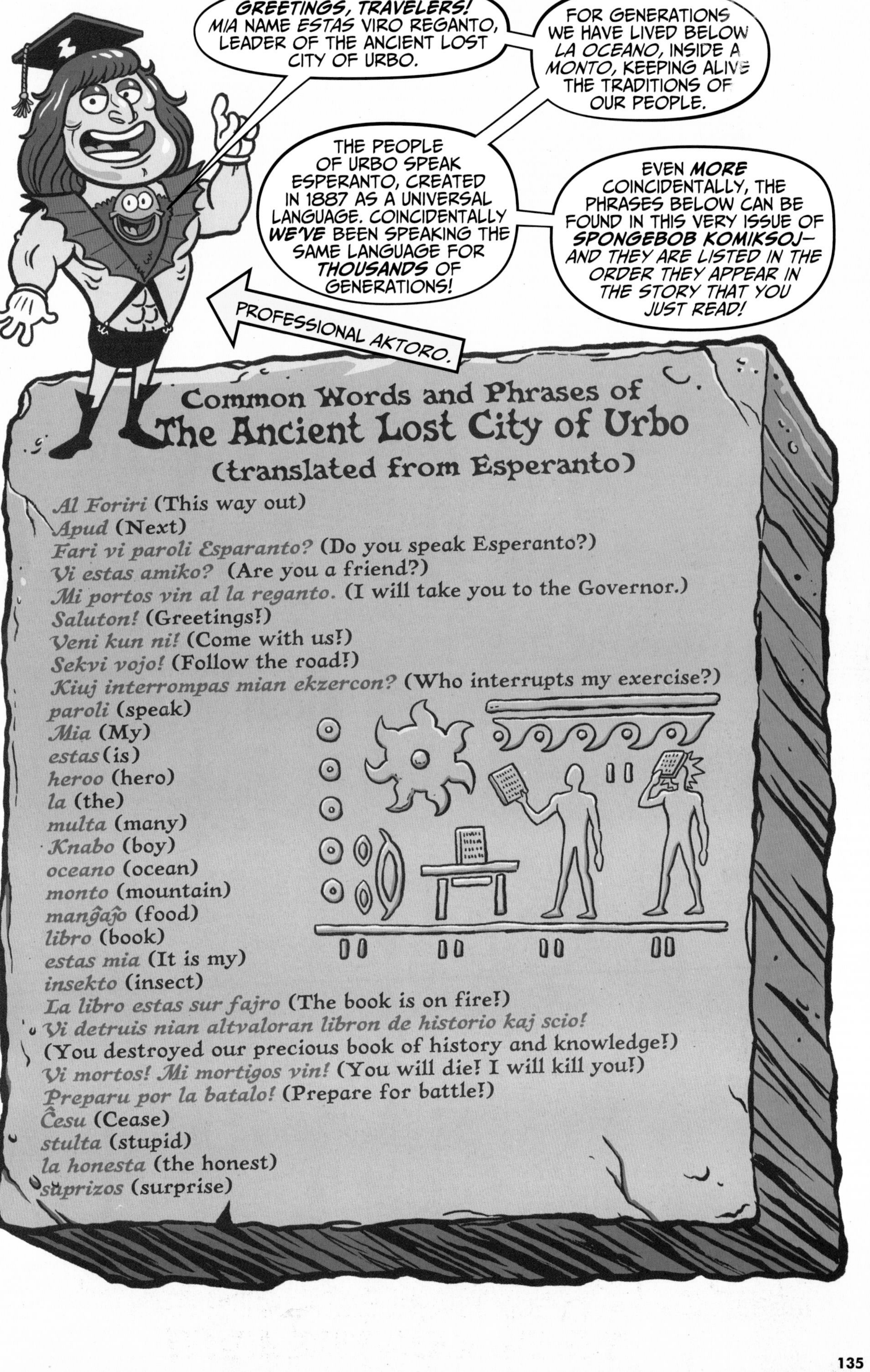
GREETINGS, TRAVELERS! MIA NAME ESTAS VIRO REGANTO, LEADER OF THE ANCIENT LOST CITY OF URBO.
FOR GENERATIONS WE HAVE LIVED BELOW LA OCEANO, INSIDE A MONTO, KEEPING ALIVE THE TRADITIONS OF OUR PEOPLE.
THE PEOPLE OF URBO SPEAK ESPERANTO, CREATED IN 1887 AS A UNIVERSAL LANGUAGE. COINCIDENTALLY WE'VE BEEN SPEAKING THE SAME LANGUAGE FOR THOUSANDS OF GENERATIONS!
EVEN MORE COINCIDENTALLY, THE PHRASES BELOW CAN BE FOUND IN THIS VERY ISSUE OF SPONGEBOB KOMIKSOJ—AND THEY ARE LISTED IN THE ORDER THEY APPEAR IN THE STORY THAT YOU JUST READ!
PROFESSIONAL AKTORO.
Common Words and Phrases of
The Ancient Lost City of Urbo
(translated from Esperanto)
Al Foriri (This way out)
Apud (Next)
Fari vi paroli Esparanto? (Do you speak Esperanto?)
Vi estas amiko? (Are you a friend?)
Mi portos vin al la reganto. (I will take you to the Governor.)
Saluton! (Greetings!)
Veni kun ni! (Come with us!)
Sekvi vojo! (Follow the road!)
Kiuj interrompas mian ekzercon? (Who interrupts my exercise?)
paroli (speak)
Mia (My)
estas (is)
heroo (hero)
la (the)
multa (many)
Knabo (boy)
oceano (ocean)
monto (mountain)
manĝaĵo (food)
libro (book)
estas mia (It is my)
insekto (insect)
La libro estas sur fajro (The book is on fire!)
Vi detruis nian altvaloran libron de historio kaj scio! (You destroyed our precious book of history and knowledge!)
Vi mortos! Mi mortigos vin! (You will die! I will kill you!)
Preparu por la batalo! (Prepare for battle!)
Ĉesu (Cease)
stulta (stupid)
la honesta (the honest)
suprizos (surprise)

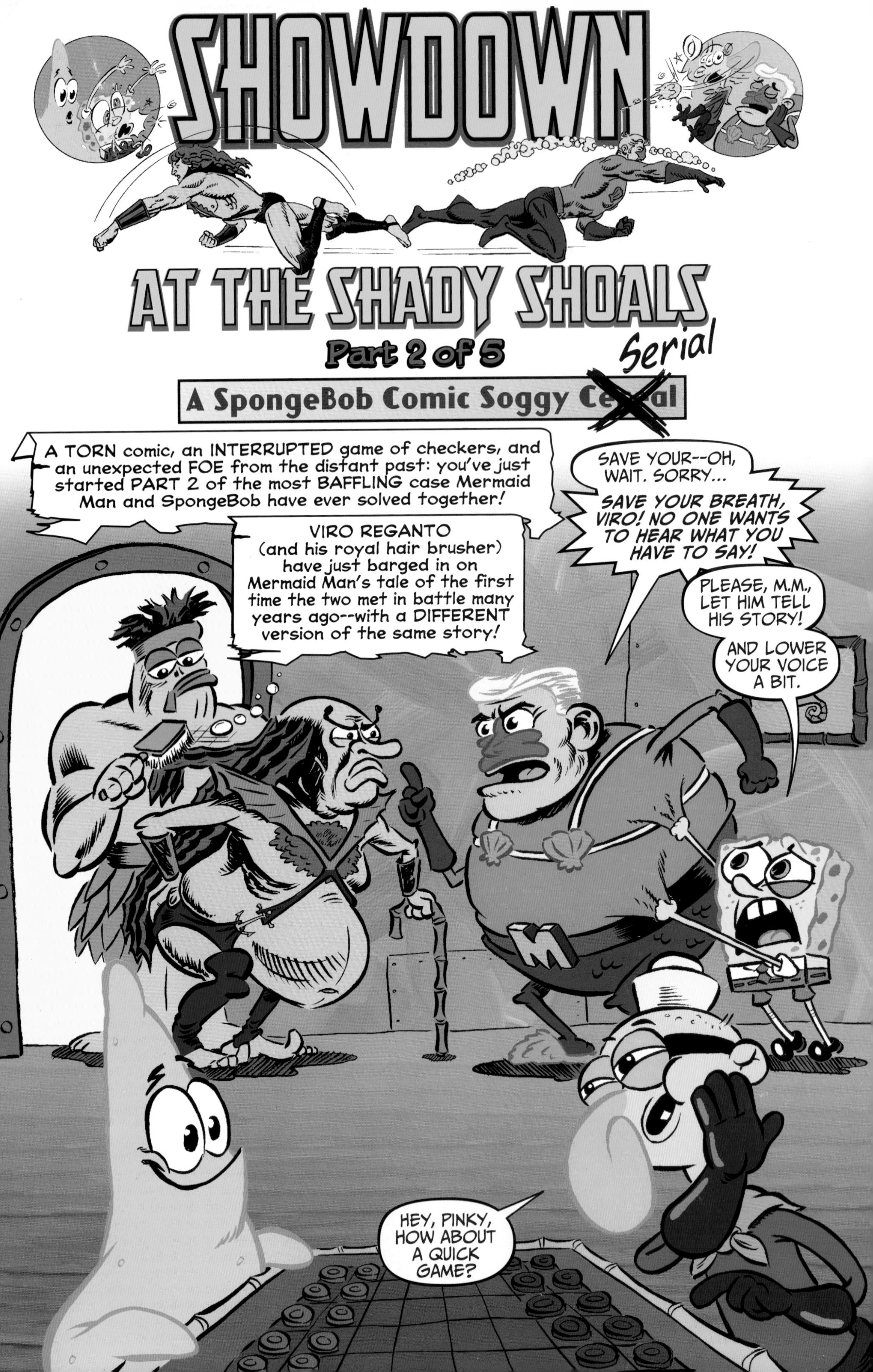
SHOWDOWN
AT THE SHADY SHOALS
Part 2 of 5
A SpongeBob Comic Soggy Cereal Serial
A TORN comic, an INTERRUPTED game of checkers, and an unexpected FOE from the distant past: you've just started PART 2 of the most BAFFLING case Mermaid Man and SpongeBob have ever solved together!
VIRO REGANTO (and his royal hair brusher) have just barged in on Mermaid Man's tale of the first time the two met in battle many years ago--with a DIFFERENT version of the same story!
SAVE YOUR--OH, WAIT. SORRY...
SAVE YOUR BREATH, VIRO! NO ONE WANTS TO HEAR WHAT YOU HAVE TO SAY!
PLEASE, M.M., LET HIM TELL HIS STORY!
AND LOWER YOUR VOICE A BIT.
HEY, PINKY, HOW ABOUT A QUICK GAME?

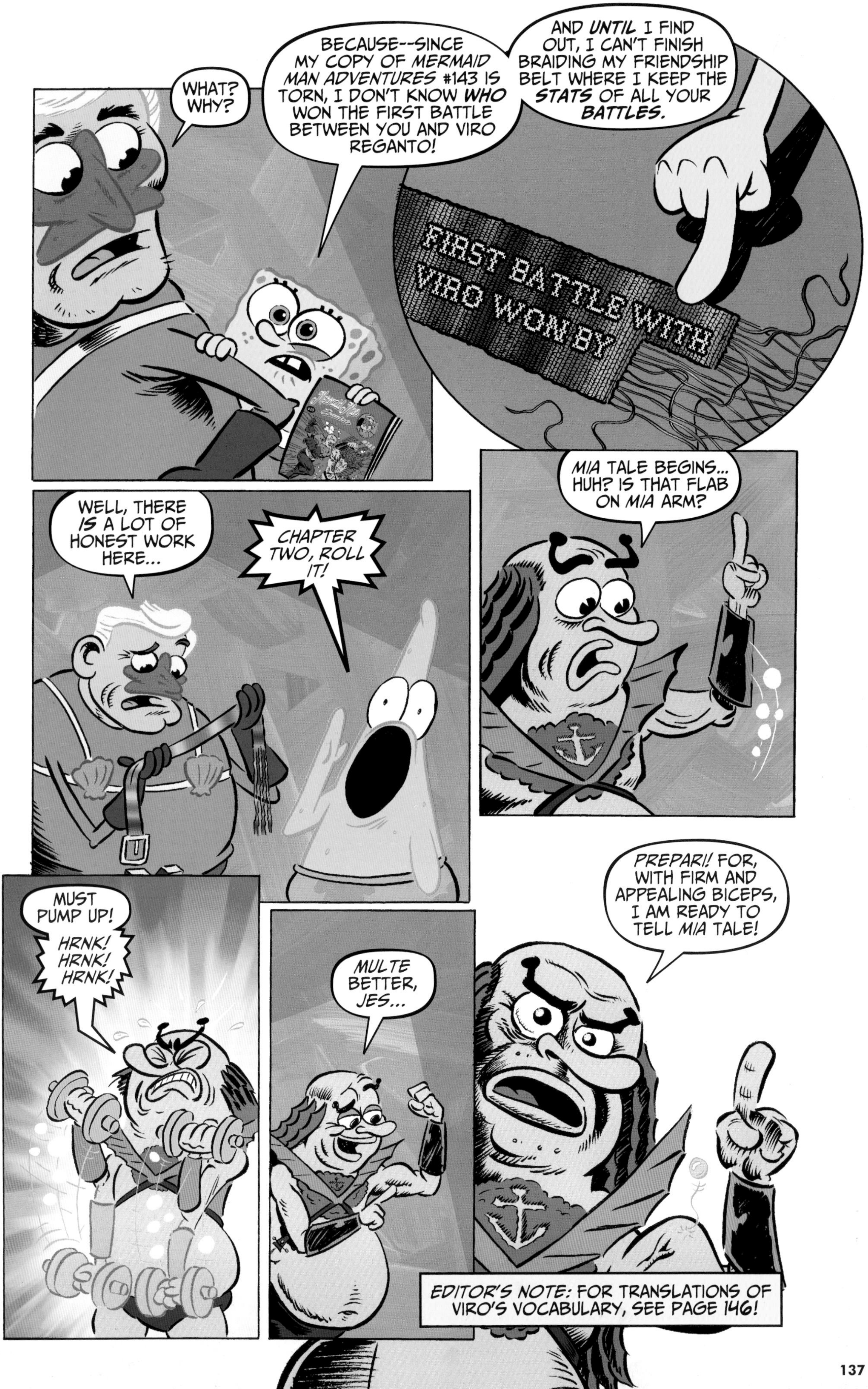
WHAT? WHY?
BECAUSE--SINCE MY COPY OF MERMAID MAN ADVENTURES #143 IS TORN, I DON'T KNOW WHO WON THE FIRST BATTLE BETWEEN YOU AND VIRO REGANTO!
AND UNTIL I FIND OUT, I CAN'T FINISH BRAIDING MY FRIENDSHIP BELT WHERE I KEEP THE STATS OF ALL YOUR BATTLES.
FIRST BATTLE WITH VIRO WON BY
WELL, THERE IS A LOT OF HONEST WORK HERE...
CHAPTER TWO, ROLL IT!
MIA TALE BEGINS... HUH? IS THAT FLAB ON MIA ARM?
MUST PUMP UP!
HRNK! HRNK! HRNK!
MULTE BETTER, JES...
PREPARI! FOR, WITH FIRM AND APPEALING BICEPS, I AM READY TO TELL MIA TALE!
EDITOR'S NOTE: FOR TRANSLATIONS OF VIRO'S VOCABULARY, SEE PAGE 146!

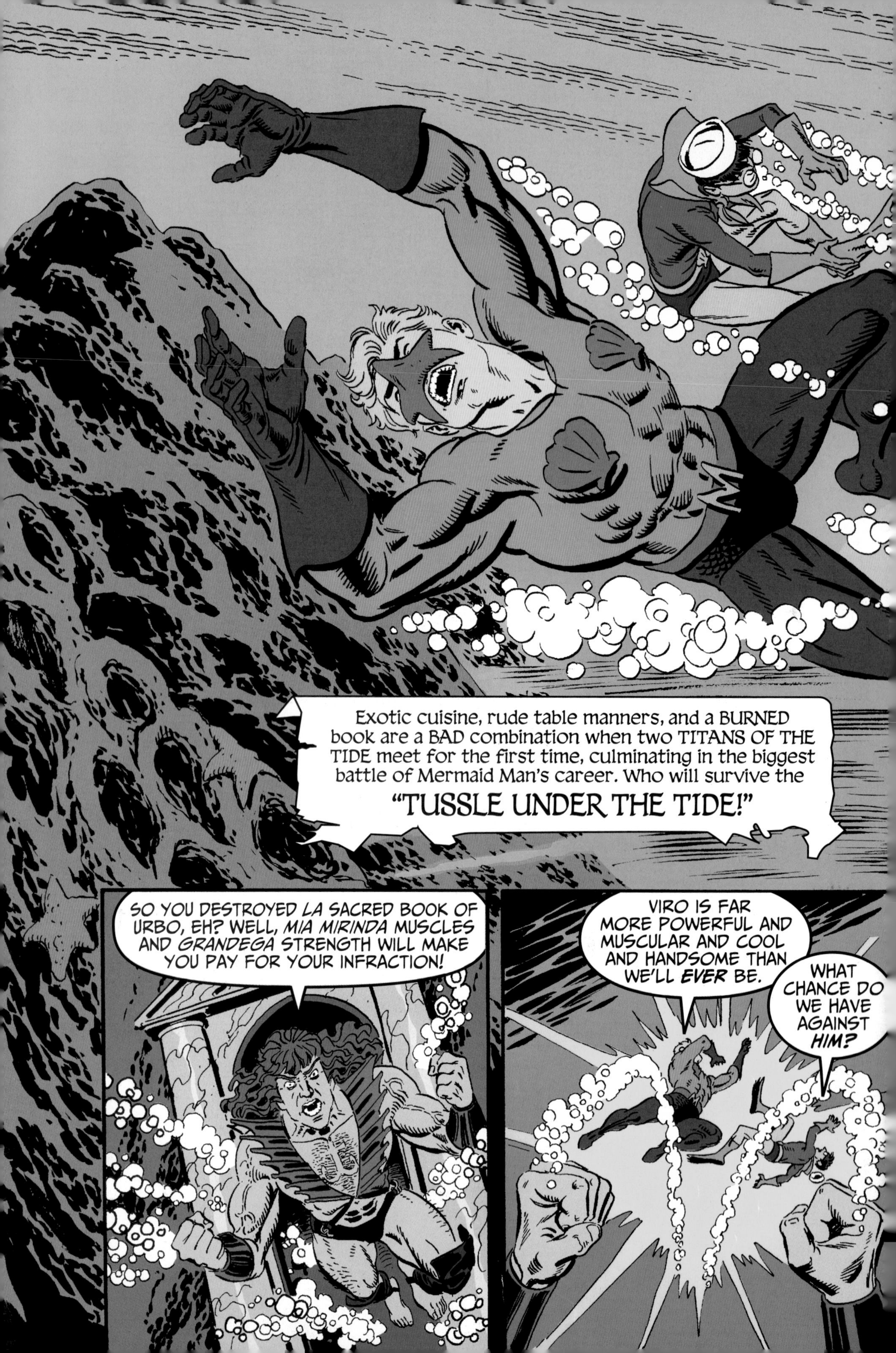

Exotic cuisine, rude table manners, and a BURNED book are a BAD combination when two TITANS OF THE TIDE meet for the first time, culminating in the biggest battle of Mermaid Man's career. Who will survive the
"TUSSLE UNDER THE TIDE!"
SO YOU DESTROYED LA SACRED BOOK OF URBO, EH? WELL, MIA MIRINDA MUSCLES AND GRANDEGA STRENGTH WILL MAKE YOU PAY FOR YOUR INFRACTION!
VIRO IS FAR MORE POWERFUL AND MUSCULAR AND COOL AND HANDSOME THAN WE'LL EVER BE.
WHAT CHANCE DO WE HAVE AGAINST HIM?

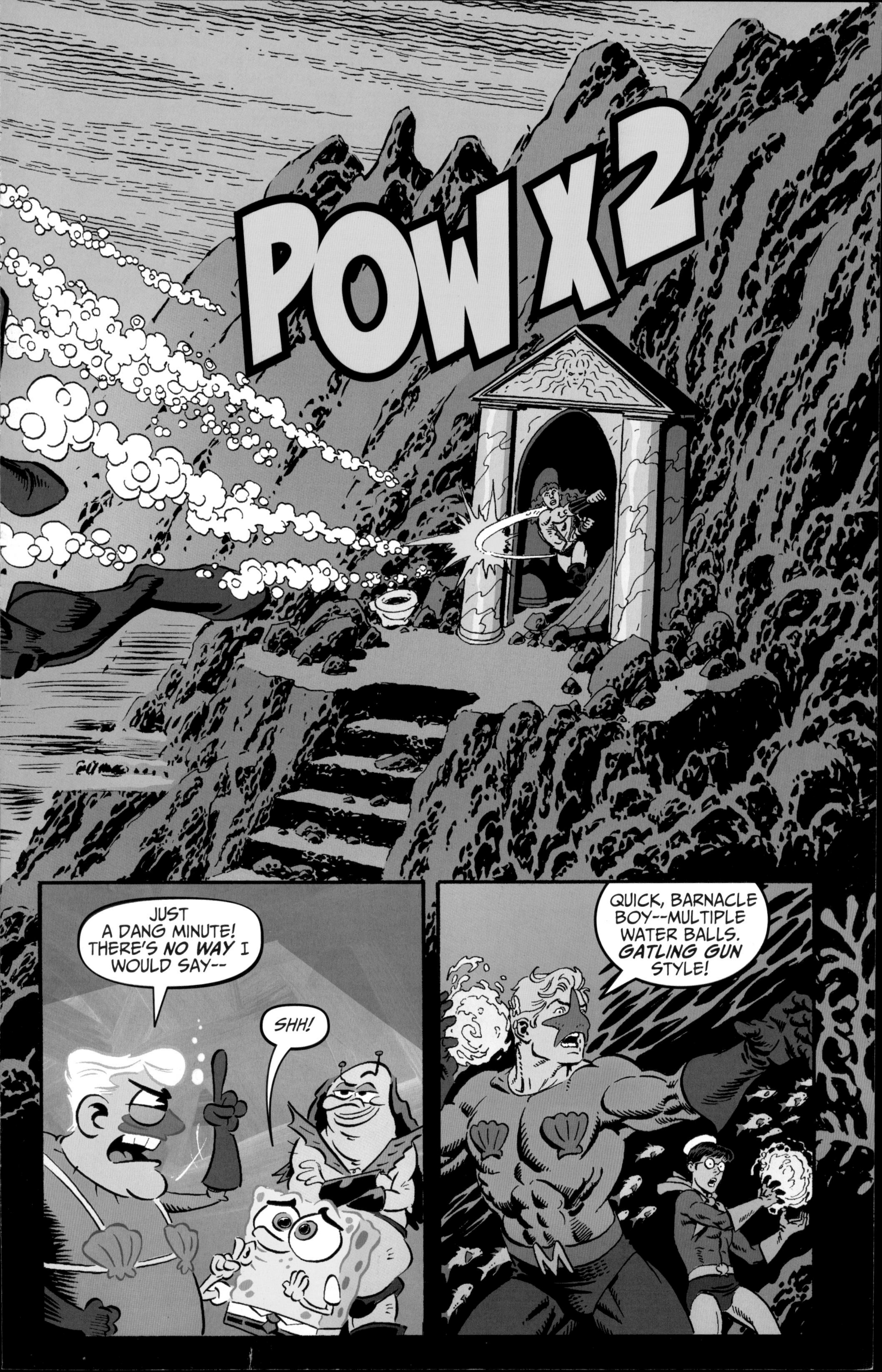
POW X 2
JUST A DANG MINUTE! THERE'S NO WAY I WOULD SAY--
SHH!
QUICK, BARNACLE BOY--MULTIPLE WATER BALLS. GATLING GUN STYLE!

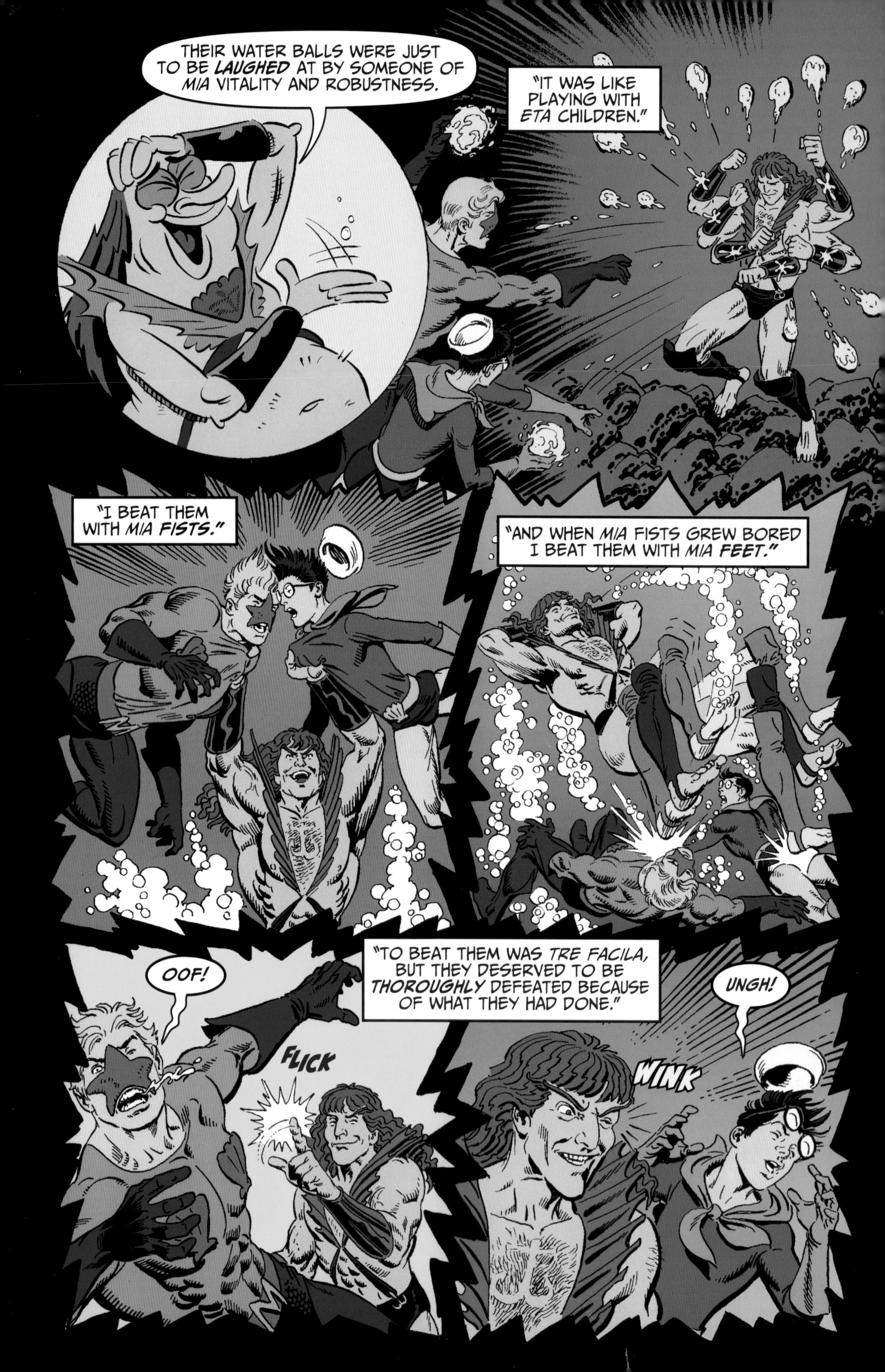
THEIR WATER BALLS WERE JUST TO BE LAUGHED AT BY SOMEONE OF MIA VITALITY AND ROBUSTNESS.
"IT WAS LIKE PLAYING WITH ETA CHILDREN."
"I BEAT THEM WITH MIA FISTS."
"AND WHEN MIA FISTS GREW BORED I BEAT THEM WITH MIA FEET."
OOF!
"TO BEAT THEM WAS TRE FACILA, BUT THEY DESERVED TO BE THOROUGHLY DEFEATED BECAUSE OF WHAT THEY HAD DONE."
UNGH!
FLICK
WINK

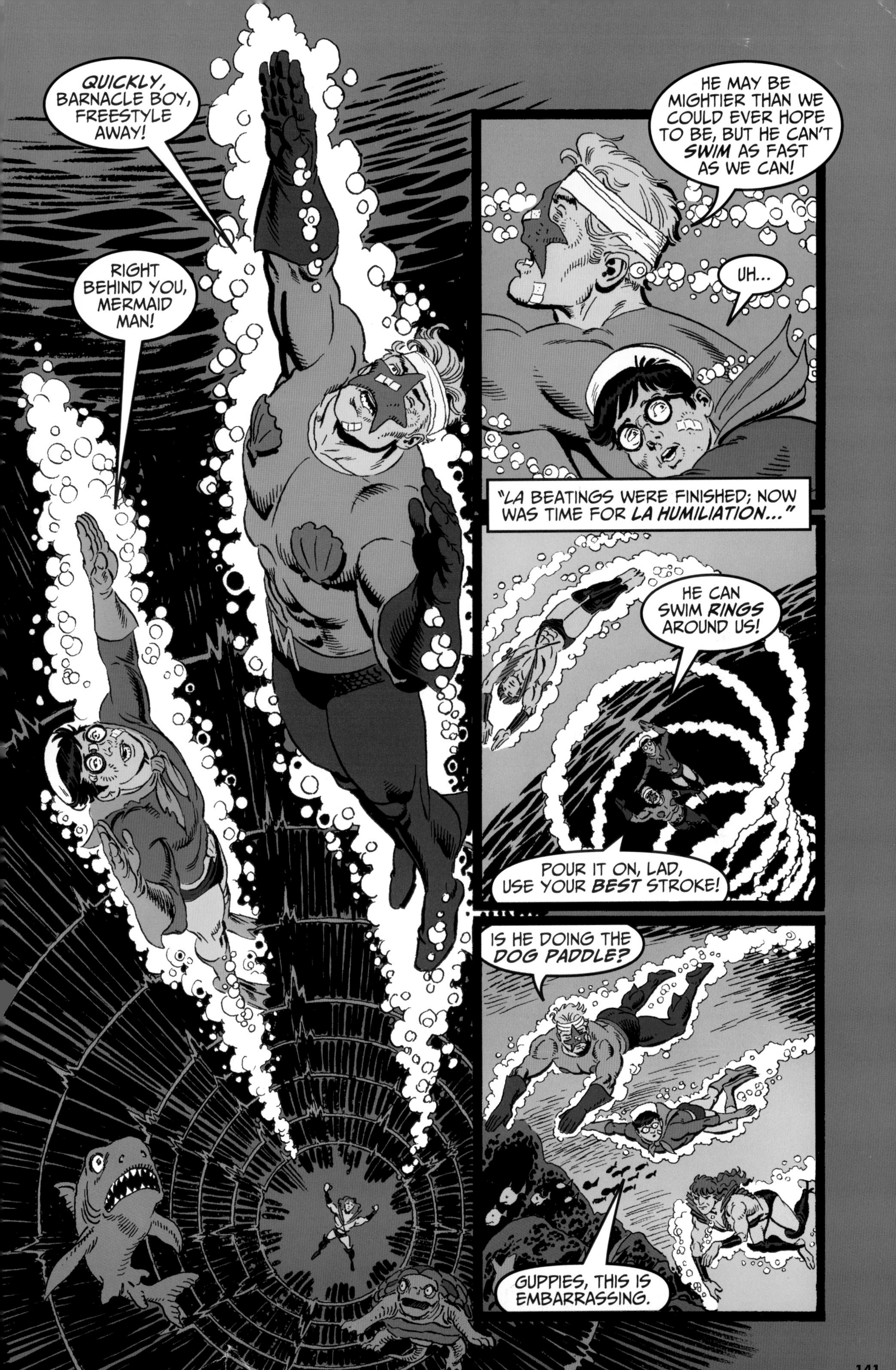
QUICKLY, BARNACLE BOY, FREESTYLE AWAY!
RIGHT BEHIND YOU, MERMAID MAN!
HE MAY BE MIGHTIER THAN WE COULD EVER HOPE TO BE, BUT HE CAN'T SWIM AS FAST AS WE CAN!
UH...
"LA BEATINGS WERE FINISHED; NOW WAS TIME FOR LA HUMILIATION..."
HE CAN SWIM RINGS AROUND US!
POUR IT ON, LAD, USE YOUR BEST STROKE!
IS HE DOING THE DOG PADDLE?
GUPPIES, THIS IS EMBARRASSING.

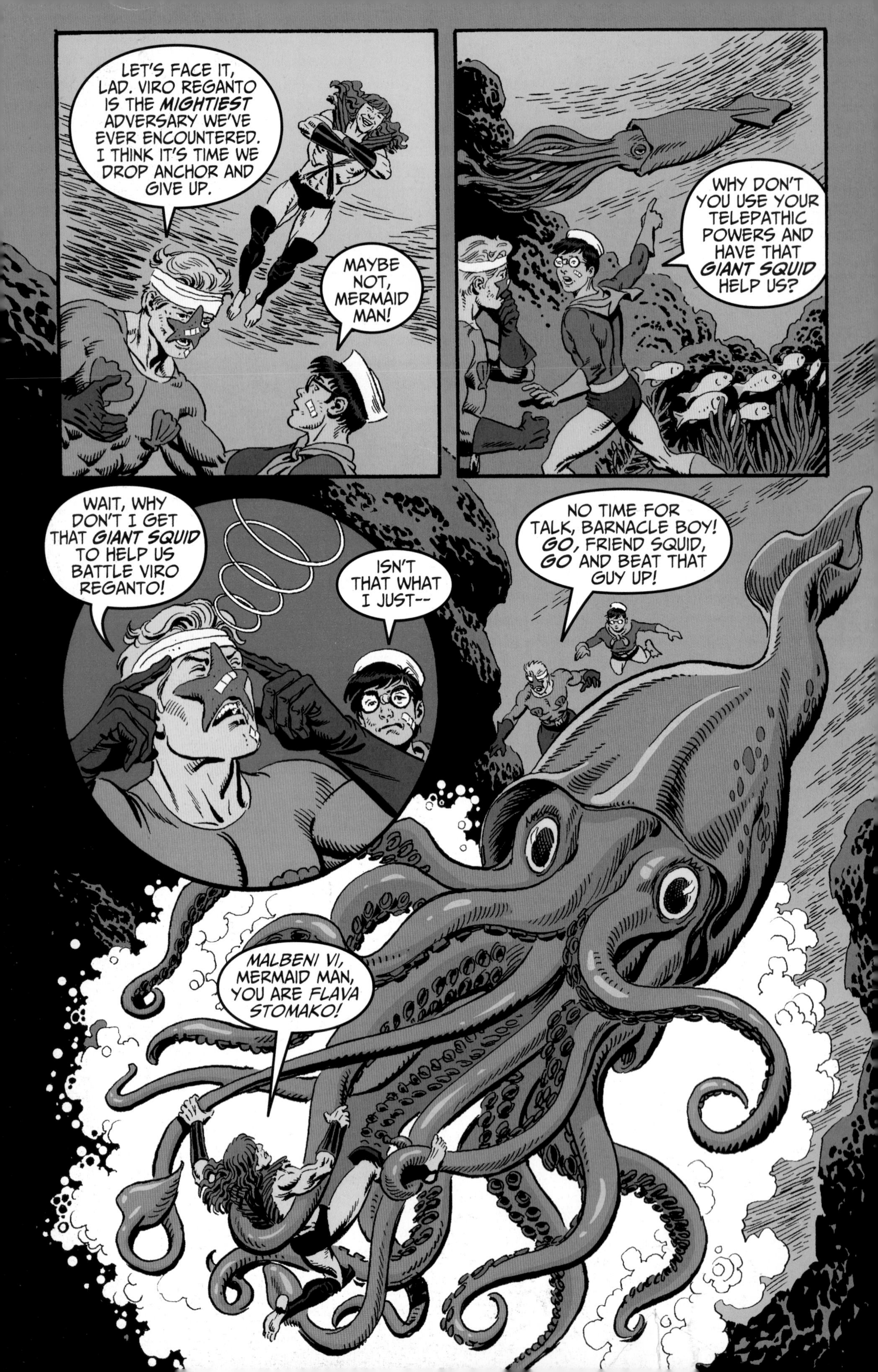
LET'S FACE IT, LAD. VIRO REGANTO IS THE MIGHTIEST ADVERSARY WE'VE EVER ENCOUNTERED. I THINK IT'S TIME WE DROP ANCHOR AND GIVE UP.
MAYBE NOT, MERMAID MAN!
WHY DON'T YOU USE YOUR TELEPATHIC POWERS AND HAVE THAT GIANT SQUID HELP US?
WAIT, WHY DON'T I GET THAT GIANT SQUID TO HELP US BATTLE VIRO REGANTO!
ISN'T THAT WHAT I JUST--
NO TIME FOR TALK, BARNACLE BOY! GO, FRIEND SQUID, GO AND BEAT THAT GUY UP!
MALBENI VI, MERMAID MAN, YOU ARE FLAVA STOMAKO!

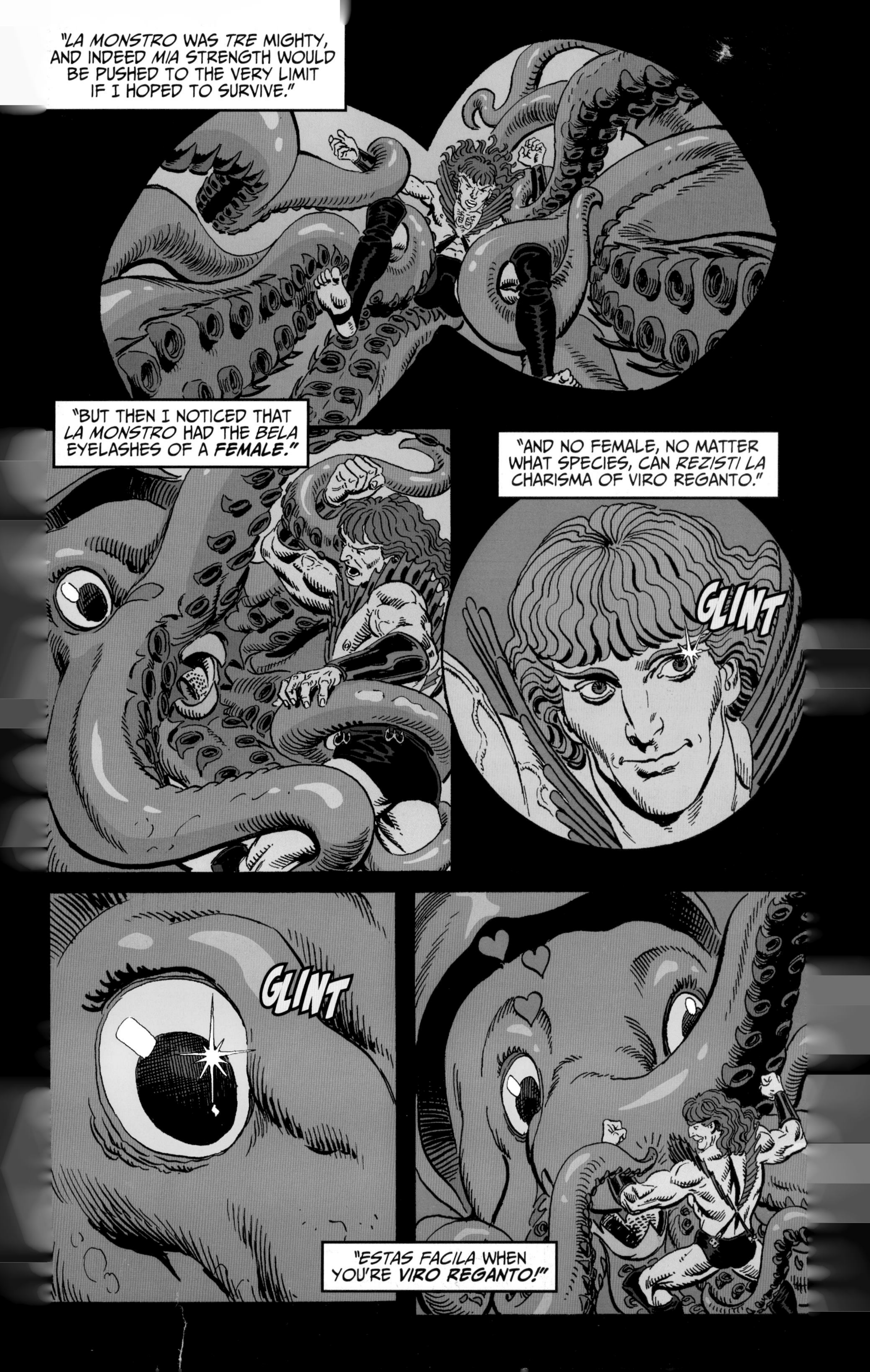
"LA MONSTRO WAS TRE MIGHTY, AND INDEED MIA STRENGTH WOULD BE PUSHED TO THE VERY LIMIT IF I HOPED TO SURVIVE."
"BUT THEN I NOTICED THAT LA MONSTRO HAD THE BELA EYELASHES OF A FEMALE."
"AND NO FEMALE, NO MATTER WHAT SPECIES, CAN REZISTI LA CHARISMA OF VIRO REGANTO."
GLINT
GLINT
"ESTAS FACILA WHEN YOU'RE VIRO REGANTO!"

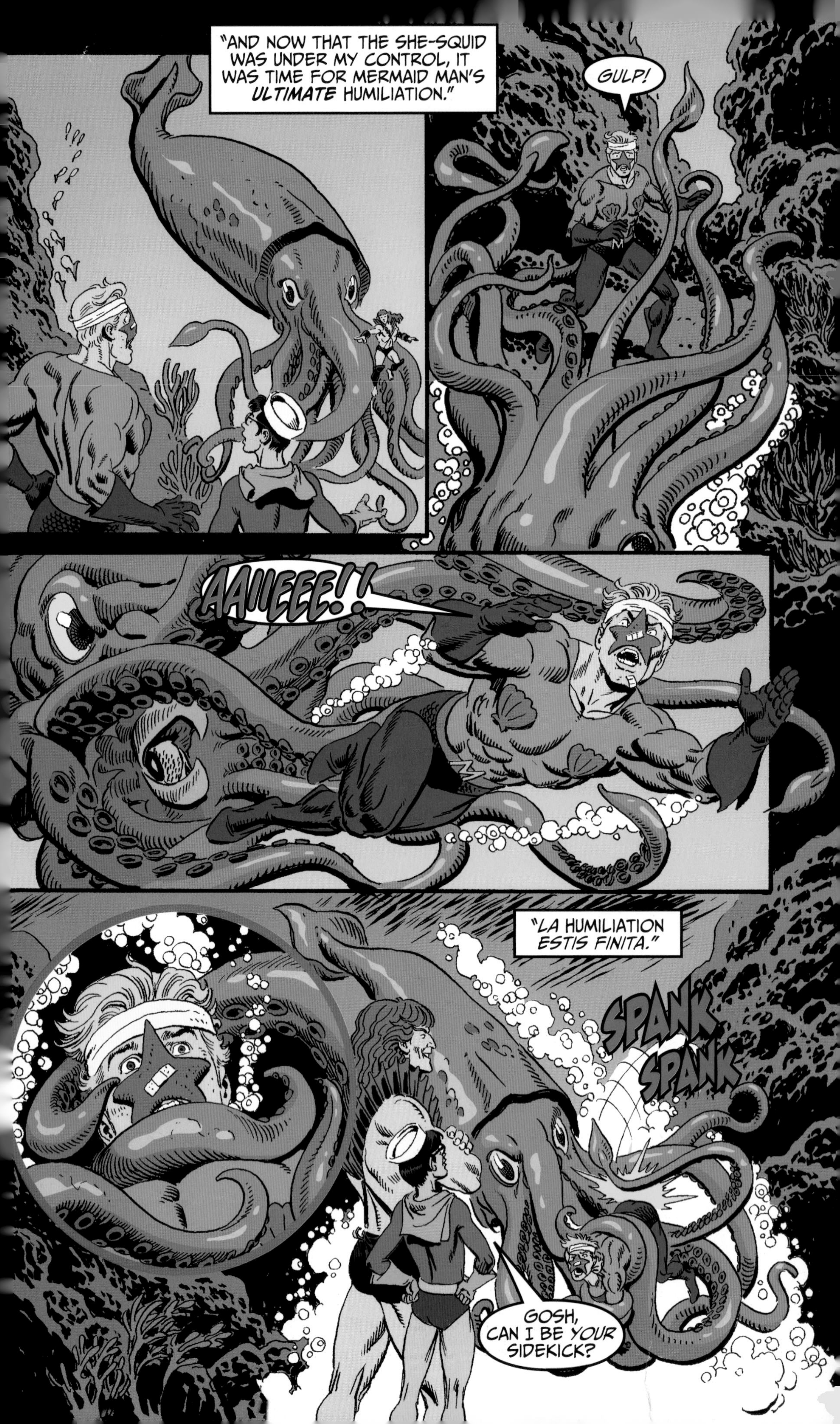
"AND NOW THAT THE SHE-SQUID WAS UNDER MY CONTROL, IT WAS TIME FOR MERMAID MAN'S ULTIMATE HUMILIATION."
GULP!
AAIIEEEE!!
"LA HUMILIATION ESTIS FINITA."
SPANK
SPANK
GOSH, CAN I BE YOUR SIDEKICK?

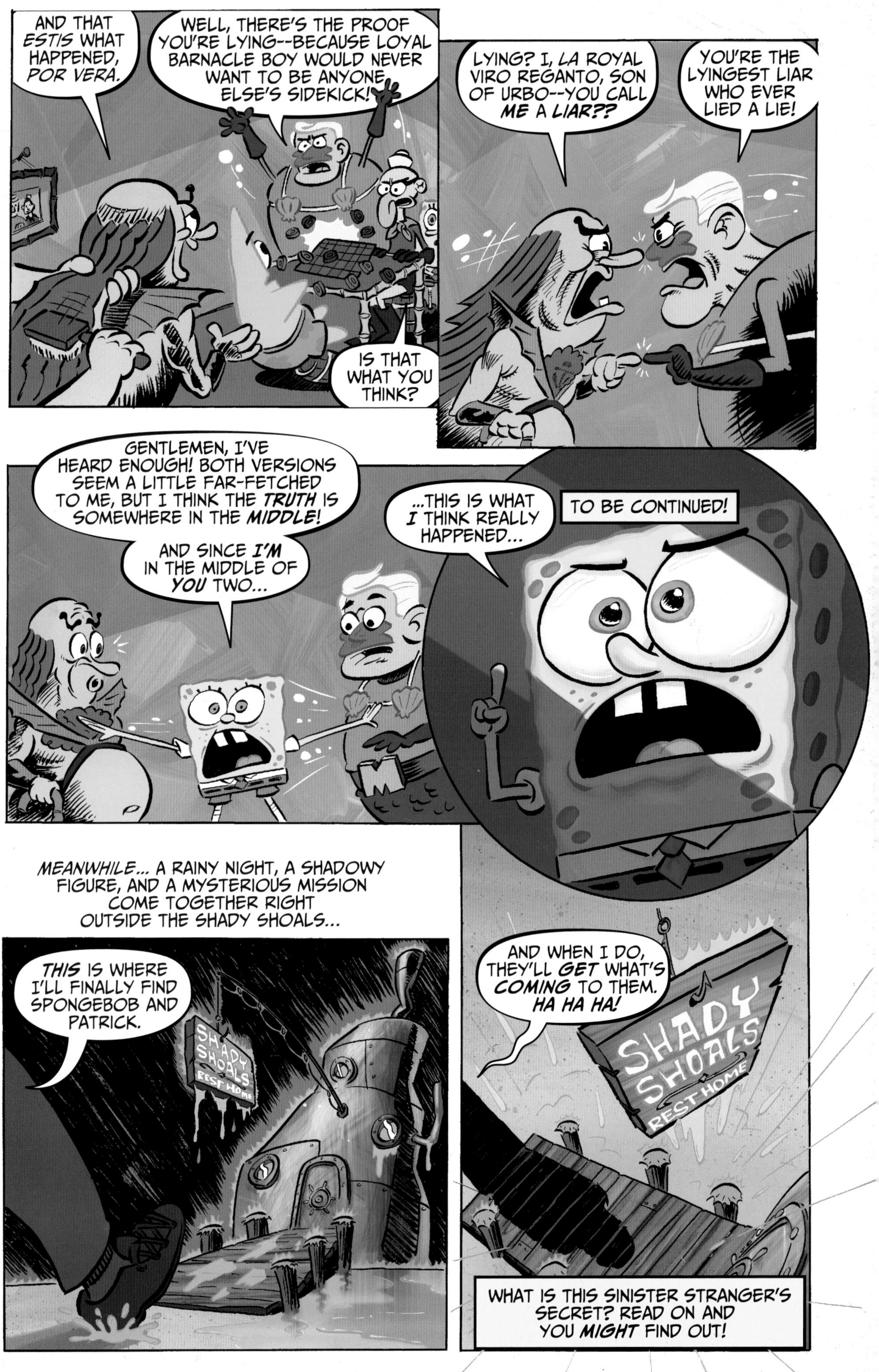
AND THAT ESTIS WHAT HAPPENED, POR VERA.
WELL, THERE'S THE PROOF YOU'RE LYING--BECAUSE LOYAL BARNACLE BOY WOULD NEVER WANT TO BE ANYONE ELSE'S SIDEKICK!
IS THAT WHAT YOU THINK?
LYING? I, LA ROYAL VIRO REGANTO, SON OF URBO--YOU CALL ME A LIAR??
YOU'RE THE LYINGEST LIAR WHO EVER LIED A LIE!
GENTLEMEN, I'VE HEARD ENOUGH! BOTH VERSIONS SEEM A LITTLE FAR-FETCHED TO ME, BUT I THINK THE TRUTH IS SOMEWHERE IN THE MIDDLE!
AND SINCE I'M IN THE MIDDLE OF YOU TWO...
...THIS IS WHAT I THINK REALLY HAPPENED...
TO BE CONTINUED!
MEANWHILE... A RAINY NIGHT, A SHADOWY FIGURE, AND A MYSTERIOUS MISSION COME TOGETHER RIGHT OUTSIDE THE SHADY SHOALS...
THIS IS WHERE I'LL FINALLY FIND SPONGEBOB AND PATRICK.
SHADY SHOALS REST HOME
AND WHEN I DO, THEY'LL GET WHAT'S COMING TO THEM. HA HA HA!
SHADY SHOALS REST HOME
WHAT IS THIS SINISTER STRANGER'S SECRET? READ ON AND YOU MIGHT FIND OUT!

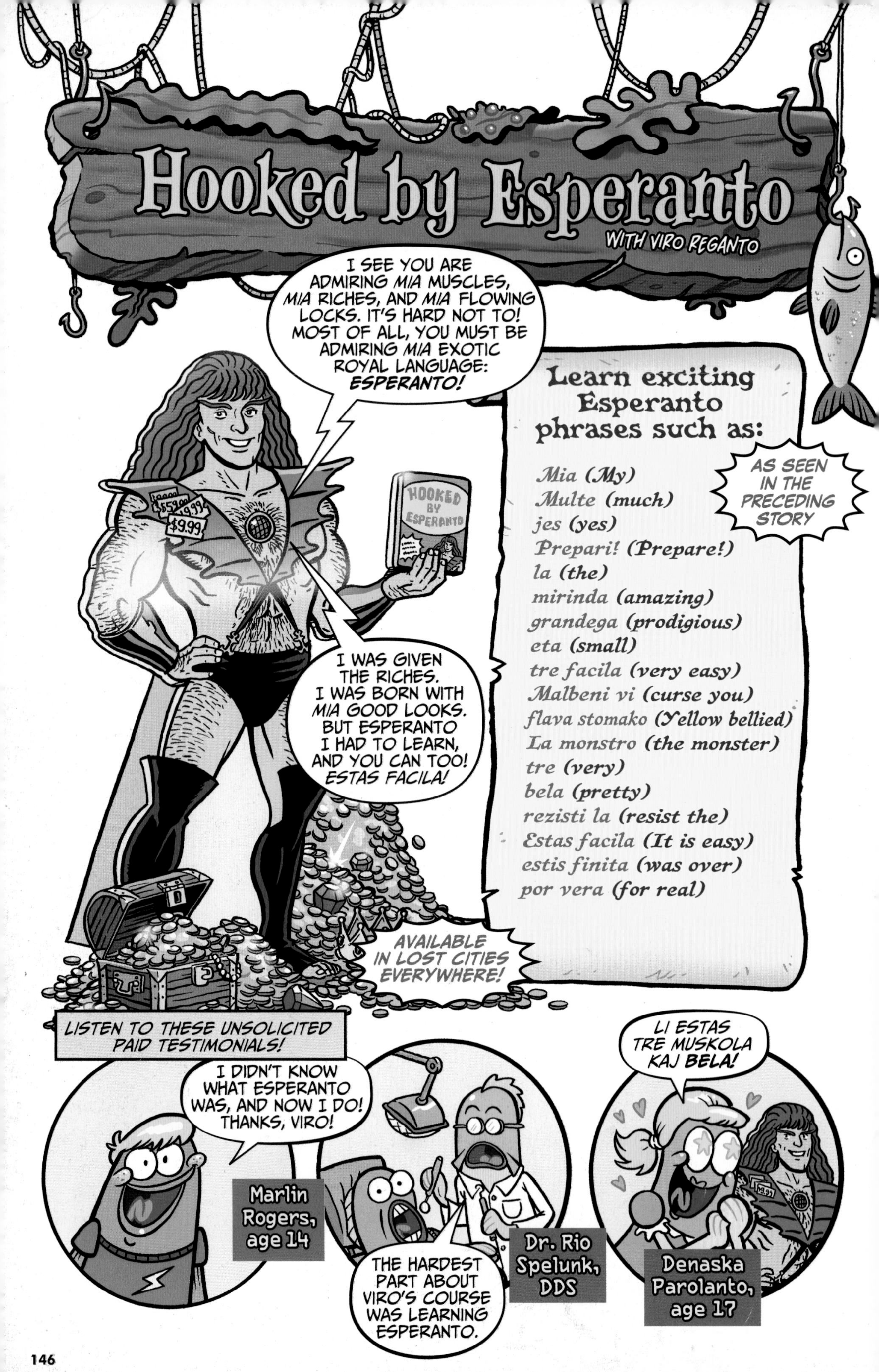
Hooked by Esperanto
WITH VIRO REGANTO
I SEE YOU ARE ADMIRING MIA MUSCLES, MIA RICHES, AND MIA FLOWING LOCKS. IT'S HARD NOT TO! MOST OF ALL, YOU MUST BE ADMIRING MIA EXOTIC ROYAL LANGUAGE: ESPERANTO!
Learn exciting Esperanto phrases such as:
AS SEEN IN THE PRECEDING STORY
Mia (My)
Multe (much)
jes (yes)
Prepari! (Prepare!)
la (the)
mirinda (amazing)
grandega (prodigious)
eta (small)
tre facila (very easy)
Malbeni vi (curse you)
flava stomako (Yellow bellied)
La monstro (the monster)
tre (very)
bela (pretty)
rezisti la (resist the)
Estas facila (It is easy)
estis finita (was over)
por vera (for real)
HOOKED BY ESPERANTO
$9.99
I WAS GIVEN THE RICHES. I WAS BORN WITH MIA GOOD LOOKS. BUT ESPERANTO I HAD TO LEARN, AND YOU CAN TOO! ESTAS FACILA!
AVAILABLE IN LOST CITIES EVERYWHERE!
LISTEN TO THESE UNSOLICITED PAID TESTIMONIALS!
I DIDN'T KNOW WHAT ESPERANTO WAS, AND NOW I DO! THANKS, VIRO!
Marlin Rogers, age 14
THE HARDEST PART ABOUT VIRO'S COURSE WAS LEARNING ESPERANTO.
Dr. Rio Spelunk, DDS
LI ESTAS TRE MUSKOLA KAJ BELA!
Denaska Parolanto, age 17

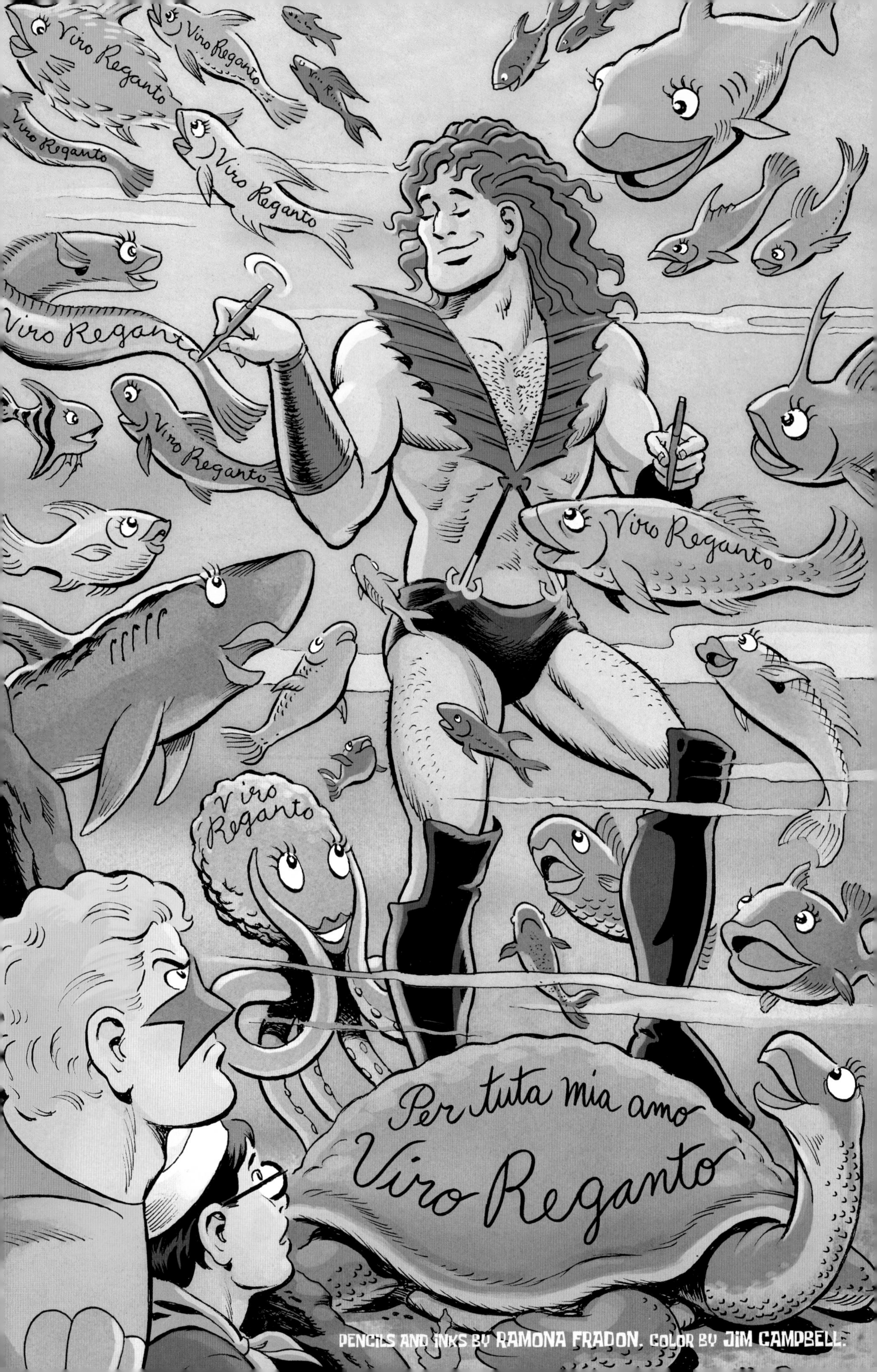
Viro Reganto
Viro Reganto
Viro Reganto
V. R.
Viro Reganto
Viro Reganto
Viro Reganto
Viro Reganto
Viro Reganto
Per tuta mia amo
Viro Reganto
PENCILS AND INKS BY RAMONA FRADON. COLOR BY JIM CAMPBELL.

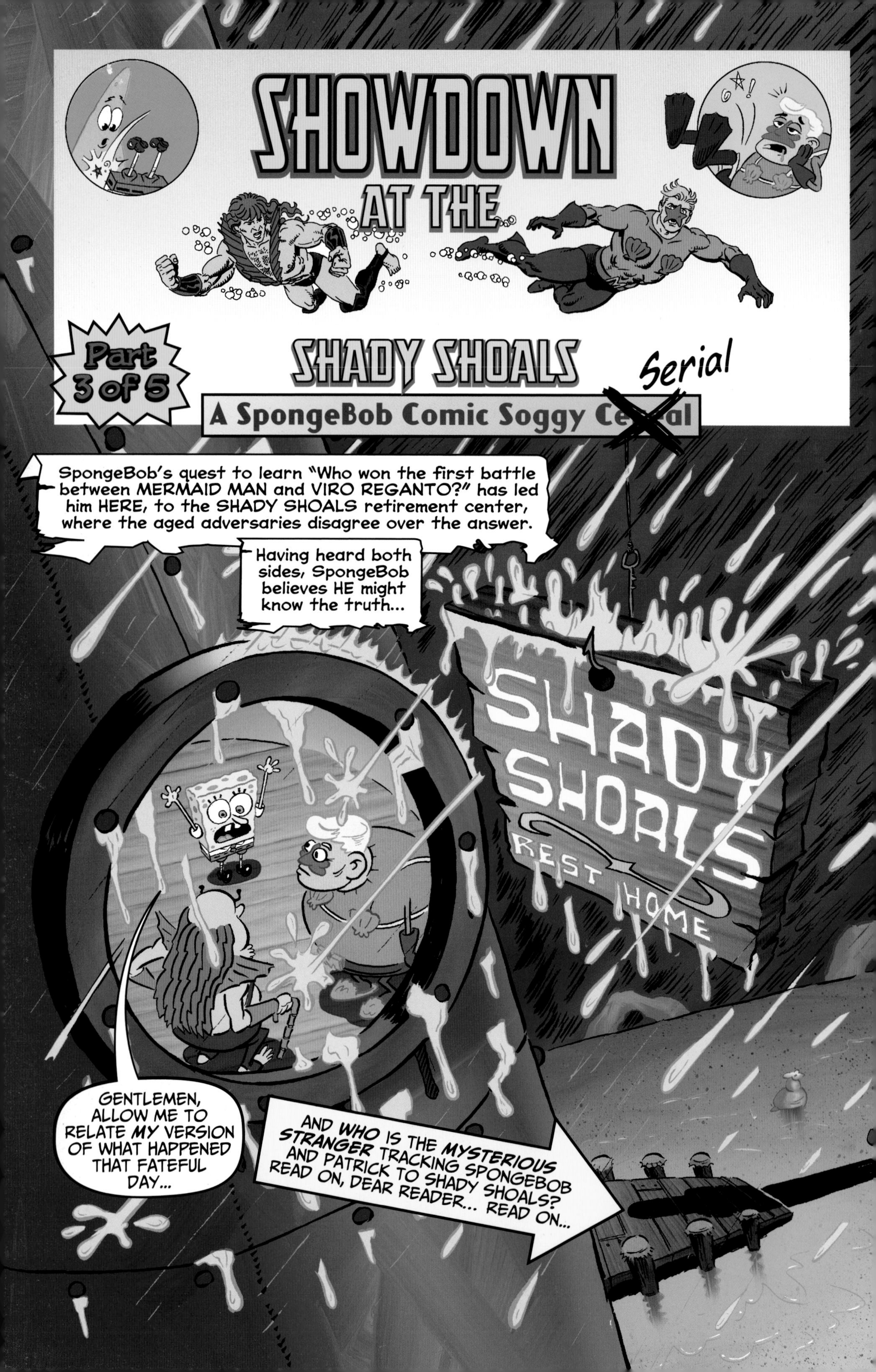
SHOWDOWN
AT THE
SHADY SHOALS
Part 3 of 5
A SpongeBob Comic Soggy Cereal
Serial
SpongeBob's quest to learn "Who won the first battle between MERMAID MAN and VIRO REGANTO?" has led him HERE, to the SHADY SHOALS retirement center, where the aged adversaries disagree over the answer.
Having heard both sides, SpongeBob believes HE might know the truth...
SHADY SHOALS REST HOME
GENTLEMEN, ALLOW ME TO RELATE MY VERSION OF WHAT HAPPENED THAT FATEFUL DAY...
AND WHO IS THE MYSTERIOUS STRANGER TRACKING SPONGEBOB AND PATRICK TO SHADY SHOALS? READ ON, DEAR READER... READ ON...

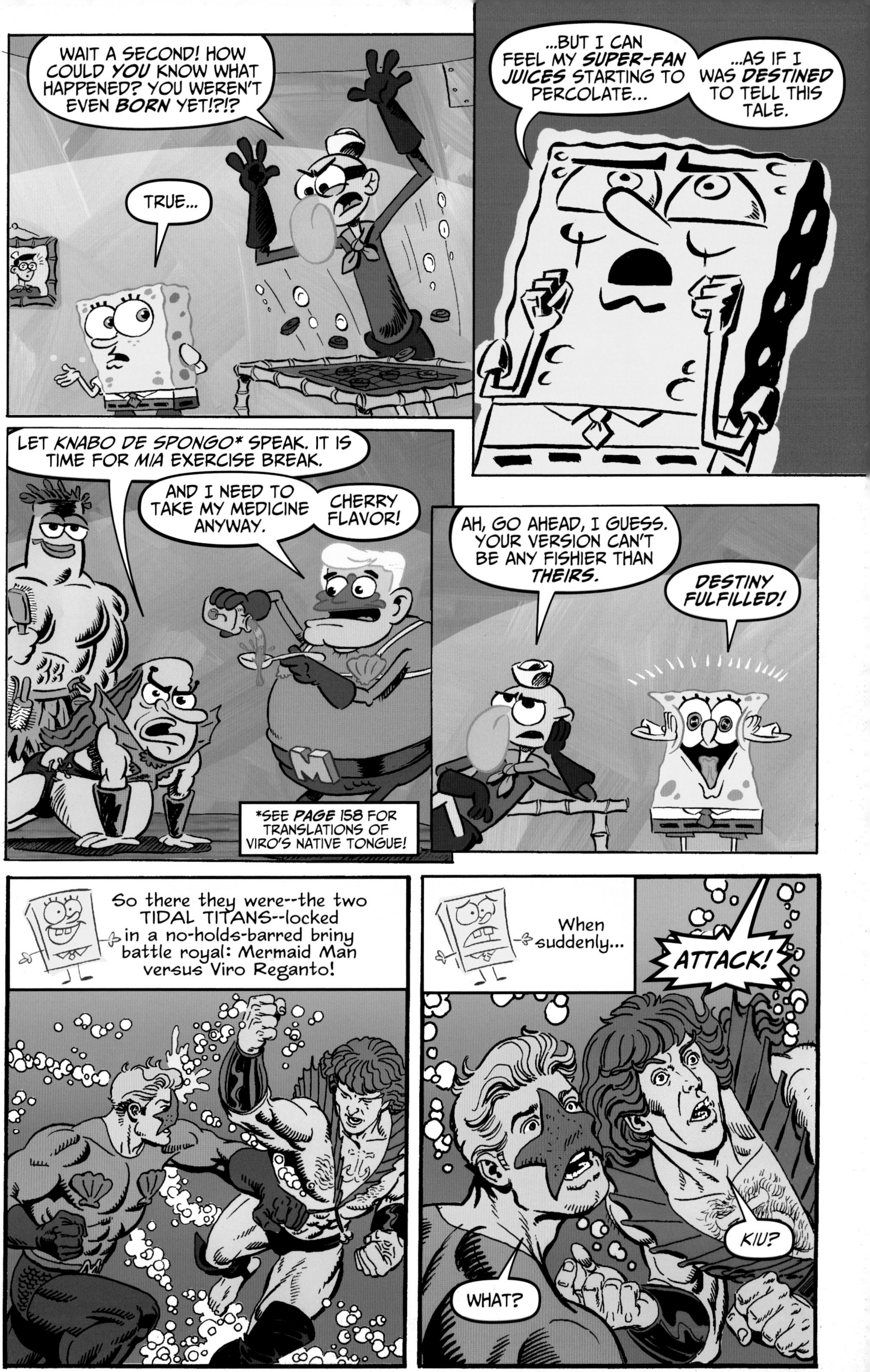
WAIT A SECOND! HOW COULD YOU KNOW WHAT HAPPENED? YOU WEREN'T EVEN BORN YET!?!?
TRUE...
...BUT I CAN FEEL MY SUPER-FAN JUICES STARTING TO PERCOLATE...
...AS IF I WAS DESTINED TO TELL THIS TALE.
LET KNABO DE SPONGO* SPEAK. IT IS TIME FOR M/A EXERCISE BREAK.
AND I NEED TO TAKE MY MEDICINE ANYWAY.
CHERRY FLAVOR!
*SEE PAGE 158 FOR TRANSLATIONS OF VIRO'S NATIVE TONGUE!
AH, GO AHEAD, I GUESS. YOUR VERSION CAN'T BE ANY FISHIER THAN THEIRS.
DESTINY FULFILLED!
So there they were--the two TIDAL TITANS--locked in a no-holds-barred briny battle royal: Mermaid Man versus Viro Reganto!
When suddenly...
ATTACK!
KIU?
WHAT?

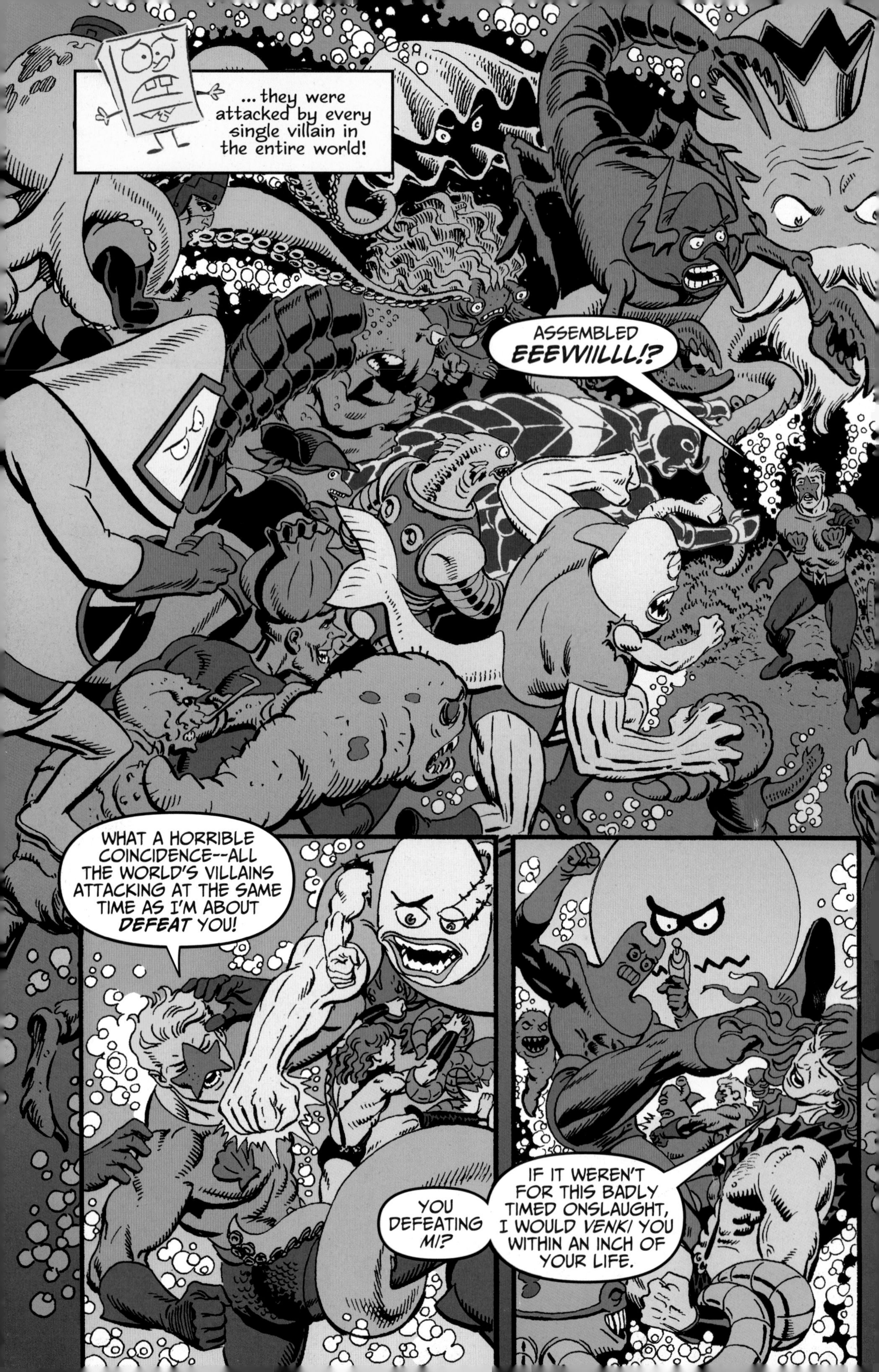
...they were attacked by every single villain in the entire world!
ASSEMBLED EEEVVIILLL!?
WHAT A HORRIBLE COINCIDENCE--ALL THE WORLD'S VILLAINS ATTACKING AT THE SAME TIME AS I'M ABOUT DEFEAT YOU!
IF IT WEREN'T FOR THIS BADLY TIMED ONSLAUGHT, I WOULD VENK! YOU WITHIN AN INCH OF YOUR LIFE.
YOU DEFEATING MI!?

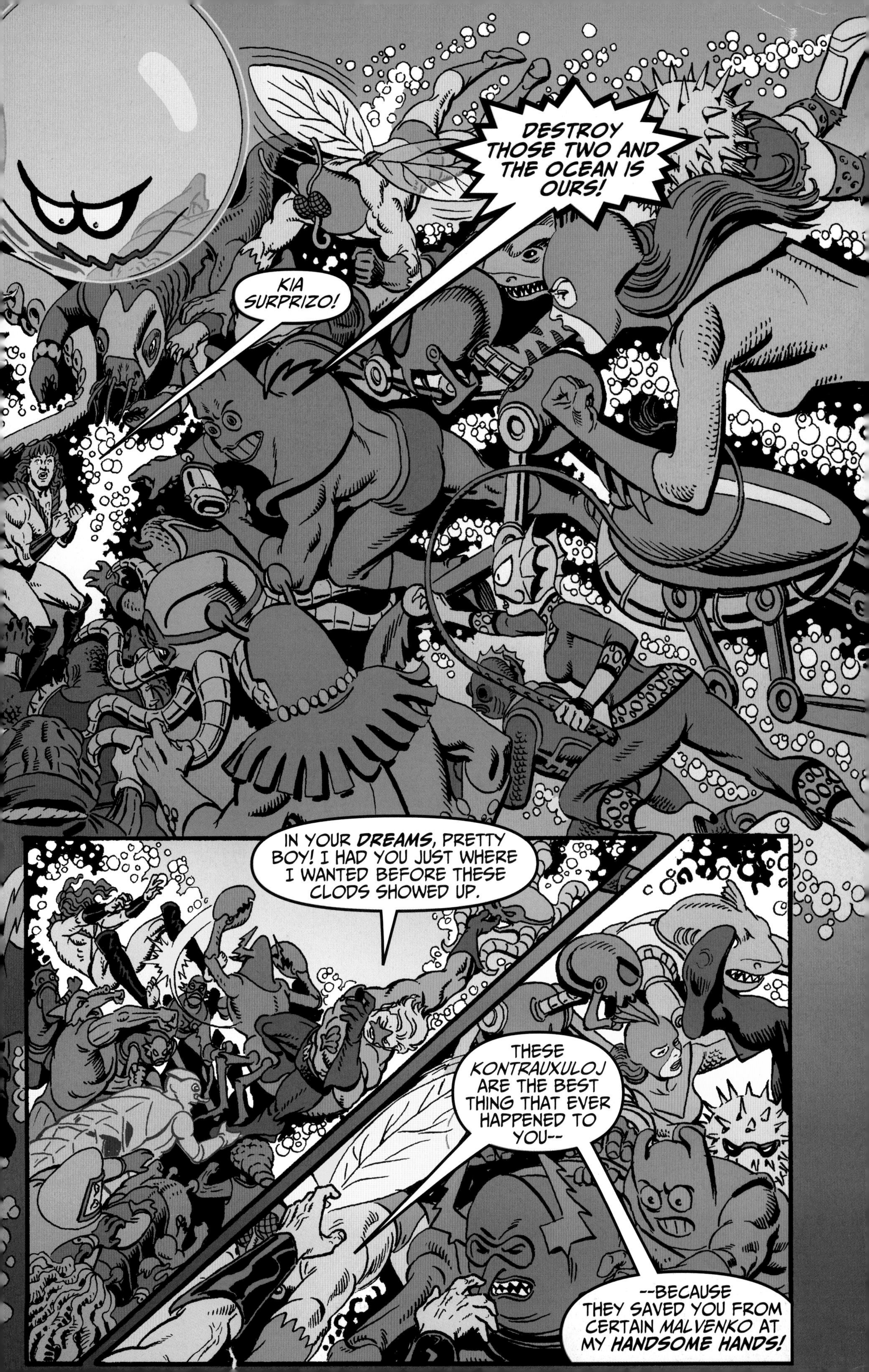
DESTROY THOSE TWO AND THE OCEAN IS OURS!
KIA SURPRIZO!
IN YOUR DREAMS, PRETTY BOY! I HAD YOU JUST WHERE I WANTED BEFORE THESE CLODS SHOWED UP.
THESE KONTRAUXULOJ ARE THE BEST THING THAT EVER HAPPENED TO YOU--
--BECAUSE THEY SAVED YOU FROM CERTAIN MALVENKO AT MY HANDSOME HANDS!

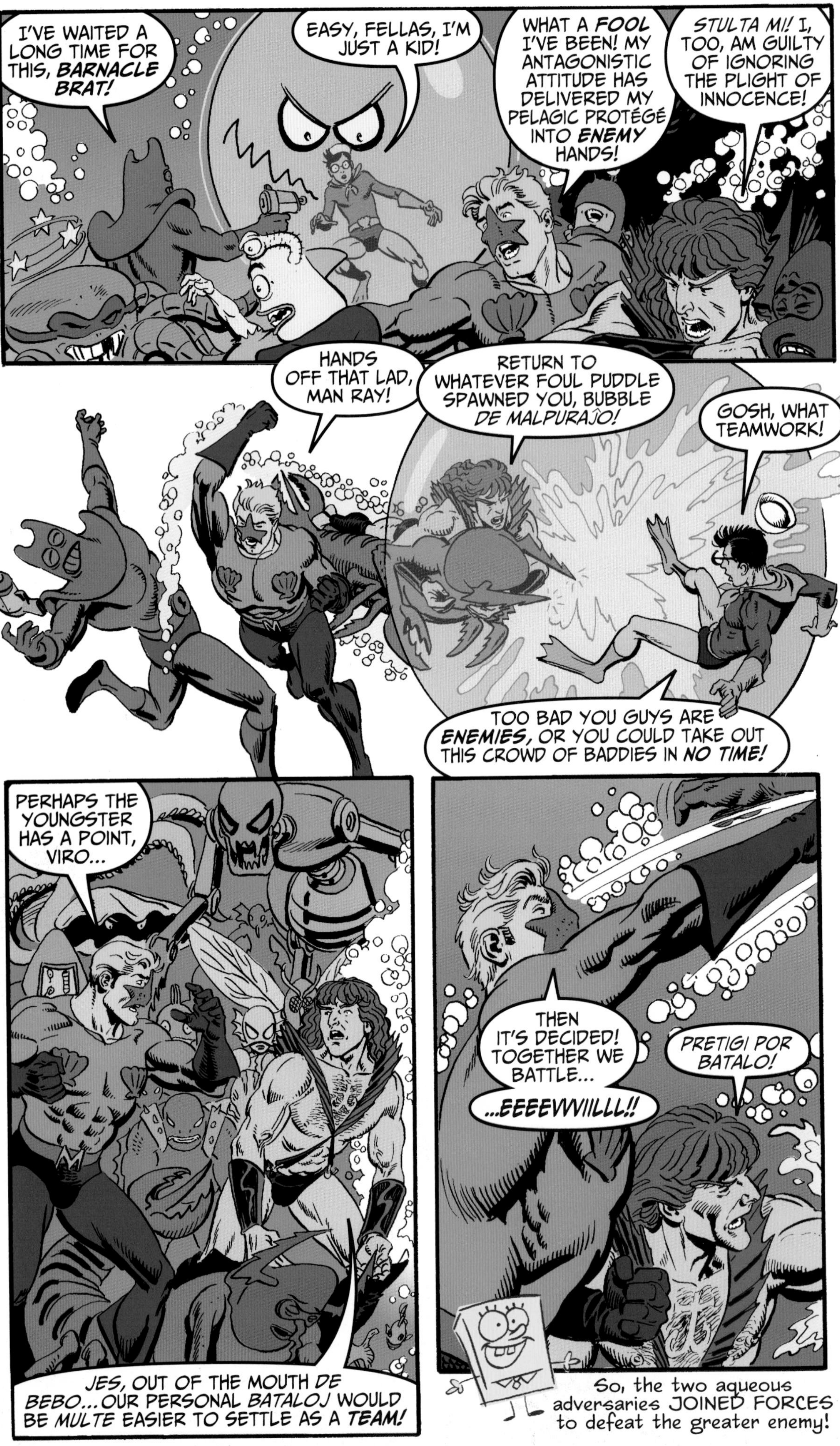
I'VE WAITED A LONG TIME FOR THIS, BARNACLE BRAT!
EASY, FELLAS, I'M JUST A KID!
WHAT A FOOL I'VE BEEN! MY ANTAGONISTIC ATTITUDE HAS DELIVERED MY PELAGIC PROTÉGÉ INTO ENEMY HANDS!
STULTA MI! I, TOO, AM GUILTY OF IGNORING THE PLIGHT OF INNOCENCE!
HANDS OFF THAT LAD, MAN RAY!
RETURN TO WHATEVER FOUL PUDDLE SPAWNED YOU, BUBBLE DE MALPURAĴO!
GOSH, WHAT TEAMWORK!
TOO BAD YOU GUYS ARE ENEMIES, OR YOU COULD TAKE OUT THIS CROWD OF BADDIES IN NO TIME!
PERHAPS THE YOUNGSTER HAS A POINT, VIRO...
JES, OUT OF THE MOUTH DE BEBO... OUR PERSONAL BATALOJ WOULD BE MULTE EASIER TO SETTLE AS A TEAM!
THEN IT'S DECIDED! TOGETHER WE BATTLE...
...EEEEVVVIILLL!!
PRETIGI POR BATALO!
So, the two aqueous adversaries JOINED FORCES to defeat the greater enemy!

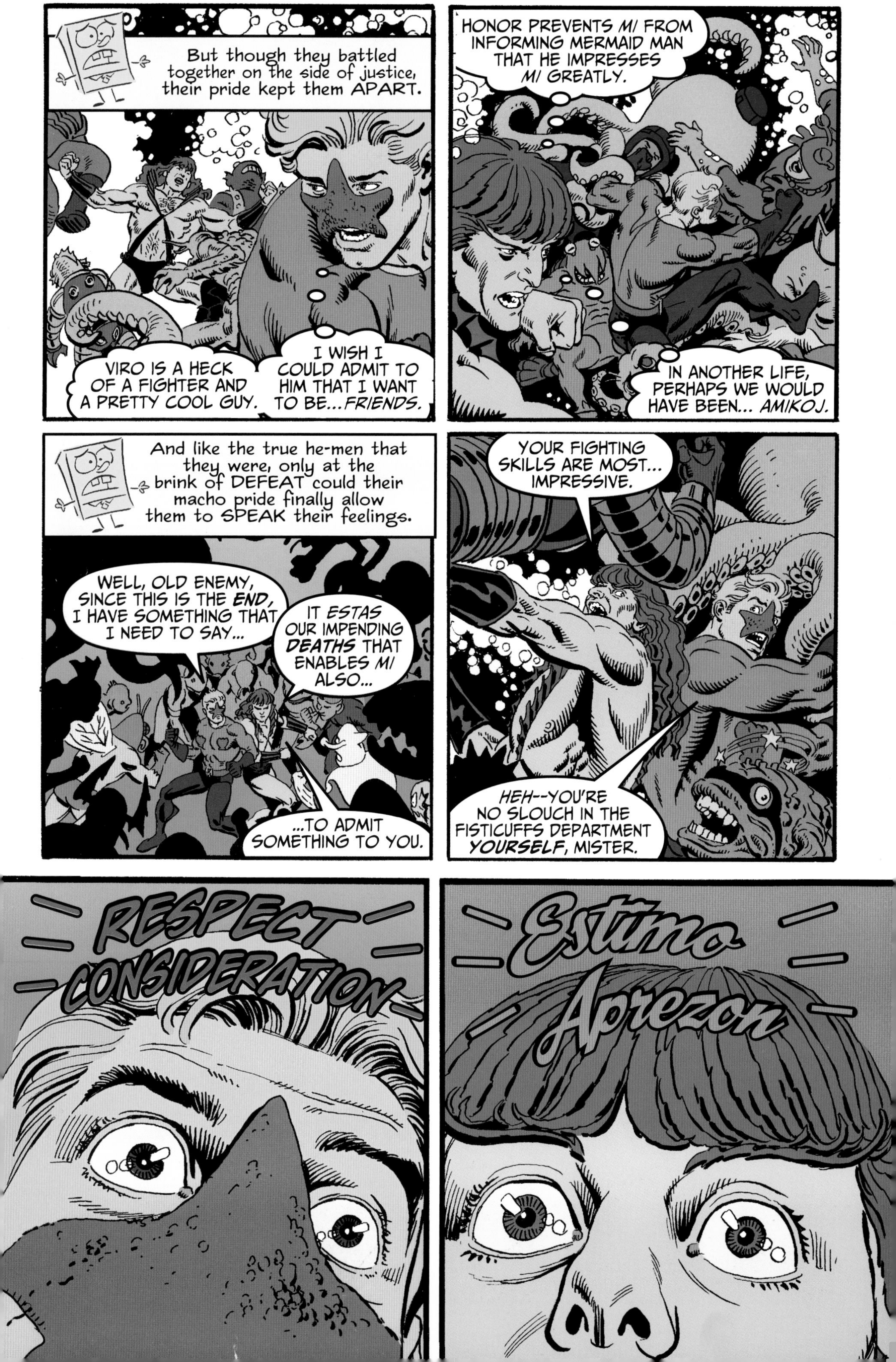
But though they battled together on the side of justice, their pride kept them APART.
VIRO IS A HECK OF A FIGHTER AND A PRETTY COOL GUY.
I WISH I COULD ADMIT TO HIM THAT I WANT TO BE... FRIENDS.
HONOR PREVENTS MI FROM INFORMING MERMAID MAN THAT HE IMPRESSES MI GREATLY.
IN ANOTHER LIFE, PERHAPS WE WOULD HAVE BEEN... AMIKOJ.
And like the true he-men that they were, only at the brink of DEFEAT could their macho pride finally allow them to SPEAK their feelings.
WELL, OLD ENEMY, SINCE THIS IS THE END, I HAVE SOMETHING THAT I NEED TO SAY...
IT ESTAS OUR IMPENDING DEATHS THAT ENABLES MI ALSO...
...TO ADMIT SOMETHING TO YOU.
YOUR FIGHTING SKILLS ARE MOST... IMPRESSIVE.
HEH--YOU'RE NO SLOUCH IN THE FISTICUFFS DEPARTMENT YOURSELF, MISTER.
RESPECT
CONSIDERATION
Estimo
Aprezon

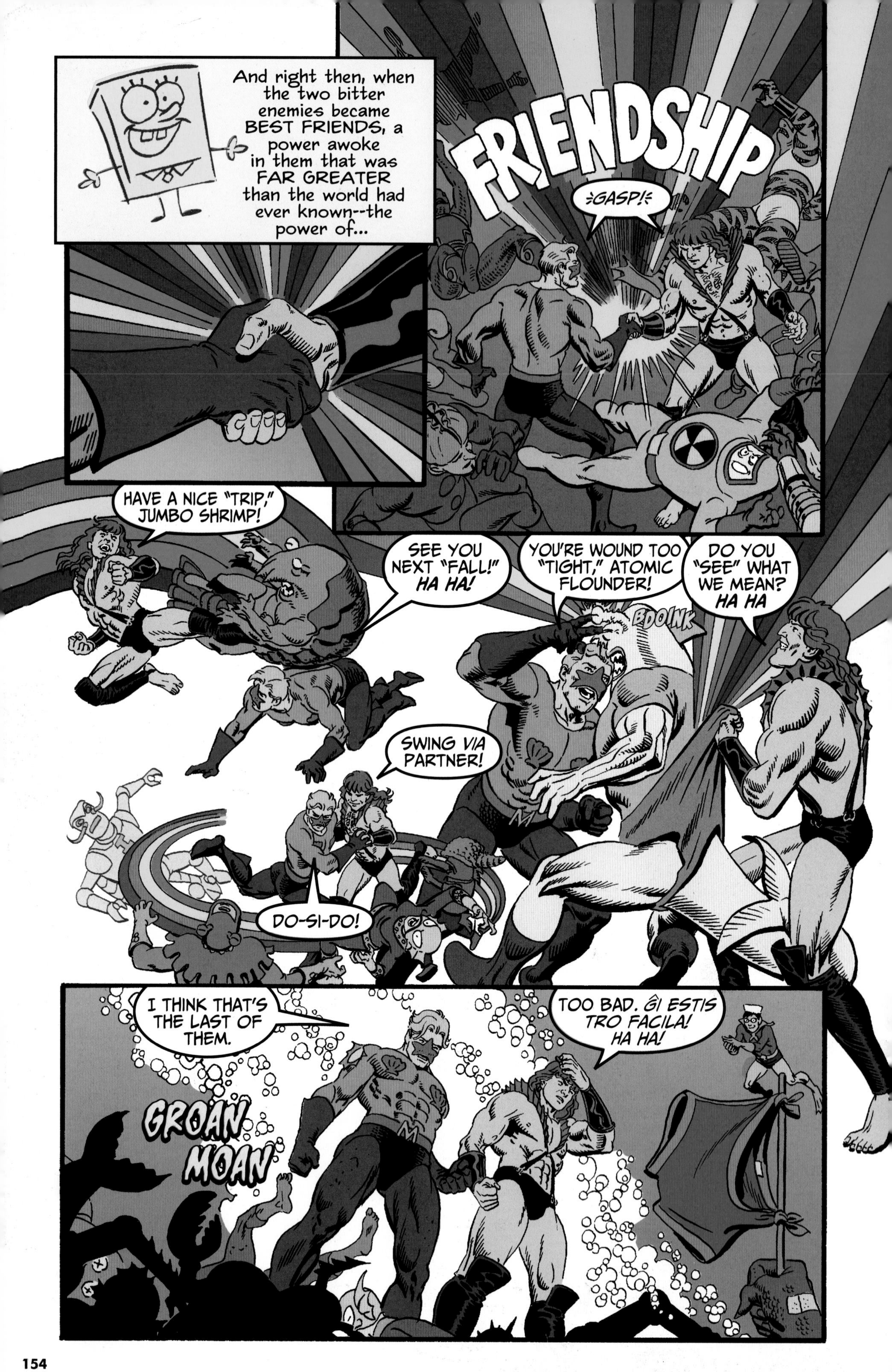
And right then, when the two bitter enemies became BEST FRIENDS, a power awoke in them that was FAR GREATER than the world had ever known--the power of...
FRIENDSHIP
GASP!
HAVE A NICE "TRIP," JUMBO SHRIMP!
SEE YOU NEXT "FALL!" HA HA!
YOU'RE WOUND TOO "TIGHT," ATOMIC FLOUNDER!
DO YOU "SEE" WHAT WE MEAN? HA HA
BDOINK
SWING VIA PARTNER!
DO-SI-DO!
I THINK THAT'S THE LAST OF THEM.
TOO BAD. ĜI ESTIS TRO FACILA! HA HA!
GROAN MOAN

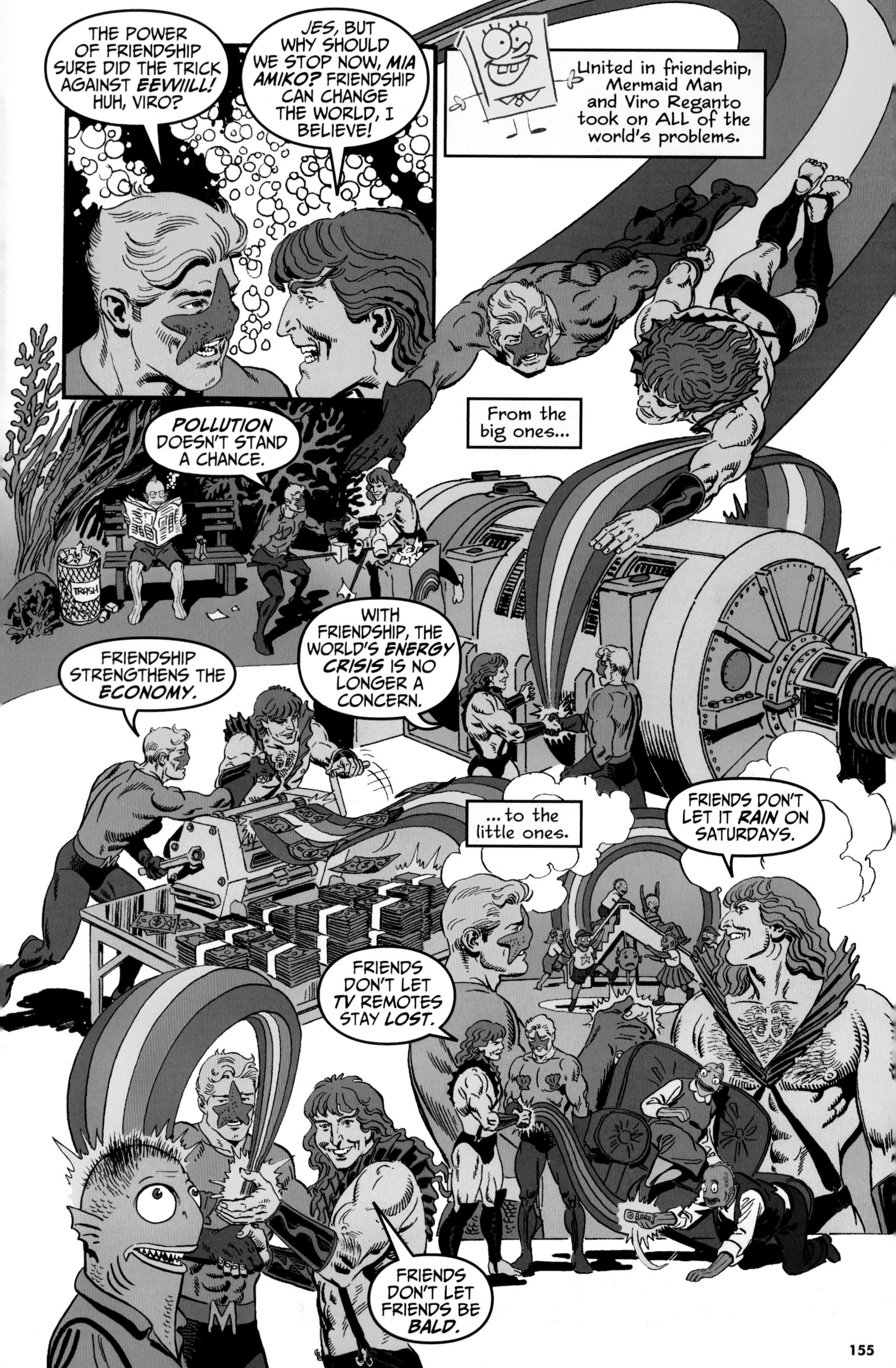
THE POWER OF FRIENDSHIP SURE DID THE TRICK AGAINST EEVVIILL! HUH, VIRO?
JES, BUT WHY SHOULD WE STOP NOW, MIA AMIKO? FRIENDSHIP CAN CHANGE THE WORLD, I BELIEVE!
United in friendship, Mermaid Man and Viro Reganto took on ALL of the world's problems.
From the big ones...
POLLUTION DOESN'T STAND A CHANCE.
TRASH
FRIENDSHIP STRENGTHENS THE ECONOMY.
WITH FRIENDSHIP, THE WORLD'S ENERGY CRISIS IS NO LONGER A CONCERN.
...to the little ones.
FRIENDS DON'T LET IT RAIN ON SATURDAYS.
FRIENDS DON'T LET TV REMOTES STAY LOST.
FRIENDS DON'T LET FRIENDS BE BALD.

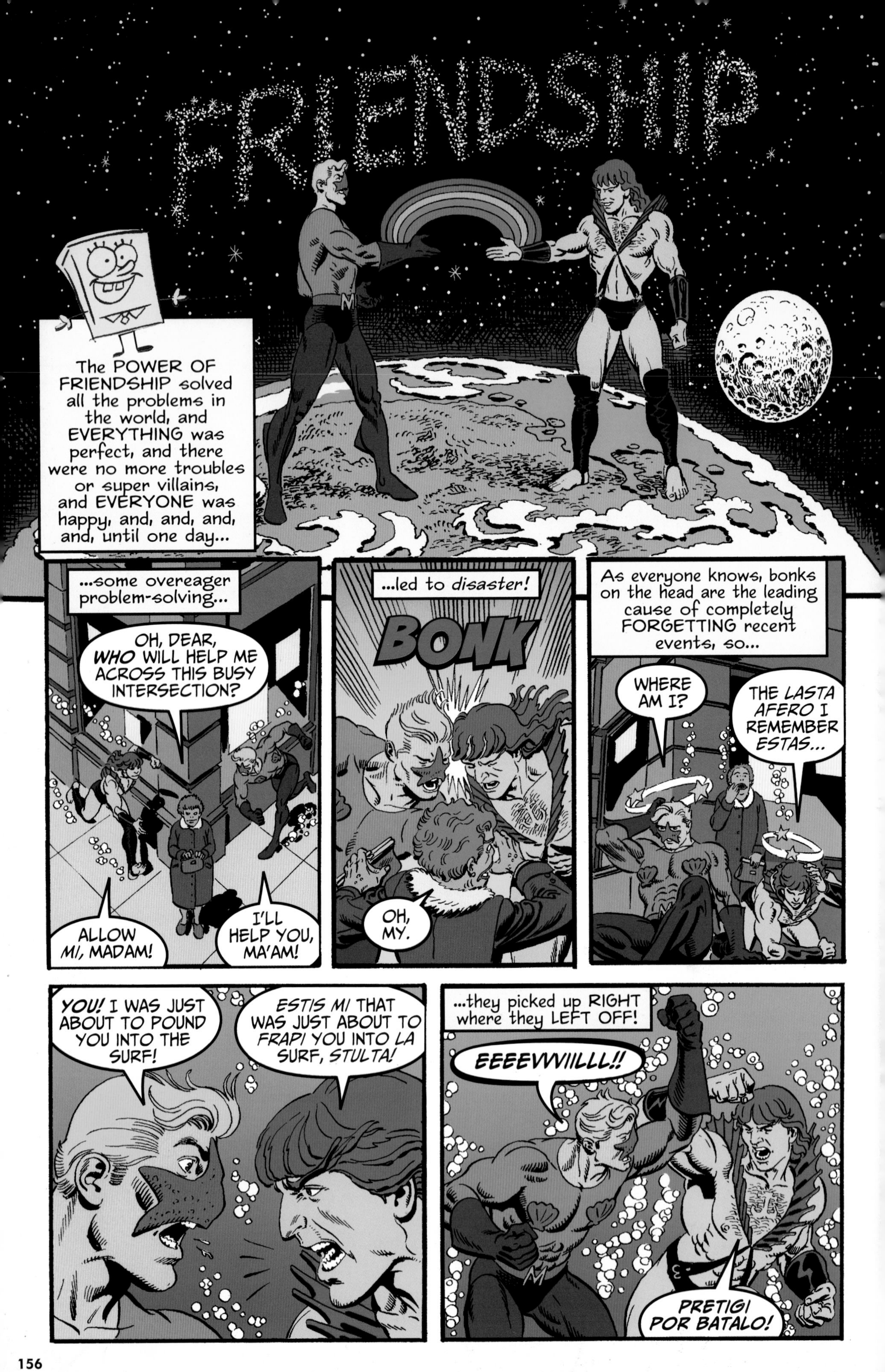
FRIENDSHIP
The POWER OF FRIENDSHIP solved all the problems in the world, and EVERYTHING was perfect, and there were no more troubles or super villains, and EVERYONE was happy, and, and, and, and, until one day...
...some overeager problem-solving...
OH, DEAR, WHO WILL HELP ME ACROSS THIS BUSY INTERSECTION?
ALLOW MI, MADAM!
I'LL HELP YOU, MA'AM!
...led to disaster!
BONK
OH, MY.
As everyone knows, bonks on the head are the leading cause of completely FORGETTING recent events, so...
WHERE AM I?
THE LASTA AFERO I REMEMBER ESTAS...
YOU! I WAS JUST ABOUT TO POUND YOU INTO THE SURF!
ESTIS MI THAT WAS JUST ABOUT TO FRAPI YOU INTO LA SURF, STULTA!
...they picked up RIGHT where they LEFT OFF!
EEEEVVVIILLL!!
PRETIGI POR BATALO!

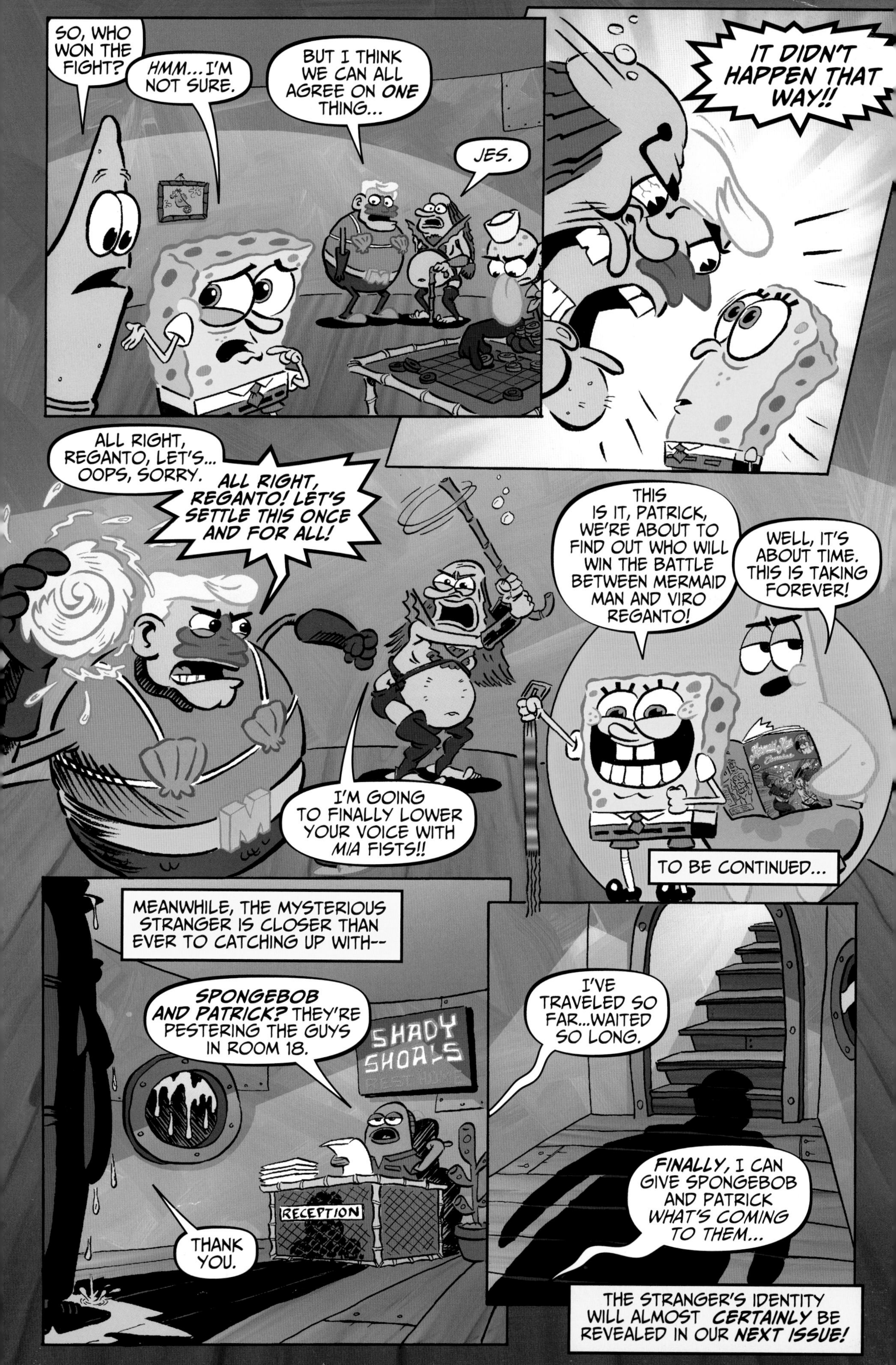
SO, WHO WON THE FIGHT?
HMM...I'M NOT SURE.
BUT I THINK WE CAN ALL AGREE ON ONE THING...
JES.
IT DIDN'T HAPPEN THAT WAY!!
ALL RIGHT, REGANTO, LET'S... OOPS, SORRY.
ALL RIGHT, REGANTO! LET'S SETTLE THIS ONCE AND FOR ALL!
I'M GOING TO FINALLY LOWER YOUR VOICE WITH M/A FISTS!!
THIS IS IT, PATRICK, WE'RE ABOUT TO FIND OUT WHO WILL WIN THE BATTLE BETWEEN MERMAID MAN AND VIRO REGANTO!
WELL, IT'S ABOUT TIME. THIS IS TAKING FOREVER!
TO BE CONTINUED...
MEANWHILE, THE MYSTERIOUS STRANGER IS CLOSER THAN EVER TO CATCHING UP WITH--
SPONGEBOB AND PATRICK? THEY'RE PESTERING THE GUYS IN ROOM 18.
SHADY SHOALS
RECEPTION
THANK YOU.
I'VE TRAVELED SO FAR...WAITED SO LONG.
FINALLY, I CAN GIVE SPONGEBOB AND PATRICK WHAT'S COMING TO THEM...
THE STRANGER'S IDENTITY WILL ALMOST CERTAINLY BE REVEALED IN OUR NEXT ISSUE!

THE LANGUAGE THAT MADE A MAN-CHOVY OUT OF "DAN" CHOVY

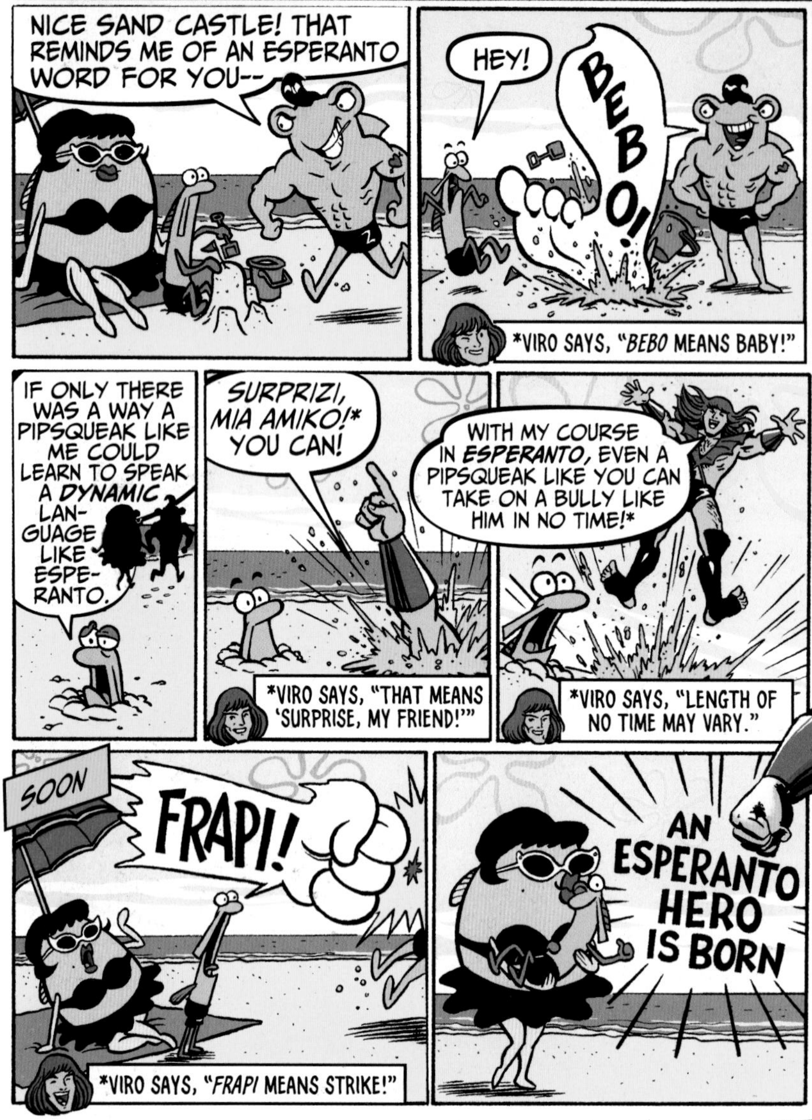

NICE SAND CASTLE! THAT REMINDS ME OF AN ESPERANTO WORD FOR YOU--
HEY!
BEBO!
*VIRO SAYS, "BEBO MEANS BABY!"
AND—
STULTA!
*VIRO SAYS, "STULTA MEANS STUPID!"
IF ONLY THERE WAS A WAY A PIPSQUEAK LIKE ME COULD LEARN TO SPEAK A DYNAMIC LANGUAGE LIKE ESPERANTO.
SURPRIZI, MIA AMIKO!* YOU CAN!
*VIRO SAYS, "THAT MEANS 'SURPRISE, MY FRIEND!'"
WITH MY COURSE IN ESPERANTO, EVEN A PIPSQUEAK LIKE YOU CAN TAKE ON A BULLY LIKE HIM IN NO TIME!*
*VIRO SAYS, "LENGTH OF NO TIME MAY VARY."
SOON
FRAPI!
*VIRO SAYS, "FRAPI MEANS STRIKE!"
AN ESPERANTO HERO IS BORN

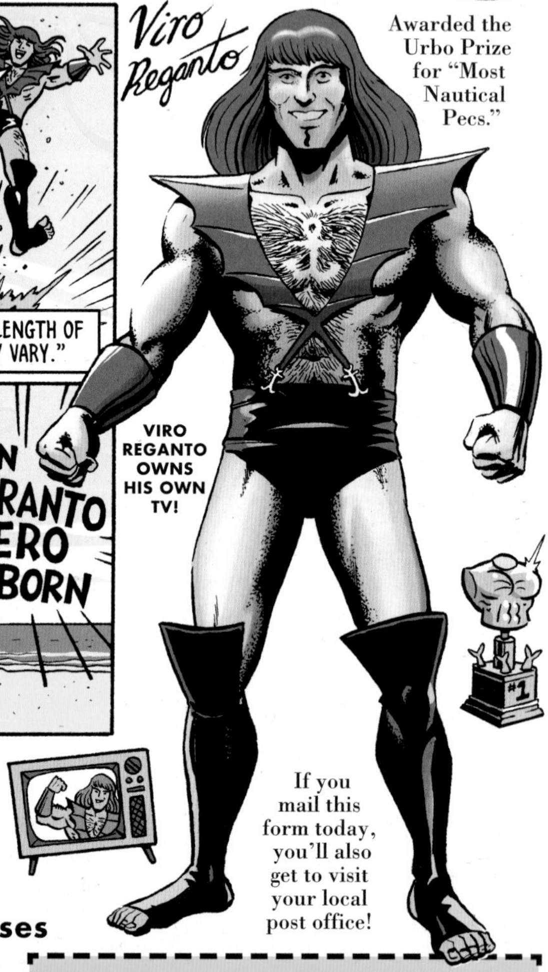

Viro Reganto
Awarded the Urbo Prize for "Most Nautical Pecs."
VIRO REGANTO OWNS HIS OWN TV!
#1
If you mail this form today, you'll also get to visit your local post office!

This Comic PROVES ESPERANTO Exists!

These amazing Esperanto words and phrases can be found in the preceding SpongeBob Comics adventure *in this order!*

Knabo de Spongo—Child of Sponge
mia—my
kiu—who
Kia surprizo!—What a surprise!
mi—me
venki—overcome
kontrauxuloj—adversaries
malvenko—defeat
stulta mi—stupid me
de malpuraĵo!—of dirt
jes—yes
de bebo—of a baby
bataloj—battles
multe—much
Pretigi por batalo!—Ready for battle!
amikoj—friends
estas—is
estimo—esteem
aprezon—appreciation
via—your
Ĝi estis tro facila!—It was too easy!
mia amiko—my friend
lasta afero—last thing
estis—was
frapi—strike

Viro Reganto's "Dynamic Esperanto"
c/o Urbo, The Lost City,
Bottom of the Ocean, Inside a Mountain.

Dear Viro Reganto,

Please turn me into a Man-chovy with these courses:

- ❑ **Esperanto**
- ❑ **Esperanto for Kids**
- ❑ **Esperanto for Adults**
- ❑ **Esperanto for Kids and Adults**
- ❑ **Esperanto for Pets**
- ❑ **Diet Esperanto**

I enclose a small chest of gold in exchange for your princely wisdom!

Print Name . . . . Age . . . .
Address . . . .
Body of Water . . . .

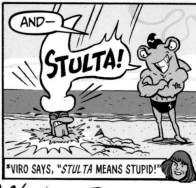

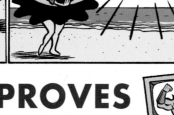

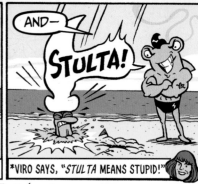

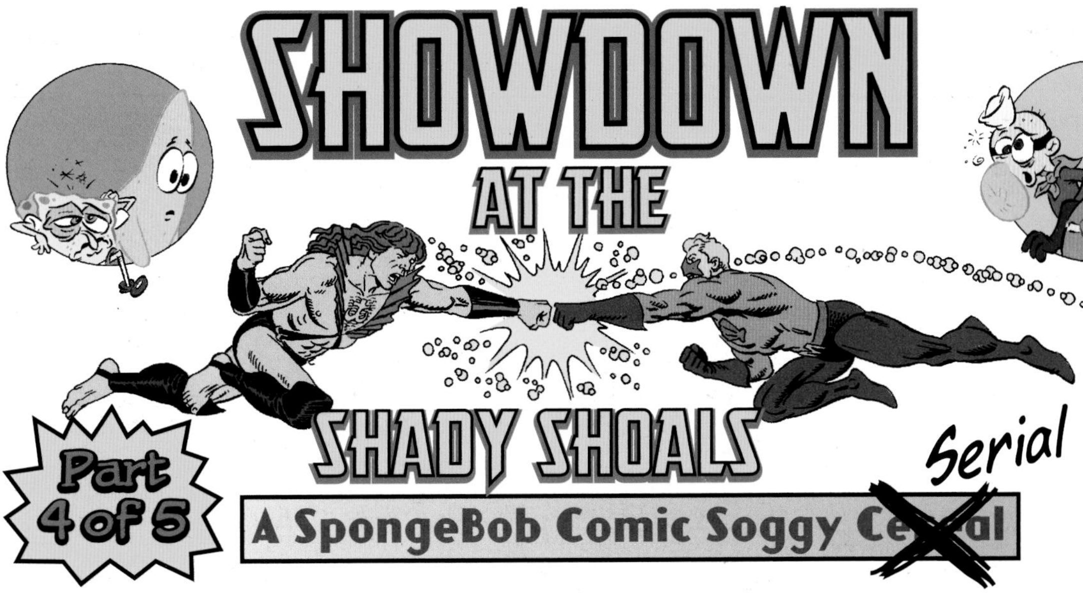
SHOWDOWN
AT THE
SHADY SHOALS
Part 4 of 5
A SpongeBob Comic Soggy Cereal
Serial

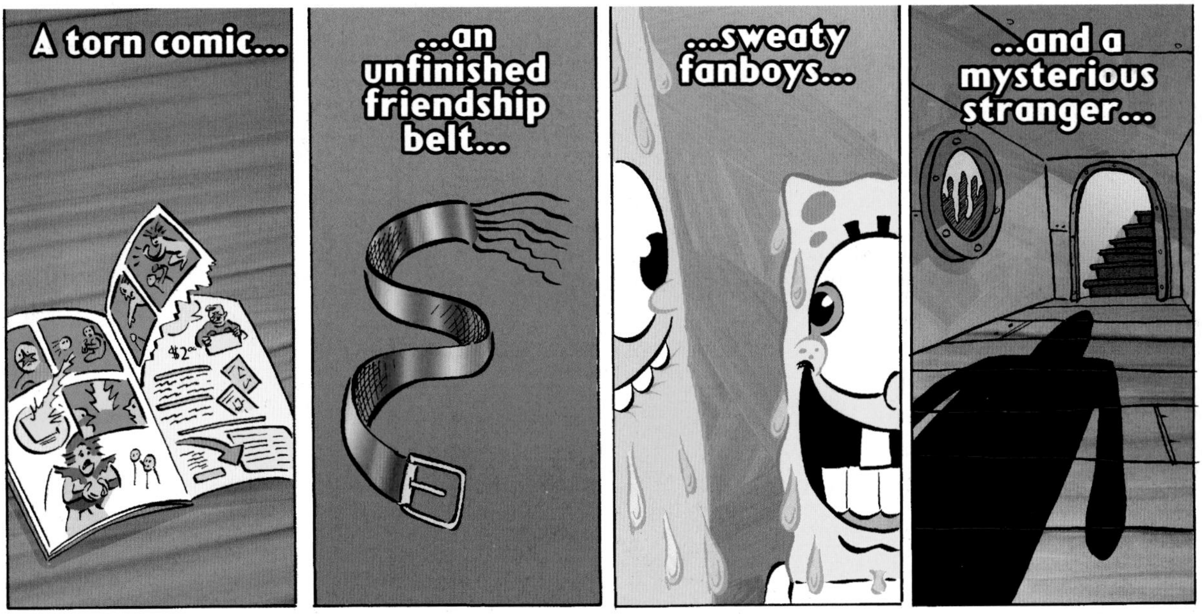
A torn comic...
...an unfinished friendship belt...
...sweaty fanboys...
...and a mysterious stranger...

...all scream for an answer; who won the first battle between Mermaid Man and Viro Reganto?

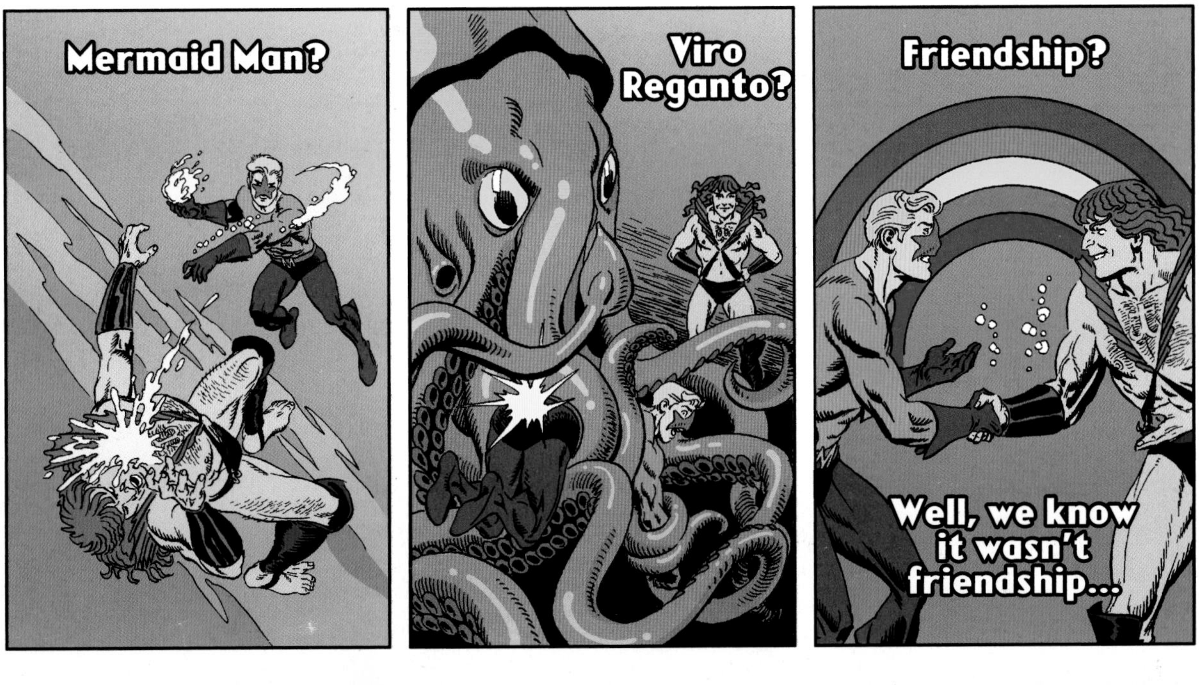
Mermaid Man?
Viro Reganto?
Friendship?
Well, we know it wasn't friendship...

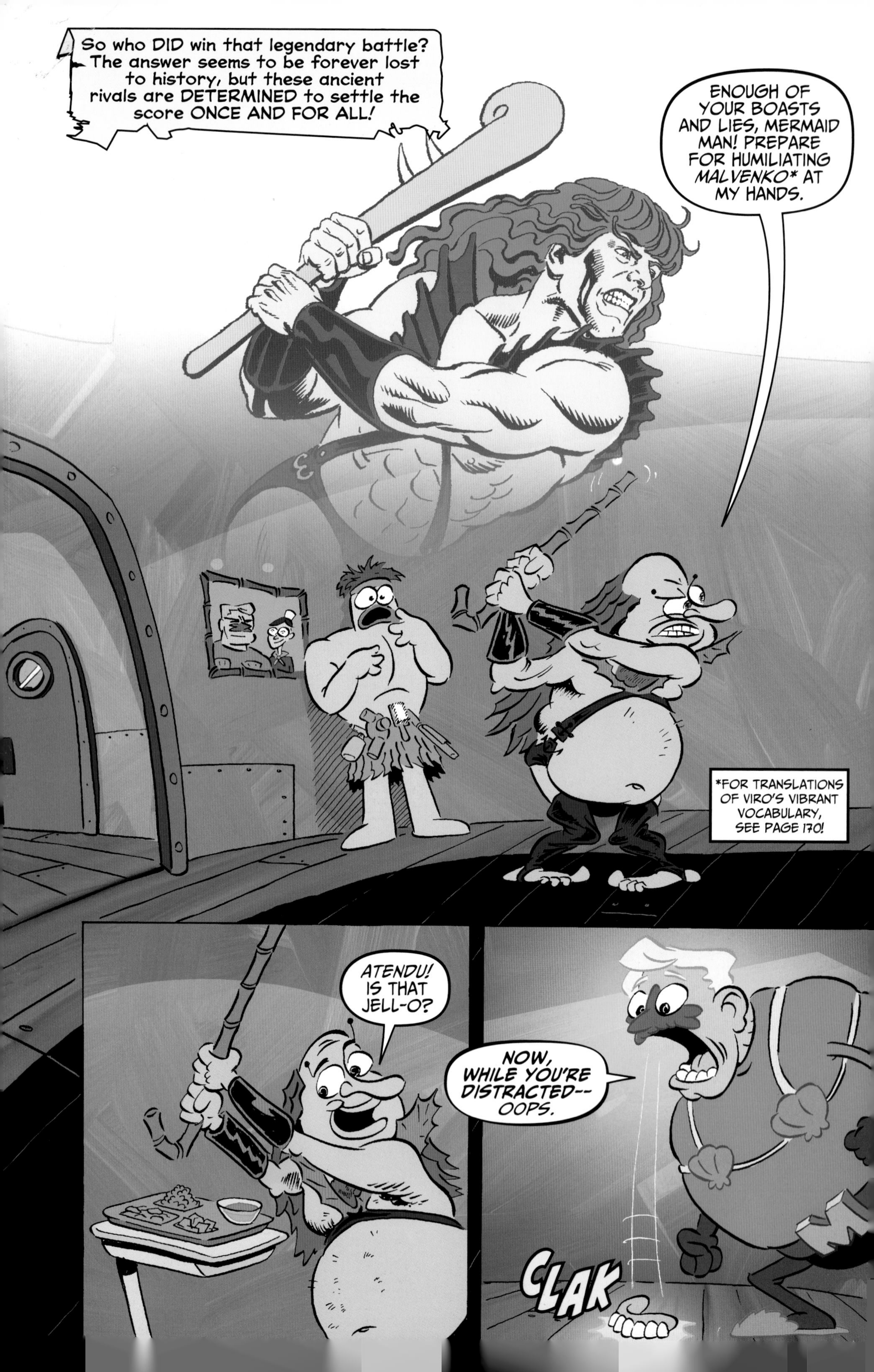
So who DID win that legendary battle? The answer seems to be forever lost to history, but these ancient rivals are DETERMINED to settle the score ONCE AND FOR ALL!
ENOUGH OF YOUR BOASTS AND LIES, MERMAID MAN! PREPARE FOR HUMILIATING MALVENKO* AT MY HANDS.
*FOR TRANSLATIONS OF VIRO'S VIBRANT VOCABULARY, SEE PAGE 170!
ATENDU! IS THAT JELL-O?
NOW, WHILE YOU'RE DISTRACTED-- OOPS.
CLAK

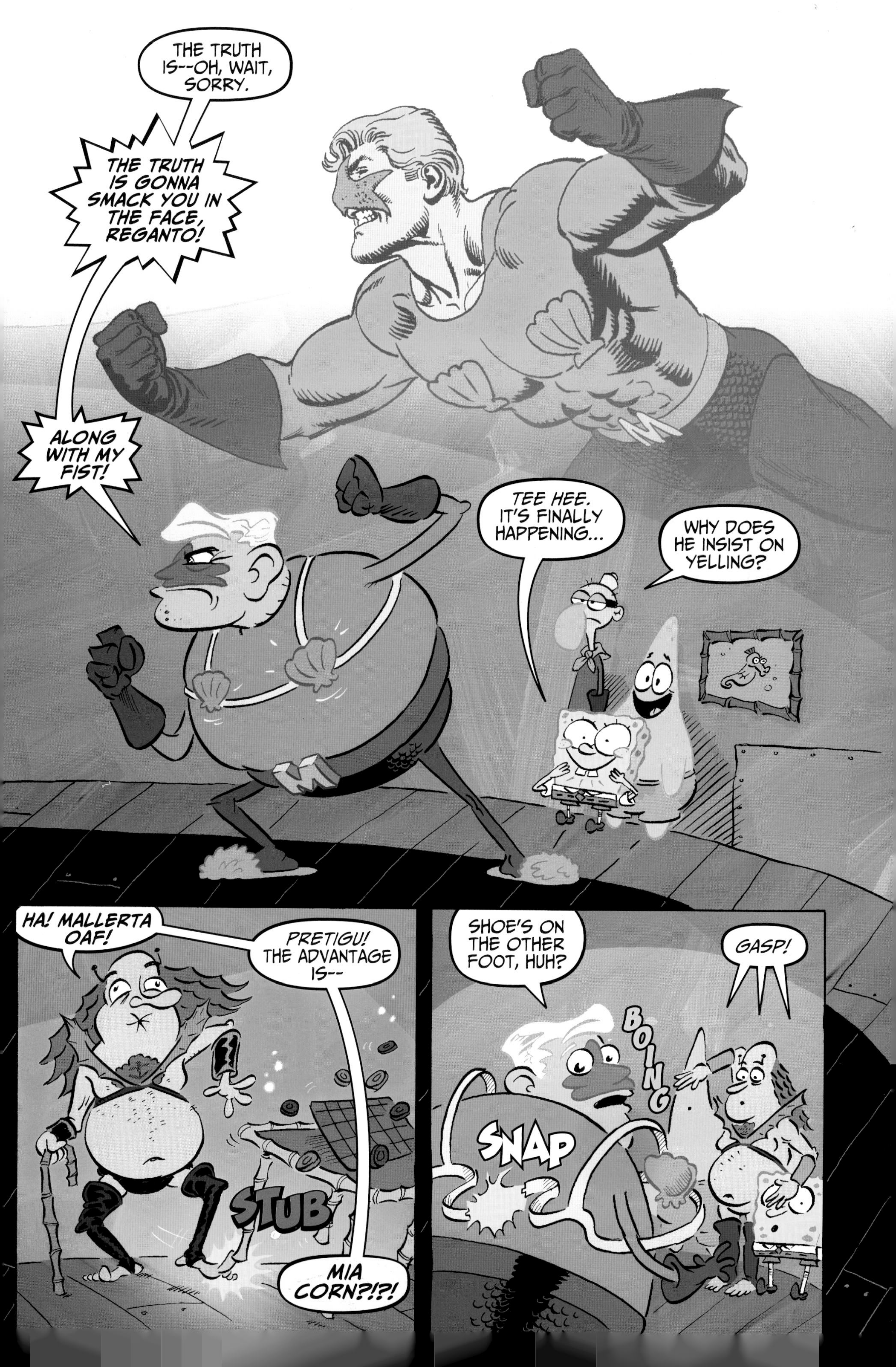
THE TRUTH IS--OH, WAIT, SORRY.
THE TRUTH IS GONNA SMACK YOU IN THE FACE, REGANTO!
ALONG WITH MY FIST!
TEE HEE. IT'S FINALLY HAPPENING...
WHY DOES HE INSIST ON YELLING?
HA! MALLERTA OAF!
PRETIGU! THE ADVANTAGE IS--
STUB
MIA CORN?!?!
SHOE'S ON THE OTHER FOOT, HUH?
GASP!
BOING
SNAP

OKAY, HOLD IT. THIS PATHETIC SPECTACLE IS GOING *NOWHERE* FAST.

SO BEFORE WE ALL MISS OUR NAPTIME...

...WE NEED TO COME UP WITH A MORE "AGE APPROPRIATE" COMPETITION.

★ The Old ★ Fogey-thon

IT'S A *BEAUTIFUL* DAY HERE AT SHADY SHOALS AS OUR COMPETITORS PREPARE FOR WHAT PROMISES TO BE A *HECK* OF A MATCH-UP.

WHY DID THAT KID CRAWL INTO OUR TV?

WELCOME TO THE FIRST ANNUAL OLD *FOGEY-THON!*

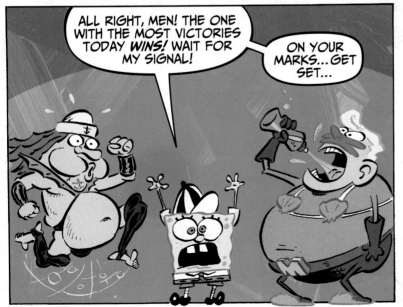

ALL RIGHT, MEN! THE ONE WITH THE MOST VICTORIES TODAY *WINS!* WAIT FOR MY SIGNAL!

ON YOUR MARKS...GET SET...

TWEET!

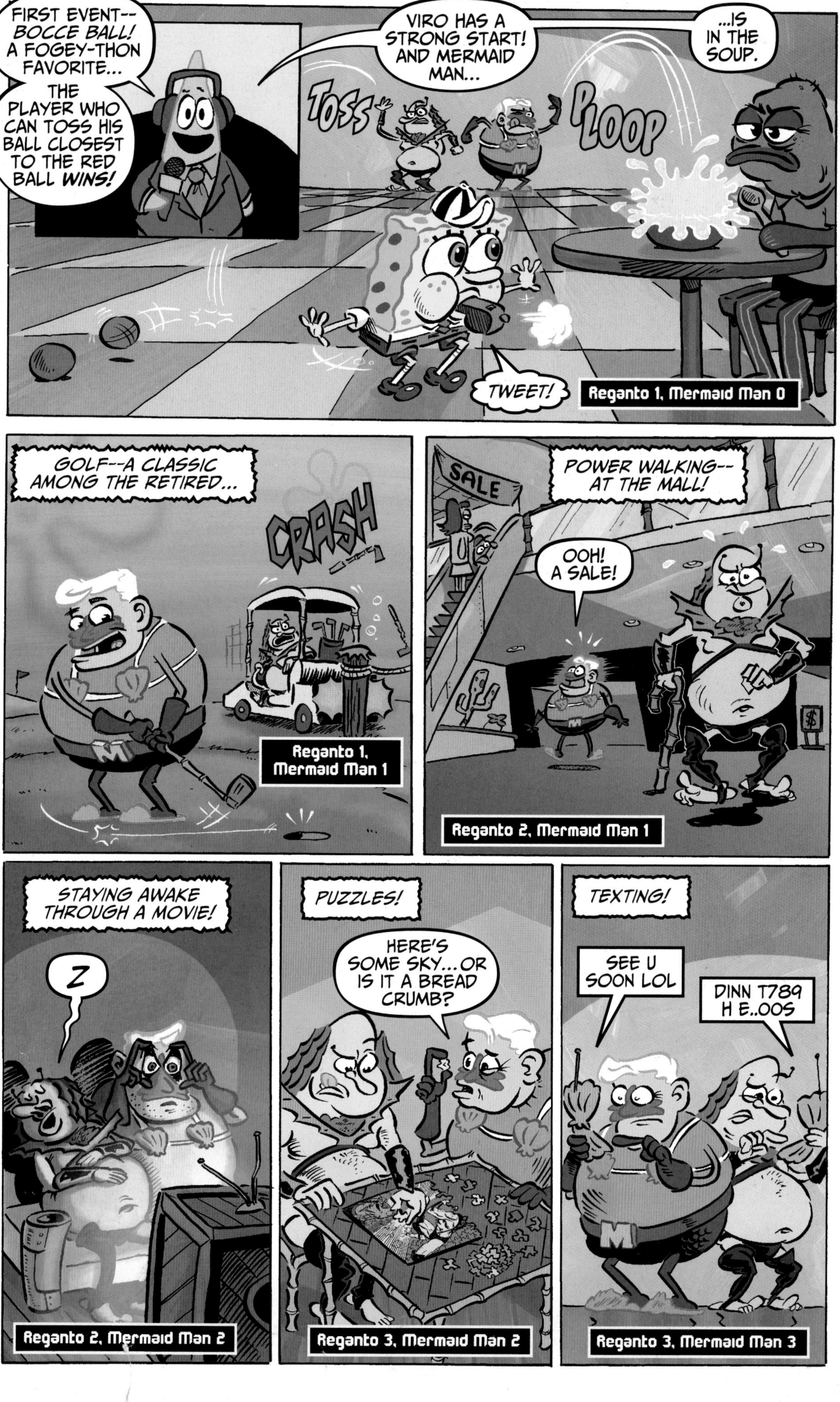
FIRST EVENT-- BOCCE BALL! A FOGEY-THON FAVORITE...
THE PLAYER WHO CAN TOSS HIS BALL CLOSEST TO THE RED BALL WINS!
VIRO HAS A STRONG START! AND MERMAID MAN...
...IS IN THE SOUP.
TOSS
PLOOP
TWEET!
Reganto 1, Mermaid Man 0
GOLF--A CLASSIC AMONG THE RETIRED...
CRASH
Reganto 1, Mermaid Man 1
POWER WALKING-- AT THE MALL!
SALE
OOH! A SALE!
Reganto 2, Mermaid Man 1
STAYING AWAKE THROUGH A MOVIE!
Z
Reganto 2, Mermaid Man 2
PUZZLES!
HERE'S SOME SKY...OR IS IT A BREAD CRUMB?
Reganto 3, Mermaid Man 2
TEXTING!
SEE U SOON LOL
DINN T789 H E..OOS
Reganto 3, Mermaid Man 3

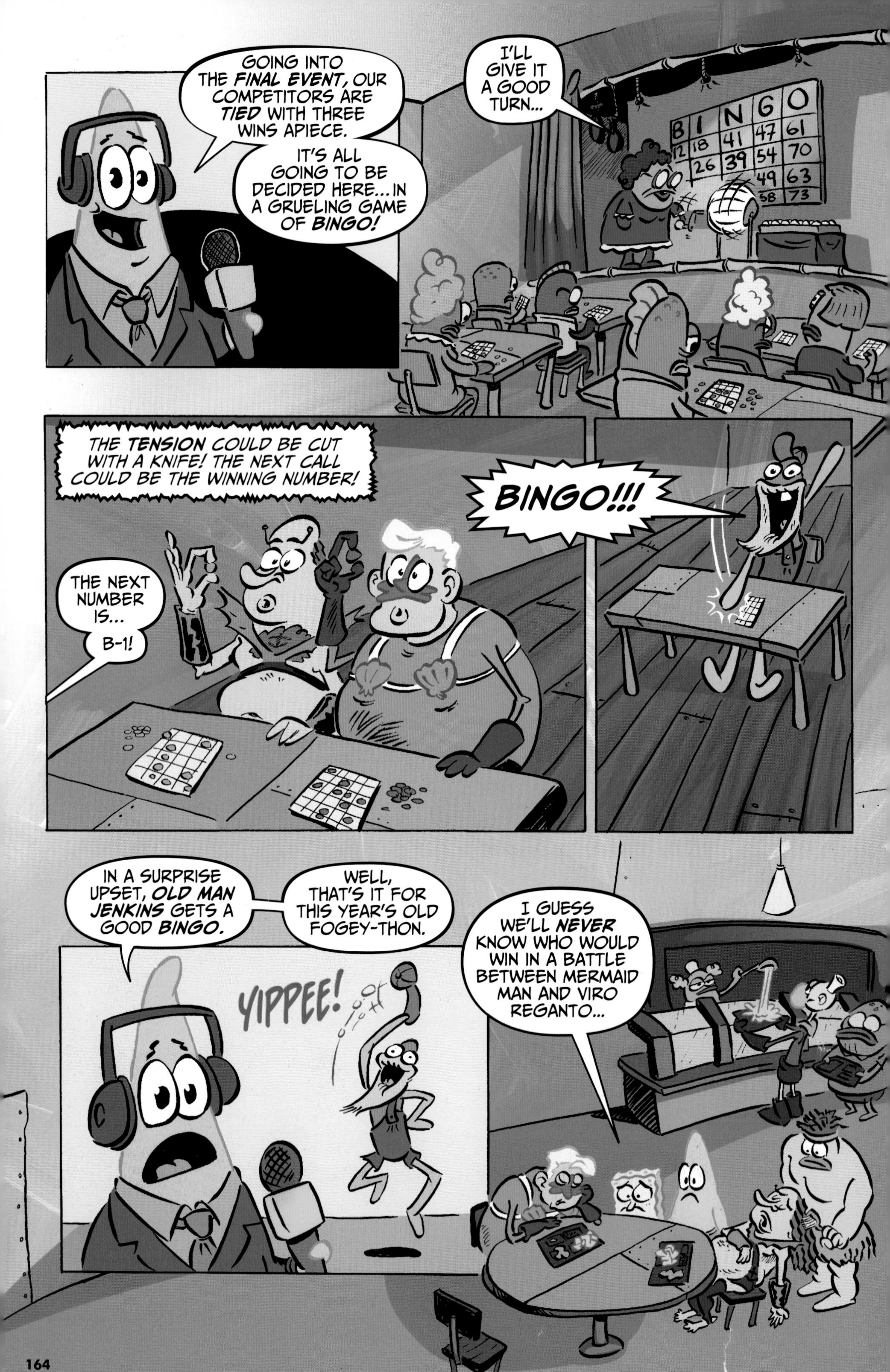
GOING INTO THE FINAL EVENT, OUR COMPETITORS ARE TIED WITH THREE WINS APIECE.
IT'S ALL GOING TO BE DECIDED HERE... IN A GRUELING GAME OF BINGO!
I'LL GIVE IT A GOOD TURN...
BINGO
THE TENSION COULD BE CUT WITH A KNIFE! THE NEXT CALL COULD BE THE WINNING NUMBER!
THE NEXT NUMBER IS...
B-1!
BINGO!!!
IN A SURPRISE UPSET, OLD MAN JENKINS GETS A GOOD BINGO.
WELL, THAT'S IT FOR THIS YEAR'S OLD FOGEY-THON.
YIPPEE!
I GUESS WE'LL NEVER KNOW WHO WOULD WIN IN A BATTLE BETWEEN MERMAID MAN AND VIRO REGANTO...

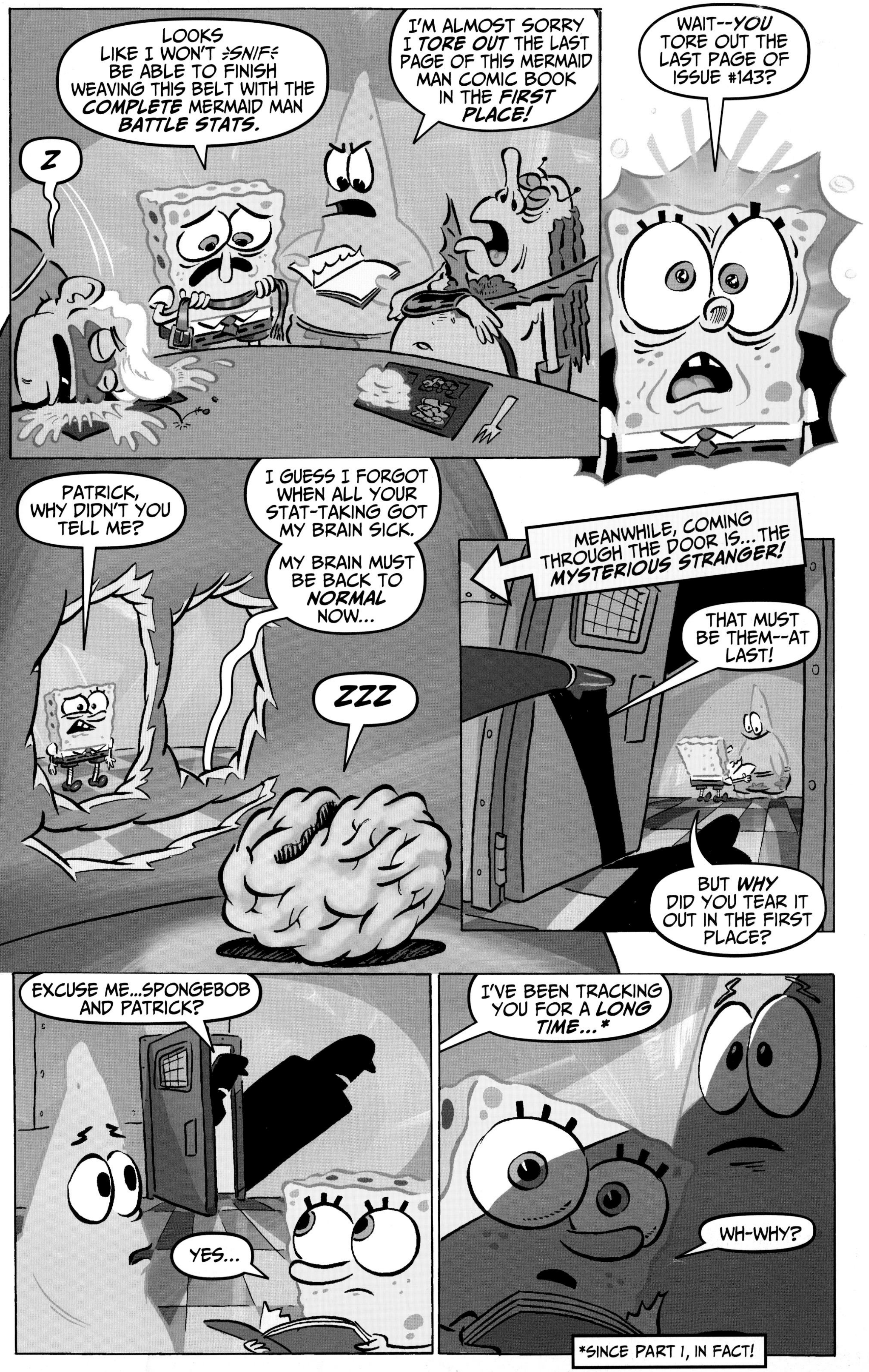
LOOKS LIKE I WON'T ⸗SNIF⸗ BE ABLE TO FINISH WEAVING THIS BELT WITH THE COMPLETE MERMAID MAN BATTLE STATS.
Z
I'M ALMOST SORRY I TORE OUT THE LAST PAGE OF THIS MERMAID MAN COMIC BOOK IN THE FIRST PLACE!
WAIT--YOU TORE OUT THE LAST PAGE OF ISSUE #143?
PATRICK, WHY DIDN'T YOU TELL ME?
I GUESS I FORGOT WHEN ALL YOUR STAT-TAKING GOT MY BRAIN SICK.
MY BRAIN MUST BE BACK TO NORMAL NOW...
ZZZ
MEANWHILE, COMING THROUGH THE DOOR IS...THE MYSTERIOUS STRANGER!
THAT MUST BE THEM--AT LAST!
BUT WHY DID YOU TEAR IT OUT IN THE FIRST PLACE?
EXCUSE ME...SPONGEBOB AND PATRICK?
YES...
I'VE BEEN TRACKING YOU FOR A LONG TIME...*
WH-WHY?
*SINCE PART 1, IN FACT!

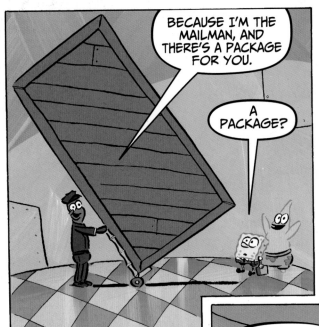

BECAUSE I'M THE MAILMAN, AND THERE'S A PACKAGE FOR YOU.

A PACKAGE?

SURE, IT WAS ORDERED FROM THE BACK OF A *COMIC BOOK!*

THE MISSING PAGE!! BUT WHO ORDERED A *SUBMARINE?*

$1.00

HEY! I ALWAYS WANTED TO EXPLORE UNDERWATER!

ONCE I TAPE THIS IN WE CAN *FINALLY* KNOW HOW THE FIRST BATTLE BETWEEN MERMAID MAN AND VIRO REGANTO *REALLY ENDED!*

I'M GONNA CHECK OUT MY NEW SUBMARINE.

HEY, IT'S ALL *RUSTY!*

WAIT, THIS SUBMARINE LOOKS KIND OF FAMILIAR...

WHAT'S THE *RETURN* ADDRESS?

KICK

PLOP

IT WAS SENT FROM THE LOST, DOMED, UNDERGROUND, SECRET CITY OF *URBO.*

URBO!? OH NO!

C'MON, OPEN...

CREEEEK

PATRICK, WAIT!!

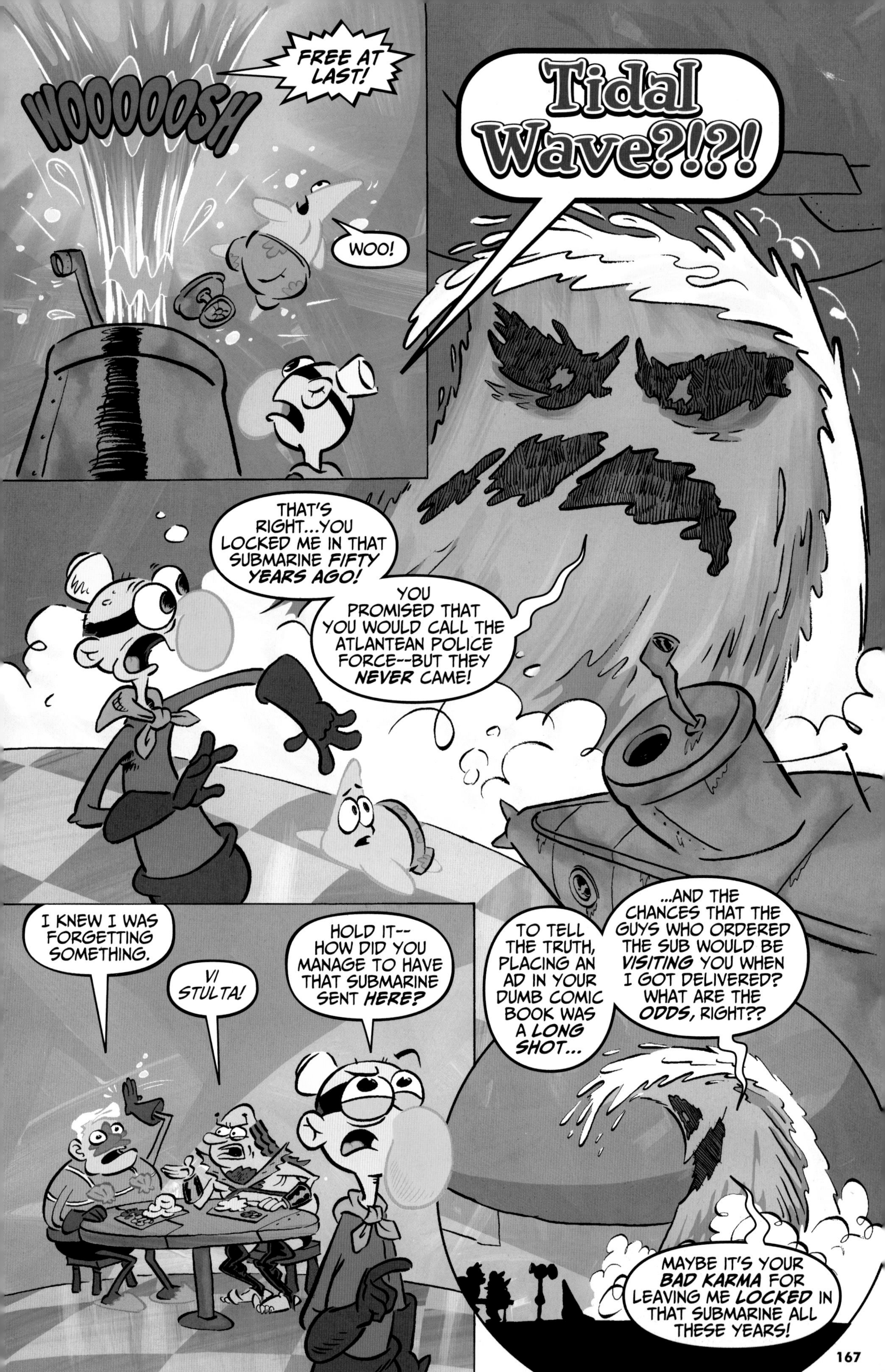
WOOOOOSH
FREE AT LAST!
Tidal Wave?!?!
WOO!
THAT'S RIGHT...YOU LOCKED ME IN THAT SUBMARINE FIFTY YEARS AGO!
YOU PROMISED THAT YOU WOULD CALL THE ATLANTEAN POLICE FORCE--BUT THEY NEVER CAME!
I KNEW I WAS FORGETTING SOMETHING.
VI STULTA!
HOLD IT--HOW DID YOU MANAGE TO HAVE THAT SUBMARINE SENT HERE?
TO TELL THE TRUTH, PLACING AN AD IN YOUR DUMB COMIC BOOK WAS A LONG SHOT...
...AND THE CHANCES THAT THE GUYS WHO ORDERED THE SUB WOULD BE VISITING YOU WHEN I GOT DELIVERED? WHAT ARE THE ODDS, RIGHT??
MAYBE IT'S YOUR BAD KARMA FOR LEAVING ME LOCKED IN THAT SUBMARINE ALL THESE YEARS!

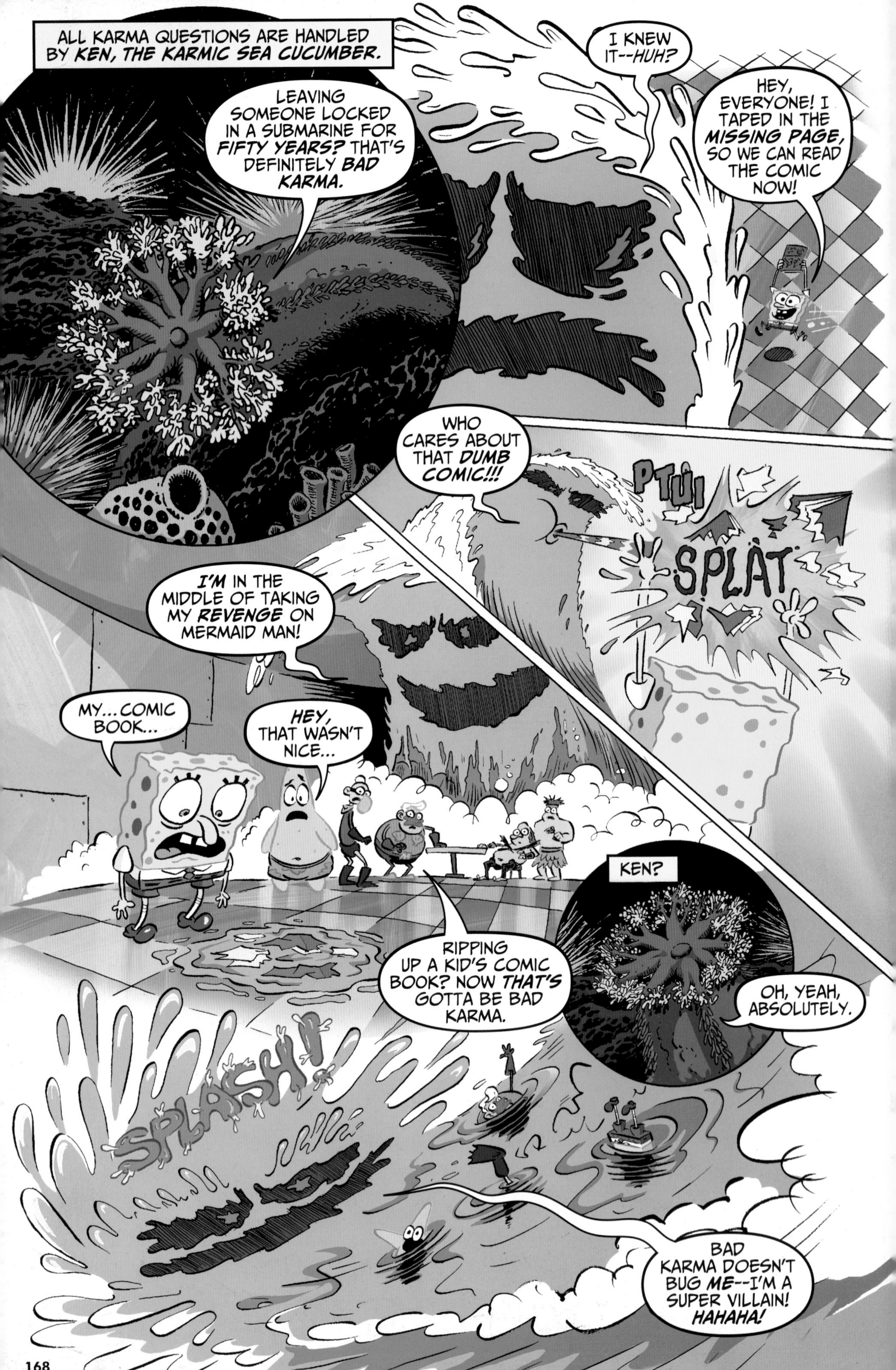

ALL KARMA QUESTIONS ARE HANDLED BY KEN, THE KARMIC SEA CUCUMBER.
LEAVING SOMEONE LOCKED IN A SUBMARINE FOR FIFTY YEARS? THAT'S DEFINITELY BAD KARMA.
I KNEW IT--HUH?
HEY, EVERYONE! I TAPED IN THE MISSING PAGE, SO WE CAN READ THE COMIC NOW!
WHO CARES ABOUT THAT DUMB COMIC!!!
PTUI
SPLAT
I'M IN THE MIDDLE OF TAKING MY REVENGE ON MERMAID MAN!
MY...COMIC BOOK...
HEY, THAT WASN'T NICE...
KEN?
RIPPING UP A KID'S COMIC BOOK? NOW THAT'S GOTTA BE BAD KARMA.
OH, YEAH, ABSOLUTELY.
SPLASH!
BAD KARMA DOESN'T BUG ME--I'M A SUPER VILLAIN! HAHAHA!

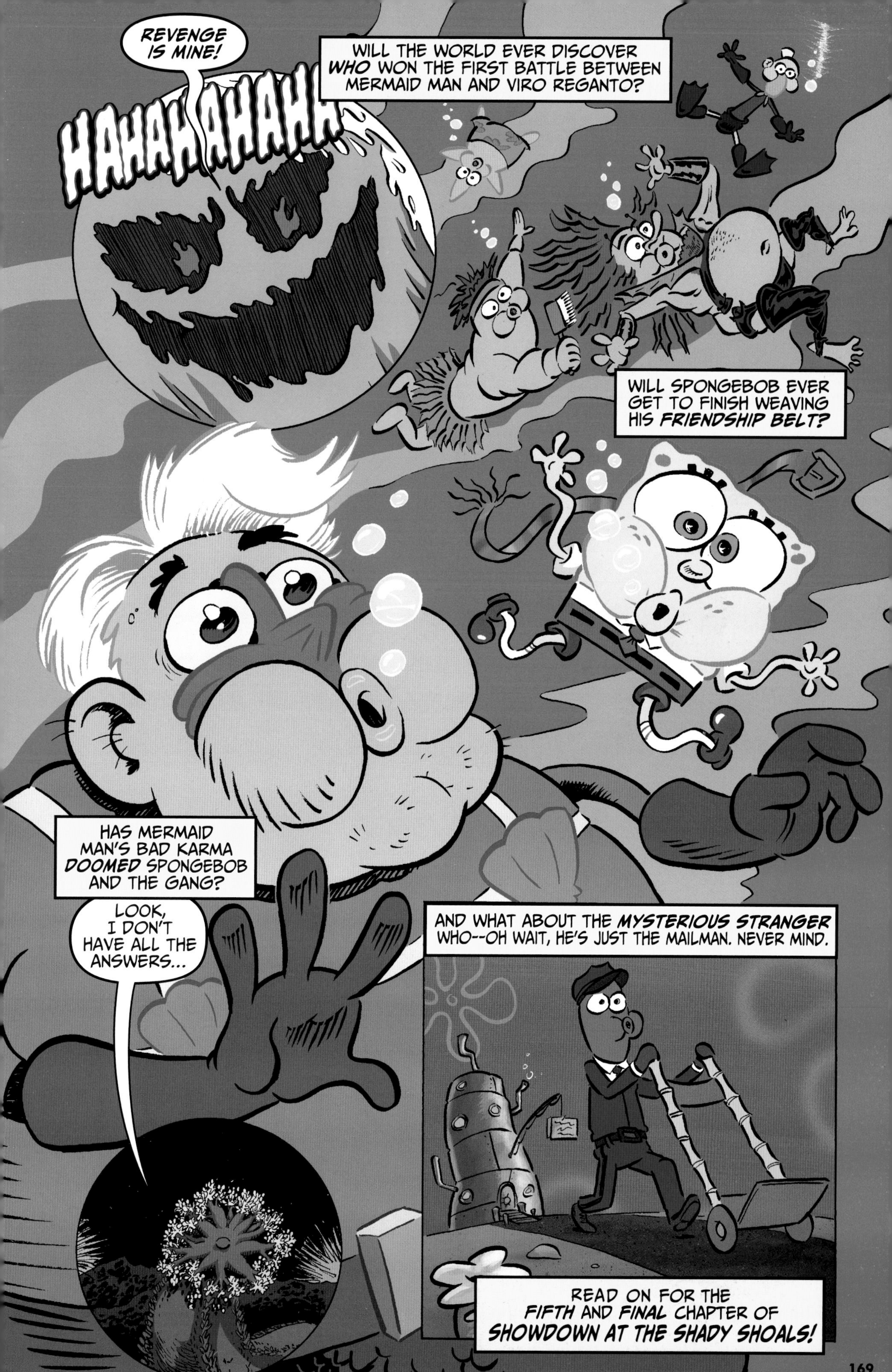
REVENGE IS MINE!
HAHAHAHAHAHA
WILL THE WORLD EVER DISCOVER WHO WON THE FIRST BATTLE BETWEEN MERMAID MAN AND VIRO REGANTO?
WILL SPONGEBOB EVER GET TO FINISH WEAVING HIS FRIENDSHIP BELT?
HAS MERMAID MAN'S BAD KARMA DOOMED SPONGEBOB AND THE GANG?
LOOK, I DON'T HAVE ALL THE ANSWERS...
AND WHAT ABOUT THE MYSTERIOUS STRANGER WHO--OH WAIT, HE'S JUST THE MAILMAN. NEVER MIND.
READ ON FOR THE FIFTH AND FINAL CHAPTER OF SHOWDOWN AT THE SHADY SHOALS!

ATTENTION BOYS AND GIRLS!

MALVENKO! (DEFEAT)
MALLERTA! (CLUMSY)
PRETIGU! (PREPARE)
MIA! (MY)
ATENDU! (WAIT)
OFFICE
VI STULTA! (YOU FOOL!)

Tired of THROWING YOUR VOICE in only ONE language? Well, now your rather specific problem is solved — with this newly patented, almost-portable device derived from *deep-sea secrets!* THE ESPERANTO VENTRILOQUISM CONTRIVANCE lets you throw your voice in a different, **STRANGE** language from a lost civilization! Fool your friends! Confuse your parents! Scare strangers!! Talk to yourself!!! EXCLAMATION POINTS!!!!!

All words and definitions shown are featured in this story of SpongeBob Comics. Esperanto Ventriloquism Contrivance not available in stores or by mail.

REAL RUSTY 50-YEAR-OLD SUBMARINE!

Over 575 feet long!

Hatch opens and closes manually!

Big enough to imprison sentient tidal wave bent on revenge!

$1.00

POSSIBLE FEATURES INCLUDE
- Entirely made of metal!
- See-through windows!
- Controls that once worked!
- Lights that probably blinked!

Found abandoned near the Ancient Lost City of Urbo, this modern wonder can now be yours. Your friends will marvel as you tour them around the bow, the stern, and the hull! You'll be the talk of the reef! This is the exact model they base better-looking replicas on!

10-DAY FREE TRIAL

Rush me my RUSTY SUBMARINE. I can use it for 10 days and if I am not satisfied I can abandon it wherever I want.

❑ SEND IT PREPAID: I have enclosed $1 plus $300,000 to help cover shipping charges.

NAME ____________________

ADDRESS ____________________

OCEAN DEPTH ____________________

SUPERHERO AFFILIATION ____________________

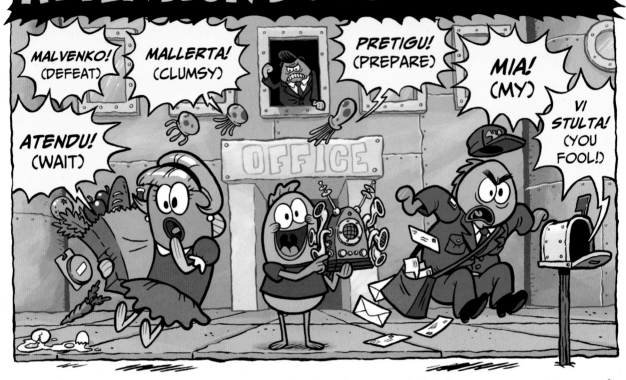

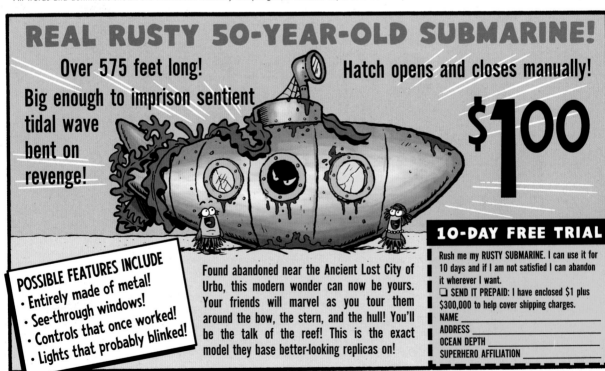

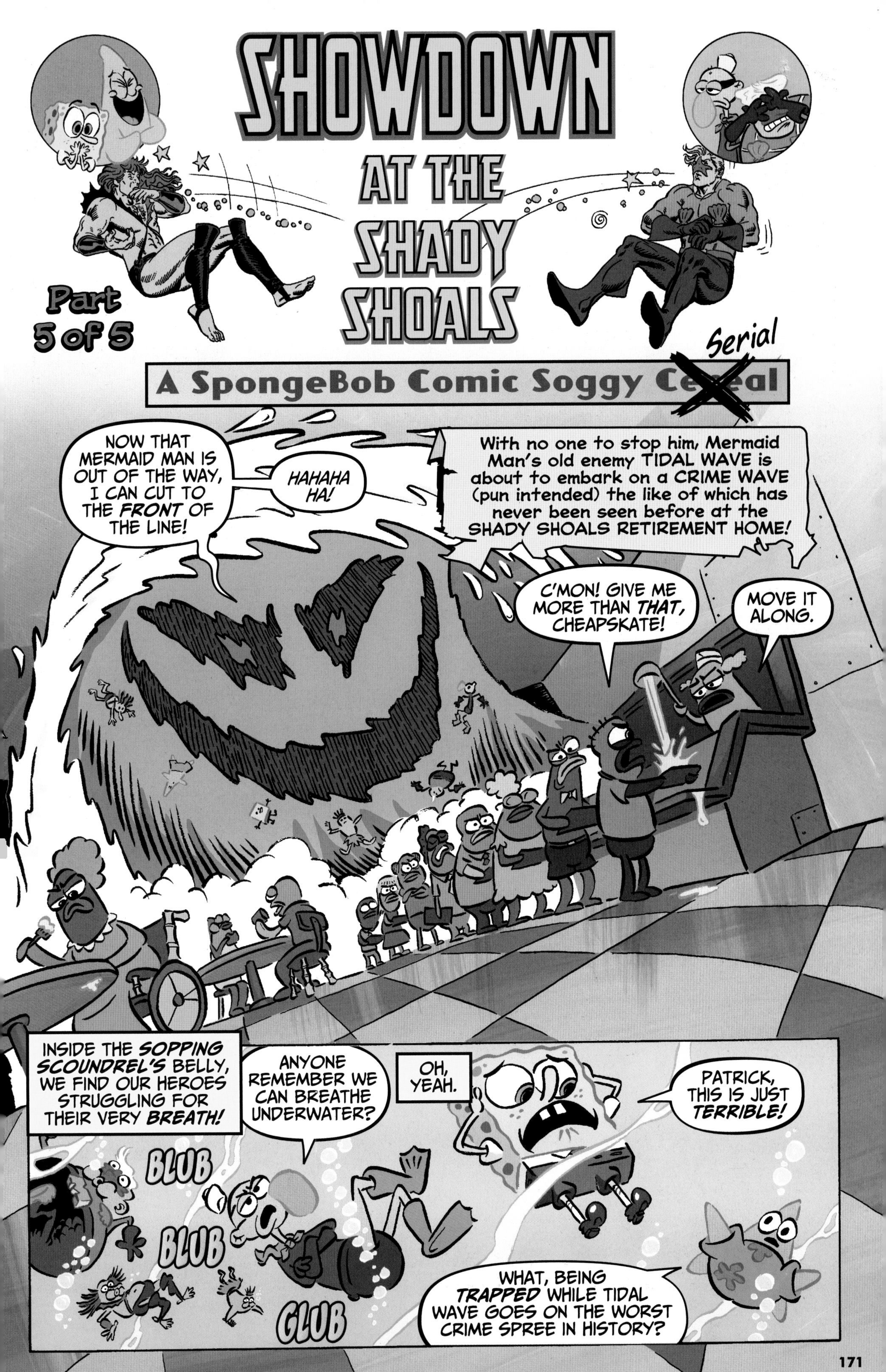
SHOWDOWN AT THE SHADY SHOALS
Part 5 of 5
A SpongeBob Comic Soggy Cereal Serial
NOW THAT MERMAID MAN IS OUT OF THE WAY, I CAN CUT TO THE FRONT OF THE LINE!
HAHAHA HA!
With no one to stop him, Mermaid Man's old enemy TIDAL WAVE is about to embark on a CRIME WAVE (pun intended) the like of which has never been seen before at the SHADY SHOALS RETIREMENT HOME!
C'MON! GIVE ME MORE THAN THAT, CHEAPSKATE!
MOVE IT ALONG.
INSIDE THE SOPPING SCOUNDREL'S BELLY, WE FIND OUR HEROES STRUGGLING FOR THEIR VERY BREATH!
ANYONE REMEMBER WE CAN BREATHE UNDERWATER?
OH, YEAH.
PATRICK, THIS IS JUST TERRIBLE!
BLUB
BLUB
GLUB
WHAT, BEING TRAPPED WHILE TIDAL WAVE GOES ON THE WORST CRIME SPREE IN HISTORY?

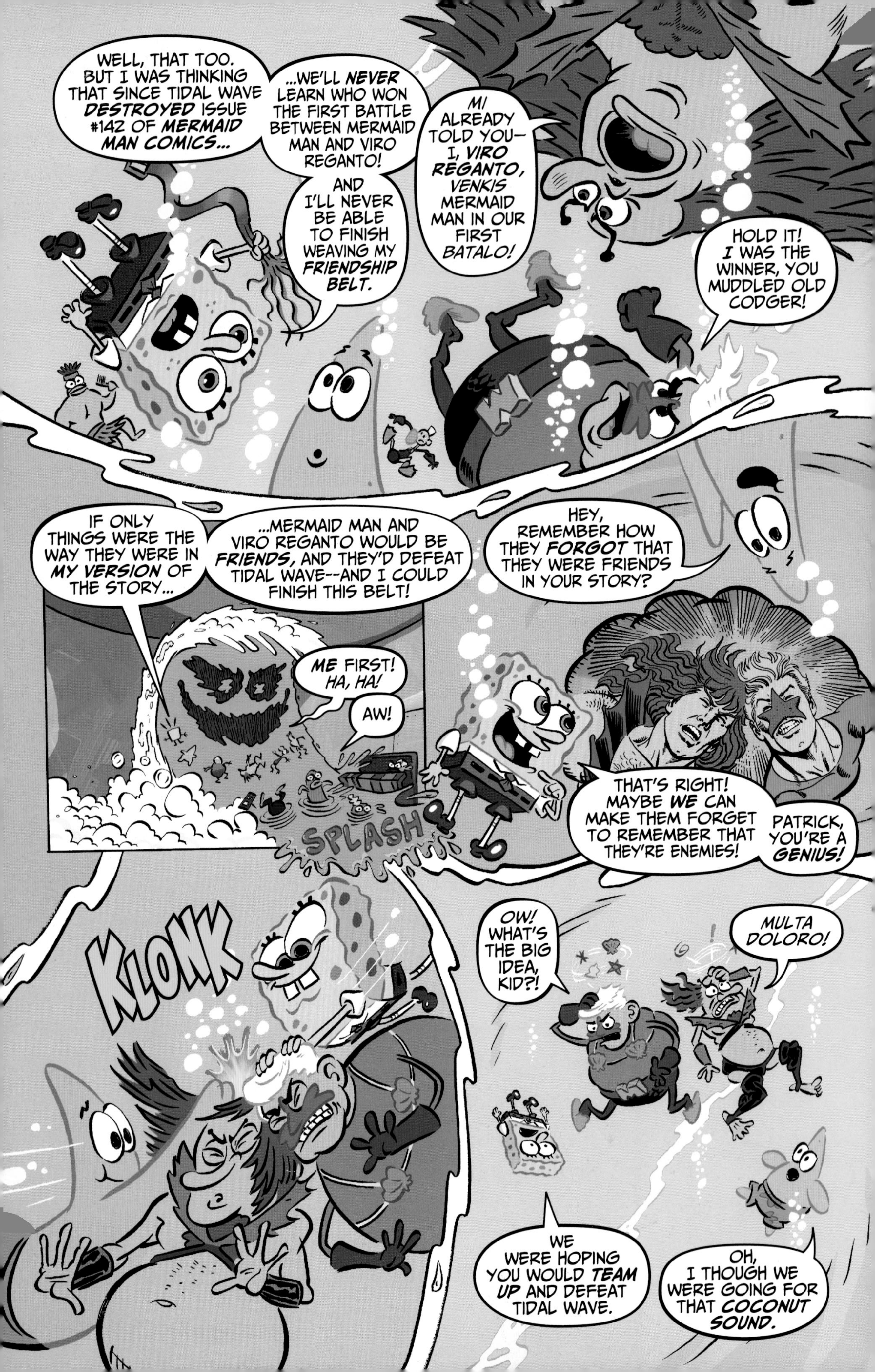

WELL, THAT TOO. BUT I WAS THINKING THAT SINCE TIDAL WAVE DESTROYED ISSUE #142 OF MERMAID MAN COMICS...
...WE'LL NEVER LEARN WHO WON THE FIRST BATTLE BETWEEN MERMAID MAN AND VIRO REGANTO!
AND I'LL NEVER BE ABLE TO FINISH WEAVING MY FRIENDSHIP BELT.
MI ALREADY TOLD YOU— I, VIRO REGANTO, VENKIS MERMAID MAN IN OUR FIRST BATALO!
HOLD IT! I WAS THE WINNER, YOU MUDDLED OLD CODGER!
IF ONLY THINGS WERE THE WAY THEY WERE IN MY VERSION OF THE STORY...
...MERMAID MAN AND VIRO REGANTO WOULD BE FRIENDS, AND THEY'D DEFEAT TIDAL WAVE--AND I COULD FINISH THIS BELT!
ME FIRST! HA, HA!
AW!
SPLASH
HEY, REMEMBER HOW THEY FORGOT THAT THEY WERE FRIENDS IN YOUR STORY?
THAT'S RIGHT! MAYBE WE CAN MAKE THEM FORGET TO REMEMBER THAT THEY'RE ENEMIES!
PATRICK, YOU'RE A GENIUS!
KLONK
OW! WHAT'S THE BIG IDEA, KID?!
MULTA DOLORO!
WE WERE HOPING YOU WOULD TEAM UP AND DEFEAT TIDAL WAVE.
OH, I THOUGH WE WERE GOING FOR THAT COCONUT SOUND.

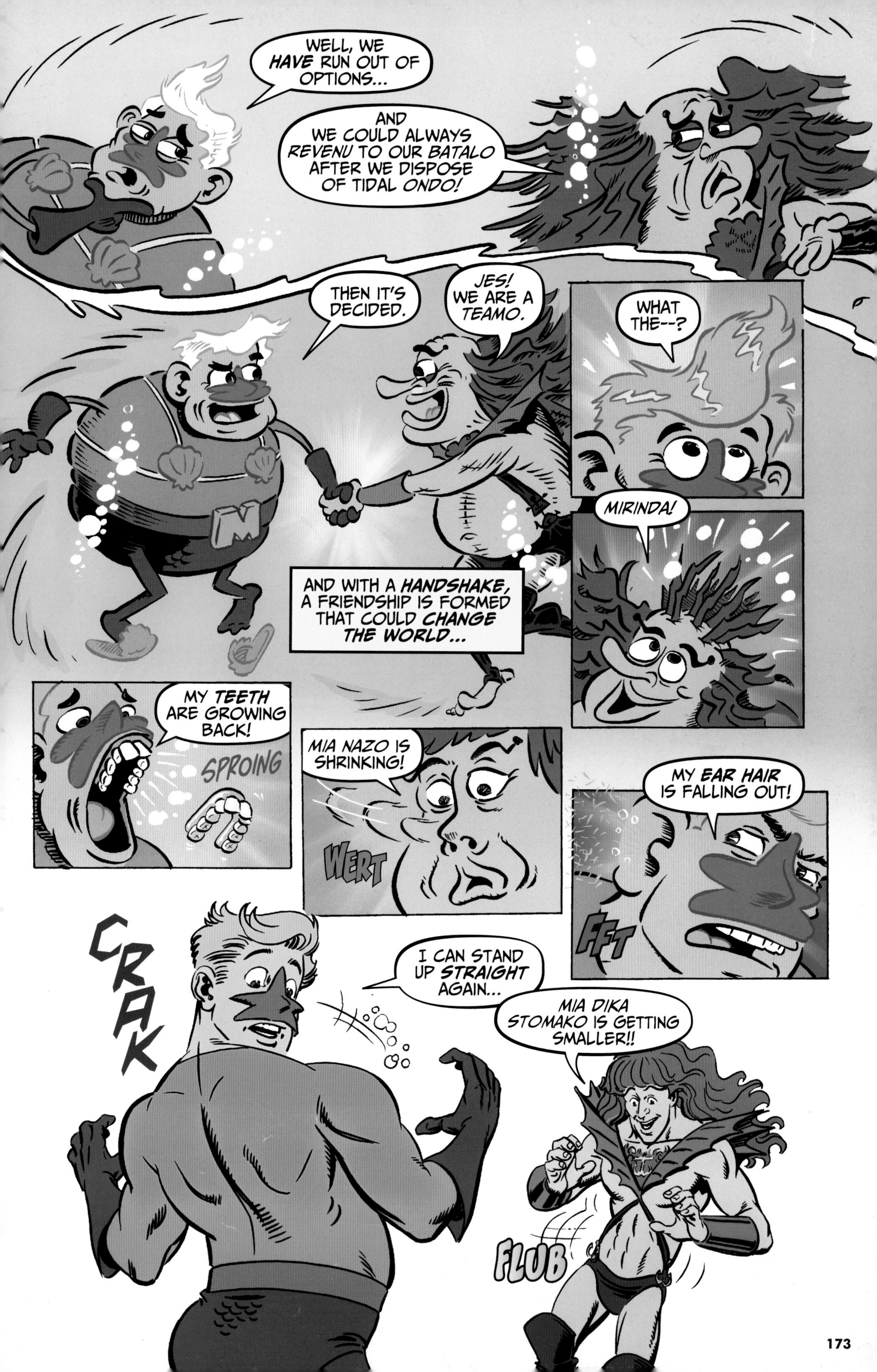
WELL, WE HAVE RUN OUT OF OPTIONS...
AND WE COULD ALWAYS REVENU TO OUR BATALO AFTER WE DISPOSE OF TIDAL ONDO!
THEN IT'S DECIDED.
JES! WE ARE A TEAMO.
AND WITH A HANDSHAKE, A FRIENDSHIP IS FORMED THAT COULD CHANGE THE WORLD...
WHAT THE--?
MIRINDA!
MY TEETH ARE GROWING BACK!
SPROING
MIA NAZO IS SHRINKING!
WERT
MY EAR HAIR IS FALLING OUT!
FFT
CRAK
I CAN STAND UP STRAIGHT AGAIN...
MIA DIKA STOMAKO IS GETTING SMALLER!!
FLUB

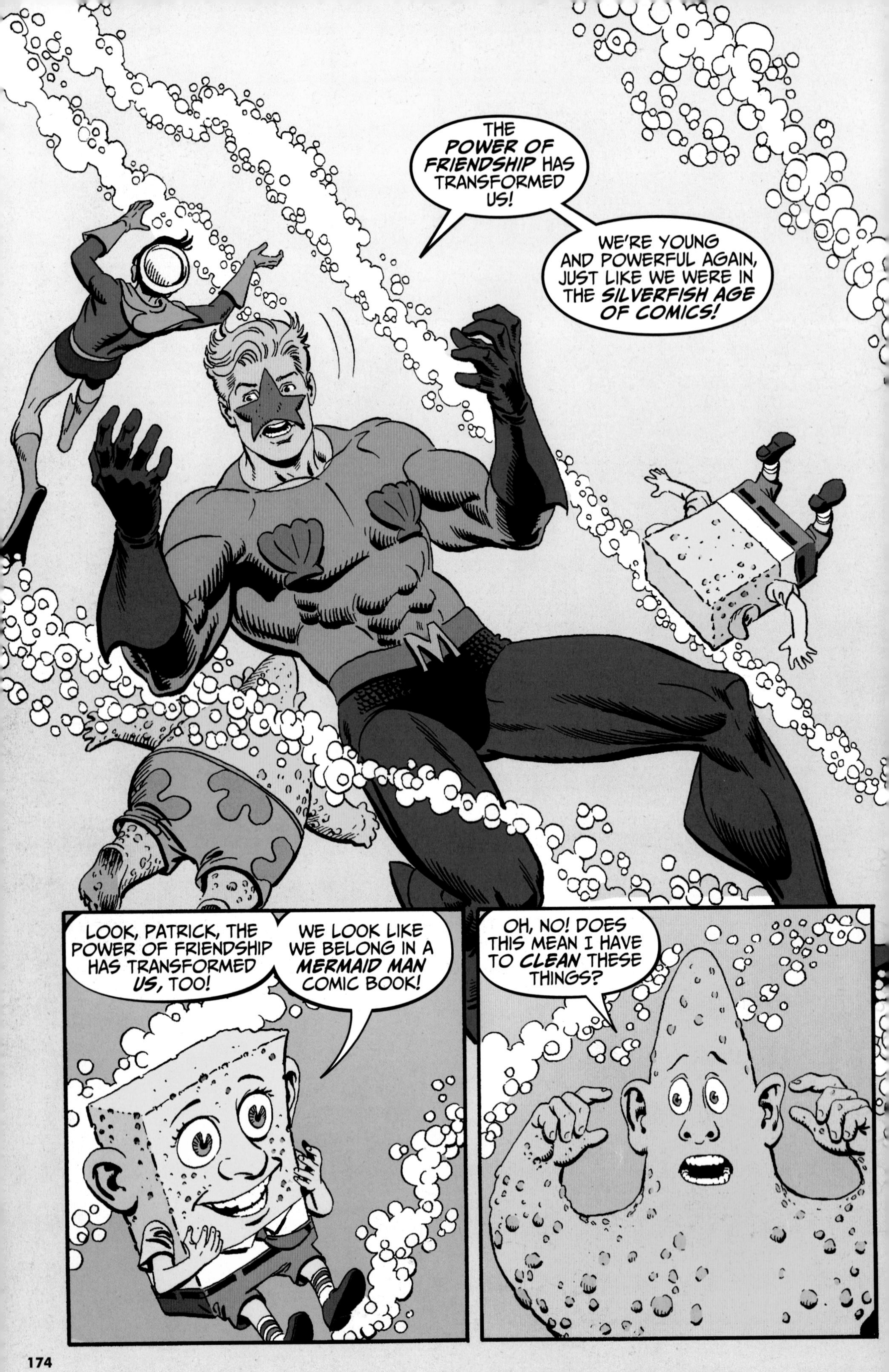

THE POWER OF FRIENDSHIP HAS TRANSFORMED US!
WE'RE YOUNG AND POWERFUL AGAIN, JUST LIKE WE WERE IN THE SILVERFISH AGE OF COMICS!
LOOK, PATRICK, THE POWER OF FRIENDSHIP HAS TRANSFORMED US, TOO!
WE LOOK LIKE WE BELONG IN A MERMAID MAN COMIC BOOK!
OH, NO! DOES THIS MEAN I HAVE TO CLEAN THESE THINGS?

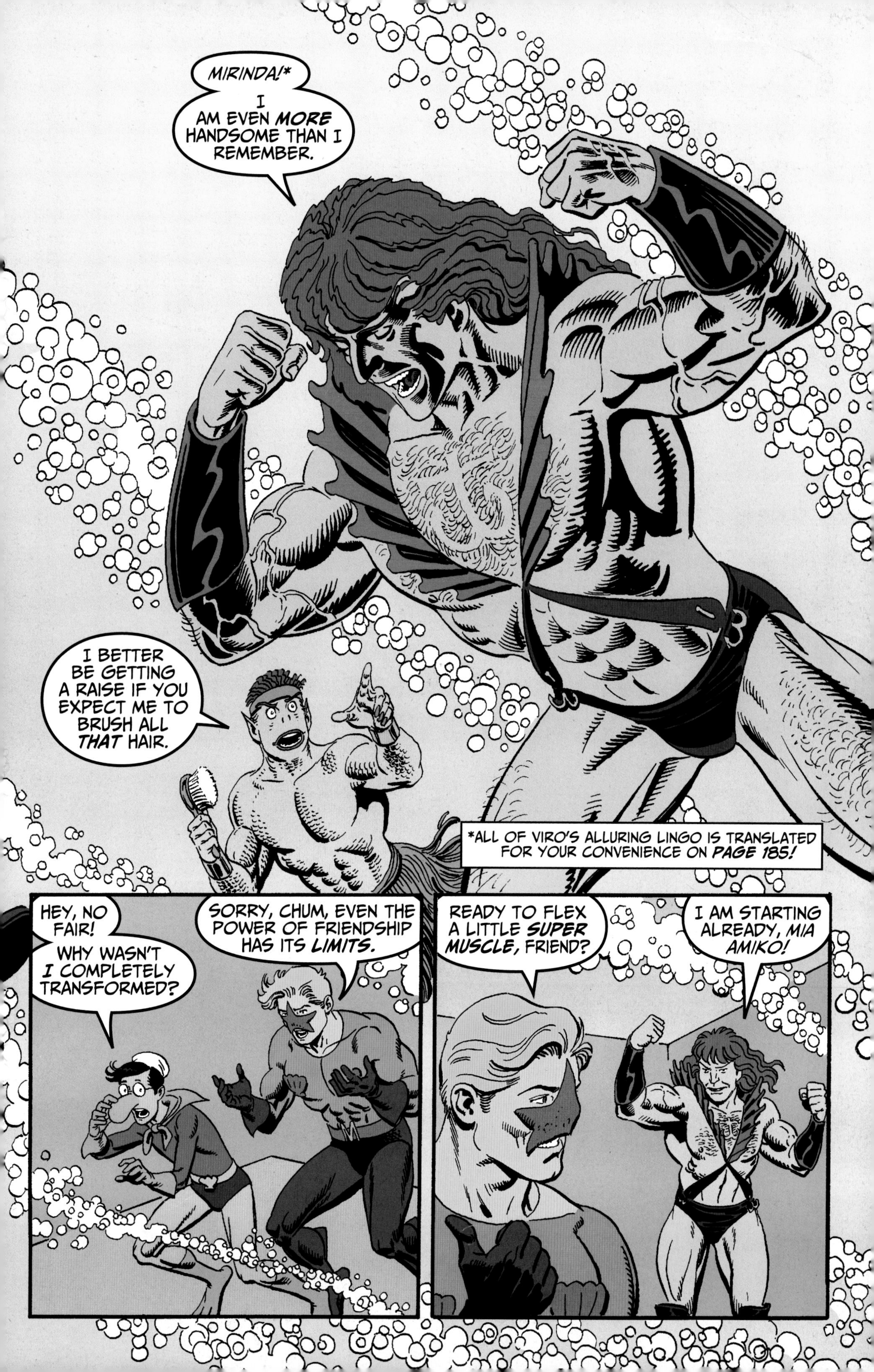
MIRINDA!*
I AM EVEN MORE HANDSOME THAN I REMEMBER.
I BETTER BE GETTING A RAISE IF YOU EXPECT ME TO BRUSH ALL THAT HAIR.
*ALL OF VIRO'S ALLURING LINGO IS TRANSLATED FOR YOUR CONVENIENCE ON PAGE 185!
HEY, NO FAIR!
WHY WASN'T I COMPLETELY TRANSFORMED?
SORRY, CHUM, EVEN THE POWER OF FRIENDSHIP HAS ITS LIMITS.
READY TO FLEX A LITTLE SUPER MUSCLE, FRIEND?
I AM STARTING ALREADY, MIA AMIKO!

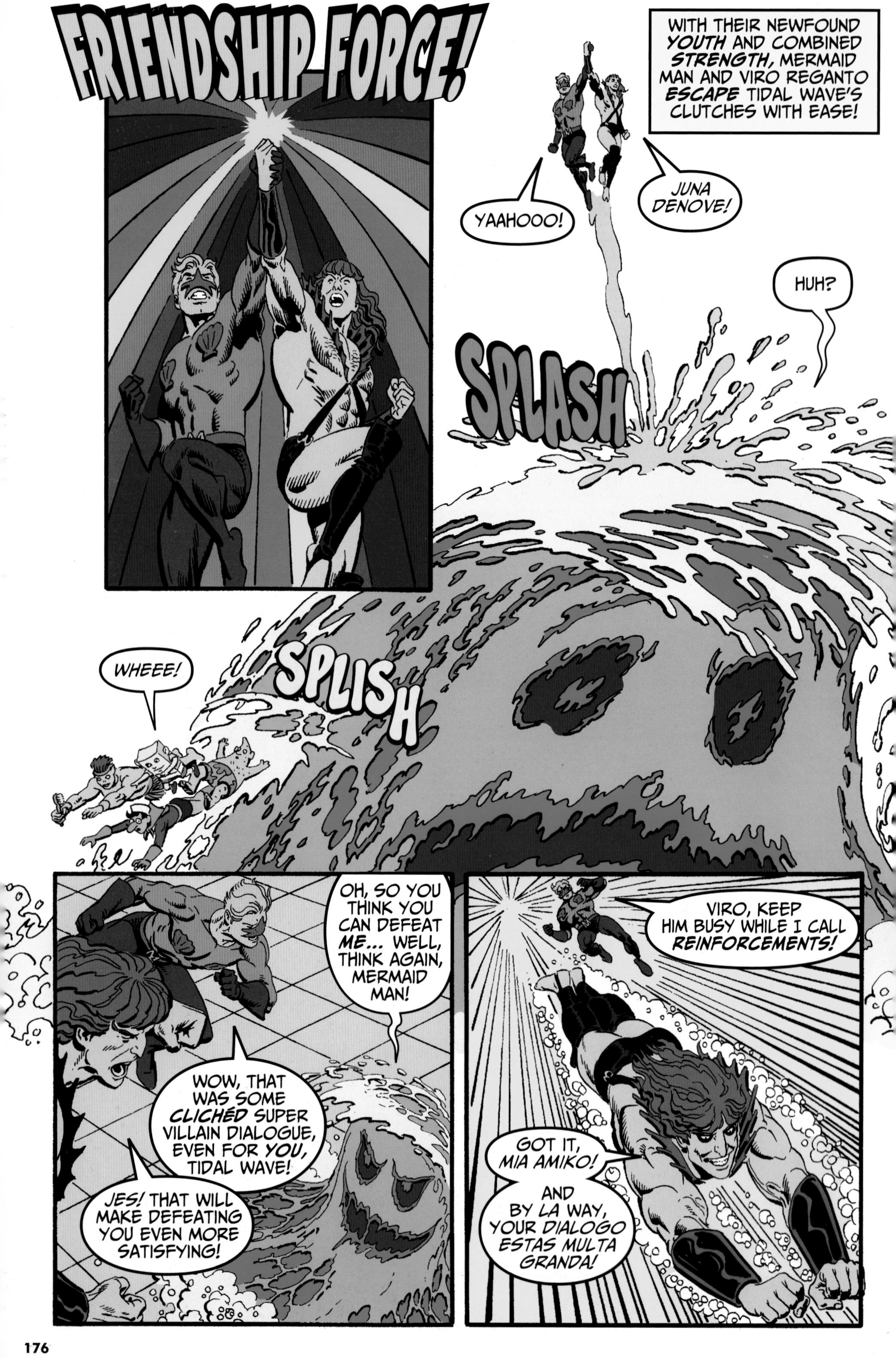
FRIENDSHIP FORCE!
WITH THEIR NEWFOUND YOUTH AND COMBINED STRENGTH, MERMAID MAN AND VIRO REGANTO ESCAPE TIDAL WAVE'S CLUTCHES WITH EASE!
YAAHOOO!
JUNA DENOVE!
HUH?
SPLASH
WHEEE!
SPLISH
OH, SO YOU THINK YOU CAN DEFEAT ME... WELL, THINK AGAIN, MERMAID MAN!
WOW, THAT WAS SOME CLICHÉD SUPER VILLAIN DIALOGUE, EVEN FOR YOU, TIDAL WAVE!
JES! THAT WILL MAKE DEFEATING YOU EVEN MORE SATISFYING!
VIRO, KEEP HIM BUSY WHILE I CALL REINFORCEMENTS!
GOT IT, MIA AMIKO!
AND BY LA WAY, YOUR DIALOGO ESTAS MULTA GRANDA!

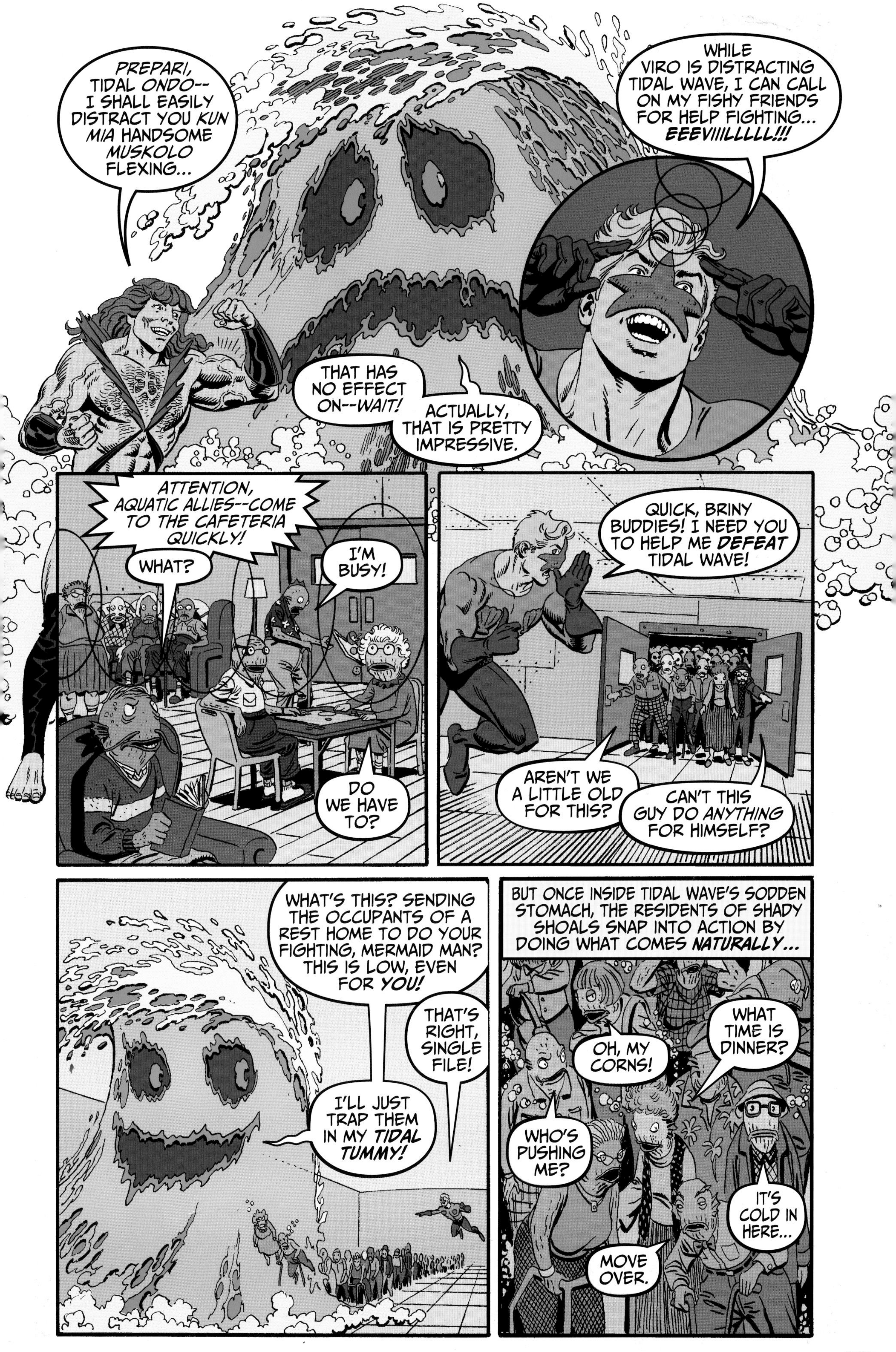
PREPARI, TIDAL ONDO-- I SHALL EASILY DISTRACT YOU KUN MIA HANDSOME MUSKOLO FLEXING...
WHILE VIRO IS DISTRACTING TIDAL WAVE, I CAN CALL ON MY FISHY FRIENDS FOR HELP FIGHTING... EEEVIIIILLLLL!!!
THAT HAS NO EFFECT ON--WAIT!
ACTUALLY, THAT IS PRETTY IMPRESSIVE.
ATTENTION, AQUATIC ALLIES--COME TO THE CAFETERIA QUICKLY!
WHAT?
I'M BUSY!
DO WE HAVE TO?
QUICK, BRINY BUDDIES! I NEED YOU TO HELP ME DEFEAT TIDAL WAVE!
AREN'T WE A LITTLE OLD FOR THIS?
CAN'T THIS GUY DO ANYTHING FOR HIMSELF?
WHAT'S THIS? SENDING THE OCCUPANTS OF A REST HOME TO DO YOUR FIGHTING, MERMAID MAN? THIS IS LOW, EVEN FOR YOU!
THAT'S RIGHT, SINGLE FILE!
I'LL JUST TRAP THEM IN MY TIDAL TUMMY!
BUT ONCE INSIDE TIDAL WAVE'S SODDEN STOMACH, THE RESIDENTS OF SHADY SHOALS SNAP INTO ACTION BY DOING WHAT COMES NATURALLY...
OH, MY CORNS!
WHAT TIME IS DINNER?
WHO'S PUSHING ME?
IT'S COLD IN HERE...
MOVE OVER.

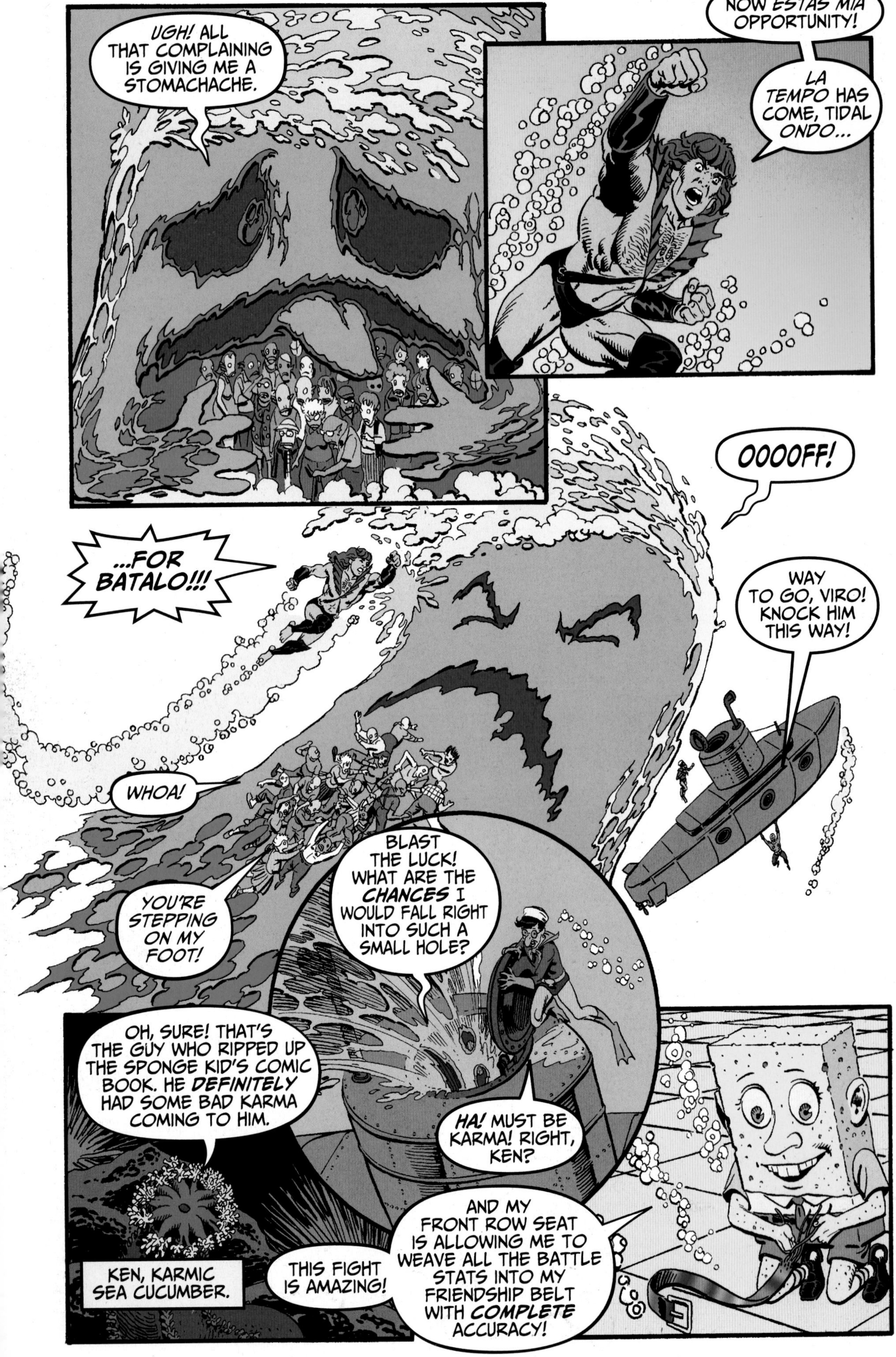
UGH! ALL THAT COMPLAINING IS GIVING ME A STOMACHACHE.
NOW ESTAS MIA OPPORTUNITY!
LA TEMPO HAS COME, TIDAL ONDO...
...FOR BATALO!!!
OOOOFF!
WAY TO GO, VIRO! KNOCK HIM THIS WAY!
WHOA!
YOU'RE STEPPING ON MY FOOT!
BLAST THE LUCK! WHAT ARE THE CHANCES I WOULD FALL RIGHT INTO SUCH A SMALL HOLE?
OH, SURE! THAT'S THE GUY WHO RIPPED UP THE SPONGE KID'S COMIC BOOK. HE DEFINITELY HAD SOME BAD KARMA COMING TO HIM.
HA! MUST BE KARMA! RIGHT, KEN?
KEN, KARMIC SEA CUCUMBER.
THIS FIGHT IS AMAZING!
AND MY FRONT ROW SEAT IS ALLOWING ME TO WEAVE ALL THE BATTLE STATS INTO MY FRIENDSHIP BELT WITH COMPLETE ACCURACY!

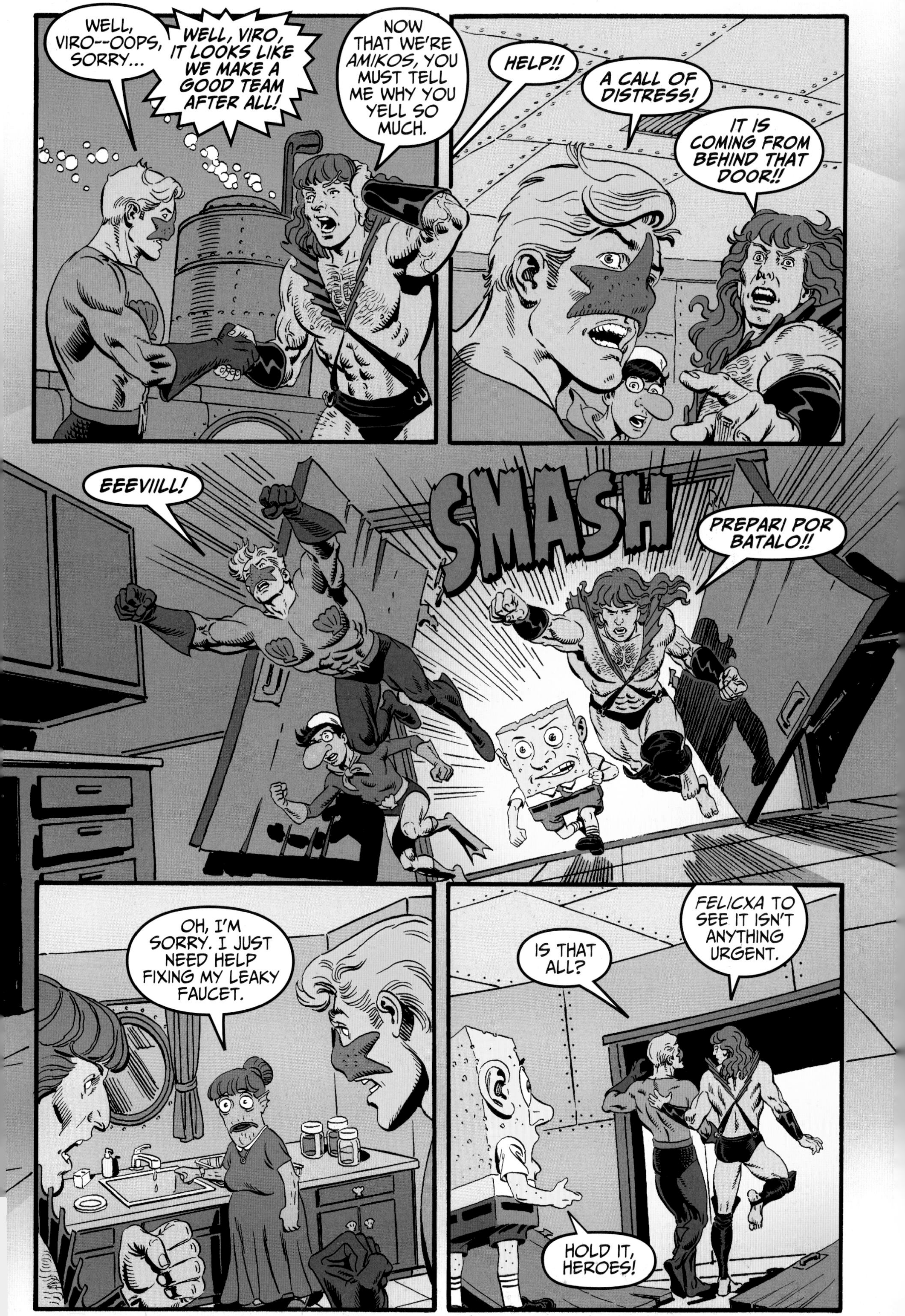
WELL, VIRO--OOPS, SORRY...
WELL, VIRO, IT LOOKS LIKE WE MAKE A GOOD TEAM AFTER ALL!
NOW THAT WE'RE AMIKOS, YOU MUST TELL ME WHY YOU YELL SO MUCH.
HELP!!
A CALL OF DISTRESS!
IT IS COMING FROM BEHIND THAT DOOR!!
EEEVIILL!
SMASH
PREPARI POR BATALO!!
OH, I'M SORRY. I JUST NEED HELP FIXING MY LEAKY FAUCET.
IS THAT ALL?
FELICXA TO SEE IT ISN'T ANYTHING URGENT.
HOLD IT, HEROES!

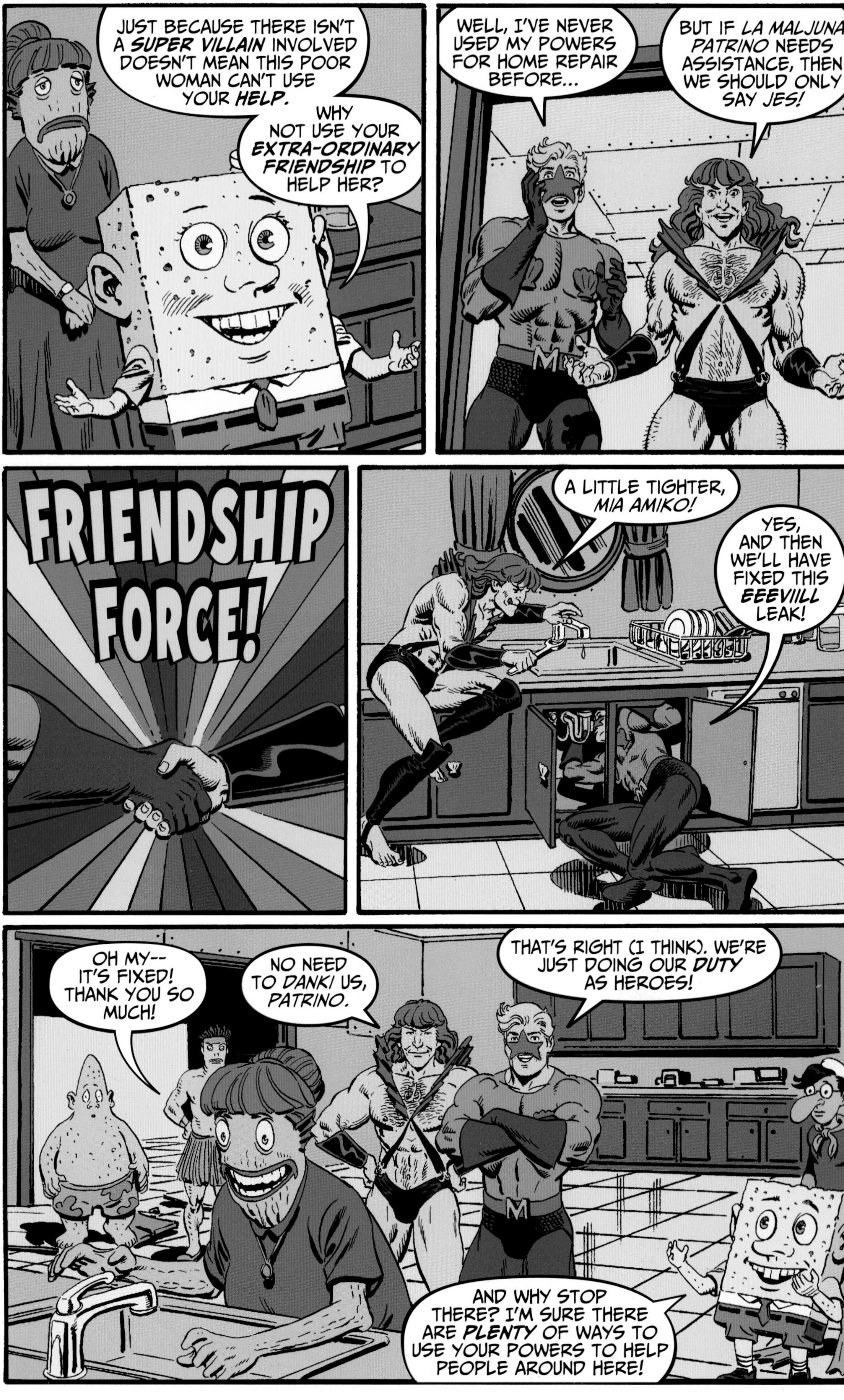
JUST BECAUSE THERE ISN'T A SUPER VILLAIN INVOLVED DOESN'T MEAN THIS POOR WOMAN CAN'T USE YOUR HELP.
WHY NOT USE YOUR EXTRA-ORDINARY FRIENDSHIP TO HELP HER?
WELL, I'VE NEVER USED MY POWERS FOR HOME REPAIR BEFORE...
BUT IF LA MALJUNA PATRINO NEEDS ASSISTANCE, THEN WE SHOULD ONLY SAY JES!
FRIENDSHIP FORCE!
A LITTLE TIGHTER, MIA AMIKO!
YES, AND THEN WE'LL HAVE FIXED THIS EEEVIILL LEAK!
OH MY-- IT'S FIXED! THANK YOU SO MUCH!
NO NEED TO DANKI US, PATRINO.
THAT'S RIGHT (I THINK). WE'RE JUST DOING OUR DUTY AS HEROES!
AND WHY STOP THERE? I'M SURE THERE ARE PLENTY OF WAYS TO USE YOUR POWERS TO HELP PEOPLE AROUND HERE!

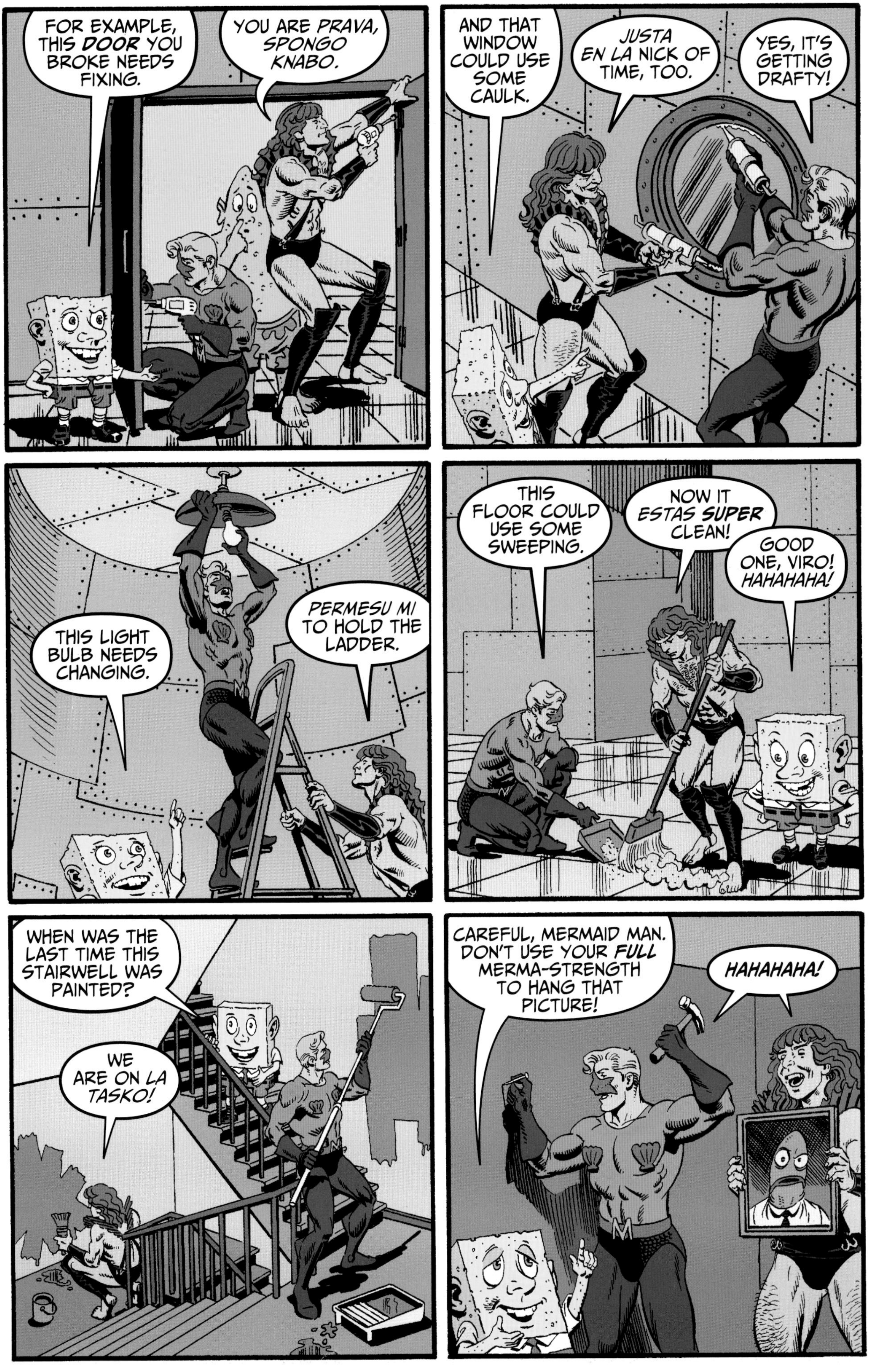
FOR EXAMPLE, THIS DOOR YOU BROKE NEEDS FIXING.
YOU ARE PRAVA, SPONGO KNABO.
AND THAT WINDOW COULD USE SOME CAULK.
JUSTA EN LA NICK OF TIME, TOO.
YES, IT'S GETTING DRAFTY!
THIS LIGHT BULB NEEDS CHANGING.
PERMESU MI TO HOLD THE LADDER.
THIS FLOOR COULD USE SOME SWEEPING.
NOW IT ESTAS SUPER CLEAN!
GOOD ONE, VIRO! HAHAHAHA!
WHEN WAS THE LAST TIME THIS STAIRWELL WAS PAINTED?
WE ARE ON LA TASKO!
CAREFUL, MERMAID MAN. DON'T USE YOUR FULL MERMA-STRENGTH TO HANG THAT PICTURE!
HAHAHAHA!

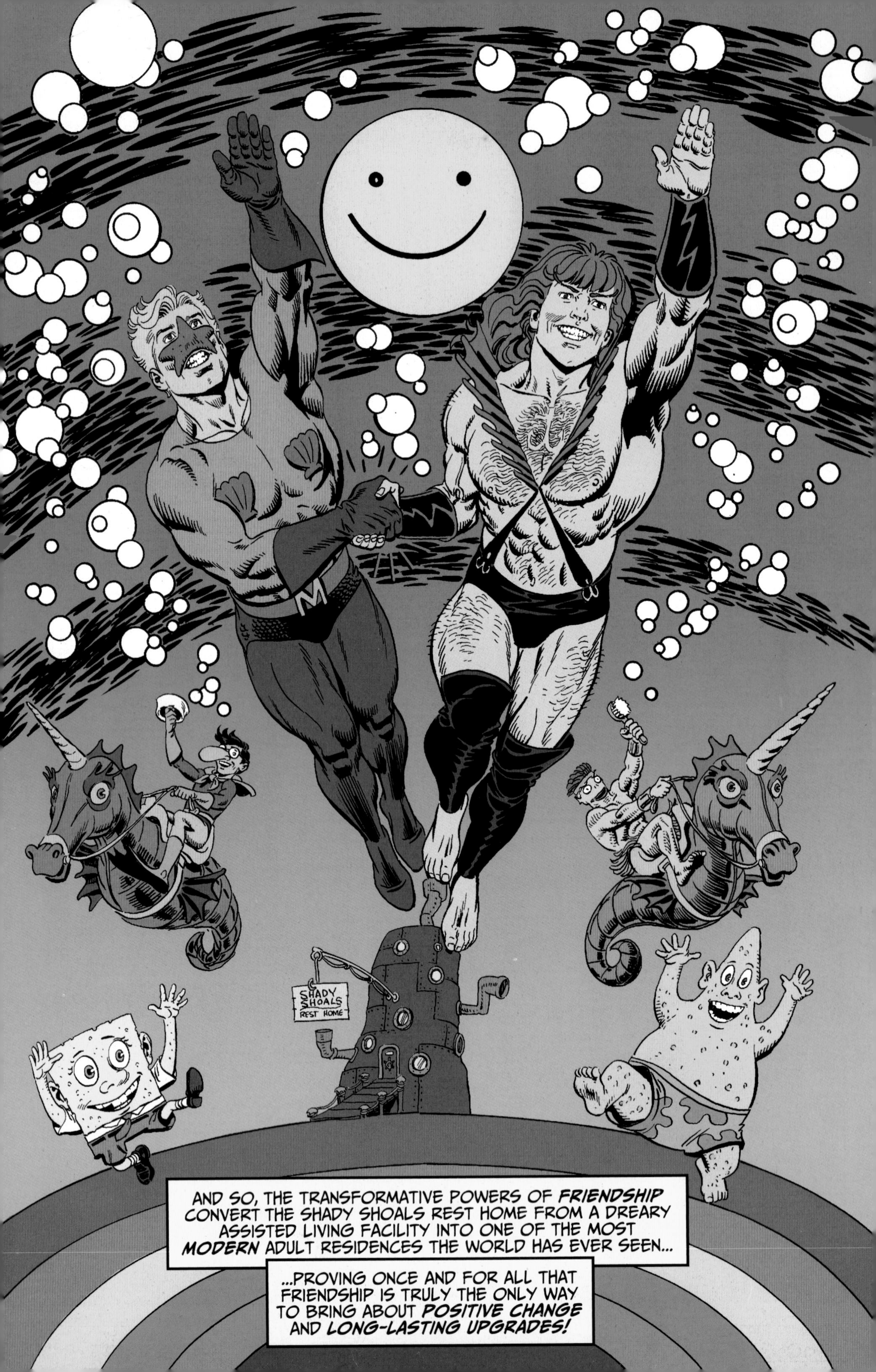
SHADY SHOALS REST HOME
AND SO, THE TRANSFORMATIVE POWERS OF *FRIENDSHIP* CONVERT THE SHADY SHOALS REST HOME FROM A DREARY ASSISTED LIVING FACILITY INTO ONE OF THE MOST *MODERN* ADULT RESIDENCES THE WORLD HAS EVER SEEN...
...PROVING ONCE AND FOR ALL THAT FRIENDSHIP IS TRULY THE ONLY WAY TO BRING ABOUT *POSITIVE CHANGE* AND *LONG-LASTING UPGRADES!*

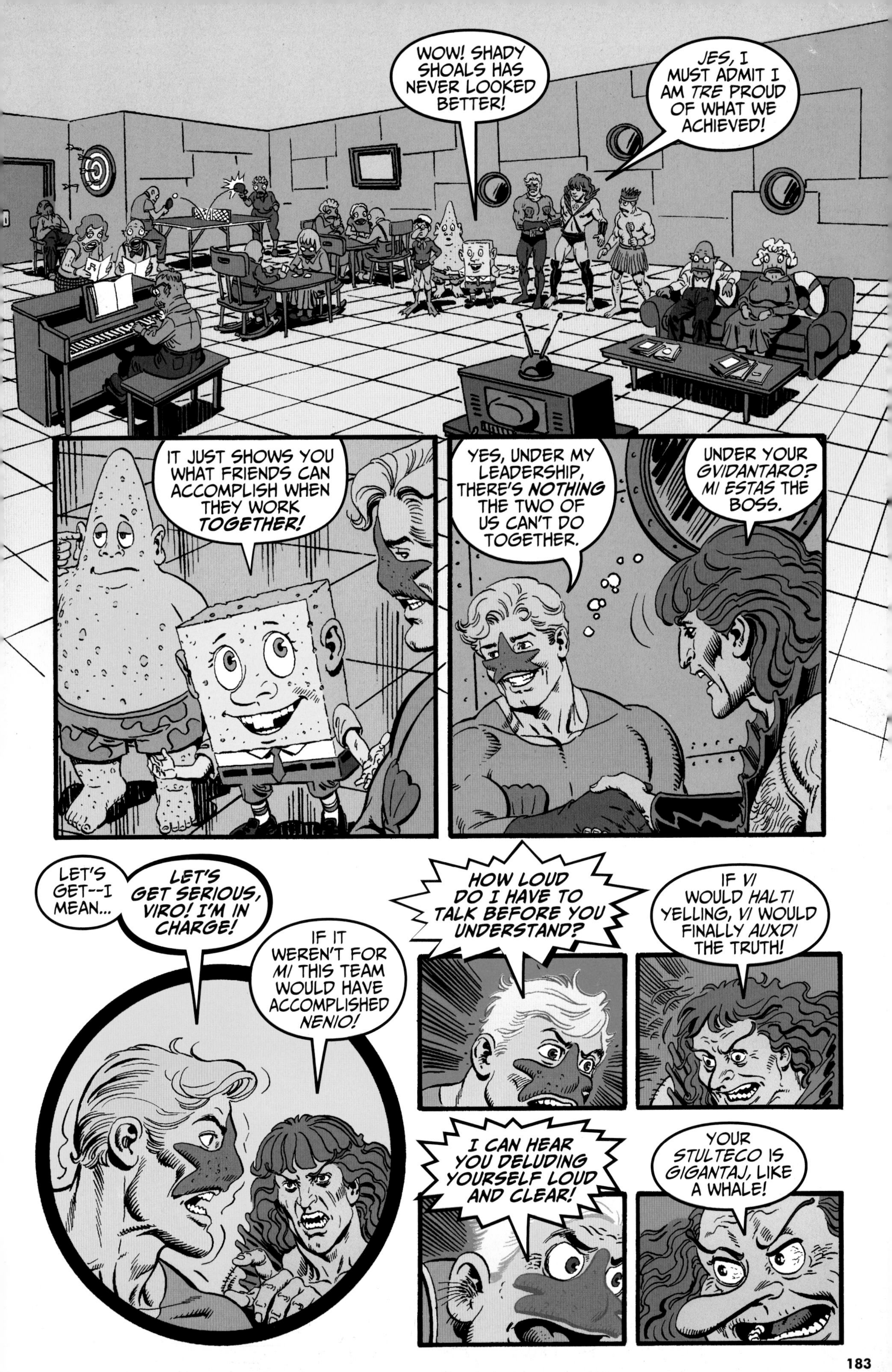
WOW! SHADY SHOALS HAS NEVER LOOKED BETTER!
JES, I MUST ADMIT I AM TRE PROUD OF WHAT WE ACHIEVED!
IT JUST SHOWS YOU WHAT FRIENDS CAN ACCOMPLISH WHEN THEY WORK TOGETHER!
YES, UNDER MY LEADERSHIP, THERE'S NOTHING THE TWO OF US CAN'T DO TOGETHER.
UNDER YOUR GVIDANTARO? MI ESTAS THE BOSS.
LET'S GET--I MEAN...
LET'S GET SERIOUS, VIRO! I'M IN CHARGE!
IF IT WEREN'T FOR MI THIS TEAM WOULD HAVE ACCOMPLISHED NENIO!
HOW LOUD DO I HAVE TO TALK BEFORE YOU UNDERSTAND?
IF VI WOULD HALTI YELLING, VI WOULD FINALLY AUXDI THE TRUTH!
I CAN HEAR YOU DELUDING YOURSELF LOUD AND CLEAR!
YOUR STULTECO IS GIGANTAJ, LIKE A WHALE!

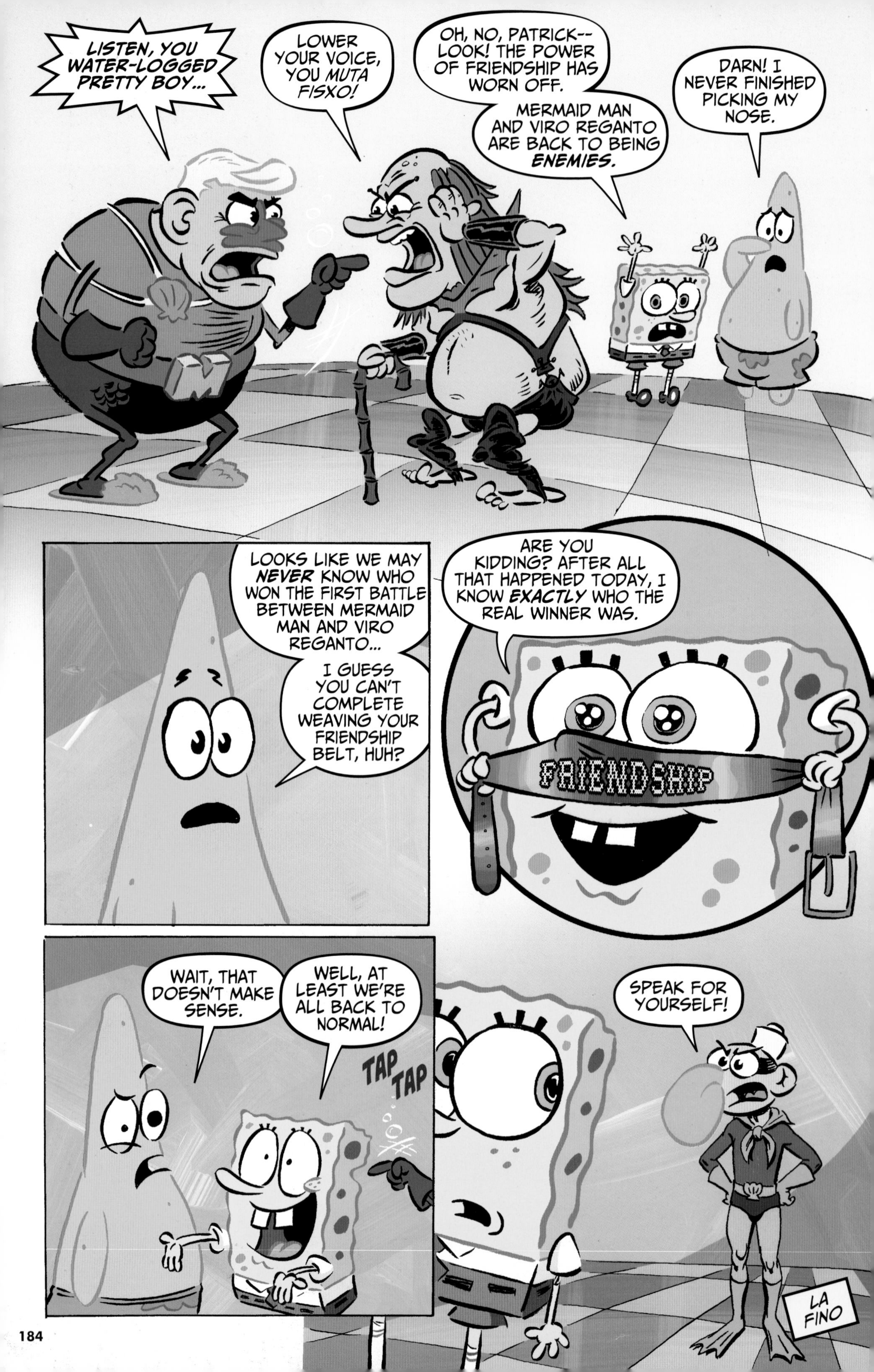
LISTEN, YOU WATER-LOGGED PRETTY BOY...
LOWER YOUR VOICE, YOU *MUTA FISXO!*
OH, NO, PATRICK-- LOOK! THE POWER OF FRIENDSHIP HAS WORN OFF.
MERMAID MAN AND VIRO REGANTO ARE BACK TO BEING ***ENEMIES.***
DARN! I NEVER FINISHED PICKING MY NOSE.
LOOKS LIKE WE MAY ***NEVER*** KNOW WHO WON THE FIRST BATTLE BETWEEN MERMAID MAN AND VIRO REGANTO...
I GUESS YOU CAN'T COMPLETE WEAVING YOUR FRIENDSHIP BELT, HUH?
ARE YOU KIDDING? AFTER ALL THAT HAPPENED TODAY, I KNOW ***EXACTLY*** WHO THE REAL WINNER WAS.
FRIENDSHIP
WAIT, THAT DOESN'T MAKE SENSE.
WELL, AT LEAST WE'RE ALL BACK TO NORMAL!
TAP TAP
SPEAK FOR YOURSELF!
LA FINO

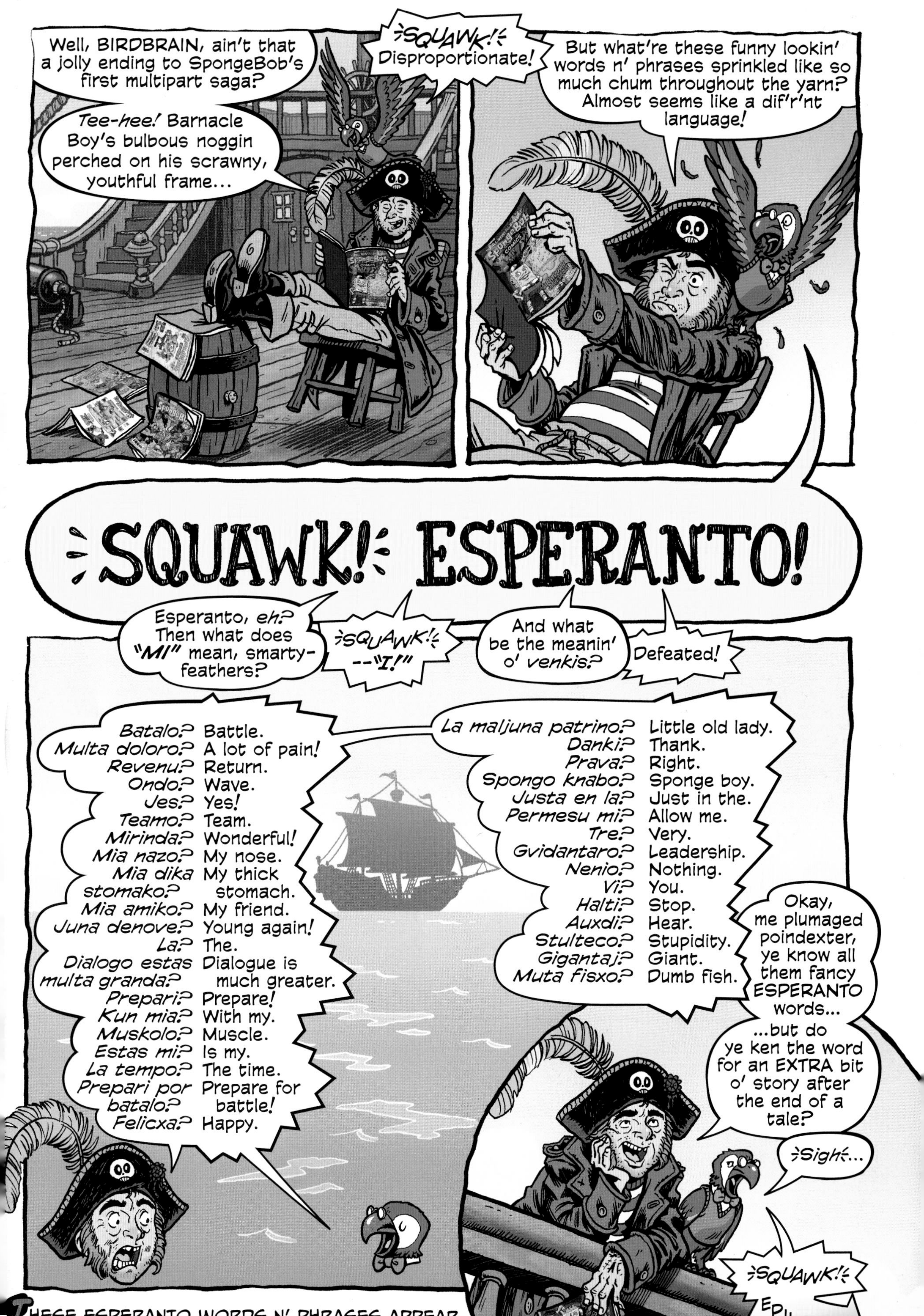

Well, BIRDBRAIN, ain't that a jolly ending to SpongeBob's first multipart saga?
SQUAWK! Disproportionate!
Tee-hee! Barnacle Boy's bulbous noggin perched on his scrawny, youthful frame...
But what're these funny lookin' words n' phrases sprinkled like so much chum throughout the yarn? Almost seems like a dif'r'nt language!
SQUAWK! ESPERANTO!
Esperanto, eh? Then what does "MI" mean, smarty-feathers?
SQUAWK! --"I!"
And what be the meanin' o' venkis?
Defeated!
Batalo? Battle.
Multa doloro? A lot of pain!
Revenu? Return.
Ondo? Wave.
Jes? Yes!
Teamo? Team.
Mirinda? Wonderful!
Mia nazo? My nose.
Mia dika stomako? My thick stomach.
Mia amiko? My friend.
Juna denove? Young again!
La? The.
Dialogo estas multa granda? Dialogue is much greater.
Prepari? Prepare!
Kun mia? With my.
Muskolo? Muscle.
Estas mi? Is my.
La tempo? The time.
Prepari por batalo? Prepare for battle!
Felicxa? Happy.
La maljuna patrino? Little old lady.
Danki? Thank.
Prava? Right.
Spongo knabo? Sponge boy.
Justa en la? Just in the.
Permesu mi? Allow me.
Tre? Very.
Gvidantaro? Leadership.
Nenio? Nothing.
Vi? You.
Halti? Stop.
Auxdi? Hear.
Stulteco? Stupidity.
Gigantaj? Giant.
Muta fisxo? Dumb fish.
Okay, me plumaged poindexter, ye know all them fancy ESPERANTO words...
...but do ye ken the word for an EXTRA bit o' story after the end of a tale?
Sigh...
SQUAWK! EPILOGUE!
THESE ESPERANTO WORDS N' PHRASES APPEAR IN THE PRECEDING STORY IN THIS ORDER!

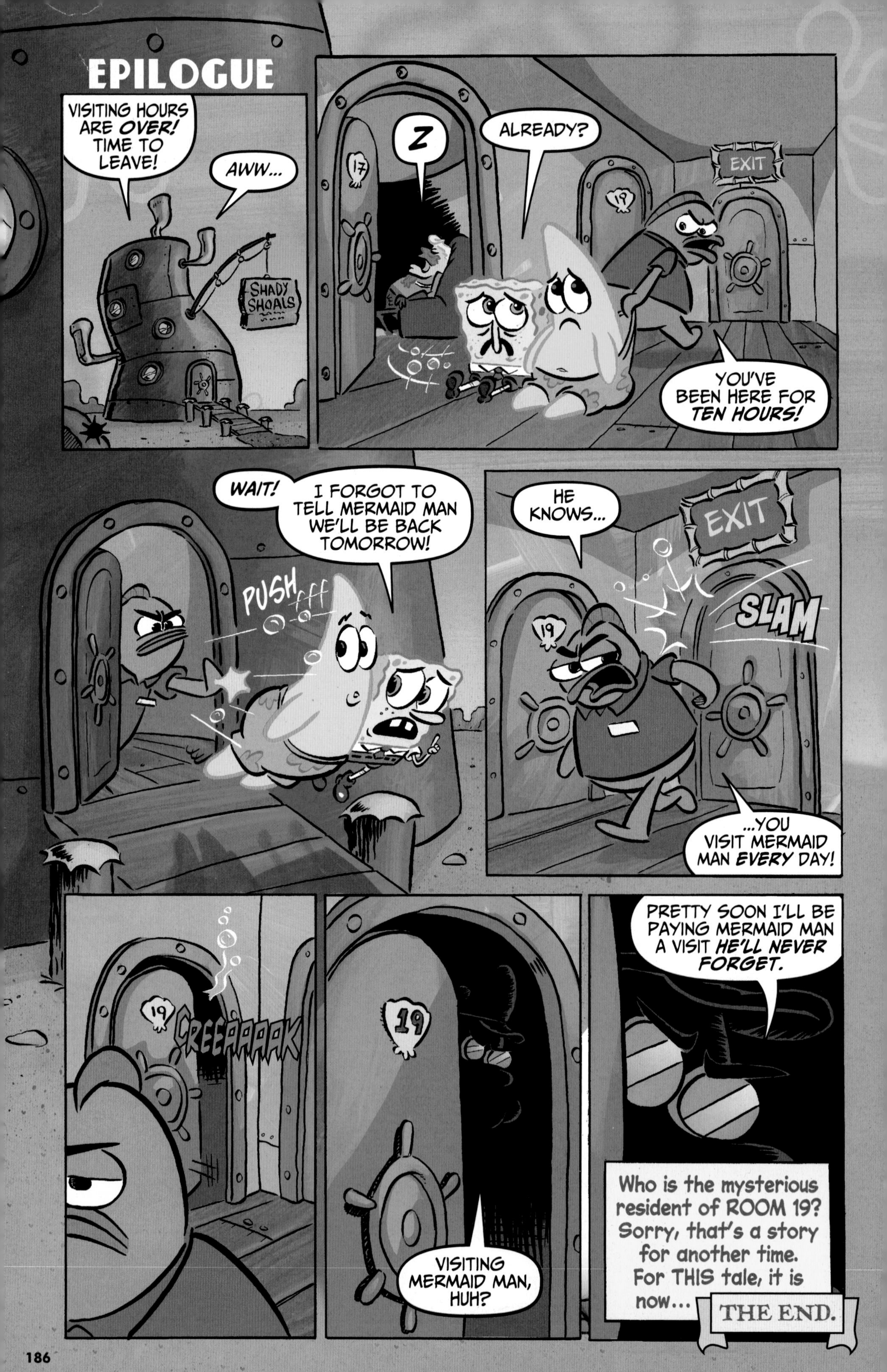
EPILOGUE
VISITING HOURS ARE OVER! TIME TO LEAVE!
AWW...
SHADY SHOALS
Z
ALREADY?
EXIT
YOU'VE BEEN HERE FOR TEN HOURS!
WAIT!
I FORGOT TO TELL MERMAID MAN WE'LL BE BACK TOMORROW!
PUSH
HE KNOWS...
EXIT
SLAM
...YOU VISIT MERMAID MAN EVERY DAY!
CREEAAAAK
VISITING MERMAID MAN, HUH?
PRETTY SOON I'LL BE PAYING MERMAID MAN A VISIT HE'LL NEVER FORGET.
Who is the mysterious resident of ROOM 19? Sorry, that's a story for another time. For THIS tale, it is now...
THE END.

BONUS PINUP GALLERY

Featuring

pinups by the saltiest artists
this side of the Mariana Trench!

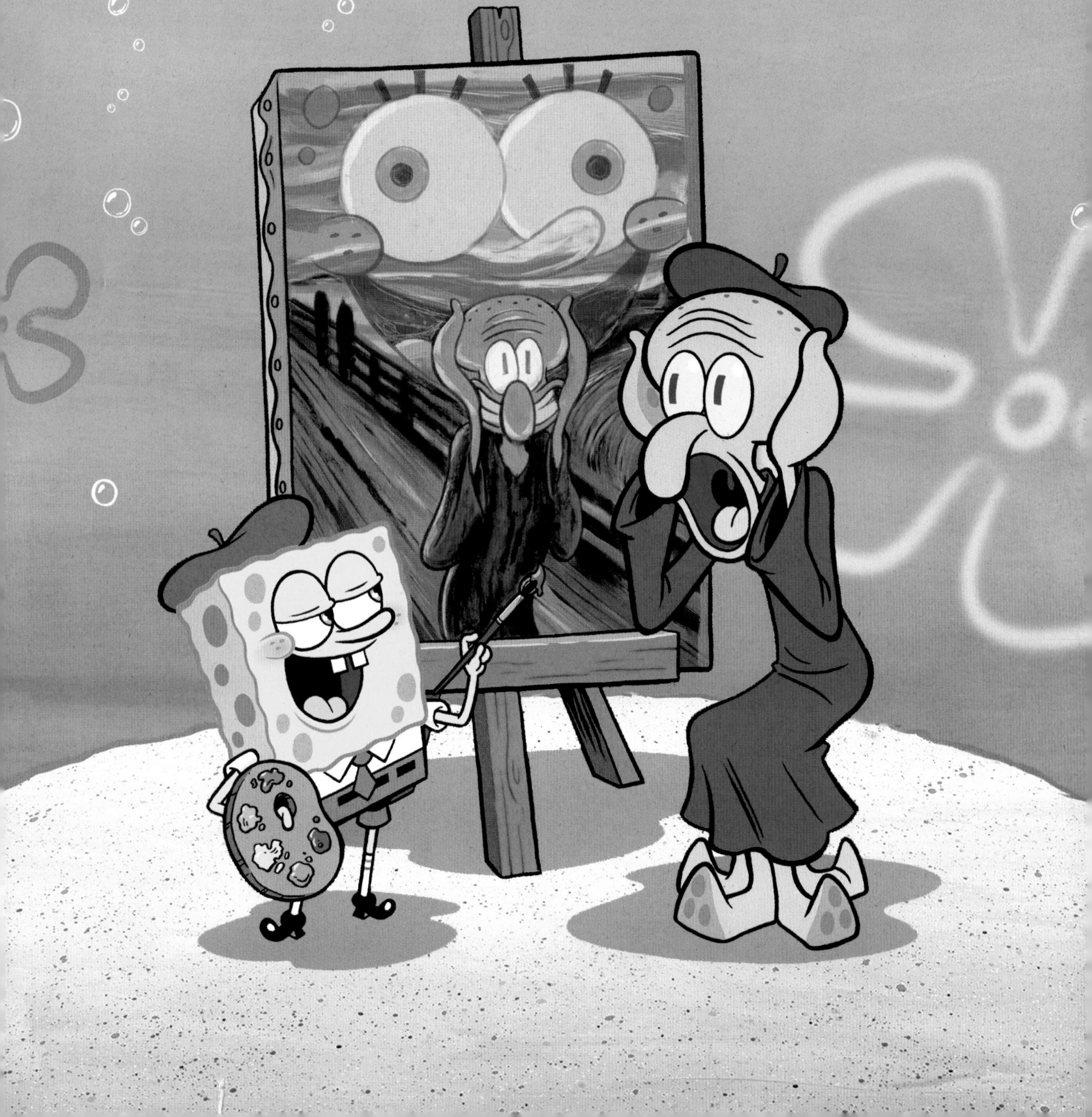

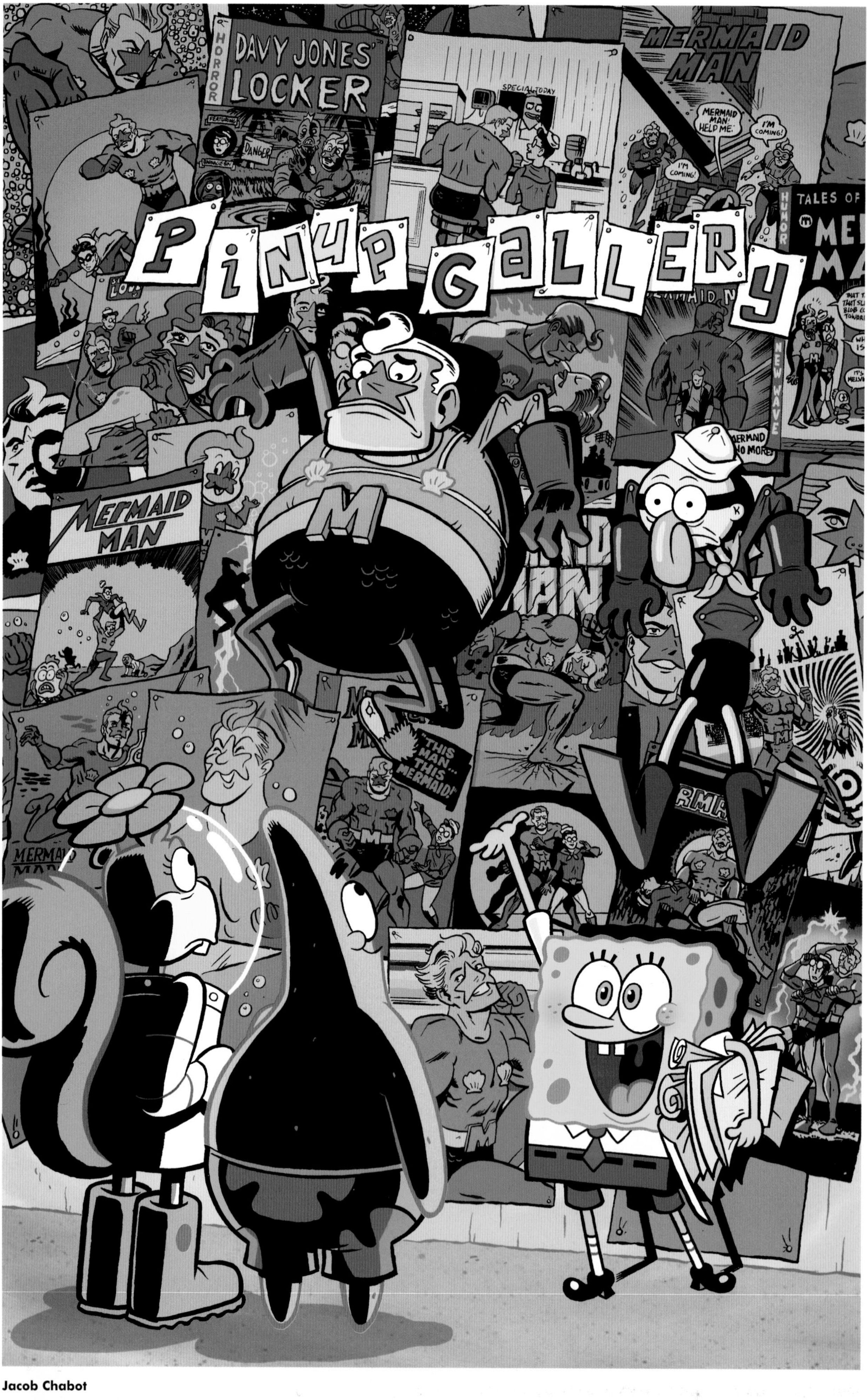
Pinup Gallery
DAVY JONES' LOCKER
HORROR
DANGER
SPECIAL TODAY
MERMAID MAN
MERMAID MAN! HELP ME!
I'M COMING!
I'M COMING!
TALES OF
HUMOR
NEW WAVE
MERMAID NO MORE
MERMAID MAN
"THIS MAN... THIS MERMAID!"
MERMAID MAN

Jacob Chabot

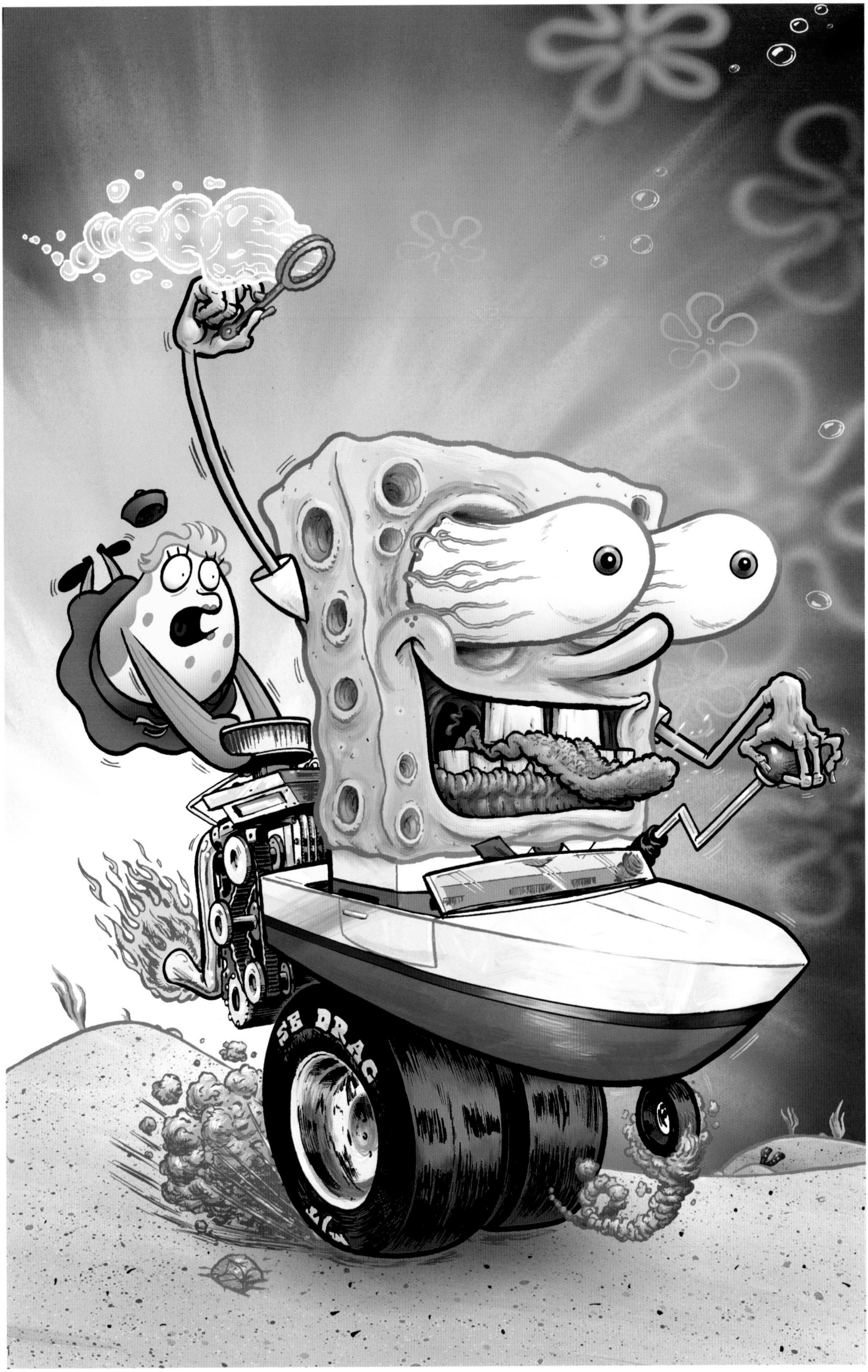
SB DRAG

SPONGEBOB COMICS NO. 2 COVER by **Brian Smith**. Colors by **Mark Martin**

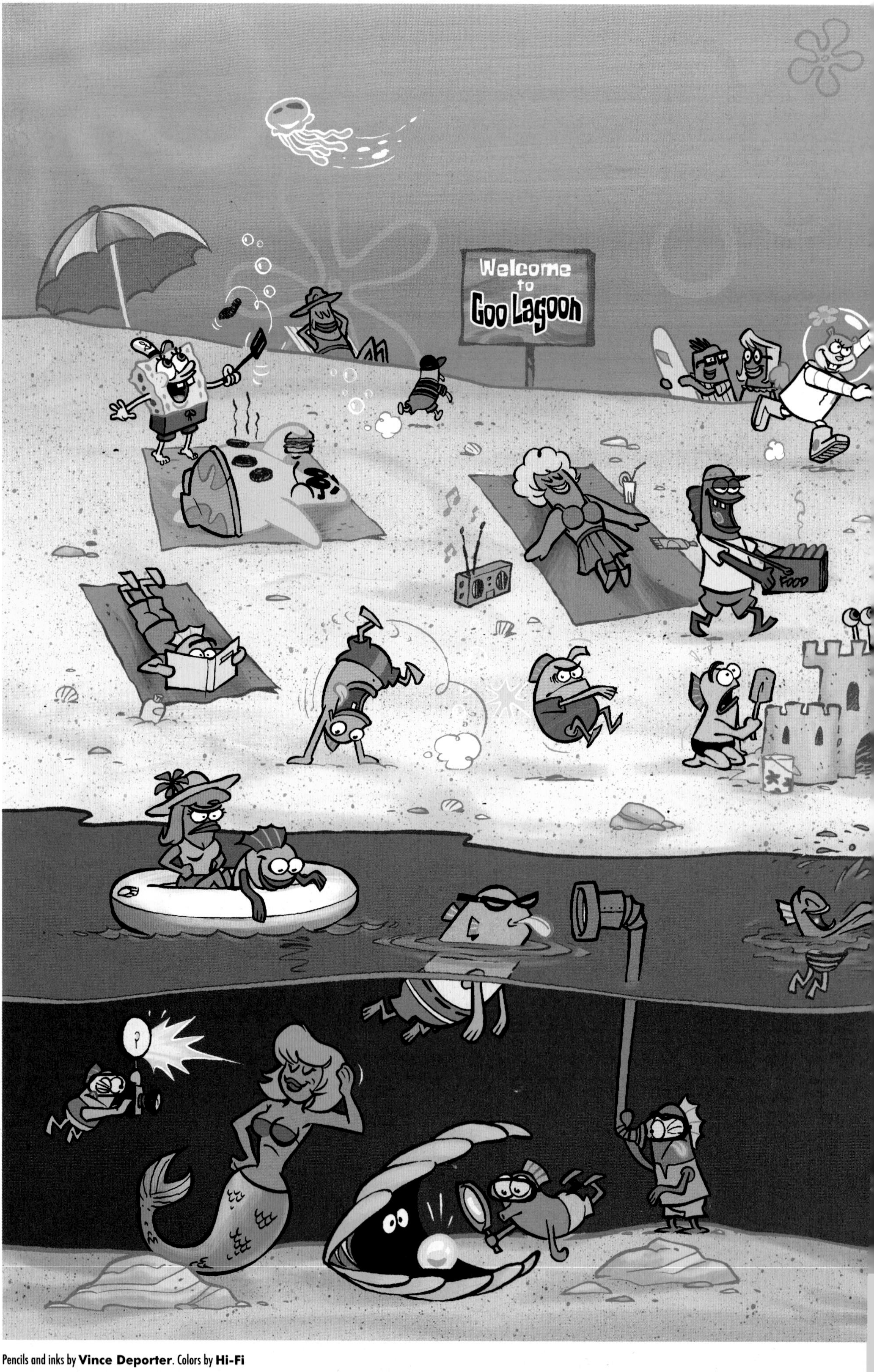
Welcome to Goo Lagoon
FOOD

Pencils and inks by **Vince Deporter**. Colors by **Hi-Fi**

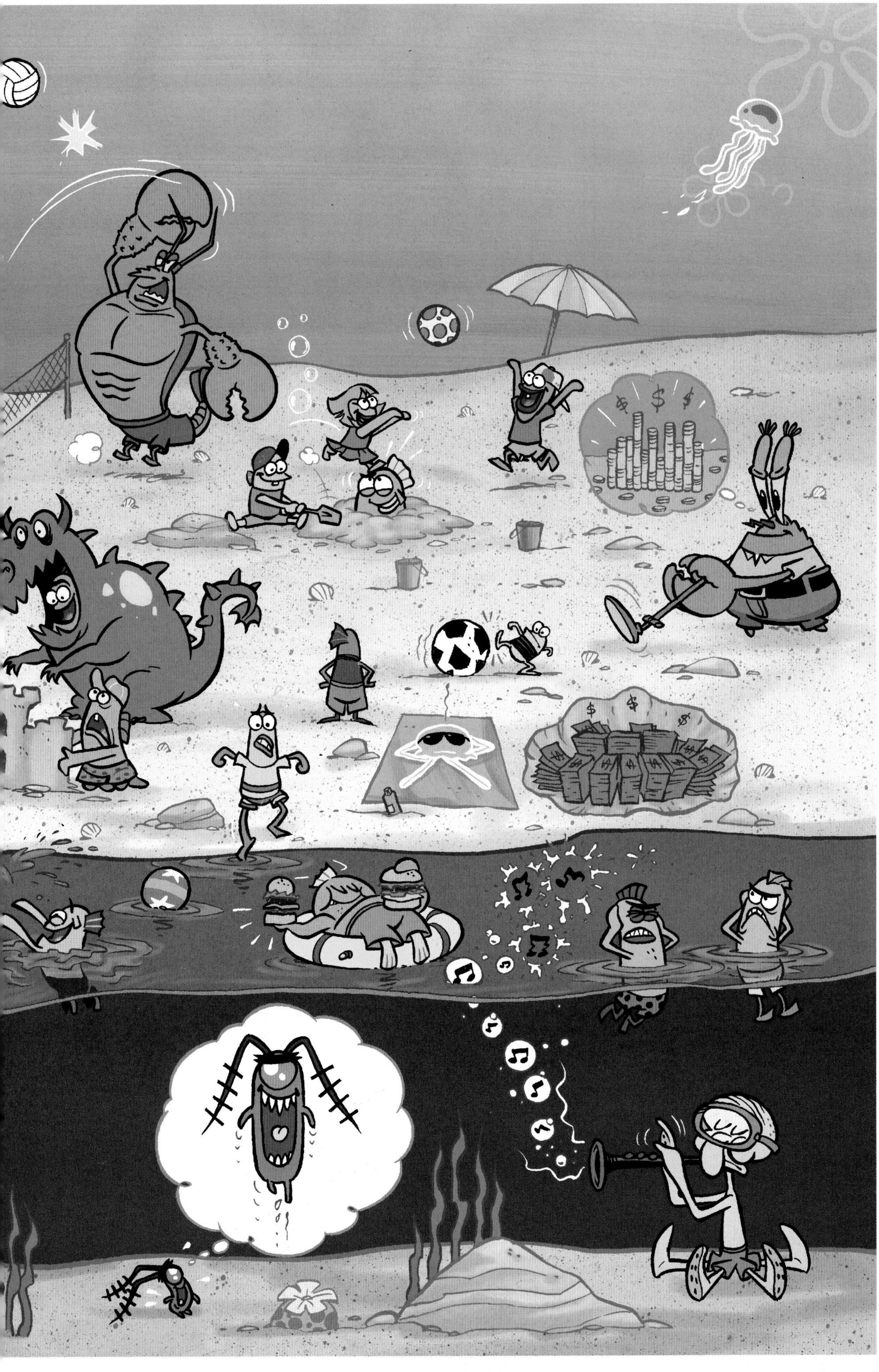

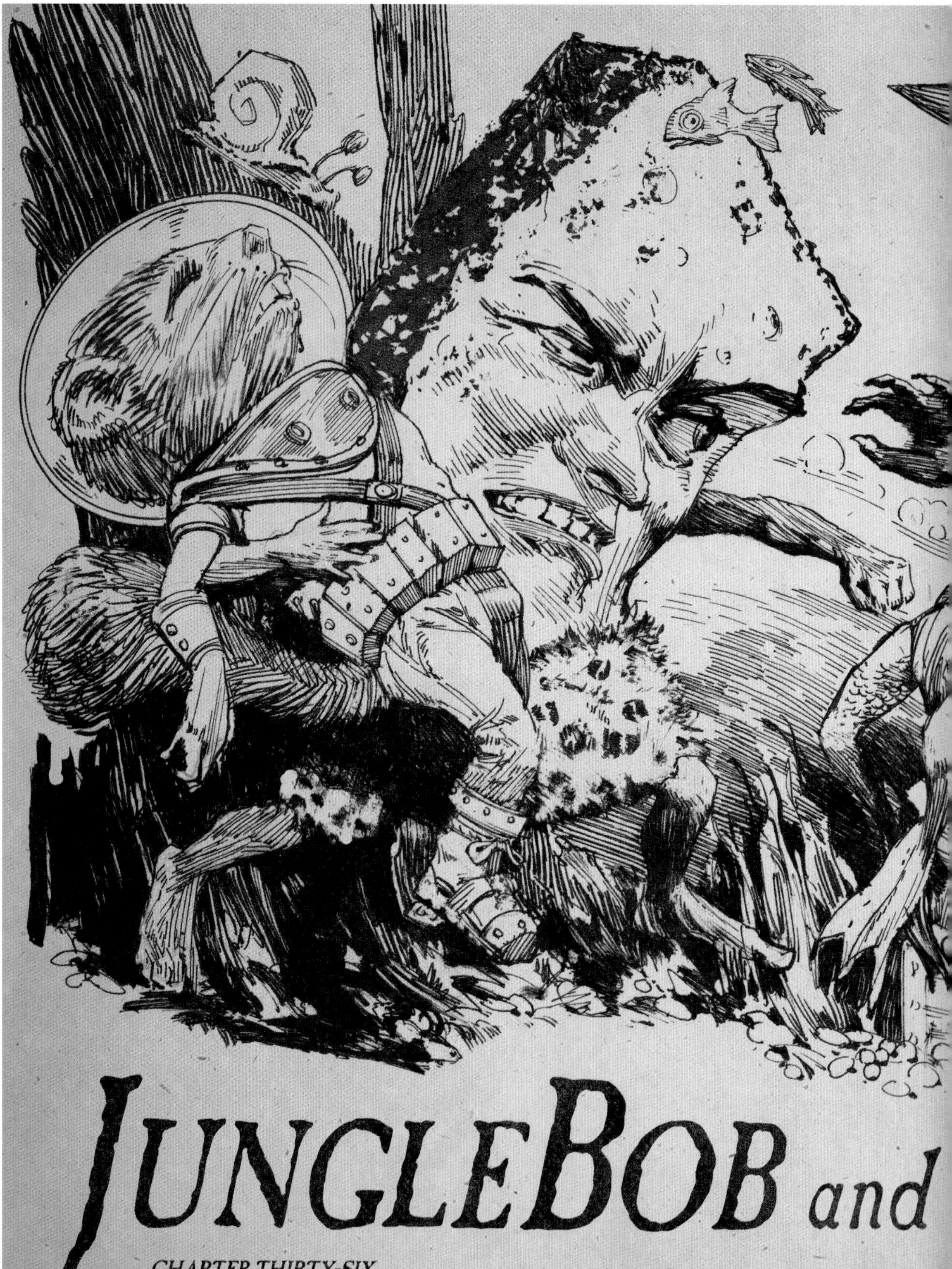

JUNGLEBOB and

CHAPTER THIRTY-SIX

N'Gari the little gastropod suddenly squirmed less slowly than usual. His master, JungleBob LoinCloth, who had returned to the kelp wilderness, instantly understood that the snail's contortions meant danger was close at hand. With catfish-like reflexes and grim resolve etched deeply across his golden brow, the lord of the kelp forest girded his square-clothed loins for battle.

Suddenly a school of Tsunami Pirate Fish poured

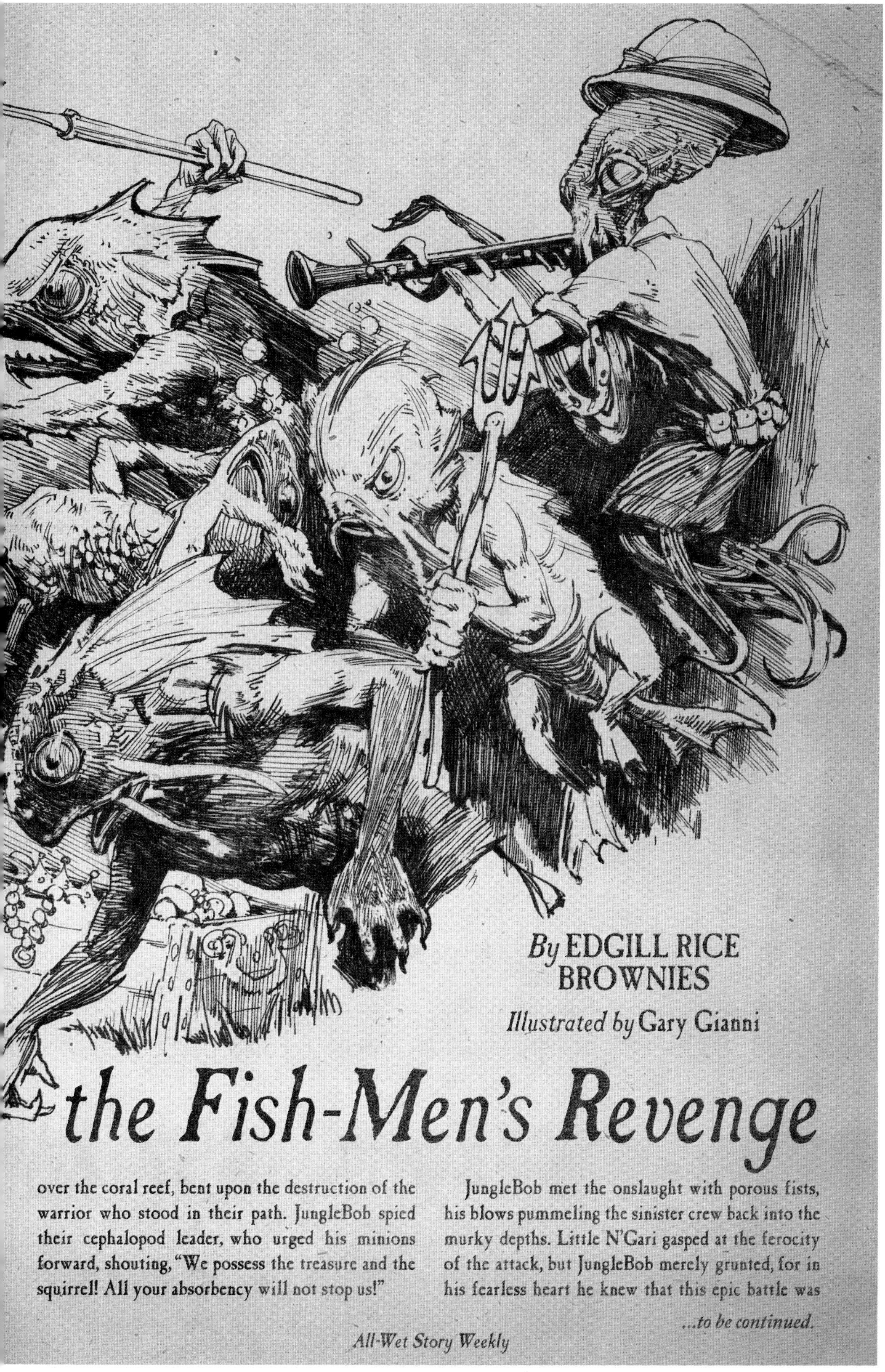

By EDGILL RICE BROWNIES

Illustrated by Gary Gianni

the Fish-Men's Revenge

over the coral reef, bent upon the destruction of the warrior who stood in their path. JungleBob spied their cephalopod leader, who urged his minions forward, shouting, "We possess the treasure and the squirrel! All your absorbency will not stop us!"

JungleBob met the onslaught with porous fists, his blows pummeling the sinister crew back into the murky depths. Little N'Gari gasped at the ferocity of the attack, but JungleBob merely grunted, for in his fearless heart he knew that this epic battle was

...to be continued.

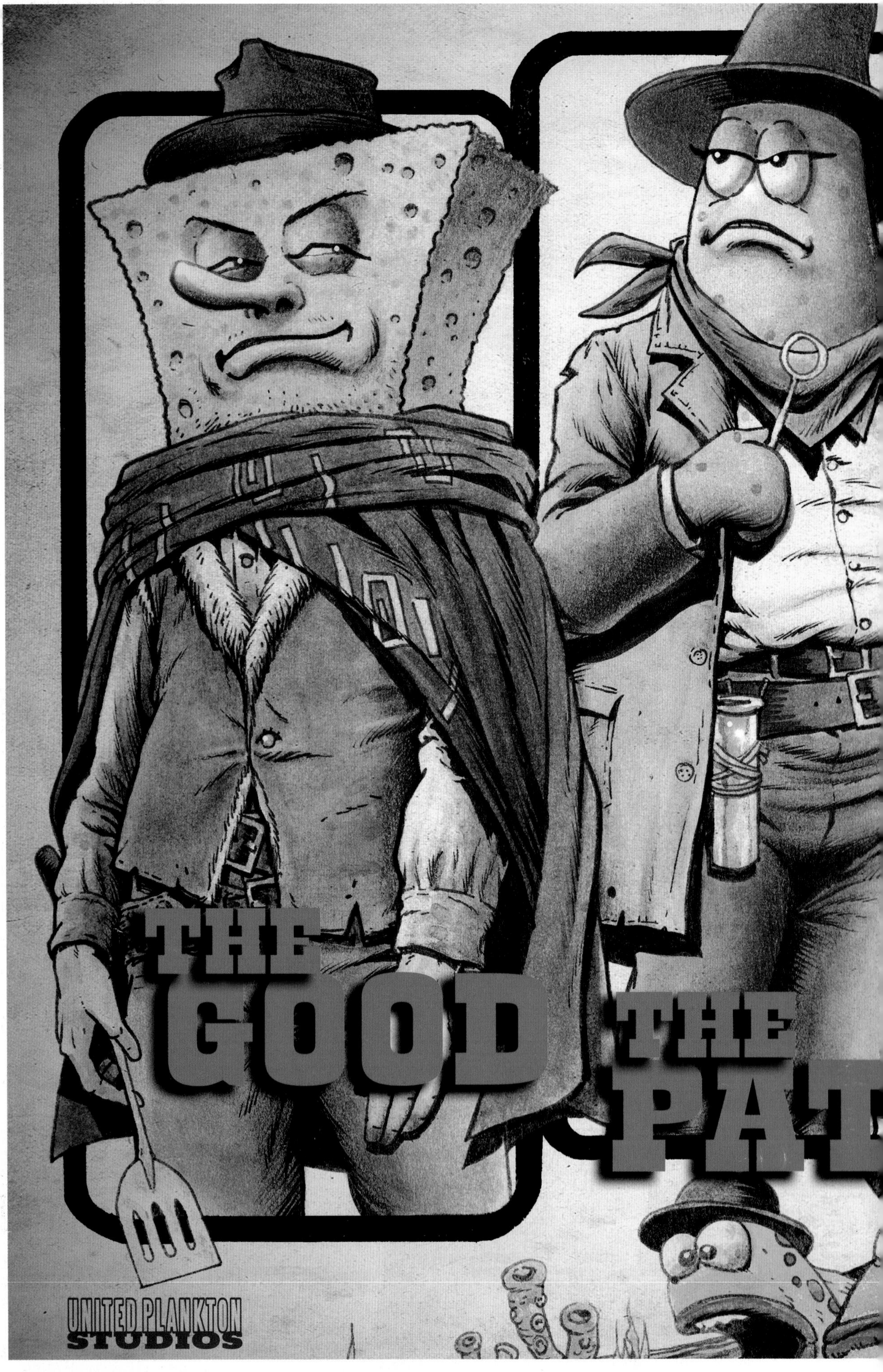
THE GOOD
THE PAT
UNITED PLANKTON STUDIOS

Tim Truman. Lettering by Paul Tutrone

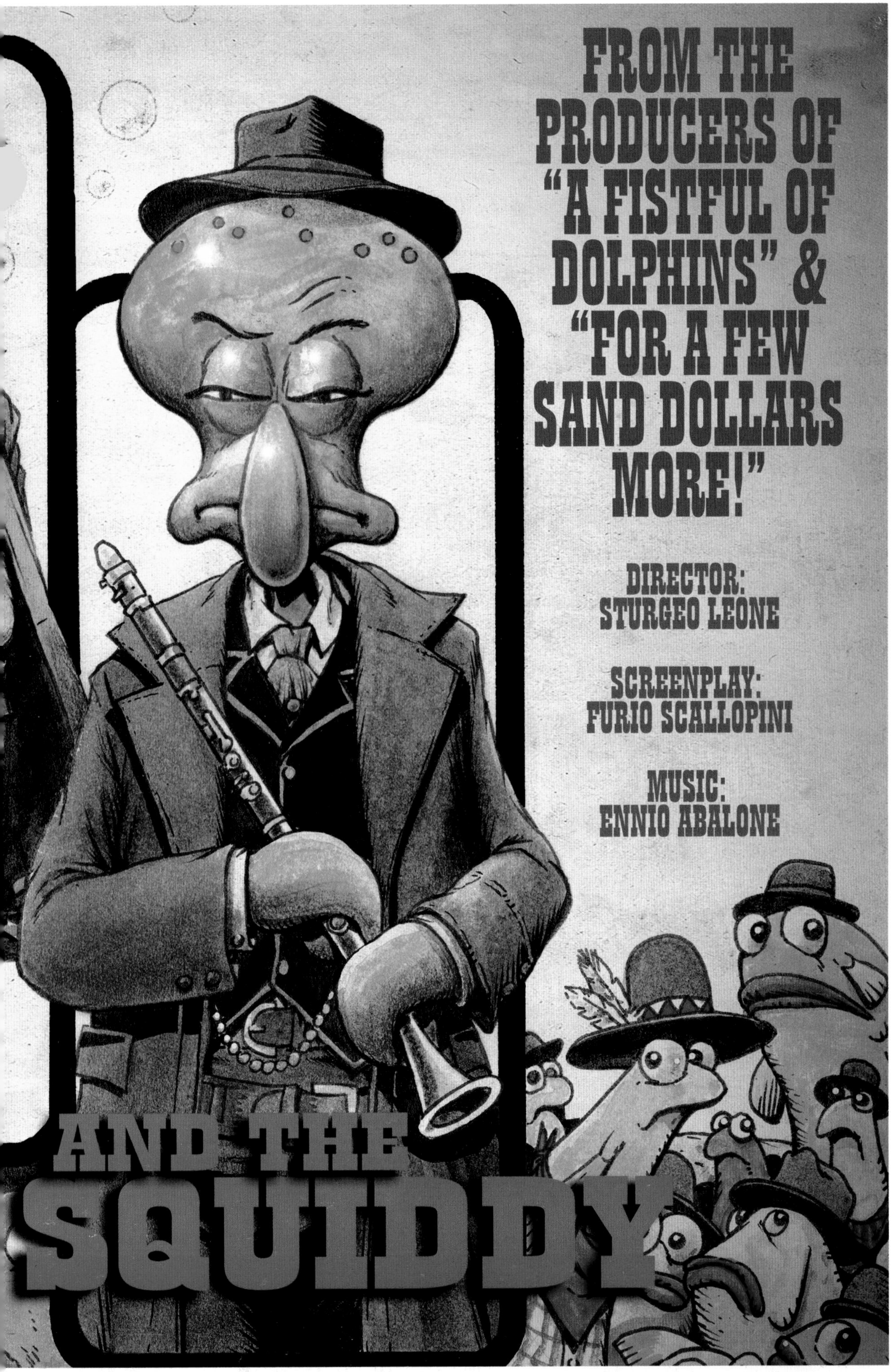
FROM THE PRODUCERS OF "A FISTFUL OF DOLPHINS" & "FOR A FEW SAND DOLLARS MORE!"
DIRECTOR: STURGEO LEONE
SCREENPLAY: FURIO SCALLOPINI
MUSIC: ENNIO ABALONE
AND THE SQUIDDY

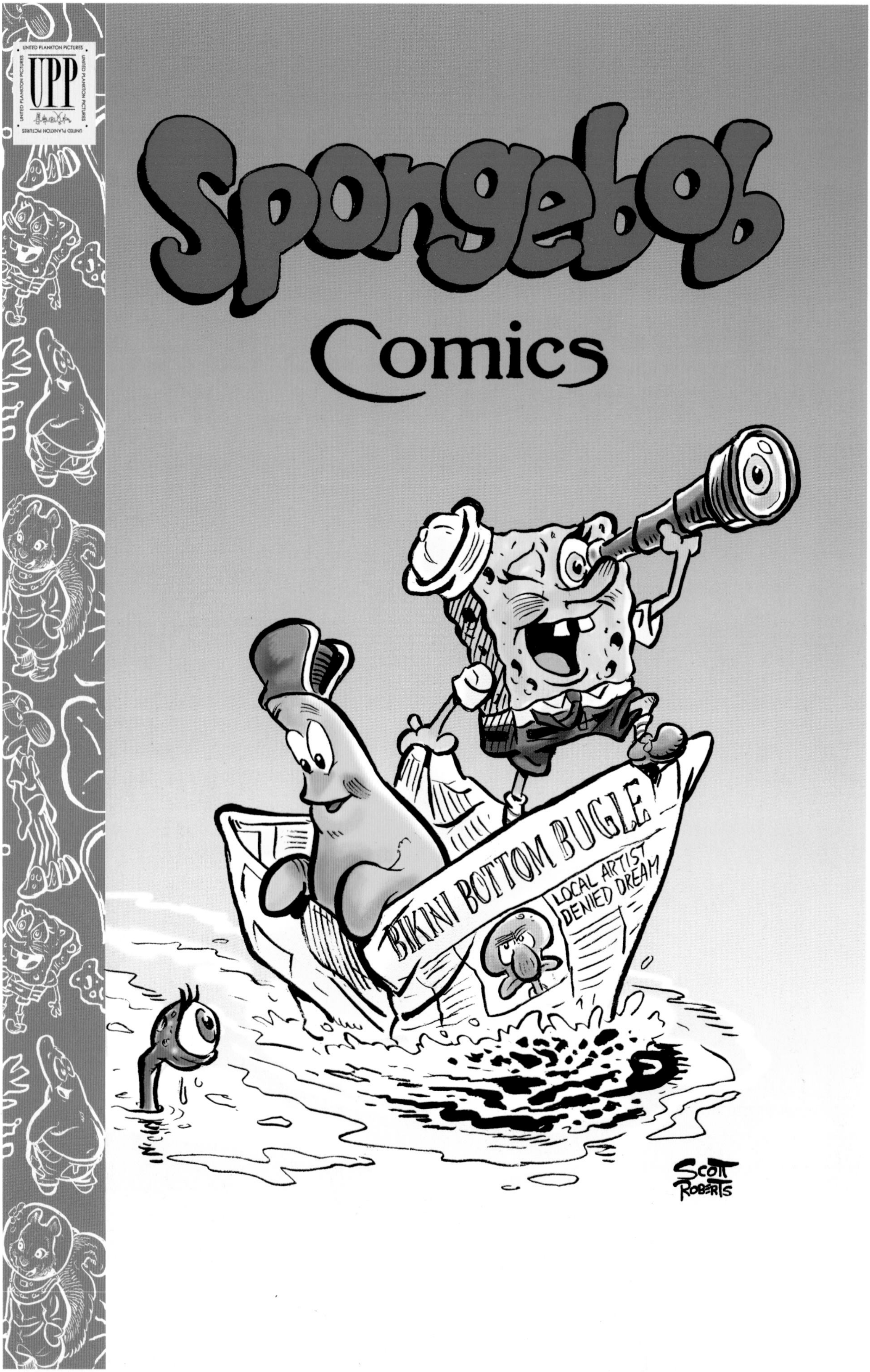
UNITED PLANKTON PICTURES
UPP
Spongebob
Comics
BIKINI BOTTOM BUGLE
LOCAL ARTIST DENIED DREAM
SCOTT ROBERTS

Scott Roberts

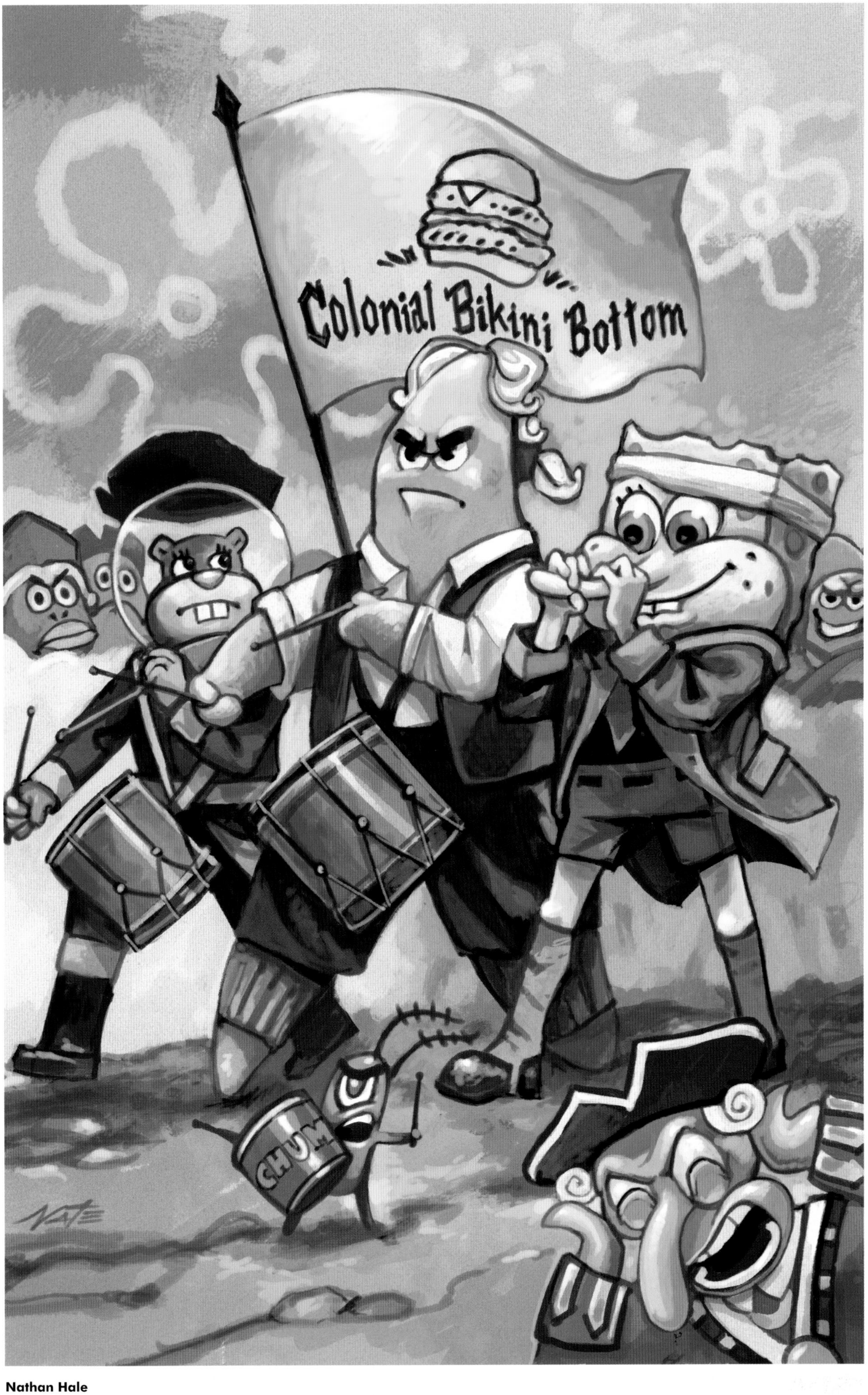
Colonial Bikini Bottom
CHUM
NATE

Nathan Hale

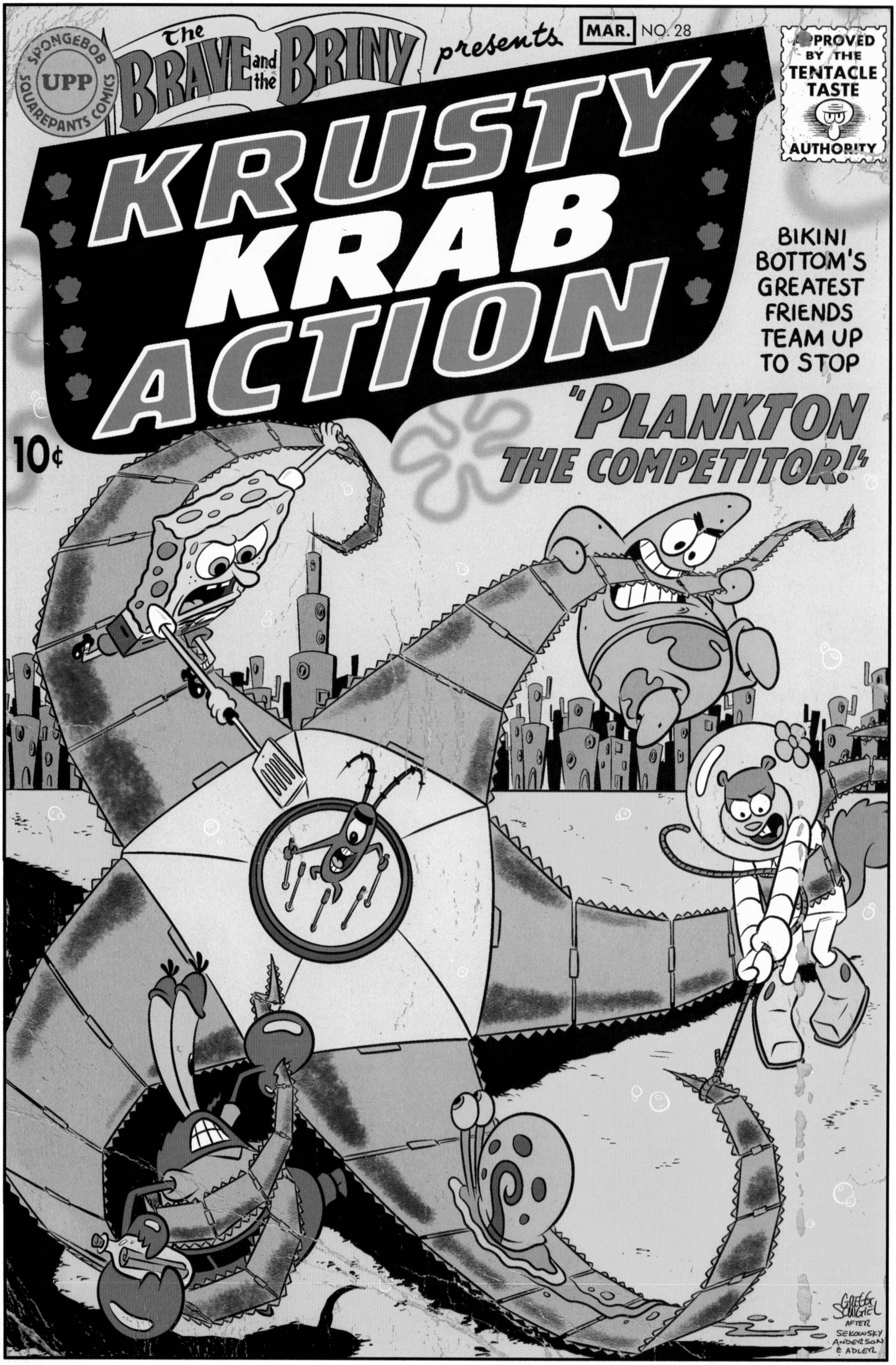

SPONGEBOB SQUAREPANTS COMICS
UPP
The BRAVE and the BRINY presents
MAR. NO. 28
APPROVED BY THE TENTACLE TASTE AUTHORITY
KRUSTY KRAB ACTION
BIKINI BOTTOM'S GREATEST FRIENDS TEAM UP TO STOP
"PLANKTON THE COMPETITOR!"
10¢
GREGG SCHIGIEL
AFTER SEKOWSKY ANDERSON & ADLER

Gregg Schigiel

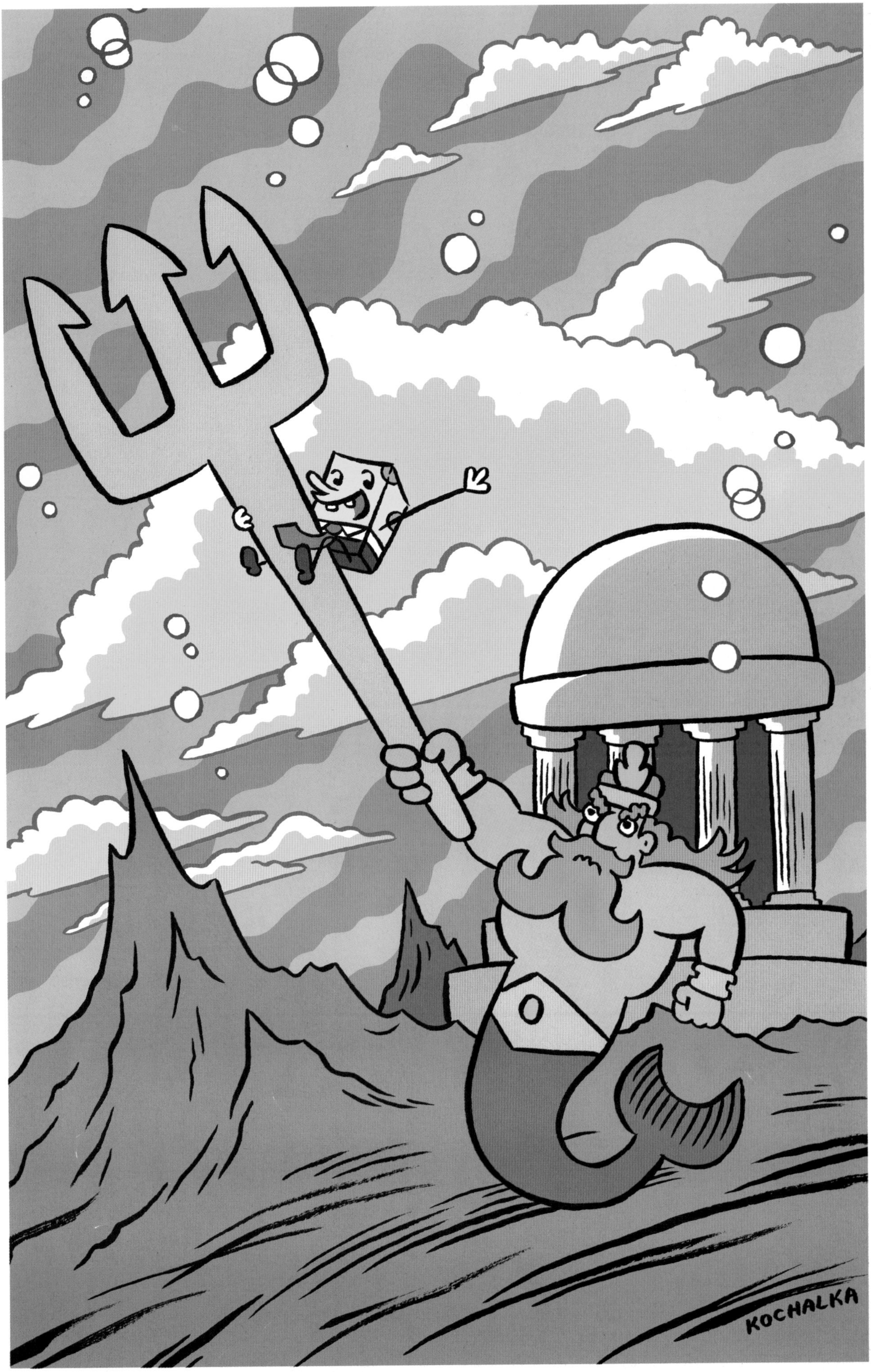
KOCHALKA

James Kochalka

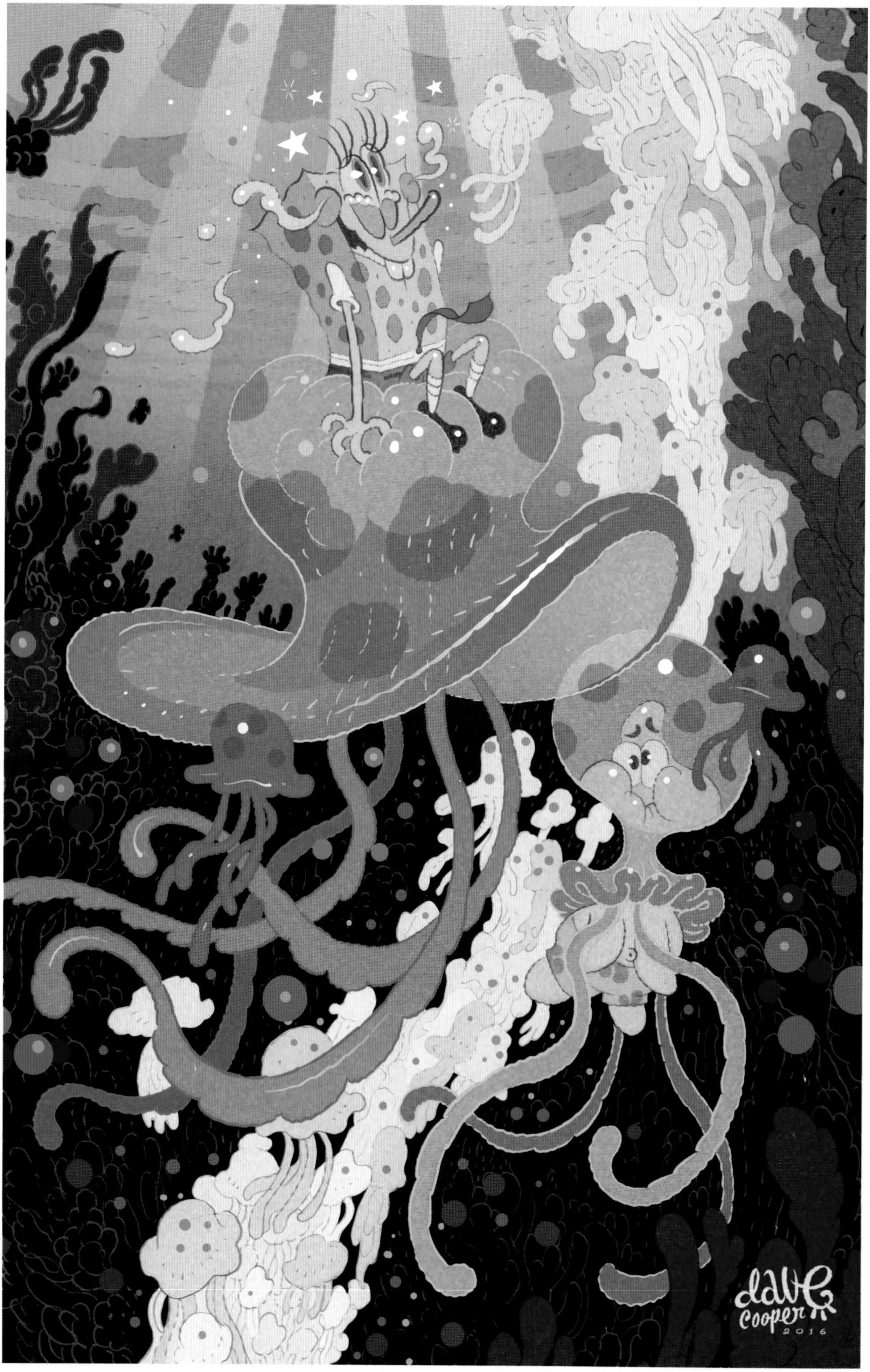
dave
cooper
2016

Dave Cooper

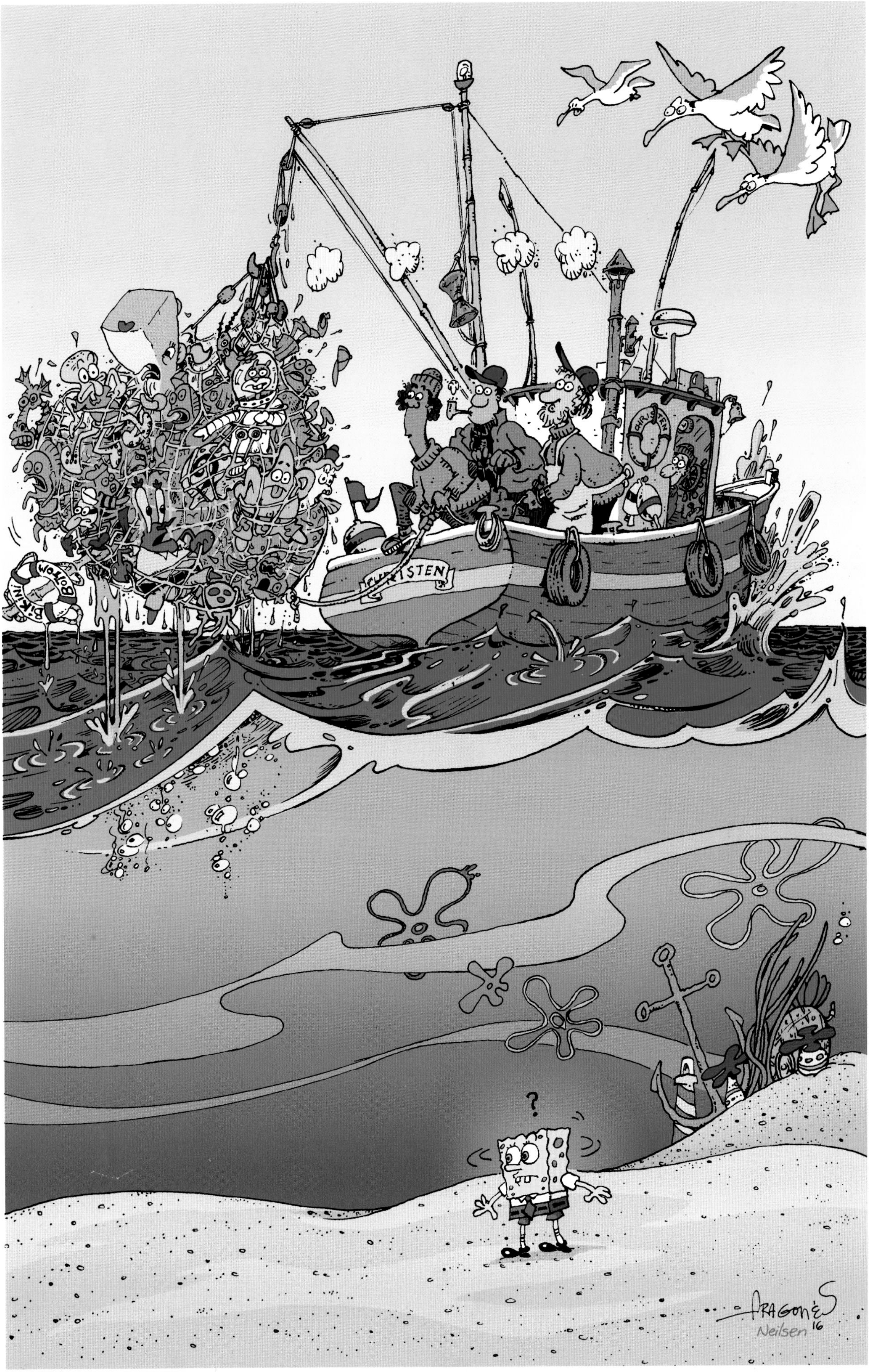

CHRISTEN
CHRISTEN
BIKINI BOTTOM
?
ARAGONÉS
Neilsen '16

Pencils and inks by **Sergio Aragonés.** Colors by **Rick Neilsen**

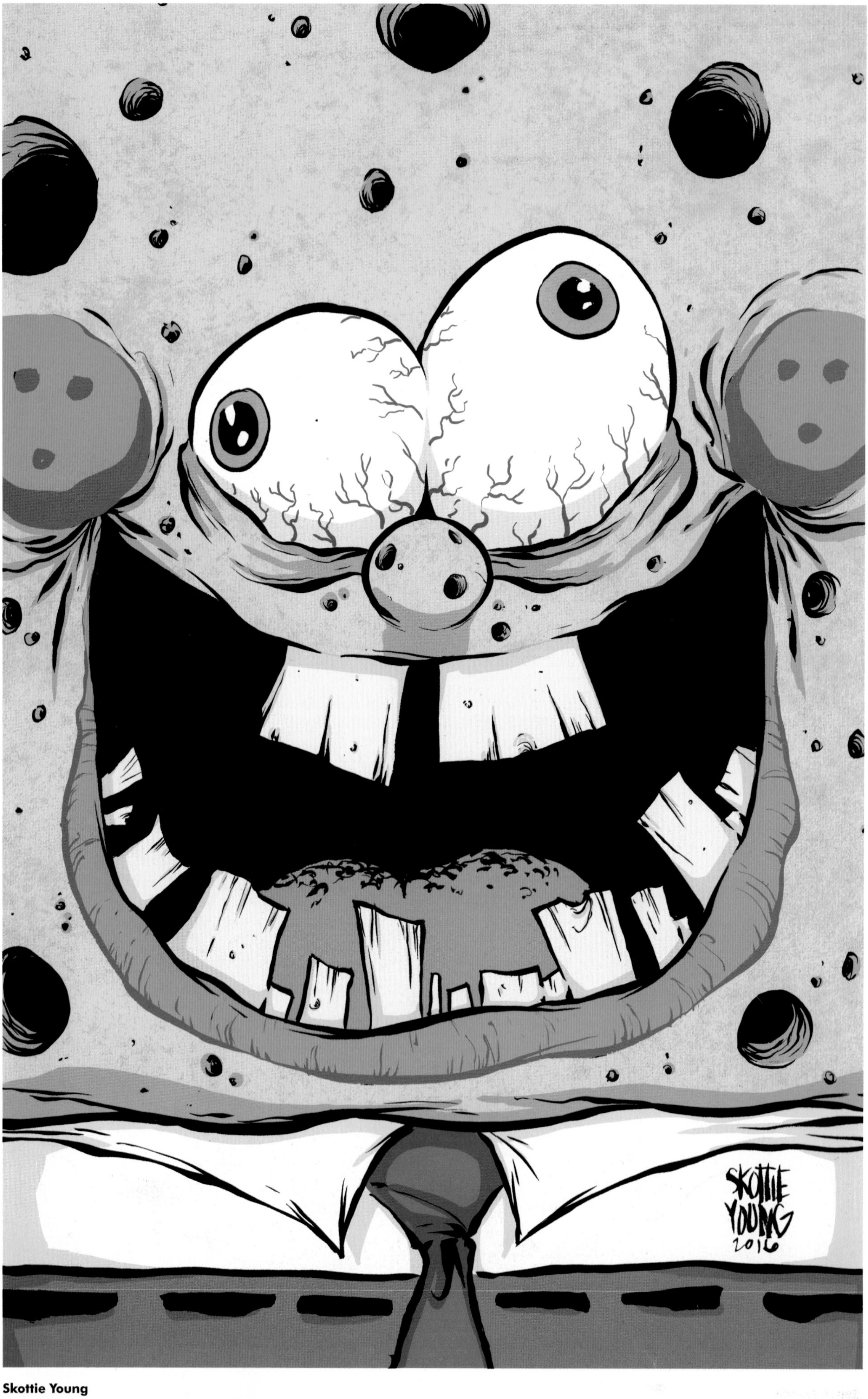
SKOTTIE YOUNG 2016

Skottie Young

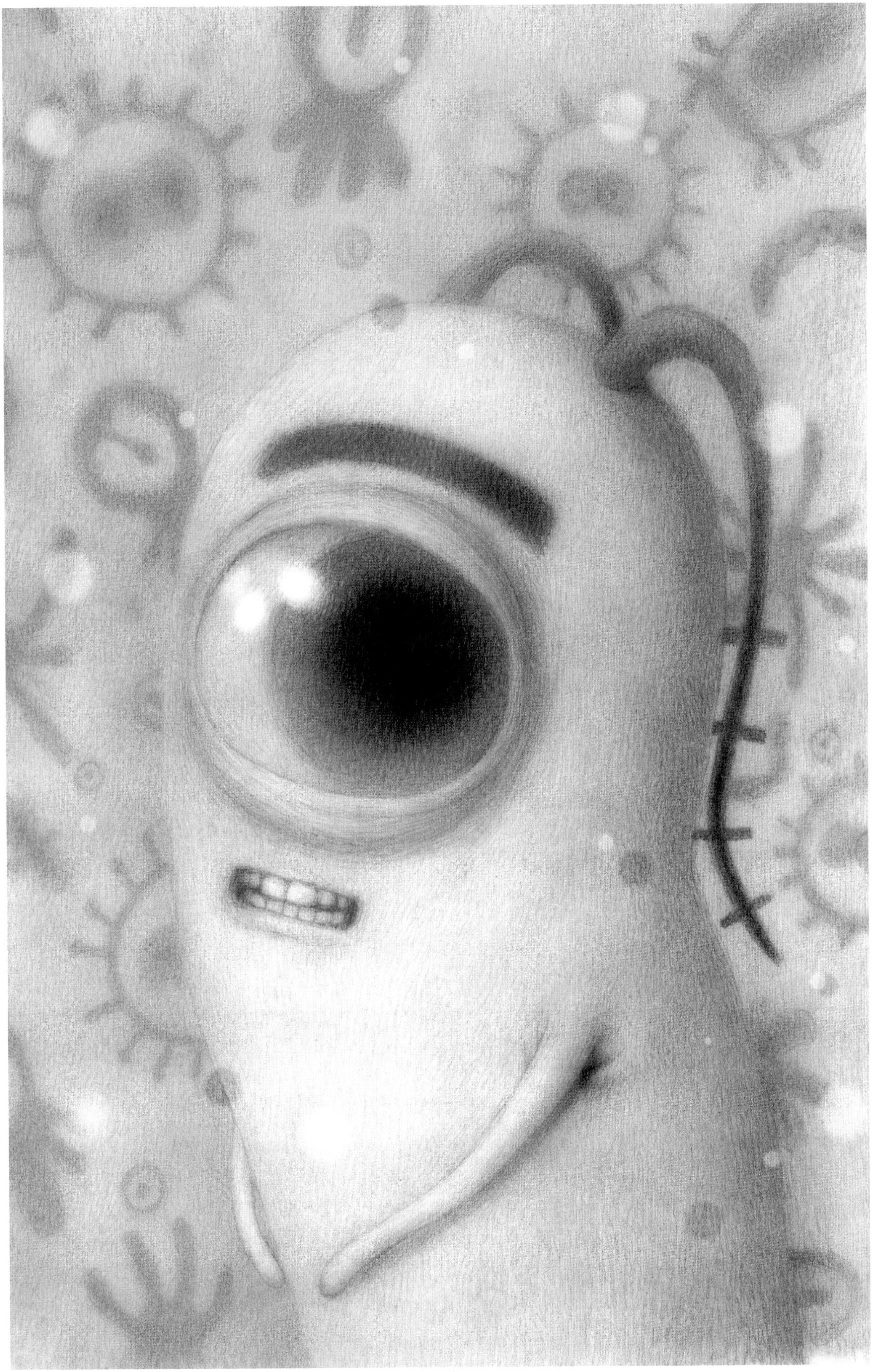

Reneé French

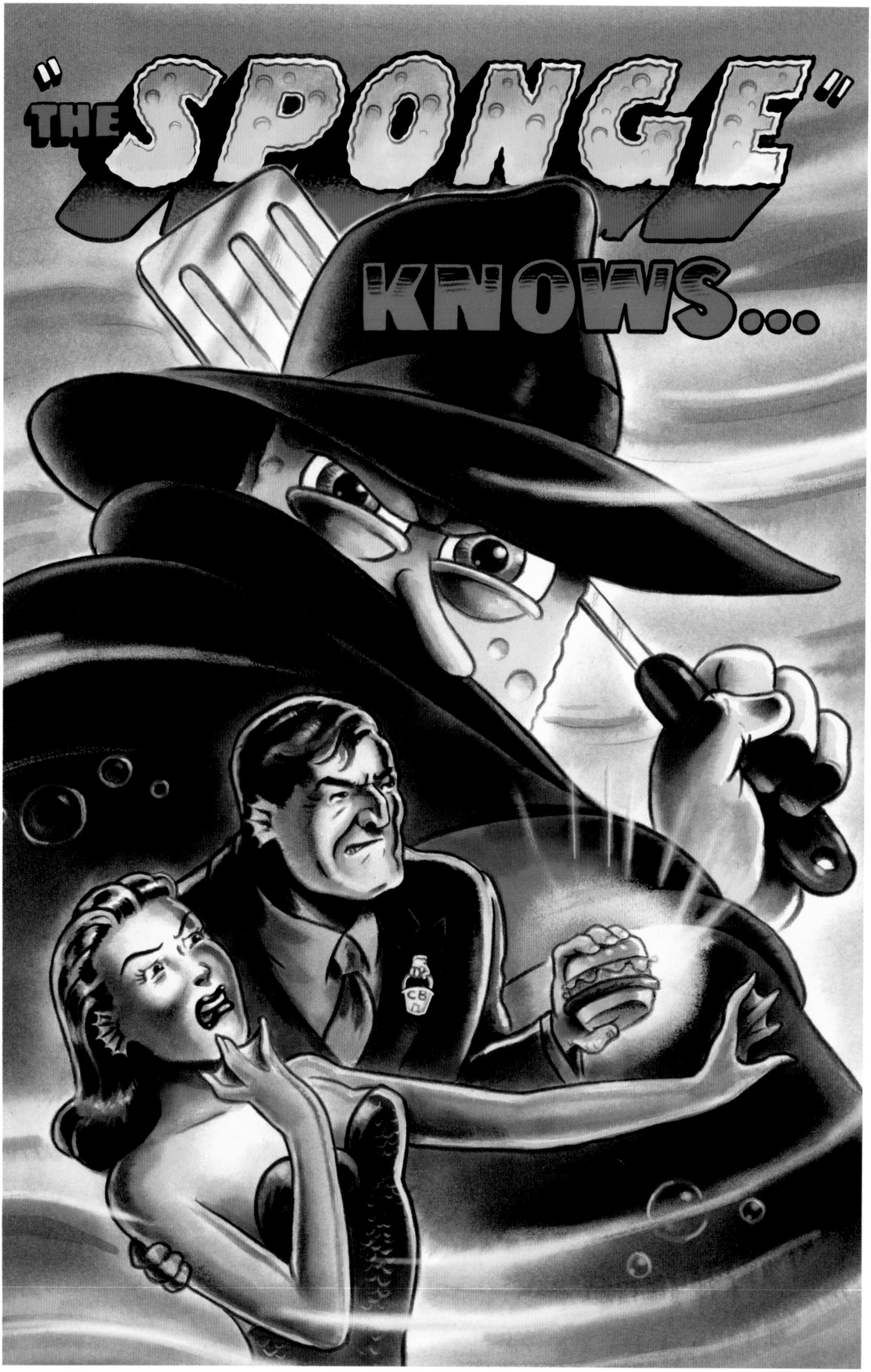
"THE SPONGE"
KNOWS...

Ross MacDonald

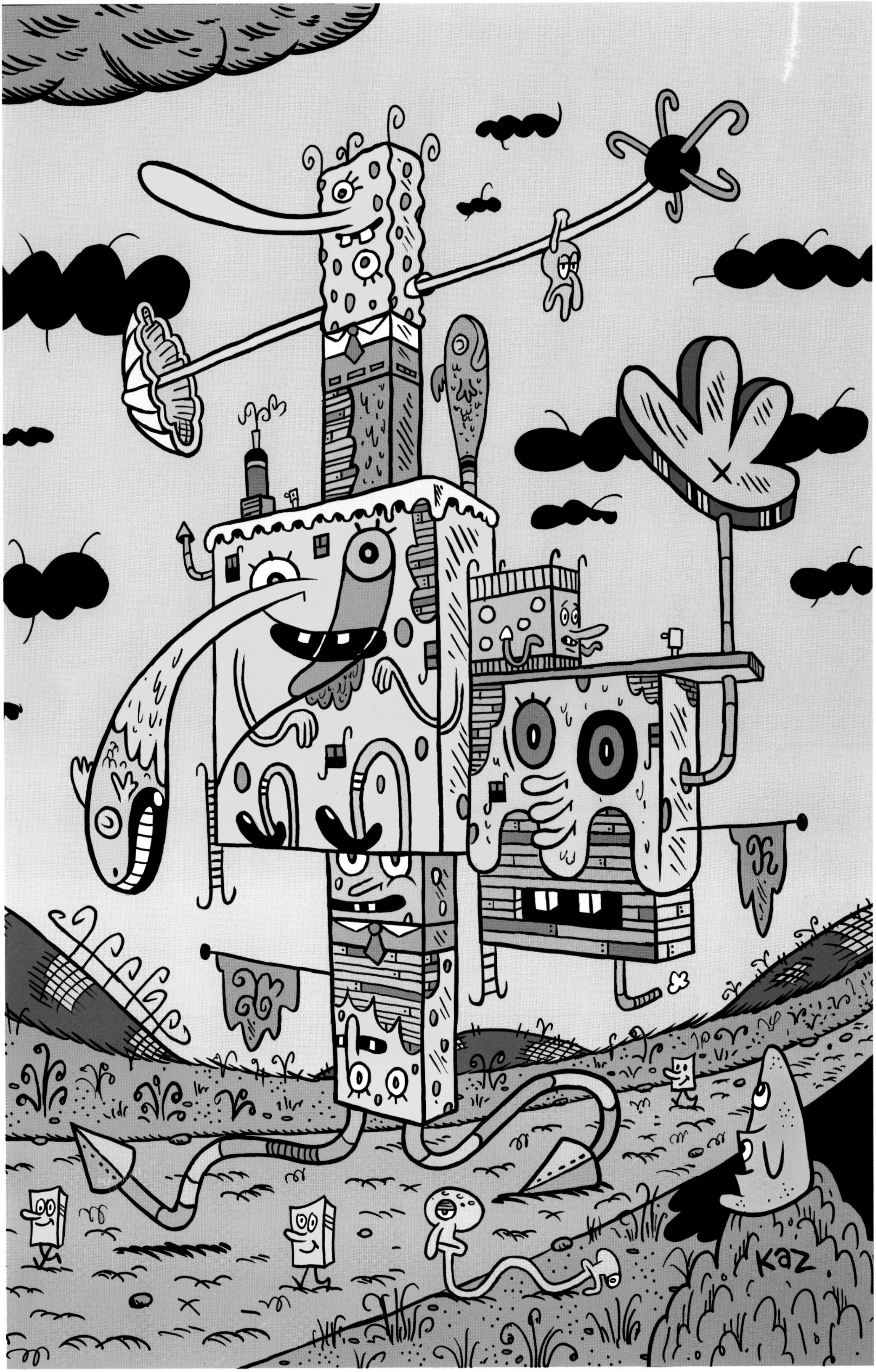
KAZ

Kaz

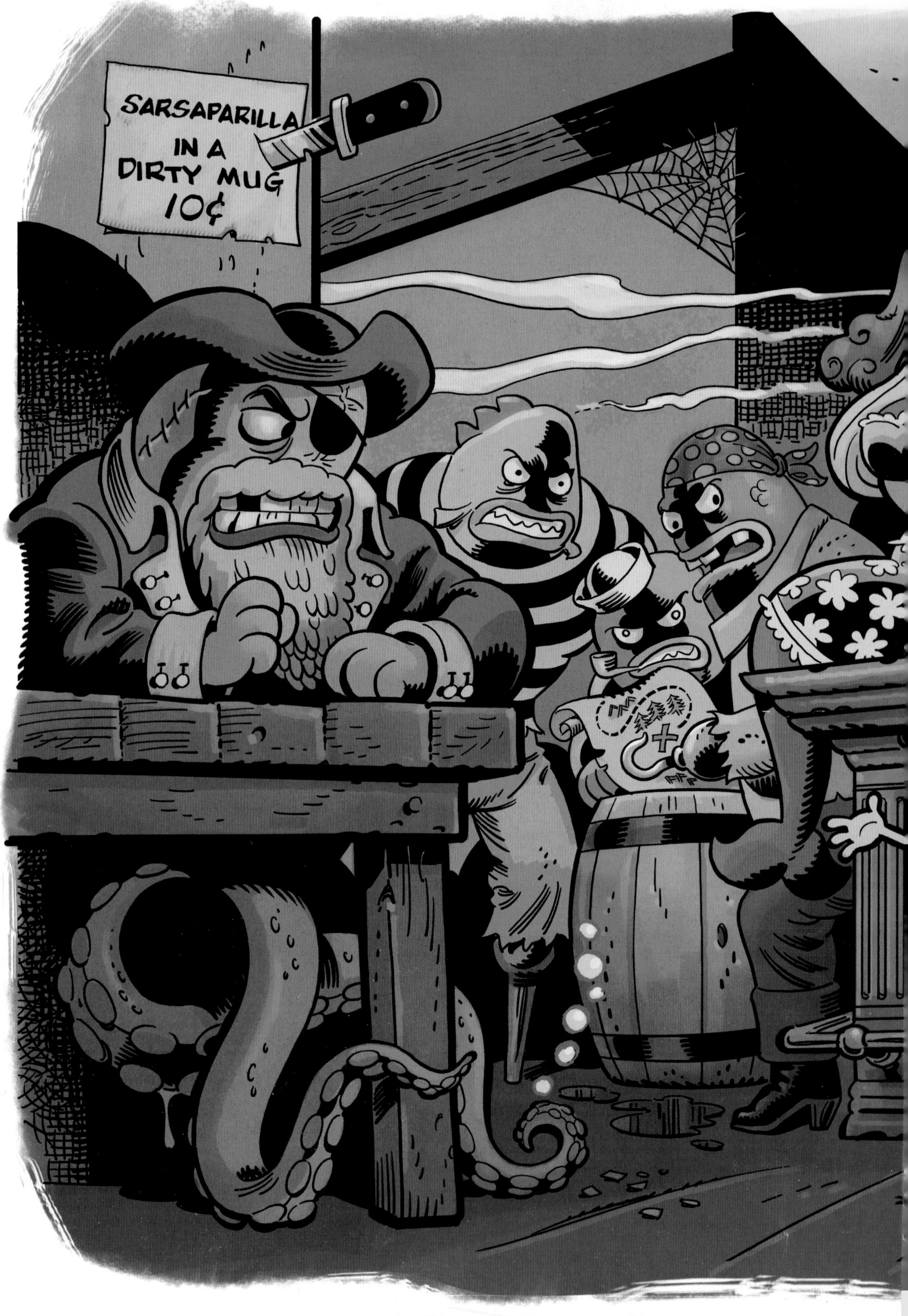
SARSAPARILLA IN A DIRTY MUG 10¢

"Soda jerk! Ice cream

Gag and pencils by **Hilary Barta**. Inks by **Stephen DeStefano**. Colors by **Jason Millet**

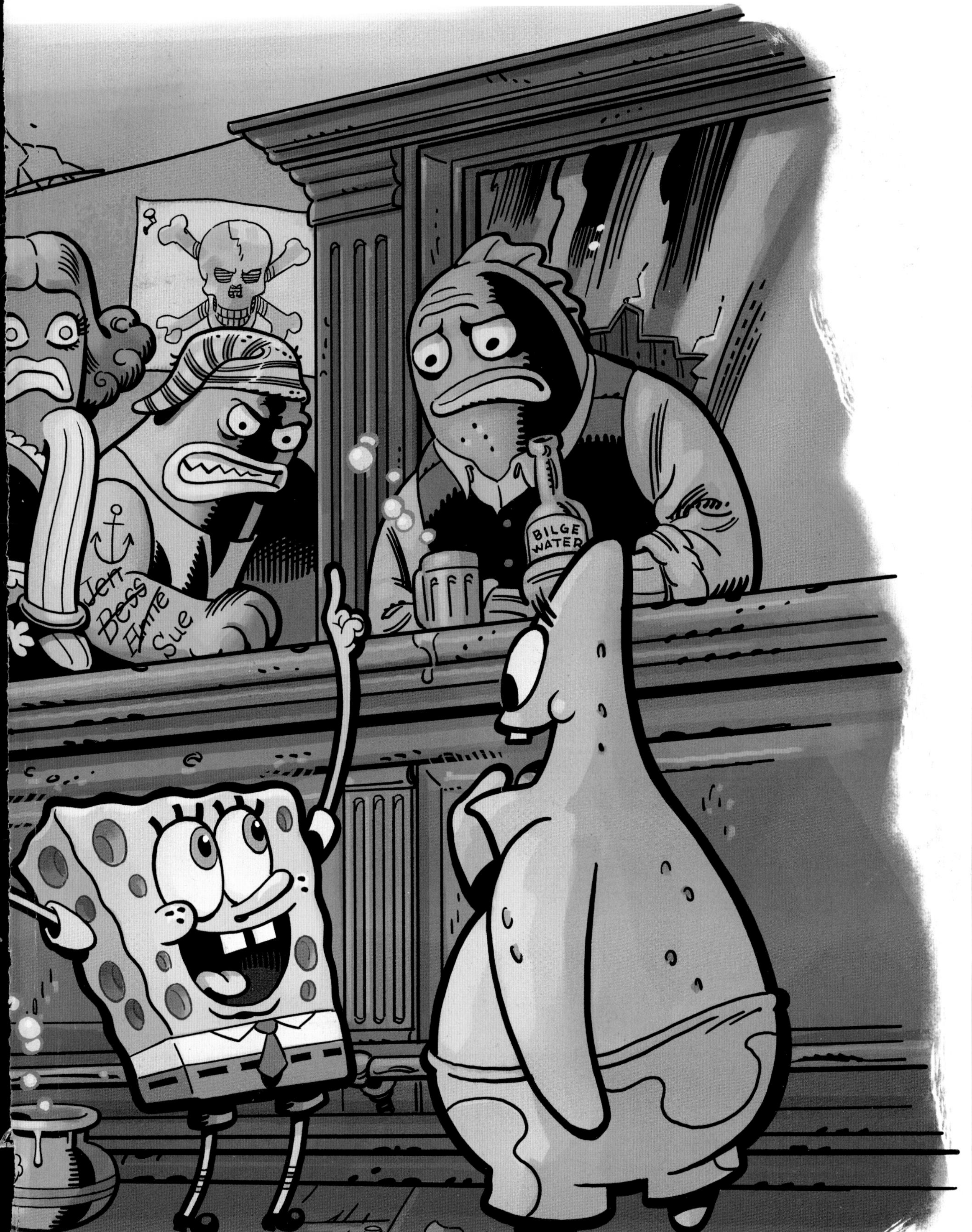
BILGE WATER
Jeff
Bess
Ernie
Sue

Sundaes for everyone!"

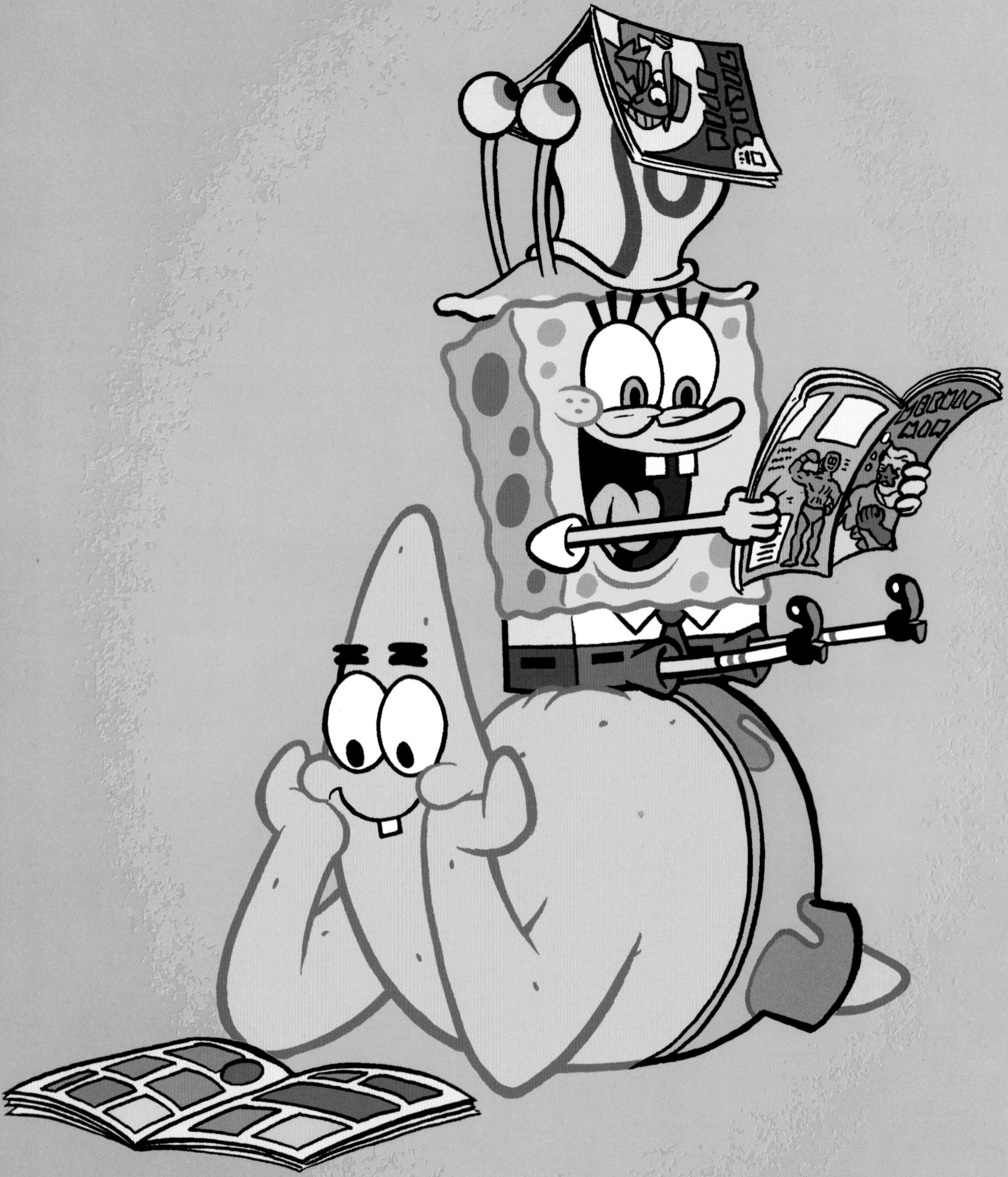

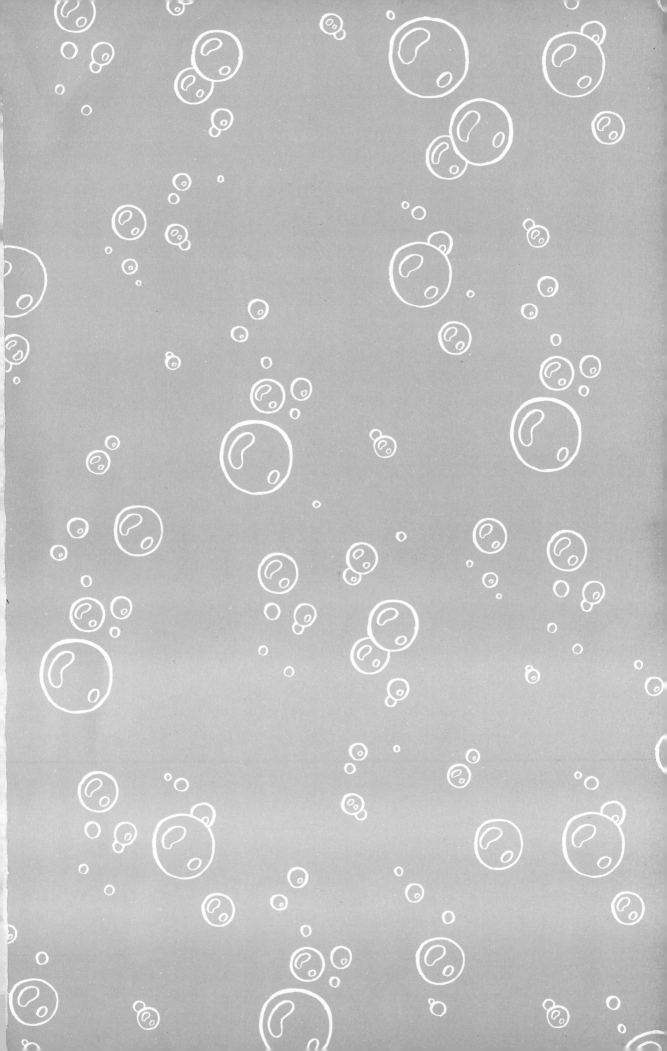

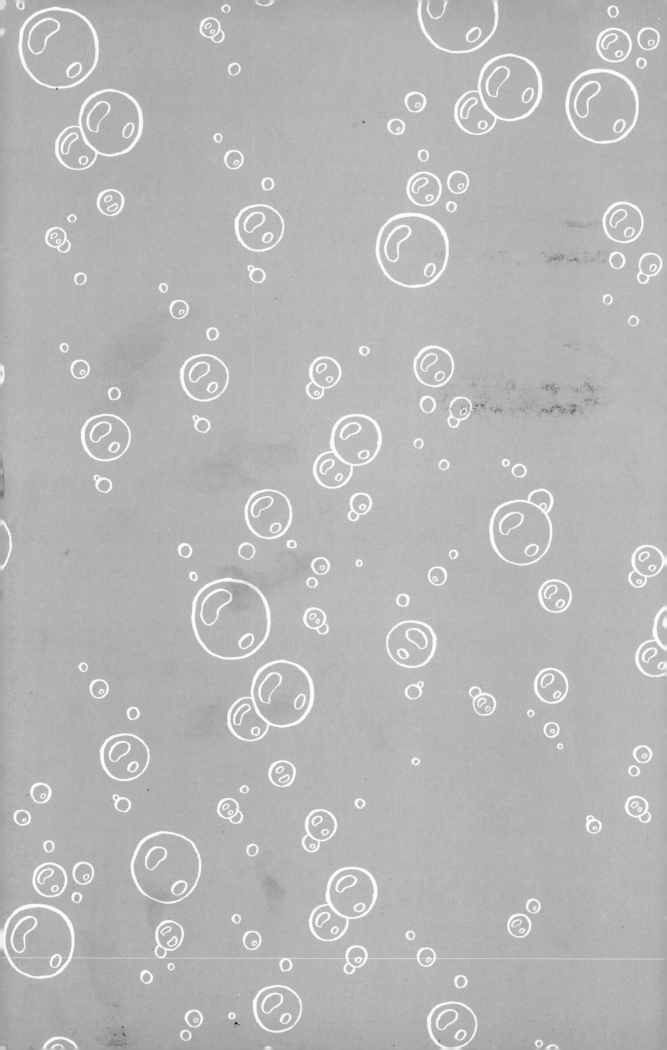